The UN role in promoting democracy

The UN role in promoting democracy: Between ideals and reality

Edited by Edward Newman and Roland Rich

United Nations University Press

TOKYO · NEW YORK · PARIS

United Nations University Press
United Nations University, 53-70, Jingumae 5-chome,
Shibuya-ku, Tokyo, 150-8925, Japan
Tel: +81-3-3499-2811   Fax: +81-3-3406-7345
E-mail: sales@hq.unu.edu
general enquiries: press@hq.unu.edu
www.unu.edu

United Nations University Office in North America
2 United Nations Plaza, Room DC2-2062, New York, NY 10017, USA
Tel: +1-212-963-6387   Fax: +1-212-371-9454
E-mail: unuona@ony.unu.edu

United Nations University Press is the publishing division of the United Nations University.

Cover design by Sese-Paul Design

Printed in the United States of America

UNUP-1104
ISBN 92-808-1104-5

Library of Congress Cataloging-in-Publication Data

The UN role in promoting democracy : between ideals and reality / edited by Edward Newman and Roland Rich.
    p.   cm.
 Includes bibliographical references and index.
 ISBN 9280811045 (pbk.)
 1. United Nations. 2. Democratization—Case studies. I. Newman, Edward, 1970– II. Rich, Roland.
 JZ4984.5.U53   2004
 321.8—dc22   2004015271

Contents

List of tables and figures

Acknowledgements

This volume is the result of a research project jointly organized by the Peace and Governance Programme of the United Nations University (UNU) and the Centre for Democratic Institutions (CDI) at the Australian National University (ANU). The editors wish to acknowledge the intellectual and material support received throughout this long and challenging project from their host institutions. Their gratitude extends to many people, starting with Professor Ramesh Thakur, Senior Vice Rector of the UNU, and Professor Ian McAllister, then Director of the ANU's Research School of Social Sciences.

Thanks must also go to the contributors of this volume. Any analysis of contemporary developments falls prey to the speed of events under review. The contributors accepted the challenge and scrambled determinedly to keep up. This should have been a sufficient difficulty, but they also needed to negotiate the requirements of their often over-demanding editors. The editors thank them for their unfailing professionalism and good humour.

Many people were consulted and many opinions sought in the drafting of this volume of essays. They cannot all be mentioned and, indeed, some requested anonymity. The editors would nevertheless like to thank some who gave of their time and wisdom – Boutros Boutros-Ghali, Danilo Turk, David Malone, Francisco da Costa Guterres, Hilary Charlesworth, and John Sanderson.

Finally, a special note of gratitude needs to be extended to those who gave their personal encouragement and support. Edward Newman would like to thank his colleagues Yoshie Sawada and Gareth Johnston. Roland Rich extends his gratitude to Nelly Lahoud.

Edward Newman   Roland Rich
Tokyo   Canberra
March 2004

Part I

Thematic perspectives

1

Introduction: Approaching democratization policy

Roland Rich and Edward Newman

Democracy, in both theory and practice, is the subject of a huge field of literature.[1] Within this literature, the international dimensions of democracy are increasingly understood and explored. Democracy has even come to be seen by some practitioners as something of a political panacea.[2] It is widely accepted as a universal value.[3] Yet the role of the United Nations – the embodiment of international society – in the promotion of democracy remains understudied, even though the organization has adopted democracy promotion as an important objective:

The phenomenon of democratization has had a marked impact on the United Nations. Just as newly-independent States turned to the United Nations for support during the era of decolonization, so today, following another wave of accessions to Statehood and political independence, Member States are turning to the United Nations for support in democratization. While this has been most visible in the requests for electoral assistance received since 1989 from more than 60 States – nearly one-third of the Organization's Membership – virtually no area of United Nations activity has been left untouched. The peace-keeping mandates entrusted to the United Nations now often include both the restoration of democracy and the protection of human rights. United Nations departments, agencies and programmes have been called on to help States draft constitutions, create independent systems for the administration of justice, provide police forces that respect and enforce the rule of law, de-politicize military establishments, and establish national institutions for the promotion and protection of human rights. They also have been asked by many States engaged in democratization to help

3

encourage and facilitate the active participation of citizens in political processes, and to foster the emergence of a productive civil society, including responsible and independent communications media.[4]

This volume explores and questions the modalities, effectiveness, and controversies of the UN's work in promoting and assisting democracy. It considers if the United Nations can help to build the foundations of democracy and whether, as an "external actor", it can have a substantive positive impact upon the development of democratic governance inside countries. The issues involved are approached from various angles. Thematic studies examine how the United Nations operates from the viewpoint of international law and within the theory and practice of democracy promotion. Focused chapters look specifically at techniques such as the operating mandates under which the United Nations works, the transitional authorities through which it operates, and the electoral design choices open to it. The volume also examines experience in this field through a series of case studies. "The pathway to any democracy is idiosyncratic, beset by a host of domestic political and cultural concerns particular to the nation in question."[5] And thus five case studies are selected to span time and space. The case studies are from three continents and begin with the UN's first efforts in this field, in Namibia, then pass through Cambodia, Kosovo, and East Timor, and end with what was thought, when this research project was first mapped out, to be the latest case, Afghanistan. Even as the eventual outcome of the democratization process in Afghanistan remains in the balance, the world's attention has shifted dramatically to the new challenge of 2003 – Iraq. While it is impossible for this volume to await the outcome of the post-war state-building process in Iraq, that situation is already casting its shadow over the UN system and indeed the international system as a whole. Clearly many of the issues raised in this volume will come under severe test in Iraq.

There is a natural tendency for high-profile cases to monopolize attention. These are the cases that demand attention from decision-makers, the media, and the public alike. But they do not tell the whole story of the democratization process and the UN's role therein. There are therefore also chapters on the work of the United Nations Development Programme and of the Electoral Assistance Unit of the Political Affairs Division of the UN Secretariat, explaining how the UN's work in democratization is a daily chore with long-term horizons. These chapters provide a useful counterweight to the balance of the book that mainly describes and analyses the dramatic and large operations.

The thrust of this project is therefore to ask, and hopefully to respond constructively, to the where, when, what, and how questions of the UN's involvement with democratization. The aim is to provide insights and provoke debate through critical analysis. But before launching into the analytical issues and attempting to draw conclusions, there is a preliminary question that should be addressed.

Why should the United Nations be involved in democratization?

The word "democracy" does not appear in the UN Charter. It is not one of the stated purposes of the United Nations to foster democracy, to initiate the process of democratization, or to legitimize other actors' efforts in this field. Democracy is not a precondition for UN membership; candidate members need only be "peace-loving states which accept the obligations in the present Charter and ... are able and willing to carry out these obligations".[6] Many members of the United Nations are not multiparty democracies in their domestic political structures, and many more could not be said to be liberal democracies. The United Nations is silent on other features of domestic political organization. It is agnostic as between republics and constitutional monarchies. It does not choose between presidential or parliamentary systems. It is ambivalent on the issue of bicameral as opposed to unicameral parliaments. Yet it propagates electoral democracy as the basic governance template for all nations to follow and the members appear to accept this view, or at least the UN's espousal of this view.

To understand the UN's penchant for democracy it might be worthwhile to look at the basic purposes of the United Nations as set out in the Preamble to the Charter and ask whether the UN's work in favour of democracy flows from these purposes.

"The scourge of war"

The UN's first purpose is to save succeeding generations from the scourge of war. Does democratization help avoid war? This is the question addressed by the debate on democratic peace theory. The basic thesis draws on concepts first advanced in the eighteenth century by Immanuel Kant on perpetual peace and on recent empirical work analysing international wars since 1817.[7] The conclusion from the study of wars over the past two centuries is that while democratic states often go to war against non-democratic states, they generally remain at peace with each other. The length of the period under study and the apparent consistency and strength of the observation of this "democratic peace" have led some scholars to draw the conclusion that democratization will have a substantial peace dividend.[8]

An acceptance of democratic peace theory would fully justify the UN's efforts in this area. The proposed link between peace and democracy would mean the UN's democratization work could be seen as a proactive means of ending the threat of the scourge of war. It clearly addresses the very purpose for which the United Nations was established. There are two ways of judging the theory: examining how widely it is accepted in the academic community, and gauging the extent to which policy-makers know, accept, and rely on it.

Samuel Huntington summarizes the importance of the issue when he says, "the democratic peace thesis is one of the most significant propositions to come out of social science in recent decades. If true, it has crucially important implications for both theory and policy."[9] The strength of the thesis comes from the robustness of the statistical evidence in support, largely provided by R. J. Rummel.[10] One way of reading Rummel's findings is to conclude that between 1816 and 1991, of the 353 pairings of nations fighting in major international wars, none occurred between two democracies. Such a startling statistical correlation is rare in the social sciences and provides a powerful foundation for democratic peace theory.

Debate continues, however, about the possible reason why consolidated democracies do not go to war against each other. Argumentation revolves around a number of hypotheses.[11] One theory claims that the checks and balances inherent in democratic decision-making act as a brake on decisions to go to war which is doubly effective when both sides of an argument are applying the brakes. Or perhaps there is a greater identification amongst the citizens of consolidated democracies, leading the peoples to a more sympathetic disposition towards each other through shared beliefs, making each less like "the other" and more like "us". Rational choice theorists also posit explanations based on democracies' greater competence in reaching non-zero-sum outcomes of not going to war. These debates are in the hands of social theorists and are unlikely to lead to any settled conclusions for a while.

There has been significant academic criticism of the democratic peace theory. Some of it inevitably focuses on the underlying definitions employed by Rummel and others to allow them to come to their conclusion.[12] More disturbing is the argument that while there may be some truth in the proposition in so far as consolidated democracies are concerned, transitional democracies have shown themselves to be particularly war-like.[13] For the United Nations, this poses an acute dilemma. If democratization is based on the purpose of securing world peace, one of the short-term consequences may be an upsurge of war. Another prob-lem with democratic peace theory is that it deals solely with interstate conflict and has little to say about internal national conflicts. Because many of the current trouble spots the United Nations must deal with are within the context of a single nation-state, democratic peace theory has little to offer in this regard.

The next question is the extent to which democratic peace theory has entered the policy domain. An important signal in this regard was President Clinton's 1994 State of the Union address, in which he based a key plank of his foreign policy on this theory when he said: "Ultimately, the best strategy to ensure our security and to build a durable peace is to support the advance of democracy elsewhere." Democracy-building worldwide became a key plank of the Clinton years, culminating in the launching of the Community of Democracies, which had as one of its underlying premises "the interdependence between peace, development, human rights and democracy".[14]

The Bush administration maintained an interest in democracy as an organizing principle in its foreign policy and has continued to support the Community of Democracies initiative, but, distracted by issues of terrorism, Afghanistan, and Iraq, the enthusiasm waned. Democracy promotion nevertheless continues to be a significant plank of the foreign policy and international development programmes of most Western democracies, and democratic peace theory is a key motivation.[15] Support can also be discerned among developing countries, given that 60 of the 115 participants and observers at the 2002 Seoul Ministerial Conference of the Community of Democracies were developing countries.[16]

One can conclude that there is solid backing, both academic and in practice, for the proposition that democratization will help avoid the scourge of war. But in neither field is the support complete, nor can it be said that a consensus has formed around this proposition. The United Nations is on solid ground in its democratization rationale based on this theory, but perhaps further justification is required in the other purposes of the United Nations.

"Faith in fundamental human rights"

The UN's second purpose revolves around respect for human rights. The question thus becomes whether it is established and accepted that there is a linkage between democracy and human rights. There is now a considerable body of literature on this subject[17] and an authoritative pronouncement by UN members in the 1993 Vienna Declaration and Plan of Action,[18] which established the clear link between human rights and democracy when it declared in paragraph 8:

Democracy, development and respect for human rights and fundamental free-doms are interdependent and mutually reinforcing. Democracy is based on the freely expressed will of the people to determine their own political, economic, social and cultural systems and their full participation in all aspects of their lives. In the context of the above, the promotion and protection of human rights and fundamental freedoms at the national and international levels should be universal and conducted without conditions attached. The international community should support the strengthening and promoting of democracy, development and respect for human rights and fundamental freedoms in the entire world.

The interdependence of human rights and democracy manifests itself in several ways. There is a strong argument that individuals have a right to participate in "genuine periodic elections" as required under Article 25 of the International Covenant on Civil and Political Rights. The meaning of "genuine periodic elections" is also becoming clearer with the recent decisions of the Human Rights Committee and the Commission on Human Rights spelling out that these must be free and fair multi-party elections.[19]

Another linkage is emerging in the suggested right to democratic gov-ernance forcefully posited by Thomas Franck.[20] The argument in favour of this thesis flows not only from the perspective of individual entitlement but also from the perspective of international legitimacy being conferred on governments coming to office by democratic means.[21] Yet until the right to democratic governance is enshrined in a widely adopted legal instrument, it is difficult to dispense with the term "emerging" in de-scribing its place in the panoply of human rights.

A further linkage is the understanding in human rights law, as articu-lated in the Universal Declaration of Human Rights, that democratic practice can mediate any limitations on the exercise of human rights.[22] Article 29 sets out the means of limiting the exercise of human rights, authorizing only "such limitations as are determined by law solely for the purpose of securing due recognition and respect for the rights and free-doms of others and of meeting the just requirements of morality, public order and the general welfare of a democratic society".

A final linkage may exist through the operation of the right of self-determination. Common Article 1 of the two major human rights cove-nants enshrines the right of self-determination for "all peoples" and asserts that "by virtue of that right they freely determine their political status". There have been suggestions that a form of internal self-determination is developing, providing the people of a state with a continuing right to self-determination in the choice of political systems and leaders.[23] This could well become yet another foundation for democracy in human rights law. But at present the more common interpretation of this right makes it more analogous to a right of decolonization than to a continuing right to democratic choice.[24]

The linkage between human rights and democracy is certainly sufficiently strong to be yet another rationale for the UN's involvement in democratization. The practice of the United Nations is increasingly to link the two issues in its work and to design interventions and supporting programmes with the effect of reinforcing respect for human rights with the building of democratic governance processes.

"To promote social progress and better standards of life"

Having found strong support for the propositions that democracy promotes peace and human rights, perhaps the most difficult question arises at this point when considering the third fundamental purpose of the United Nations: does democracy promote development? Initial thinking was that democracy depends on development, and that a certain level of income enjoyed by a large urban middle class was required before democracy could take hold.[25] This rather élitist concept of the flowering of democracy was a fundamental influence on the early shape of the international community's development assistance strategy, placing emphasis on economic growth, creation of export industries, and trickle-down models of social uplift. Jagdish Bhagwati wrote an influential book in 1966 in which he argued that developing countries faced a "cruel dilemma" because they had to choose between democracy and development.[26]

That early thinking has been replaced by a more sophisticated analysis. Bhagwati himself has had a change of heart and now believes that "the quality of democracy greatly affects the quality of development".[27] Other commentators stopped using the concept of development as a precondition for democracy and instead speak of certain factors, such as literacy rates, limited income inequality, and substantial economic activity independent of the state, as facilitating the development of democracy.[28] Amartya Sen points out the error of seeing democracy as an end product of a largely economic process. He argues that it was wrong to ask if a country is "fit for democracy"; the correct way to look at the issue of economic and social development is to understand that a country becomes "fit through democracy".[29]

The relationship between democracy and development will remain a subject of continuing research by theorists. The link between governance and development is now well established, and it is being complemented by a growing acceptance of the link between democracy and good governance. There is certainly a sufficient acceptance of the link to be another justification of why the United Nations is involved in democratization work.

There may remain continuing questions about the extent of the relevance of democracy to each of the three purposes of the United Nations discussed above. But when the link between democracy and these three major purposes of the United Nations is seen together, it constitutes a powerful case. All the more so when one considers the reinforcing nature of peace, human rights, and development to each other and the role that democracy plays in achieving each of these goals.

Outline of the volume

The first section of the volume raises a comprehensive range of issues, challenges, and controversies related to democracy promotion and assistance. These thematic papers deal with the genealogy, normative context, and justification of democracy promotion, the legal and political framework, and some of the difficulties of this activity. They highlight the strengths and weaknesses of the UN's democracy promotion, and set the scene for the case studies that follow.

Tom J. Farer's chapter, "The promotion of democracy: International law and norms", considers if the normative framework of the United Nations permits it to influence the institutions and structures of governance within member states, if it has the legal authority to promote or defend "democratic" forms of government, and, if so, by what means. Farer demonstrates that the United Nations has indeed acted to influence the allocation of authority and power within states. The organization was a major facilitator for self-determination, and its capacity to promote democratic forms of government when it has the consent of the affected state has been demonstrated. Only where democracy promotion does not enjoy the consent of the target state can there be any reasonable doubt about the legal authority of the United Nations or its agents, in line with the domestic jurisdiction clause of the UN Charter. Even then, state sovereignty has never been inviolable; it has never been absolute in the sense of precluding one state from taking any legitimate interest in what was going on in another, including issues relating to governance and human rights.

In concrete terms, the 1948 Universal Declaration on Human Rights states that "the will of the people shall be the basis of the authority of government ... [and] shall be expressed in periodic and genuine elections which shall be by universal and equal suffrage". Regional and global norms, institutions, and legal instruments have furthered this democratic entitlement. The United Nations has taken a role in the coercive promotion of human rights as well as in more functional technical assistance. In terms of coercive action, this chapter examines the cases of Somalia,

Haiti, and Sierra Leone and the implications they hold for the legal status of democracy and democracy-promoting activities. Finally, Farer's chapter examines the legal basis of a number of assertions that suggest a central – and potentially coercive – UN role in democracy promotion. These propositions are:

- that the United Nations should refuse to seat representatives of states in cases where they have overthrown a government elected in internationally monitored and certified elections
- among the member states of treaty regimes that have made democratic government a condition of participation, intervention in order to defend or restore a government elected in an internationally monitored and certified process is presumptively legitimate and should not be deemed an "enforcement action" under Article 53 of the Charter
- requests for Security Council authorization of military intervention to establish or restore elected governments that are not members of pro-democracy treaty regimes should be denied unless they are related to the occurrence in the target state of crimes against humanity or a humanitarian crisis resulting from the collapse of political order
- military intervention to overthrow a widely recognized unelected government not engaged in crimes against humanity should continue to be characterized as "aggression"
- in peace operations the United Nations should continue to treat democratic governance as the only plausible basis for a sustainable politics in conflicted societies, while recognizing that the particular form of democracy must be shaped primarily by the local context.

The decision-making process and language of UN mandates are of enormous importance to the development of the legal and normative framework of UN democracy promotion and assistance. Roland Rich's chapter, "Crafting Security Council mandates", examines the evolution of Security Council terminology relating to state-building operations and democracy assistance, and demonstrates how Security Council resolutions are the product of both law and politics. The terms of Council mandates are critical to establishing the legality of the UN's actions. Subsequently, the question of who drafts the resolutions is an important element in determining objectives and intentions. In the post-Cold War world, the Council has been operating in a far more collegial manner. Nevertheless, the influence of the major powers in drafting resolutions is clear, and there are often concerns of "permanent five" dominance. A critical question of this chapter is whether there is a coherent and cumulative process that builds on the style and terminology of the previous resolutions to establish an intentional pattern. The chapter suggests that there has indeed been a cumulative process. By looking at the language of resolutions in cases including Namibia, Angola, Western Sahara, East

Timor, Haiti, Kosovo, and Sierra Leone, Rich shows how the terminology is increasingly leaning towards the importance of governance in long-term solutions to conflict and instability.

However, this is not without problems. Mandates are constructed based on certain premises. One of those premises is the coherence of the political agreement negotiated by the disputing parties. If the agreements are negotiated in bad faith, or are beyond the ability of the signatories to implement, or are overtaken by subsequent events, the mandate that flows from them may be inappropriate. As a result of this, or because of the nature of building a consensus, resolutions are sometimes ambiguous. On the basis of experience, the chapter makes a number of conclusions: mandates need to be appraised on their clarity and practicality, with measurable targets in terms of performance, cost, timeliness, and closure. They must also have a defined division of labour.

Much of the UN's work in democracy assistance involves modest technical guidance and support. However, in exceptional circumstances, the United Nations is entrusted with a major role in upholding public authority, security, and governance. Simon Chesterman's chapter, "Building democracy through benevolent autocracy", considers the challenges of consultation and accountability in major UN transitional administrations such as in Bosnia, Eastern Slavonia, Kosovo, and East Timor. This chapter is guided by a number of core questions: how does one help a population prepare for democratic governance and the rule of law by imposing a form of benevolent autocracy? And to what extent should the transitional administration itself should be bound by the principles that it seeks to encourage in the local population?

In the case of Kosovo, Chesterman observes that the OSCE Ombudsperson came to a damning conclusion on UNMIK'S record:

UNMIK is not structured according to democratic principles, does not function in accordance with the rule of law, and does not respect important international human rights norms. The people of Kosovo are therefore deprived of protection of their basic rights and freedoms three years after the end of the conflict by the very entity set up to guarantee them.

There is a paradox here: consultation and accountability and local representation are central to democracy, yet in post-conflict situations democracy must be balanced against peace and stability. This chapter considers the different forms of consultation with local populations that have evolved in the various operations as a necessary precursor to the transfer of some or all power to local actors. It also examines whether a transitional administration itself can or should be held accountable for its actions in either a legal or a political sense. Chesterman concludes that there is a contradiction between the means and the ends of transitional administration, which stems from a reluctance to acknowledge the military force that gives it legitimacy. He argues that it is misleading to expect the international presence in territories such as Bosnia and Herzegovina, Kosovo, and East Timor to depend on local consent or "ownership". Consent of the local population is not the starting point. Accountability of international actors will necessarily be limited during the opening phases of an operation.

Elections are a mainstay of democratic politics; according to some definitions of democracy, they are the defining characteristic. In any context an electoral system attempts to result in a system of government that combines and balances a number of values: accountability, participation, pluralism, representation, stability, efficiency. The timing and modalities of electoral assistance are critical. Benjamin Reilly's chapter, "Elections in post-conflict societies", argues that elections are not always conducive to post-conflict peace-building. He observes that variations in electoral procedures can play a key role in determining whether political competition evolves along extremist or centrist lines, and hence in developing moderate and broad-based political parties. Three main areas of variation are crucial influences on the shape of post-conflict politics in most countries. First, there is the question of timing: should post-conflict elections be held as early as possible, so as to fast-track the process of establishing a new regime? Or should they be postponed until peaceful political routines and issues have been able to come to prominence? Second, there are the mechanics of elections themselves: who runs the elections? How are voters enrolled? What electoral formula is used? Third, there is the issue of political parties. Especially in cases of weak civil society, political parties are the key link between masses and élites, and play a crucial role in building a sustainable democratic polity. As Reilly observes, "there is the overarching issue of under what circumstances elections help to build a new democratic order, and under what circumstances they can undermine democracy and pave the way for a return to conflict".

Laurence Whitehead's chapter, "Democratization with the benefit of hindsight: The changing international components", reflects on the arguments and presumptions of the "democratic transitions" theories and how they relate to the international dimensions of democracy and democratization. In fact he observes that much of the seminal literature on democratization neglected the role of international actors and norms. Democratization was viewed as internally driven and most likely to succeed when external destabilizing pressures could be minimized. The relevant unit of analysis was therefore the state (or national political regime), and attention was focused on those states that possessed sufficient internal autonomy to screen out international intrusions. The situation today appears quite different. In re-evaluating democratic transition, Whitehead considers the balance between the external and internal drivers of regime change; the privileged site of state sovereignty as the main locus of attention; the new emphasis on democracy as security, rather than democracy as liberation; and the consequent appropriation of democratic discourse and rhetoric as justification for potentially neo-imperial initiatives that can now apparently be pursued unilaterally, without regard for countervailing responses.

The second section of the volume, Perspectives from the United Nations, provides an analysis of the practical work of the United Nations in democracy assistance, and some consideration of the conceptual and practical challenges; the chapters are also written from within the constraints that exist for authors writing as UN staff members. Robin Ludwig begins this section with an overview of UN electoral work in "The UN's electoral assistance: Challenges, accomplishments, prospects". She demonstrates how, since 1989, the United Nations has become an important source of international support and expertise in the conduct of democratic elections. This built in some ways upon the experience of decolonization and the UN Charter "principle of equal rights and self-determination of peoples". The end of the Cold War gave real impetus to international democracy assistance. The United Nations was called upon to assume a new, more active role in peacemaking and conflict resolution, and growing international emphasis was also placed on its work in the promotion and protection of human rights. At the same time, international negotiations on a variety of long-term conflicts began to show signs of success, and the issue of governance and democracy became integral with long-term conflict settlement. Nevertheless, as Ludwig observes, the beginnings of UN electoral assistance were not uncontroversial, due to sensitivities relating to sovereignty and interference in domestic affairs.

Nevertheless, in 1991 the General Assembly adopted a resolution entitled "Enhancing the effectiveness of the principle of periodic and genuine elections". With this resolution, the General Assembly established an organizational structure for the provision of electoral assistance. A UN focal point for electoral assistance activities was established, and the mechanisms and processes of electoral assistance were developed. Ludwig describes how that process works – starting from a written request by a member state to the Secretary-General, or to the focal point. The varying forms of assistance described by Ludwig include the supervision of elections, verification of elections, organization and conduct of elections, coordination and support for elections, domestic election observation, and technical assistance. Ludwig concludes that one of the most important lessons of UN electoral experience over the past decade is the evolution of a more realistic view of the role that elections can play in the creation of democracy. In the early 1990s many in the international community believed that the successful conduct of an election would establish the basis for the growth of a viable democracy. Experience demonstrated, however, that although elections contribute substantially to democratization, elections alone are not enough.

Edward Newman's chapter, "UN democracy promotion: Comparative advantages and constraints", raises a number of conceptual and practical challenges related to democracy assistance and considers the potential of various actors, especially the United Nations. His chapter considers if "external" international actors – such as hegemonic states, global organizations, regional organizations, financial institutions, and NGOs – can have a decisive, substantial, and enduring impact upon domestic transition and democratization, or whether assistance programmes only have a positive impact where the society in question is already moving towards democracy. He considers if top-down government assistance programmes are the most effective, or those that work with civil society and nongovernmental groups, and whether the promotion of democracy in post-conflict and divided societies has a significant role in conflict settlement and reconciliation. Newman also considers what values or models of democracy external agents such as the United Nations or the USA bring with them to the democratization process, and how successful democracy assistance activities have been in terms of consolidating democracy in transitional societies.

This chapter concludes that the United Nations has had a modestly successful although not dramatic impact upon the countries in which it has assisted democracy and democratization. However, the extent to which durable institutions have been created in some of these cases is questionable, and the quality of democracy – in terms of accountability, transparency in political decision-making, participation and inclusion, and a constructive civil society – is also questionable. In most cases the United Nations can only facilitate progress when local conditions are conducive to this. When conditions are not, or when the UN's approach is not entirely appropriate for the nature of local conditions, success is unlikely. UN assistance is most fruitful when a convergence of forces – both within the society and internationally – coalesce around a democratic future and broad acceptance of democratic rules of the game.

Richard Ponzio's chapter deals with "UNDP experience in long-term democracy assistance". He describes how the UNDP made the promotion of democratic governance a core operational activity in the 1990s. Focusing on development assistance, this has involved support for electoral management bodies and parliaments to facilitate constitutional reforms and decentralization processes, giving primacy to building indigenous

governing capacity. This often stands in marked contrast with – but complementary to – short-term interventions to stabilize a country and build
the foundations for recovery and peace. His chapter provides a short review of the evolution of the UNDP's involvement in long-term democracy assistance, and raises a number of research questions in scrutinizing
two distinct types of UNDP engagement, namely electoral systems support and assistance to legislative bodies. What is the UNDP's record in
building indigenous capacity within formal and informal democratic institutions? To what extent is it possible to draw conclusions and "best
practices" from limited experience in different contexts? In examining
these questions, the chapter contributes to the broader and more complicated question: does the UN system, through agencies such as the
UNDP, have a decisive and enduring impact upon democratization in a
country?

While each country setting poses unique challenges, some global lessons
can be gleaned from UNDP successes and failures in election-related activities since the 1970s. The UNDP's emerging comparative advantage
lies in helping countries establish independent and permanent electoral
bodies through long-term institutional capacity development. Electoral
assistance has provided the UNDP and the UN system with a strategic
entry point for broader, long-term democratic governance programming.
Successful elections are critical in establishing political legitimacy within
countries seeking to make a transition towards democracy and away from
more authoritarian (and sometimes violent) rule. Effective civic and
voter-education programmes, both prior to and following elections, help
expand democratic participation. Donor coordination and resource mobilization are UNDP services that can be essential to the preparation of
an election. And the UNDP provides valuable support to the implementation of technical assistance programmes for elections.

The final section of the volume deals with cases of major UN democracy assistance, spanning a broad historical and geographic range. The
authors have all been personally engaged in the issues, they have a stake
in the outcomes, and they provide an immediacy to their chapters that
is often missing from the analyses of the more dispassionate observer.
Henning Melber's chapter, "Decolonization and democratization: The
United Nations and Namibia's transition to democracy", deals with one
of the first such cases. The historical context was important to the UN's
electoral assistance in Namibia because this took place in the context
of the country's transition to independence. His chapter explores the
role played by the United Nations in contributing to a democratic post-
colonial political order.

Melber argues that the United Nations played a crucial, if not decisive,
role through the UN Transitional Assistance Group with supervisory

powers for the transition of Namibia to an internationally accepted sovereign state. Indeed, the United Nations can be considered as the midwife to the birth of the Republic of Namibia, proclaimed in 1990. The democratic political system established as the framework for the governing of this society has since been shaped to a considerable extent both directly and indirectly by the United Nations and its agencies involved in the process.

However, Melber argues that the United Nations was more of a broker in the transition to internationally accepted independence than an agency promoting democracy as its priority. And, like a number of other post-independence African countries, Namibia was characterized by a liberation movement turning into a political party to occupy political power. In this case SWAPO consolidated its dominant position and expanded control over the state apparatus. Its legitimacy was based on being the representative of the majority of the people. Yet Melber questions the commitment of the ruling élite to true democratic principles and values. The track records of the African liberation movements – both with regard to their internal practices during the wars of liberation as well as their lack of democratic virtues and respect for the protection of human rights once in power – are far from positive examples. Namibia's first decade of independence witnessed a constant consolidation of political power and control by the former liberation movement, and Namibia's political culture reveals more than a decade after independence some disturbing features of deterioration. Melber concludes that the Namibian case of decolonization was guided by the goal of achieving a more or less democratically legitimate transition towards independence, but not the firm entrenchment of democracy.

Sorpong Peou's chapter, "The UN's modest impact on Cambodia's democracy", concludes that the best that can be said for the UN role in democratizing Cambodian politics is that it has been "positive but modest". His chapter asserts that Cambodia would have remained undemocratic had the United Nations (and individual member states of the UN system) not intervened. In terms of the legacy of democracy assistance, Peou observes a number of positive achievements that he partly attributes to the UN presence. The constitution (largely drafted by UN advisers and adopted after the 1993 election) has survived; Cambodia continues to have a multi-party electoral system and has thus far held national elections on a regular basis; political violence has been steadily declining; and political parties seem to accept election outcomes more readily. However, this alone does not qualify Cambodian democracy as liberal and embedded. The United Nations was unable to disarm the Cambodian signatories, a circumstance that perpetuated the conflict until 1998. The United Nations by itself has had a very limited impact on the promotion of equitable media access during elections. The Cambodian authorities failed to respond to UN pressure for equitable media access, or comply with UN demands for law enforcement in relation to electoral laws. Cambodian authorities also tended to ignore repeated UN calls for political justice. In short, Peou argues that the UN success in promoting democracy should not be exaggerated. Cambodia's cultural and socio-economic factors made it difficult for the United Nations to play a more effective role in the country. At the time of the UN's arrival Cambodia had no genuine democratic culture, and there were clear limitations in terms of what the United Nations could achieve.

Ylber Hysa's chapter, "Kosovo: A permanent international protec-torate?", addresses a complex case of international democracy assistance. Democracy assistance activities in Kosovo have occurred against a back-ground of vicious state persecution, ethnic conflict, secessionist pressures, and international military involvement. This is not an auspicious context for the fostering of pluralism and democratic values. Nevertheless, in the wake of the NATO military campaign a broad range of reconstruction efforts were initiated, including education, police and security, supporting civil society, and democracy assistance. This has involved a number of very delicate challenges, relating to the position of the remaining minor-ity Serbs in Kosovo and their willingness – or not – to participate in the democratic process, the need to establish a secure environment, the transformation and demilitarization of the Kosovar guerilla movement, the reconstruction of the economy, and elections.

Hysa concludes that the UN interim mission in Kosovo is a unique and ambitious UN engagement. Not only is it a peacemaking and peace-keeping mission, but at the same time it is a mission engaged in the ad-ministration and building of democratic institutions. It has required the creation of a completely new administration that started with a transi-tional phase and ended with the emergence of free local and general elections. Even though the United Nations is seized with the importance of its mission in Kosovo, its bureaucratized structure and a multiplicity of external actors place it in a poor position to discharge the ambitious objective set for it by the international community. Ultimately, he con-cludes, it must be the people of Kosovo who determine the fate of their land and who must provide the decisive input for the successful democ-ratization of Kosovo.

A case that learnt lessons from Kosovo – although not necessarily all the right lessons – was the UN's involvement in East Timor. Tanja Hohe's chapter, "Delivering feudal democracy in East Timor", describes how the UN Transitional Administration in East Timor (UNTAET) had been given a mandate to rebuild and administer a country that was re-duced to ruins by the Indonesian military and local militias after a successful vote by the East Timorese for independence in 1999. A central theme of her chapter is that state-building and democratization are particularly difficult to achieve. She argues that whilst certain institutions were successfully established, UN state-building in East Timor was ultimately insufficient and inappropriate in its approach. It ignored local realities and functioned without specialized local knowledge. The international community focused solely on the establishment of Western institutions at the national level, which were not appropriate to local conditions.

An uninformed international community was not aware of how different local politics was from the forms taken by modern democratic states, and how these indigenous traits could undermine any state-building programme. The result, she argues, is that the institutions of Western democracy have not taken root in East Timor. The result of the mix of local social hierarchy, national political factions competing for exclusive authority, and the UN's centralization and absolutism has been the establishment of a type of feudal political culture. While internal constraints of the UN organization have been widely addressed, the intricacies of local realities on the ground are an additional dimension yet to be adequately appreciated. The grass-roots therefore need special attention, as this is where the majority of the population live and their understanding is an important ingredient for success. Their participation in the state-building process and a basic understanding of state institutions are crucial. The United Nations, she argues, has not yet developed effective methods to involve local populations, and has not even focused adequately on this problem.

Finally, Amin Saikal focuses on the United Nations and democratization in Afghanistan, which reflects a quite different case to Kosovo and East Timor. He recalls that the United Nations has had a long involvement in Afghanistan, directed at bringing peace and stability to the country. Whilst previous efforts have been modest, the US-led military intervention in Afghanistan in 2002 opened an opportunity for the United Nations to play a central role in helping the Afghans to settle their internal differences and build a lasting, popularly legitimated political order. However, the attempt to promote democracy is fraught with difficulty. The Afghan people, who are made up of various traditional Muslim micro-societies, divided along ethno-tribal, linguistic, sectarian, and personality lines, have never had a tradition or culture of democracy. Saikal's chapter explores the history of the Afghan conflict and the UN's role in search of a peaceful end to it; and evaluates the UN's role in the post-Taliban settlement of the Afghan conflict in terms of helping the Afghans to create the necessary conditions for the growth of a stable and workable political order. Finally, he discusses the steps which have been taken in which the United Nations has been involved in support of democratization in Afghanistan. Perhaps one of the most critical questions in Afghanistan concerns the nature of its state and society. Resolution 1378, adopted on 14 November 2001, authorized the United Nations to play a "central role" in helping the Afghan people to establish a transitional administration for the formation of a new government. But Afghanistan continues to provide a classic case of a weak state with a strong society, according to Saikal. Historically, Afghanistan's micro-societies have operated both individually and in alliance with one another, and the dynamics of their relations amongst themselves and with a central authority have been critical in defining the powers of the central authority and the nature of the Afghan state.

There is no chapter on Iraq, the war having concluded and the reconstruction effort begun as this volume was nearing completion. It is already clear that the situation in Iraq presents the United Nations and the international community with its sternest test. Among the many challenges being faced is the challenge of democratization. As one commentator has already pointed out:

Iraq has all the characteristics that have impeded democratic transitions elsewhere: a large, impoverished population deeply divided along ethnic and religious lines; no previous experience with democracy; and a track record of maintaining stability only under the grip of a strongly autocratic government. The United States enjoys no clear advantage in trying to develop a new political system for Iraq. It has no historical ties to the country and little understanding of Iraqi culture and society. Many Iraqis resent the United States as an occupying power.[30]

Pulling the strands together

The five case studies, the description of UN development assistance for democracy-building, and the various thematic chapters are eloquent testimony to a simple truth: the United Nations is engaged in a vast and ambitious enterprise. The people engaged in this work come from many different walks of life. They include political leaders and civil society leaders, soldiers and police, lawyers and judges, international civil servants and local bureaucrats, development specialists and democracy specialists. Given the number of talented people involved over the past dozen years, it is not surprising that this volume does not pretend to have discovered a large truth that somehow eluded all its predecessors. That is because there is no magic formula for success. But pulling together the strands of the various chapters provides interesting insights. The chapters were written from particular country or specialist perspectives.

They were written by academics, practitioners, and engaged activists. Yet common themes emerge from the chapters that may assist in further refining and improving the UN's work in the field. The themes can usefully be grouped under three broad headings: managing time, making trade-offs, and mastering techniques.

Managing time

Time is never an ally; it is always the remorseless enemy. This is true of virtually every situation the United Nations must deal with, from building states out of the rubble of war to assisting local authorities prepare for impending elections. In dealing with democratization questions, the United Nations works to many timetables, each more pressing than the last. Militant groups are often standing-off uneasily waiting for an opportunity to seize a speedy victory rather than engage in the tortuously slow work of compromise and reconciliation. Local people are impatient for security and normality to return to their lives. Peacekeepers and parachuted civil administrators are working through their allotted time before their successors begin their own steep learning curves. The major financial contributors are nervously watching the meter tick, knowing that each day represents millions of dollars in costs to their taxpayers. And the international community, fed by a frenetic media, finds it hard to maintain focus for long as it is beckoned to switch its attention to the next urgent situation.

Working to this time pressure, the United Nations and its fellow democracy promoters are confronted with the problem of promoting democracy while all the time knowing that the eventual solution will ultimately only be found in generational change. Democracy is far more than the holding of a transitional or post-conflict election. It is the building of a political system that has to survive the inevitable manipulation from insiders, the necessary alternation among power holders, and the attempts at usurpation by ambitious groups. It is a political system that must surmount the disappointment of defeated candidates, the continuing despair of marginalized communities, and the exasperation of the intelligentsia with the slow pace of reform. Democracy is both a system of working institutions and a viable political culture. Both aspects need time to establish themselves profoundly in any polity. The amount of time needed for such profound change cannot be measured in a financial year, a mandate period, or even a five-year plan. It is generational. Yet, of course, the United Nations does not have the luxury of that much time.

The most striking manifestation of the problem of management of time by the United Nations in its major national democracy-building programmes can be summarized in two words pregnant with consequences:

"exit strategy". The problem that led to the push for exit strategies can perhaps best be seen from one of the continuing UN peacekeeping programmes, the UN Military Observer Group in India and Pakistan. Set up in 1949, UNMOGIP was deployed to supervise the cease-fire agreed between India and Pakistan in the state of Jammu and Kashmir. Since renewed hostilities in 1971, UNMOGIP monitors the cease-fire called for by the UN Security Council. So, over half a century later, even though one of the two disputing parties considers the mandate to have lapsed, the international community continues to pay almost $10 million each year to have 68 international personnel "supervise" a cease-fire.[31] UNMOGIP has simply become part of the scenery. Its continued existence is not due to what it might be able to achieve but because of the possible diplomatic difficulties of ending the mission. Hence the understandable call for exit strategies.

Many of the case studies and thematic chapters point to problems posed by the pressure to bring major UN operations in the field to a close. The tendency to see the post-conflict national elections as a proper time for such a withdrawal places great pressure to hold the election as quickly as possible and then leave the local political forces to grapple with a new and difficult system. Cost pressures and changing priorities as new crises emerge add to the momentum for withdrawal of the United Nations. The question needs to be asked as to whether it is wise to jeopardize a significant investment by withdrawing precipitously. There are criticisms that this was the case in Cambodia, and fears that this may be the case in East Timor.[32] Yet where a region has the resources and will-power to support a more deliberate and engaged strategy, as do the Europeans in the Balkans, time pressure becomes far less pressing, horizons broaden, and democratization plans become more elaborate.

Accepting the inevitability of pressure for an exit strategy, the United Nations needs to plan around this with a well-thought-through entry strategy. A coherent entry strategy entails an understanding of the limits of UN effectiveness, an appreciation of the areas of UN comparative advantage, and a system of setting priorities and following a process of sequencing. The entry strategy begins with the international debate and passes through the drafting of the mandate. There is a tendency in the course of this process to adopt unrealistically ambitious goals and time-frames. These can lead to situations where the United Nations is virtually the sole actor with the task of turning an entire society around – a recipe for failure. With mounting experience in the field, the United Nations is increasingly accepting that its task is more often than not that of the coordinator of and the bringer of legitimacy to a broad effort involving regional civilian and military organizations, donor agencies, specialized agencies, humanitarian organizations, non-governmental organizations, and local civil society. The UN value added is thus in the leadership role it undertakes and the confidence it builds in all parties through its involvement.

The reality the United Nations faces in building such coalitions is that national interests and international politics will determine the level of enthusiasm in any given situation. There was at one time an unwritten practice that peacekeeping forces should come from areas far away from the trouble spot, that the countries involved in peacekeeping be disinterested in the outcome of the local dispute, and that international citizenship rather than national interest should be the determining factor for involvement. Recent practice has tended to sweep away this concept. Today it tends to be the coalitions of the willing that undertake the tough peace-building jobs. They are self-selected on the basis of direct national interest in the outcome. Thus the Balkans can attract European attention, Haiti has US involvement, and East Timor has a protector in Australia. But the diminution of international citizenship as the motivating factor for disinterested involvement and its replacement with national interests usually based on proximity can leave many other parts of the world in difficulty. Rwanda and the Democratic Republic of Congo are examples.

Managing time boils down to good mission design. It requires realistic mandates and good planning. The larger the mission, the more effort is required for coalition-building. Perhaps most of all, it requires a high degree of competence on the part of the United Nations as the leader in the field. This in turn requires an understanding of trade-offs and techniques.

Making trade-offs

One of the recurrent criticisms of UN efforts, echoed in a number of the case studies, is an unstated assumption that the United Nations is somehow entering a political vacuum that simply needs to be filled with its own leadership. The assumption is particularly easy to make in situations of weak states or where occupying powers have been vanquished, leaving an absence of administrative machinery. There is a temptation in such situations to think of the area as a type of governance *tabula rasa* where the new administering power may construct a new political order beginning with first principles.

But as we can see in Afghanistan, weak states can have strong societies. As became quickly evident in Kosovo, in the shadow of the formal occupation administration that was swept away, there exists a parallel informal local administration. And as is clear in East Timor, a quarter of a century of Indonesian administration did not destroy traditional village governance processes. The first trade-off that has to be made is a balance between notions of a universal template of governance and the reality of local politics. Even acephalous polities have politics.

The UN administration also often quickly finds itself facing another trade-off situation: the trade-off between impartiality and the reality that there is often a liberation organization that has fought long and hard and now awaits the spoils. The question becomes one of how to manage SWAPO, or Fretilin, or the Kosovo Liberation Army. There is no point in pretending that such organizations lose their *raison d'être* simply because their foe is vanquished. The better view is that they need to be integrated into society in as transparent and orderly a way as possible. This will entail including established leaders in consultation machinery, incorporating parts of such forces into the police or army, and allowing political organizations to test their popularity at the polls. There is a corollary trade-off here. The UN role in democratization is largely undertaken through capacity-building processes. Yet an essential ingredient for success is local ownership of the issues and results. There may be instances when a less ostensibly efficient system is put in place that gives significant decision-making power to local actors, even in transition situations, and allows them to learn from their own mistakes.

Clearly the United Nations cannot be expected to get it right every time. Getting right the balance between principle and pragmatism is a great political art. Perhaps in Cambodia the acceptance of the participation of the Khmer Rouge in the political process simply delayed for nearly a decade the ultimate UN responsibility to bring to book those guilty of genocide. Perhaps in Cambodia also, acceding to the demand of the incumbent Cambodian People's Party to share in power even though they had been the losers in the UN-organized election has simply slowed the democratization process. The choice was between power-sharing and perhaps a return to arms, and in such a choice the peace imperative will usually prevail. There is therefore often a critical trade-off between security and politics.

In examining the work of the United Nations in the field, the greatest pressure comes from the inescapable priority to assure a certain level of security before any efforts of democratization can take hold. Democracy needs a functioning state in which to operate, and it needs security at least sufficient to allow a free and fair vote to take place. The participation of the people of East Timor in their act of self-determination in August 1999, despite militia harassment, demonstrates the courage people will display to have a say in their political future.[33] Such a vote was only possible because the presence of UNAMET provided the population with some reassurance of a secure environment for the vote, though UNAMET was helpless in the face of the fury unleashed by its result. And where it is not possible to assure a workable level of security, as in Somalia, there can be no effective democratization process.

Time and again the cases demonstrate the necessity for priority to be given to the military and police efforts. There can be no question about this. Criticism is possible, however, where the enforcement effort has so dominated the process of change that there is little energy left for the democracy-building task. One wonders whether this problem may affect Afghanistan. Defeating the Taliban government that had harboured the al-Qaeda leadership was an operation that had virtually the entire world behind it, but the subsequent state-building efforts are not nearly as riveting. The security situation is still not satisfactory in rural Afghanistan, and there is a question mark over whether the United Nations and the international community will stay the course and successfully rebuild the civilian infrastructure that underpins democracy.

Mastering techniques

After a decade of practice in promoting democracy, the United Nations can be expected to have come close to understanding and wielding the appropriate techniques. The structural issues involved concern those of consultation, institutional design, transition processes, circuit-breaker in intractable conflicts, reconciliation initiatives, establishing rule of law, and transferring skills. Every situation the United Nations faces has its own particularities and the United Nations needs to be a master of the general and a country specialist at the same time. The United Nations arrives in-country armed with a basket of universal values and norms, yet often is confronted by groups motivated by a culturally specific moral order, often distorted by years of national trauma. Does the United Nations have the right kitbag of techniques and attitudes to deal with these situations?

First and foremost among the UN's assets are its people. Beginning with the Secretary-General himself, the United Nations needs to put the right people in place. Kofi Annan has demonstrated his skills in many difficult situations. Having spent a career at the United Nations and having lived through the peacekeeping crises of the early 1990s, Annan came with a broad vision of the UN's role, tempered by an understanding of what the United Nations could realistically be expected to achieve. One of the Secretary-General's most important tasks is to put the right people in place as the special representative of the Secretary-General (SRSG). A consistent theme emerging from a study of UN activism in the field is the impact of the personality and style of the SRSG. The decision in 2003 to appoint Sergio Vieira de Mello as SRSG to Iraq for a four-month period is testimony to the critical importance of the position. Vieira de Mello had only recently been appointed as the UN High Commissioner for Human Rights, one of the highest-profile positions in the UN system, and yet Annan considered it so important to have an experienced campaigner in the Iraq position that he was prepared to take the risk of withdrawing Vieira de Mello from Geneva. The reason for Annan's surprising decision can be seen in Vieira de Mello's success in his recent assignment in East Timor and the Secretary-General's appreciation of the role of the SRSG. It may be partly for reasons of his undoubted abilities that Vieira de Mello was tragically targeted for assassination.

The SRSG has virtual monarchical powers in the transition process and, as history judges a monarch's reign in part through that individual's personality, so must the SRSG's reign be assessed. Experience shows that the best profile for a successful SRSG is to have a UN insider who knows how to get the most out of a stubbornly inflexible system. The SRSG also needs to find a way to connect with local actors, often through a shared maternal language, while being seen by those actors as unconnected with the politics of the situation. The SRSG clearly must be a good manager, effective communicator, and a successful coalition-builder. Vieira de Mello had these qualities, as does Lakhdar Brahimi in Afghanistan. The initial SRSG in Kosovo, Bernard Kouchner, was also seen in a positive light in many quarters, while his successor, Hans Haekkerup, had more difficulty connecting with local politics. The third SRSG in Kosovo, Michael Steiner, seems to have made a strong start. The SRSG in Cambodia, Yasushi Akashi, did as well as could be expected with a relatively weak mandate and, heading the first major operation in the post-Cold War period, he suffered from the inexperience of the UN Secretariat in New York in handling the mission as well as some questionable appointments in the field.[34]

The Secretary-General and the SRSGs are supported by thousands of people in New York and in the field. The roles they assume range from the soldier authorized to employ force to fulfil a Security Council requirement to the official advising local electoral officials on best practice in ballot-paper design. At this point, one must ask whether a workforce of expatriates, not sharing the same cultural or educational background and speaking in several different languages, is comparatively the best group to undertake the range of tasks required. One of the chapters in this volume looks in detail at this question, and others approach it from various thematic and case-based viewpoints. A case can be made that the UN system necessarily produces a "Tower of Babel" of misunderstandings and confusion that can never compare favourably in efficiency with the best national bureaucracies. If, however, one looks at the work being performed not as "tasks" but as a "role", a different perspective emerges. The point here is that the United Nations and its people are most important as the vectors between the situation on the ground and the norms, values, and aspirations of the international community. The legitimacy the United Nations brings with it is as important in this process as the skills it employs.

But even in this context, the skills need to be developed and exercised effectively. The United Nations will at times lack the necessary skills. This is obviously the case in enforcement operations, where the United Nations lacks the military skills of countries such as the USA, France, or Australia, or of organizations like NATO or the Military Observer Group (ECOMOG) of the Economic Community of West African States. It can also be the case in capacity-building programmes, where partnerships with international financial institutions, global civil society organizations, or bilateral donor agencies and their consultants may be the best way to deliver results. Again, the United Nations adds legitimacy to such operations as well as oversight in delivery. The element of legitimacy can often be employed in the UN's consciousness-raising role. The UNDP's global *Human Development Report 2002,* on the theme "Deepening democracy in a fragmented world", had significant impact in setting an agenda for democracy in many national and regional debates. The *Arab Human Development Report 2002*, written by Arab specialists, had considerable impact in a region which has not yet seen the full impact of the third wave of democratization. As one of the authors, Rima Khalaf Hunaidi, notes:

the *Arab Human Development Report* has received unprecedented attention. In the Arab world and many Western capitals, virtually no major newspaper has failed to give it extensive coverage, and the broadcast media have been equally generous.[35]

No national or academic report could have had similar impact.

One area where the analysts in this volume find fault is with the way the United Nations discharges its accountability function. The UN's ultimate overseer is the membership of the organization. But having 191 masters does not presage having efficient oversight, particularly where the process of review of the work of the organization is highly political. There are also internal processes of oversight in the budgetary and personnel areas that parallel similar mechanisms in organizations of such size. These are clearly important, but they suffer from the fact that they share a broad world view – they do not see the world the way the recipients of UN assistance see it. Connecting with and being responsive to local people is perhaps the UN's greatest challenge and one it is not meeting well enough. The consultation processes are often too *ad hoc* or too personalized in terms of the relationship of local political leaders with the SRSG. One of the effects of the tendency to personalization of the process is that it often leaves resignation or the threat thereof as the only means of protest. The United Nations cannot be expected overnight to turn traumatized societies into pluralist utopia and hold monthly referenda, but it can be expected to encourage élites and volunteers to debate the issues and start the process of building deliberative democracy. It can also be expected to study the local situation more closely and gain a better understanding of local perspectives.

There are mechanisms available to the United Nations in this regard. The independent ombudsperson, as instituted in Kosovo, is an excellent initiative that can play a crucial role of representing local people dealing with a new, confusing, and sometimes opaque administration. The use of local media outlets is another means of involving local communities in the governance debate. Depending on local practice, other techniques such as petitions, gatherings of traditional leaders, or meetings with NGOs can also improve the communication process. The various "lessons-learned" processes within the United Nations are available to examine best practice in consultation processes.[36] The United Nations would be selling short all the energy it puts into these processes if it adopts a "we always know best" approach.

Defining the UN role in democratization

The present volume attempts in various ways to assess how well the United Nations is performing in its democracy-promotion role. The aim of the exercise is neither to praise nor to chastise the United Nations but to analyse how best it can contribute to this important ambition. Another way of looking at the issue is to ask whether the United Nations is indispensable to global democratization efforts. This is a better question than the riddle often posed in justification of the United Nations by its supporters: is the situation better after UN involvement? This is far too glib a question, as it takes no account of the tremendous resources the United Nations is employing and the reasonable expectation of a return from those assets.

A survey of the case studies and programmes described in this volume raises a fundamental difficulty that can be posited in the following simple question: is the United Nations only able to advance democratization in relatively small societies? There seems to be a correlation between the size of the problem and the degree of UN achievement. The success stories like Namibia, Kosovo, and East Timor are all societies of modest population size. The problems in these societies are no less complex than in other cases, but the breadth of the problem is somehow manageable.

An academic case for UN indispensability has recently been made in relation to another small society that is of critical importance to future global peace efforts, Palestine. In rejecting the ability of the USA to resolve the question of Palestine on a bilateral basis, even though it clearly has the most influence on all the parties involved, an influential academic has made the case for a UN trusteeship over Palestine as the only way of overseeing the process of statehood and democracy-building. The Kosovo and East Timor situations were seen as the relevant precedents.[37]

But the situations the United Nations finds most testing are those of large nations like Afghanistan, Congo, and Iraq. If the United Nations can only successfully deal with the small islands, the sparsely populated territories, and the ethnic enclaves then it will fail the indispensability test. The case of Cambodia becomes ever more telling in this regard. It can currently neither be regarded a success nor a failure, as Cambodia's UN-nurtured democratic forms are not matched by a local democratic spirit. But Cambodia shows that the United Nations does have the ambition to tackle the large problems. The future of Afghanistan, Congo, and Iraq will tell us much more about the extent of the UN role in global democracy promotion.

Until there is an answer to this key question, we must content ourselves with a list of the significant roles the United Nations plays in this field. It can bring international legitimacy to the international community's efforts, even when it pronounces itself after the event as in Kosovo, and even where it remains ambivalent about the legality of the preceding actions as in Iraq. This legitimacy is transferable to the UN's agents and partners, making it one of the UN's principal assets. The United Nations also has the role of a conveyor of norms and values. It is the vector between the principles its members espouse and the reception of these principles on the ground. The vector role can most successfully be performed if the conveying agents are materially disinterested in the results, a description that is difficult to ascribe to powerful neighbouring states undertaking bilateral democratization efforts. The UN's international legitimacy enhances its role as a vector of ideals and ideas. The balance of this volume examines how the United Nations has undertaken its role in propagating one of the great ideals of our age, democracy.

Notes

1. Space does not allow even a cursory citation of the most important works, but to mention some: Dahl, Robert. 1971. *Polyarchy: Participation and Opposition*. New Haven: Yale University Press; Diamond, Larry. 1999. *Developing Democracy: Toward Consolidation*. Baltimore: Johns Hopkins University Press; Held, David. 1996. *Models of Democracy*, 2nd edn. Cambridge: Polity Press; Huntington, Samuel P. 1991. *The Third Wave: Democratization in the Late Twentieth Century*. Norman: University of Oklahoma Press; Lijphart, Arend. 1999. *Patterns of Democracy: Government Forms and Performance in Thirty-six Countries*. New Haven: Yale University Press; O'Donnell, Guillermo, Philippe Schmitter, and Laurence Whitehead (eds). 1986. *Transitions from Authoritarian Rule: Prospects for Democracy*, 4 vols. Baltimore: Johns Hopkins University Press.

2. The US Department of State has a policy to "promote democracy as a means to achieve security, stability, and prosperity for the entire world". See www.state.gov/g/drl/democ/.
3. Sen, Amartya. 1999. "Democracy as a universal value", *Journal of Democracy*, Vol. 10, No. 3.
4. "Report of the Secretary-General on the support by the United Nations system for the efforts of Governments to promote and consolidate new or restored democracies", A/51/761, 20 December 1996; reprinted under the title *Agenda for Democratization*, DPI/1867 (97.I.3), para. 5.
5. Hunt, Ben. 2000. "Democratization, international relations, and US foreign policy", in James F. Hollifield and Calvin Jillson (eds) *Pathways to Democracy – The Political Economy of Democratic Transitions*. New York: Routledge.
6. UN Charter, Article 4(1).
7. Doyle, Michael. 1983. "Kant, liberal legacies and foreign affairs", *Philosophy and Public Affairs*, Vol. 12.
8. Russett, Bruce. 1993. *Grasping the Democratic Peace*. Princeton, NJ: Princeton University Press.
9. Quoted in Brown, Michael E., Sean M. Lynn-Jones, and Steven E. Miller (eds). 1996. *Debating the Democratic Peace*. Boston, MA: MIT Press.
10. Rummel, R. J. Undated. "Libertarianism and international violence", helpfully summarized on his website at www.mega.nu:8080/ampp/rummel/dp83.htm.
11. The debate was nicely summarized by John Norton Moore in his address at the University of Virginia's Engaging the Mind lecture series, Beyond the Democratic Peace: Solving the War Puzzle, 9 September 2002, www.virginia.edu/facultysenate/speakers/2020/0203_schedule.html.
12. Layne, Christopher. 1996. "Kant or cant: The myth of the democratic peace", in Brown, Lynn-Jones, and Miller, note 9 above.
13. Mansfield, Edward and Jack Snyder. 1995. "Democratization and war", *Foreign Affairs*, Vol. 74, No. 3. The authors find that "while mature, stable democracies are safer, states usually go through a dangerous transition to democracy. Historical evidence from the last 200 years shows that in this phase, countries become more war-prone, not less, and they do fight wars with democratic states."
14. Toward a Community of Democracies Ministerial Conference, "Final Warsaw Declaration: Toward a Community of Democracies", Warsaw, Poland, 27 June 2000, www.ccd21.org/articles/warsaw_declaration.htm.
15. Burnell, Peter. 2000. "Democracy assistance: Origins and organization", in Peter Burnell (ed.) *Democracy Assistance: International Co-operation for Democratization*. London: Frank Cass.
16. See www.ccd21.org/conferences/ministerial/participants.htm.
17. See in particular Donnelly, Jack. 1999. "Human rights, democracy and development", *Human Rights Quarterly*, Vol. 21, No. 3.
18. Vienna Declaration and Plan of Action, A/CONF.157/23, 12 July 1993, para. 8.
19. Rich, Roland. 2001. "Bringing democracy into international law", *Journal of Democracy*, Vol. 12, No. 3.
20. Franck, Thomas. 1992. "The emerging right to democratic governance", *American Journal of International Law*, Vol. 86, No. 1.
21. Franck, Thomas. 2000. "Legitimacy and the democratic entitlement", in Gregory H. Fox and Brad R. Roth (eds) *Democratic Governance and International Law*. Cambridge: Cambridge University Press.
22. Rich, note 19 above.
23. Cassesse, Antonio. 1995. *Self-Determination of Peoples: A Legal Reappraisal*. Cambridge: Cambridge University Press.

24. Abdulah, Frank. 1991. "The right to decolonization", in Mohammed Bedjaoui (ed.) *International Law: Achievements and Prospects*. Paris: UNESCO.
25. Moore, Barrington. 1966. *Social Origins of Dictatorship and Democracy*. Boston, MA: Beacon Press.
26. Bhagwati, Jagdish. 1966. *Economics of Underdeveloped Countries*. New York: McGraw Hill.
27. Bhagwati, Jagdish. 1995. "New thinking on development", *Journal of Democracy*, Vol. 6, No. 4.
28. Diamond, Larry, Juan J. Linz, and Seymour Martin Lipset. 1995. *Politics in Developing Countries: Comparing Experiences with Democracy*. Boulder, CO: Lynne Rienner.
29. Sen, note 3 above.
30. Ottaway, Marina. 2003. "One country, two plans", *Foreign Policy – Special Report, From Victory to Success, Afterwar Policy in Iraq*, June.
31. See www.un.org/Depts/dpko/missions/unmogip/facts.html.
32. Forman, Shepard. 2003. "UN haste puts East Timor at risk", *International Herald Tribune*, 24 February.
33. UNAMET registered 451,792 potential voters among the population of just over 800,000 in East Timor and abroad. On voting day, 30 August 1999, some 98 per cent of registered voters went to the polls, deciding by a margin of 94,388 (21.5 per cent) to 344,580 (78.5 per cent) to reject the proposed autonomy and begin a process of transition towards independence. See www.un.org/peace/etimor/UntaetB.htm.
34. Findlay, Trevor Findlay. 1995. *Cambodia – The Legacy and Lessons of UNTAC*, SIPRI Research Report No. 9. Oxford: Oxford University Press.
35. Economic Research Forum for the Arab Countries. 2002. "The driving force behind the *Arab Human Development Report:* An interview with Rima Khalaf Hunaidi", in *Newsletter of the Economic Research Forum for the Arab Countries, Iran and Turkey*, Vol. 9, No. 2.
36. The Best Practice Unit of the UN Department of Peacekeeping Operations held a seminar in Singapore in March 2002 entitled "Local Actors in Peace-building, Reconstruction and the Establishment of the Rule of Law".
37. Indyk, Martin. 2003. "A trusteeship for Palestine", *Foreign Affairs*, May/June.

2

The promotion of democracy: International law and norms

Tom J. Farer

Does the normative framework of the United Nations ever permit it to influence significantly the allocation of authority and power within member states? More specifically, does it have the legal authority under certain conditions to promote or defend "democratic" forms of government? If such a purpose is not *ultra vires* – that is, wholly beyond the constitutional authority of the organization – what means may it employ in what circumstances and through what processes? Beyond the question of legal authority, what *should* it do to promote or defend democracy in light of the plurality of purposes and principles enumerated in its Charter and the systematic challenges to its long-term authority?

Virtually from its inception the United Nations has acted with the approval of most member states to influence the allocation of authority and power within some of them. Before the end of the Cold War it did so in the name of self-determination, a value recognized in Article 1 of the Charter and translated by organizational practice into almost a synonym for decolonization.[1] The organization initially promoted this goal by normative pressure – that is by declaring or implying the illegality of continued control over peoples and territories seized by Western states during the epoch of the West's global expansion. In the words of the landmark *Declaration on the Granting of Independence to Colonial Countries and Peoples*:

The subjection of peoples to alien subjugation, domination and exploitation constitutes a denial of fundamental human rights, is contrary to the Charter of the

United Nations and is an impediment to the promotion of world peace and co-operation.[2]

Having laid down the law, a large UN majority, increasingly composed of newly independent states, set about applying it through the organization's sub-units and under its umbrella of legitimacy. Members of the progressively growing majority created a special committee that reported on the progress towards independence in various colonial territories where it perceived progress, and, where it did not, condemned what it determined to be failures to prepare the "subjugated" inhabitants of these territories for the exercise of their self-determination rights. To assist it, the committee demanded and in some cases secured reports from the colonial powers and permission to undertake on-site enquiries. In some instances the committee and hence the United Nations became involved in the political details of decolonization, going so far as to decide for itself which indigenous political parties should be deemed legitimate representatives of the subjugated people and whether the conditions existed for the exercise of an authentic popular choice of post-colonial political status.

While declaring illegal the indefinite prolongation of colonial relationships and, in effect, recognizing the "non-self-governing territories" as latent states, UN organs never suggested that the metropolitan powers did not exercise sovereignty in those territories pending a decision by their inhabitants to become independent. Underscoring the organization's implicit concession of the occupying state's sovereignty over the territories was the position it took with respect to the former German colony of South West Africa. Stripped from Germany after the First World War by the Treaty of Versailles, responsibility for its governance had been transferred through the League of Nations to the Union of South Africa, but subject to a mandate agreement that specified, among other things, that the territory had to be governed for the benefit of the indigenous population. When, following the Second World War, South Africa imposed racial apartheid on the territory, the General Assembly concluded that South Africa had thereby violated a key condition of the mandate and purported to assume jurisdiction over the territory as the successor to the League.[3]

By contrast, it never claimed the power to transfer to itself authority over colonial territories that had not passed, however notionally, through the jurisdiction of the League. It omitted such a claim even in the case of Portugal, which, for a decade after decolonization had been completed in most of the rest of Africa, continued to insist that its African territories, primarily Angola and Mozambique, were integral parts of the sovereign Portuguese state. Since a truism of modern international law is that it abhors a vacuum of sovereignty, the failure of either of the political organs of the United Nations to claim jurisdiction implies that sovereignty remained with the colonial power pending an act of self-determination. If non-self-governing territories were formally and operationally parts of sovereign states until they opted for independence, it follows that the United Nations has created a long body of precedent for attempting to influence the allocation of authority and power within member states, in some instances without the consent of the sovereign.

The capacity of the organization to promote democratic forms of government when it has the consent of the affected state seems to be beyond reasonable dispute. If a state is free, as it obviously is, to send election observers into another state at the request of the latter's government, surely the United Nations, as an agent of the community of states, can also respond positively to such a request. Only where democracy-promoting-and-defending activities of the United Nations, or of states acting pursuant to mandates from the UN's political organs, do *not* enjoy the consent of the target state can there be any reasonable doubt about the legal authority of the United Nations or its agents. To a large degree, however, that reasonable doubt must now be cast in the past tense. It had, of course, two textual sources. One was paragraph 7 of Charter Article 2 announcing that "[n]othing contained in the present Charter shall authorize the United Nations to intervene in matters which are essentially within the domestic jurisdiction of any state" except in the event of enforcement measures ordered by the Security Council under Chapter VII of the Charter. The second source was the stated preconditions for such enforcement measures, namely a threat to or breach of the peace or an act of aggression.

With respect to the non-intervention injunction of Article 2(7), it seems to have been clear from the outset that this was going to be a moving standard. After all, the words "essentially within the domestic jurisdiction" functioned as a collective synonym for the prerogatives of territorial "sovereignty". And sovereignty had never been absolute in the sense of precluding one state from taking any legitimate interest in what was going on in another. States had, for instance, always been entitled to be concerned about the behaviour and treatment of their citizens when domiciled or passing through other states, and about the treatment of their property as well.[4] Moreover, in circumstances that steadily grew, states asserted a right to object to all kinds of activities in another that happened to injure their national interests or the interests of individual citizens.[5] And where objection proved ineffective and the threatened injury occurred, injured states had a right to compensation and to reprisal.

As economies and societies became more intertwined, a trend readily observable to the drafters of the Charter, injurious transnational effects of activities originating in any given state were going to increase at least proportionately. It was equally clear in an age of intense ideological diversity and expanding literacy and communication that transnational connections and impacts would not be limited to the material sphere. Moral and ideological ties could make events in one country resonate powerfully in many others. One thing that followed from this trend was that threats to the peace were bound to be far more protean than in previous centuries. Who, for instance, in 1945 could doubt with the wisdom of hindsight that Adolph Hitler's accession to power in 1933 had constituted a threat to the peace?

Sovereignty was and remains the international law equivalent of property ownership in national legal systems. Both translate into bundles of rights and duties qualified by the comparable rights and duties of other landowners and subject in certain circumstances to an overriding public interest.

In the event, the substance of the perceived constraints of Article 2(7) and the jurisdictional requirements for Chapter VII enforcement actions have changed precisely as one would have predicted when the Charter came into force. Change has occurred incrementally, driven by the will of the member states of the United Nations to realize the principles and purposes of the organization in a rapidly changing global context. Obviously one dimension of the changing context has been the wave of democratization that has swept round the globe. In 1950 there were no more than 22 democracies. By the end of the twentieth century, states that could arguably be characterized as real (i.e. liberal) democracies had more than doubled: 120 out of 192 recognized sovereign states accounting for 58.2 per cent of all peoples selected their leaders through elections, thus at least simulating, however unimpressively in many cases, that important facet of an authentic democracy.[6] At the behest of the member states, UN organs and agencies have played a more than marginal role in this huge expansion of democracy's reach.

The effort to bring about majority rule in South Africa is, of course, one of the clearest precedents for unconsented action to promote and defend democracy. To be sure, not every General Assembly and Security Council initiative concerning South Africa had democracy promotion as its primary purpose. For instance, the sanctions imposed by the Security Council under Chapter VII were formally justified and justifiable as means for dealing with a threat to the peace and were plainly responsive to the country's explosion of a nuclear device and to the proliferating cross-border military operations executed by the South African defence forces.[7] But the totality of UN initiatives clearly had the aim of achieving majority rule, a fact corroborated among many other ways by the termination of all coercive measures following agreement on majority rule and the conduct of an election under the transitional arrangements.

Another even earlier precedent for coercive action on behalf of majority rule was the imposition of sanctions on Southern Rhodesia following its white minority government's unilateral declaration of independence from the UK.[8] A determined lawyer might distinguish this case on the grounds that, since virtually no government recognized the breakaway regime, it formally remained an appendage of the UK and the latter had consented to sanctions as it were against a part of itself. But that argument subordinates substance to form. At the time of its declaration and for years thereafter, the Southern Rhodesian government possessed very effective control over the entire territory. Meanwhile the UK showed no disposition to challenge that control; indeed, at an early point it renounced the use of force to assert its residual sovereignty and blocked resolutions at the United Nations demanding that it reassert effective authority by force if necessary, as it appeared to be.

While immediate recognition of a secessionist government would traditionally have been deemed an intervention in the affairs of a state threatened with disintegration, in the face of conspicuous failure of will by that state's government to mount an effective challenge to the secessionists, the period during which recognition would seem "premature" could shrink rapidly, as it did in the case of East Pakistan when, with the backing of India, it succeeded in detaching itself from Pakistan and became Bangladesh. In other words, when secession is effective, most states slip naturally (because it is convenient for looking after their interests in the relevant territory) into the traditional practice of treating those who are effectively in control of a state or colonial territory as the sovereign legal authority. In short, Southern Rhodesia, although governed by a white minority regime, had all the usual indicia of a sovereign state (other than recognition) at the time the United Nations imposed sanctions. Those sanctions, together with the aid given by neighbouring and other states to the resistance movement that gradually took shape, eventually forced the minority regime to hold elections, resulting, as in the case of South Africa, in a transfer of power.

Since Southern Rhodesia's settler community did not really take shape until the twentieth century, UN involvement could without too much of a stretch be passed off as another instance of decolonization activity rather than a broader precedent for action in defence of popular sovereignty. The South African precedent is more intractable. For the Afrikaners had begun settling there almost three centuries earlier, and, like the Zulus who had preceded them into the area, they had subdued peoples who had come much earlier. Both had encountered and resisted British imperialism. If the latter were indigenous, and no one argued to the contrary, than how could the former be denied the status of another African "tribe"? If they could not, then the precedent could not be quarantined within the precinct of decolonization.

In sum, the UN's plunge into democracy promotion at end of the Cold War was precedented. Still, its scope, intensity, and explicitness certainly do manifest a striking change in the attitude of member states, which must have roots in the changed conditions of the material and ideational environment in which they exist. Activity has assumed essentially all of the forms available to the United Nations and other intergovernmental organizations. One is the declaration and clarification of legal norms. In 1948, only three years after the organization's founding, the UN member states had adopted without dissent (but with eight significant abstentions that amounted to dissenting votes)[9] the Universal Declaration of Human Rights, including its Article 21 statement that "the will of the people shall be the basis of the authority of government ... [and] shall be expressed in periodic and genuine elections which shall be by universal and equal suffrage ..." Eighteen years later the movement to translate the non-binding Declaration into hard law culminated in an overwhelming vote by member states for the International Covenant on Civil and Political Rights (ICCPR). In the Covenant, Article 21 of the Declaration uses language essentially identical to Article 25. It certainly seemed to confirm an individual right to live in and participate in the politics of a democracy. But for years after 1966, as if in appearing to declare an individual's right to live and participate in a democracy they had temporarily exhausted their moral energy, the member states willed the United Nations to do little or nothing in the normative or any other realm that could be construed as taking democracy seriously, unless, as noted above, whatever it did connected closely to combating decolonization or apartheid.

One could argue that as far as normative clarification is concerned, there has been very little for the United Nations to do, since the language of Article 25 – "Every citizen shall have the right ... to vote and to be elected at genuine periodic elections which shall be by universal and equal suffrage and shall be held by secret ballot, guaranteeing the free expression of the will of the electors" – hardly allows greater clarity of expression. Particularly when read together with Article 22's guarantee of the "right to freedom of association with others", does not Article 25 clearly affirm a "democratic entitlement" and implicitly but still clearly define it as a right to live in a state "in which the power to decide is determined by a competition for the people's votes"?[10] However clear the language of a UN-sponsored treaty – and it must be admitted that the Covenant does not state explicitly that genuine elections are those open to competition among political parties which enjoy substantially equal freedom to organize and to disseminate their views – and however numerous its ratifications (now over two-thirds of the membership), where the implied right has been widely violated and the violations just as widely ignored by the United Nations, restatement is one important way of rescuing it from inanition. During the past decade, the General

Assembly, the Human Rights Commission operating under the aegis of the Economic and Social Council, and the Human Rights Committee established by the ICCPR have all contributed to the rehabilitation of the norm of democracy. In the Cold War's immediate aftermath, the Assembly reiterated that the authority to govern stems from the will of the people and determining that will "requires an electoral process that provides equal opportunity for all citizens to become candidates and put forward their political views, individually *and in cooperation with others*"[11] (emphasis added).

Yet even in that resolution – which had the operational effect of authorizing the Secretary-General to extend electoral assistance to members requesting it – one could detect the residual tug of influential dissenters. Following the words "in cooperation with others", the Assembly added "as provided in national constitutions and laws", thus implying at least a presumption of legitimacy for restrictions and obstacles more or less carefully embedded in national legislation.

Among the organs of the United Nations, the Human Rights Commission has been the principal one driving the normative animation of Article 25. To date, arguably its most important resolution is 2000/47, in which it goes beyond its Covenant-created counterpart, the Human Rights Committee, in explicitly associating the electoral participation of "multiple parties" with "a free and fair process".[12] But even in the work of the Commission, obviously a more specialized organ than ECOSOC and one to which governments are more likely to send independent representatives with a genuine interest in human rights, we see evidence that, in the world as a whole, liberal democracy is still not an uncontested right even at the level of normative theory. The most revealing occurrence in this respect was the 1999 vote on a Cuban amendment to strike the title of a resolution reaffirming the statement in the 1993 declaration of the global human rights conference in Vienna that democracy, development, and human rights are interdependent and mutually reinforcing. The title the Cubans wanted to strike was "Promotion of the Right to Democracy". The amendment was defeated, but only by a vote of 28 to 12, with 13 abstentions. Clearly the objectionable part of the title was the word "right". A resolution the following year very similar in substance but without the provocative title passed 45 to nil with only eight abstentions.[13]

While the closeness of the 1999 vote may seem surprising, given the fact that about two-thirds of UN members are at least nominally democratic, spirited opposition is not. In the first place, a number of consequential UN members – China, Cuba, and Saudi Arabia prominent among them – openly and categorically reject the equation of legitimacy with triumph in electoral competition. In the case of Saudi Arabia, opposition is a matter of religiously based principle, the King having determined that, at least in his case, royal rule is required by the Koran.[14] On the issue of principle, China's position is less clear. It does allow non-Party-members to run and sometimes win in village elections and has not ruled out on principled grounds the extension of political competition to larger political subdivisions.[15] Party rule is stated to be essential during this epoch of dramatic economic and social change.[16] But the recent decision to open the Party to persons in the private sector[17] implies abandonment of Leninist orthodoxy, still fiercely embraced by Fidel Castro, about élite rule on behalf of the proletariat as a categorical principle of political organization.

Another form of open and in some sense principled objection to the claim of democratic entitlement, if it is construed as a right to form parties and compete through them for power, is exemplified by the position of Uganda's President Yoweri Museveni. President Museveni follows in the footsteps of the first generation of post-colonial African leaders like Julius Nyerere, Kenneth Kaunda, and Jomo Kenyatta in equating party competition with ethnic polarization, resulting in civil conflict and gross violations of human rights. Like Nyerere he advocated non-party political competition for office among individuals standing within the framework of a single political organization integrating all ethnic groups.[18] However, unlike his predecessors he recognizes a right of citizens to choose between party competition and the electoral arrangements he believes would better serve peace and development in Uganda. And he now appears resigned to such a development.

Swarming closely behind the principled opponents of a democratic entitlement, at least if it is defined in terms of the liberal democratic paradigm, lie the much larger number of states where governing élites hold elections more or less regularly and may even allow a more or less accurate tabulation of votes, but so harass and constrain the organization of opposition parties and so exploit the election-influencing potential of state organs and resources as to make their defeat extremely difficult, if not practically impossible.[19] In addition, or alternatively, they influence judicial decisions, determine the acts and omissions of prosecutors and police, and, operating behind a wall of secrecy, self-interestedly allocate financial resources.[20] Such regimes, in theory drawing legitimacy from "successful" electoral competition, may well find it difficult, even operationally counterproductive, to oppose resolutions reaffirming the expressed will of the people as the basis for governmental legitimacy. Indeed, they should embrace resolutions about democracy which, while affirming its legitimating power, treat it as if it appeared in the International Covenant on Economic, Social, and Cultural Rights (ICESCR). For the rights there enumerated are not categorical like those in the

ICCPR, imperative claims for immediate action; rather they are more like ideals towards which governments move progressively with the assistance of third parties.[21]

The pro-democracy resolutions of the Human Rights Commission generally contain language equivalent to the "progressive development" formula of the ICESCR. For instance, CHR resolution 2001/36 on "Strengthening of popular participation, equity, social justice and non-discrimination as essential foundations of democracy" welcomes "the commitment of all Member States ... to work collectively for more inclusive political processes allowing genuine participation by all citizens in all countries".[22] Another now formulaic expression that gives nominally democratic governments breathing room is the recognition that "while all democracies share common features, differences between democratic societies should be neither feared nor repressed, but cherished as a precious asset of humanity".[23]

How many states fall into this category of doubtful-to-fictitious democracies? In 1994 Larry Diamond evaluated the democratic credentials of all the Latin American and the larger Caribbean states.[24] Other than Cuba, all claimed to be democracies. Diamond defined democracy to include the forms of electoral competition and the substance of real participation in decision-making and the exercise of civil and political rights (enabling citizens to organize for political ends and to express and disseminate their views without fear of persecution). He then assigned the Latin American and Caribbean states to one of eight categories that descended from "liberal democracy" through "democracy", "partially illiberal democracy", "near democracy", "semi-democracy", and "semi-competitive authoritarian", to "authoritarian" and "state hegemonic closed".[25] Of the 22 states studied, only four in his judgement ranked in the second-highest category (none was in the first) and another five achieved the status of "partially illiberal democracy", a status he believed scraped the line below which the use of the description "democratic" would be seriously misleading. In sum, 13 of the 22 did not make the grade although they claimed to be democracies and did at least hold regular elections in which, for the most part, the votes were more or less accurately counted.

The instruments for winning elections being varied and powerful, regimes can often welcome electoral assistance, a second form of UN activity which has proliferated since 1989, without great fear of compromising their grip on office. Which is not to say that such assistance has no edge at all. It may complicate the cruder forms of electoral corruption and, having accepted it in any form, it is hard for a government then to reject electoral observers of varied sorts. Occasionally, competent electoral mechanisms plus outside observers yield real surprises, as in the Nicaraguan election of 1990, which unseated the reigning Sandinista party.[26]

One final problematical feature of the UN's recent normative activity in the field of democracy should be noted. Human rights advocates generally and pro-democracy campaigners specifically have tended to celebrate the declared integralism of democracy, development, and human rights and fundamental freedoms, seeing their stated interdependence and mutual reinforcement as a rejection of authoritarian apologetics asserting the moral and temporal primacy of economic development and poverty alleviation. The integralism formulation, stemming from the 1993 Vienna Declaration,[27] could be read as declaring human rights to be trumps and/or as endorsing the proposition that democracy is a condition of real development and poverty alleviation. Still, one can also hear the sounds of an only partial victory. For even where interdependence is conceded, it remains possible to argue that not all great things come together in exactly the same proportions at exactly the same time. While a government needs to pursue them all in good faith, can it be faulted if it progresses further towards one goal than another at any given moment? And since the goals are integral, is it fair or even reasonable to indict the relative lack of progress towards one without commending relative advance towards one or two of the others? One obvious but partial answer is that at least the personal security and non-discrimination rights enumerated in the ICCPR are not subject to suspension even in times of emergency – that is they enjoy primacy under all circumstances, whether acute or chronic.

The other problem with the integralist mantra is its reinforcement of the tendency to unpackage democracy and human rights that has marked official and a good deal of unofficial discourse for years. Democracy in the form of a right to participate in practices of self-government is, after all, one of the rights enumerated in the fundamental human rights texts. Given the charisma of the human rights label and the imperative nature of a human right, could not one argue that rhetorical separation of democracy from the body of human rights, combined with progressive development language, tends to soften or discount its claims for enforcement?

The United Nations and the coercive promotion of human rights

UN actions, other than its primarily norm-generating-and-clarifying activities, can be initially bundled under the general heading of "defence and enforcement". Their common theme is the employment or authorization of at least latently coercive measures. Measures can vary in intensity from non-recognition through diverse economic sanctions to the threat or use of force, a category further subdividable in various important ways. Because they present the tension between non-intervention and other values in starkest relief, this section will concentrate on the last set of measures, which we could call broadly "militarized coercion". But it is recognized that any neat categorization of coercive measures is artificial and possibly misleading if taken to imply that they are not to a very large degree interdependent. Non-recognition of a group claiming to be the government of a UN member can, for instance, lay the legal foundation for military assistance to its domestic rival, particularly if the latter *is* recognized. Physical blockade is sometimes a condition of even moderately effective economic sanctions. So the discussion and legal analysis of militarized sanctions will not wholly ignore the other types of coercive measures.

Militarized coercion as a UN activity assumes essentially three forms. One is an operation authorized by the Security Council (SC) *and* administered by the Secretary-General under the Council's close supervision. We could call such operations "in-house measures". Another form is authorization by the SC, pursuant to Article 53, of coercive measures proposed or already undertaken by or pursuant to regional arrangements. And a third is SC or possibly General Assembly[28] authorization of force or the threat thereof by any state or coalition of states. A further distinction of central importance is the contextual one of whether the measures are taken with or without the consent of the recognized authorities in the target state.

As noted earlier, this chapter is intended to illuminate policy options for the United Nations within the contours of extant normative constraints. The acts, omissions, and related justifications (collectively the practice) of UN organs significantly shape those constraints, since they evidence and influence the inter-subjective consensus of key actors in the global community concerning the content of customary international law and the proper interpretation of the Charter and other relevant treaties. What light does UN practice with respect to militarized coercion cast on the issue of whether there is a legal entitlement to democracy, on the content of the purported right, and on its implications for the permissibility of action by states, regional organizations, or the United Nations itself purporting to be for the defence of democracy? In order to see clearly that practice's precedental implications, one needs to step back and examine it against the broad backdrop of the international law regulating foreign intervention.

The legal regulation of foreign intervention

Some dimensions of the relevant normative cluster are clear. Others are contested. All scholars, diplomats, and government lawyers begin their analysis and advocacy with the Charter, but not all end there. Under the most constraining view, Article 2(4), in conjunction with Chapter VII generally and Article 51 in particular, prohibits military intervention unless it is incidental to defence against an armed attack or authorized by the Security Council pursuant to its jurisdiction under Chapter VII. However, even those who accept these Charter provisions as the sole parameters of the legitimate use of force disagree about whether Chapter VII limits the discretion of the Security Council to determine what facts constitute the jurisdictionally required "threat to the peace", "breach of the peace", or "act of aggression". When the SC imposed sanctions on Southern Rhodesia, a former US Secretary of State, Dean Acheson, claimed that the Council had acted arbitrarily in finding the requisite "threat to the peace", since the effective government of Rhodesia – i.e. the secessionist white-minority regime – posed no threat to its neighbours beyond being prepared to exercise its right of self-defence should it be attacked.[29] Though passionately argued, his views did not persuade either governments or most scholars. Since the Council imposed sanctions before anti-regime guerrilla movements harboured in neighbouring states (and backed by the Soviet Union and China) ignited cross-border conflict, Rhodesia was a strong early precedent for two propositions: that gross violations of human rights – in the Rhodesian case the denial of democratic rights on the basis of race – may be construed by the Council as a "threat to the peace"; and that the Council enjoys at least a strong presumption in favour of its jurisdictional fact-finding.

Another interpretive conflict point is Article 2(4). Some defenders of unilateral "humanitarian intervention" argue that an intervention limited in time and in purpose to the prevention, mitigation, or termination of gross violations of human rights is not a threat either to the territorial integrity or political independence of the target state, and, given its purpose, is consistent with the principles and purposes of the United Nations.[30] Others find space for humanitarian intervention and other unilateral enforcement projects by interpreting their way outside the Charter parameters. Unilateral enforcement of fundamental international legal norms is itself legal, they argue, because the Charter's specific limits on the use of force are by necessary interpretation contingent on the creation of a system of collective enforcement marked by close cooperation among the permanent members of the SC. Since the system failed to develop, states are left with residual legal authority to enforce crucial rights subject to SC review on a case-by-case basis.[31]

Legitimization of intervention by regional institutions

Yet another approach to justifying intervention without prior SC authorization is to invoke the supposed legitimating power of the "regional arrangements and agencies" integrated into the Charter security system

52–54 of Chapter VIII. Those Articles seem to concede to
ity of states participating in such arrangements and agencies
ious role in facilitating – through mediation, conciliation, and
as not involving the threat or use of force – the peaceful
~~~~ of regional disputes, though the collectivity may also be employed to that end by the SC. However, anticipating the case where non-
coercive measures prove insufficient and the regional actor therefore
wishes to use force either to avoid or abort a threat to the peace, Article
53 states baldly that "no enforcement action shall be taken under regional arrangements or by regional agencies without the authorization of
the Security Council". Despite that language, during the Cold War the
USA aggressively pushed a multifaceted construction of it that would
give to regional actors an effectively independent power to legitimate the
use of force in circumstances beyond collective self-defence to an armed
attack. Having successfully secured requisite majorities under the Charter of the Organization of American States (OAS) to support a partial
blockade of Cuba during the 1962 missile crisis and an invasion of the
Dominican Republic in 1965 to prevent an allegedly leftist coalition from
achieving power, and having in neither case sought SC authorization, the
USA argued as follows:

- that authorization could be after the fact
- that it could be manifested by inaction (in other words the use of force
  should be deemed ratified if it were not condemned)
- that interventions pursuant to OAS authorization were not "enforcement actions" since the latter were properly understood as actions
  ordered by an intergovernmental organization and the OAS only had
  authority to recommend (a claim which begged the question of how the
  recommendation could legitimate force where it was not a defensive
  response to an armed attack).[32]

After 1965 the USA did not again seek OAS authorization for planned
interventions until the Panama invasion of 1991, when it did so un-
successfully.[33] But in the interim it did not entirely neglect the legitimating potential of regional organizations. When invading Grenada in 1983,
the USA invoked as one justification an invitation from the Organization
of Eastern Caribbean States. The political organs of the United Nations
have responded erratically to an expansive reading of Chapter VIII.
While large majorities in the Security Council (procedurally nullified by
a US veto)[34] and the General Assembly implicitly rejected that reading
when they condemned the Grenadian intervention,[35] subsequent interventions by members of the Economic Organization of West African
States (ECOWAS), first in Liberia and later in Sierra Leone, have been
welcomed, by acts of conspicuous omission in the Liberian case and positive endorsement in Sierra Leone. Meanwhile, paradoxically, the USA

has quietly buried its previous claims about the legitimating power of the OAS. That at least seems the necessary implication of the Clinton administration's behaviour during its campaign to restore to office the elected president of Haiti.[36] With respect even to economic sanctions, it attributed to the OAS nothing more than the power to "recommend" how member states should behave. As for the use of force, the administration insisted that it required SC authorization. Yet it evinced support for the unauthorized ECOWAS intervention in Liberia.[37]

Intervention by invitation

Before turning to a full review of the precedential thrust of UN activity, two other dimensions of the general law governing the use of force should be introduced. Both before and after the Charter the generality of international lawyers have considered it permissible for one state to accept an invitation from the government of another to assist in maintaining public order.[38] The authority as it were to license armed intervention has been seen as an incident of sovereignty. Twinned examples of this largely uncontested legal proposition are the early 1960s' appeals for help addressed to the just-departed colonial power, the UK, from the newly installed post-colonial governments of Tanzania and Kenya. Julius Nyerere in the former and Jomo Kenyatta in the latter, anti-colonial paragons both, sought assistance in suppressing mutinies by their new national armies. Royal Marines, dispatched by the UK government, arrived and quickly disarmed the mutineers, who, while refusing to obey orders and issuing demands about their conditions of service, were still in their barracks.

As long as the assistance is prophylactic or the rebellion either incipient or flimsy, most scholars no less than governments have been largely unconcerned about the legal status of invited foreign intervention. But where rebels succeed in making themselves the effective authority in most or all of the country, or in an ethnically divided state where the rebels declare independence and the recognized government's prospects for restoring constitutional order on its own appear bleak, then the international legal authority of the pre-existing government of the entire territory to authorize foreign troops to cross the national borders must be questioned. Of course, the legitimizing power of an invitation altogether fails when the invitation comes from the very group the intervention succeeded in installing, a case exemplified by the Soviet invasions, respectively, of Hungary (1956) and Afghanistan (1979).

Writing in the nineteenth century, the eminent English scholar W. E. Hall contended that where a government required foreign intervention in order to deal with rebels, it should no longer be deemed to be the single locus of legitimate authority – even, he seemed to imply, when its condition is not hopeless.[39] If foreign intervention is decisive in determining who governs, he believed, then foreigners have to that extent exercised powers that lie at the heart of sovereignty. Their exercise of them is, perforce, a violation of sovereignty and should therefore be deemed illegal.

Hall championed this position before self-determination had become a legal right, a right that at a minimum is inconsistent with "foreign domination". The emergence of self-determination as a core human right might seem to give Hall's analysis *a fortiori* power in today's world but for two other developments. One is the emergence of the whole constellation of human rights, of which self-determination is simply one. The other is the contested nature of self-determination's core. While some scholars and governments would limit its operation to the protection of geographic space from external control, others argue that the value of self-determination requires the protection of political choice within that space.[40] So even where foreign intervention is decisive, *should it be deemed a form of alien domination when its purpose is to protect the outcome of a fair electoral process and/or to protect other core human rights from gross violation?*

In the absence of an impartial fact-finder and in the belief that narrowly conceived national interests normally guide intervention decisions, one might decide that Charter values are generally going to be better protected by a flat prohibition of unilateral intervention ostensibly on behalf of democracy or other human rights. Should that ban apply, however, where a state bent on intervention does not unilaterally determine that the conditions of a just intervention are operative but acts rather on the invitation of a recognized government? Or should it depend on whether that government owes its mandate to an election victory, particularly one certified by official observers from the United Nations or a regional organization?

Pacted interventions

The other legal issue that bears on the limits of democracy defence and promotion is the validity of intervention pacts.[41] The pacts are general licences to intervene on behalf of a formally democratic constitutional order given by certain states to each other and embedded in a treaty. The US intervention in Grenada, although justified in part as a means of restoring democracy on the island, protecting US citizens,[42] and enhancing human rights, seemed to be driven primarily by ideology and classic notions of *realpolitik*. Nevertheless, it was also a response to what appears to have been genuine concern among the small democratic island states of the eastern Caribbean about their vulnerability to coups mounted by either their miniature security forces or a handful of well-armed thugs.[43] A defence-of-democracy pact that would include Canada and European nations with interests in the Caribbean, as well as the USA and the area's small states, and would specify criteria and procedures required for the activation of the pact, would be a way of reconciling the genuine security interests of democratic states with the danger of arbitrary unilateral intervention by the regional hegemon.

Whatever its policy merits, would such a pact be legally effective to legitimate intervention against a *de facto* government which, having seized power, withdraws from the pact and invokes sovereignty as a bar to intervention? It could be argued, as the author has suggested elsewhere,[44] that since a state can extinguish its sovereignty altogether by merging into another state, it should logically be able simply to reduce the scope of its sovereign prerogatives. But as was coincidentally noted, the a priori argument was not wholly persuasive, because the sovereign rights relinquished could be seen as essential to the existence of sovereignty. In other words, a state that has given away the right to territorial integrity and political independence, the result of giving a licence to intervene that the government cannot withdraw at will, is missing a key constituent of sovereignty. However much they may differ in size, wealth, and military power, all sovereigns are equal in terms of the possession of certain attributes, certain rights and responsibilities inherent in the very idea of sovereignty. Take or give away any piece of the core and you have an anomaly, an entity that claims to be a sovereign state but lacks the key attributes of one.

This clash of a priori arguments is inconclusive. The policy arguments may also be inconclusive, but at least they are more interesting and germane. It seems that there are, in essence, two policy-based objections to the pact. One is that such pacts, whatever their criteria and procedures, will often provide a cloak for the subordination of weak states and thereby reduce political independence from a categorical and universal to a contingent phenomenon. Even if the right of intervention is reciprocal, in practice it will be the prerogative of the strong. True, the danger of abuse will be greatest where the pact is between only two states. Adding others and requiring a heavily weighted majority to support an intervention certainly reduces the risk. But where the pact includes a state with economic, political, and military resources far in excess of all other members combined, it is vulnerable to abuse.

The difficulty with this argument is its inconsistency with the actual history of an organization fitting the paradigm, namely the Organization of American States. Despite the asymmetry of means between the USA and all the other members combined, since the late 1960s Washington has acted on the premise that it cannot command a two-thirds majority in favour of armed intervention. That undoubtedly explains why the USA never sought OAS authorization for its covert war against Nicaragua during the 1980s. When the administration of George Bush did seek OAS approval for military action against General Noriega of Panama, it failed to secure it.[45]

A second objection is the availability of procedural safeguards, which could reduce sharply the risk of abuse. The most important safeguard would engage the Security Council to review and certify the propriety of the pact's origins as well as its applications. Such pacts could be flawed by an element of coercion in their creation. If smaller states need to be dragooned into reciprocal intervention pacts, for instance by a powerful state's threat to give military assistance to latent or actual rebellions, there is already a violation of Article 2(4) of the UN Charter and thus a threat to or breach of the peace. The Council could encourage submission of pacts for vetting by taking the formal position that interventions without an invitation from the *de facto* government pursuant to such pacts are prima facie illegal where the pact was not reviewed *ab initio* and certified to be an agreement voluntary on all sides.

The other objection is more subtle and profound, and it reaches beyond pacts to affect all possible institutional arrangements for the coercive defence and promotion of democracy. It goes to the key premises of such arrangements: that the democratic entitlement has a determinate, easily identifiable, and non-contestable core; that democracy should be powerfully privileged over all other forms of government; and that coercive intervention can often play a key role in establishing or maintaining democracy. The challenge to these premises raises huge questions that can at best be addressed skeletally within the compass of this chapter. That discussion will be reserved for the recommendations section at the end.

Coercive action by the United Nations: The record to date

With this legal backdrop in place, the chapter now turns to UN involvement during the past decade in activities that seem relevant to judgements about the legal status of democracy and democracy-promoting activities and relevant also to predictions, assessments, and proposals concerning the future behaviour of the United Nations, of regional arrangements and agencies, and of individual states. The three most directly relevant cases are Somalia, Haiti, and, most recently, Sierra Leone. Democracy – in one instance its establishment, in the other two its re-establishment – was in these three cases more than incidental to the realization of other ends. Indeed, it seems fair to say that the defence and promotion of democracy was the driving force behind UN action and the actions of other key actors.

Somalia

There were two interventions in Somalia, one immediately succeeding the other.[46] The first, UNITAF, was carried out by an *ad hoc* coalition led by the USA and authorized by the SC, allegedly pursuant to its authority under Chapter VII.[47] Its purpose was humanitarian: to facilitate delivery of rations and other essentials to areas of acute famine. The second, UNOSOM II, also authorized under Chapter VII, had as its main purpose assisting the Somali people in re-establishing democratic institutions.[48] Neither intervention could have been consensual because Somalia had no recognized or *de facto* government. This fact, the absence of any central authority, has more than anything else limited the resonance of Somalia as a precedent for international pro-democracy intervention. For just as there was no government to consent, there was none to object. Therefore the normal tension between national sovereignty and external involvement in the nation's political order was muted.

The absence of an objecting voice entitled to speak for the state was probably crucial for the acquiescence in the SC of at least one permanent member, the People's Republic of China, since it is acutely sensitive to actions seen by it to encroach on traditional notions of sovereignty. But although there was no state there were politically organized factions, one of which opposed action by the United Nations to implement a phased movement to democratic governance to which it and the main opposition coalition had previously agreed.[49]

If the United Nations had been guided in this humanitarian peace operation by the spirit of its earlier peacekeeping activities, at every step of the way it would have limited its role to promoting agreement among competitive, mutually suspicious élites, abjuring any distinct institutional vision informed by widely shared values. In the event it broke with that traditional role of value-neutral conciliator. This is evident not only or primarily in its decision to proceed on its own to construct an independent judiciary and police force and to organize district elections. A still more dramatic shift in behaviour was its actually bringing to this enterprise a distinct, value-laden conception of political reconstruction. It did not simply broker the agreement among faction leaders which it subsequently cited as the basis for proceeding in the face of opposition from the coalition led by General Mohamed Farrah Aideed. It imprinted on that agreement a sense of democracy as a participatory enterprise. Against the preferences of certain faction leaders, it pushed successfully, with the informed support of the SC, for the inclusion in the political process of women, independent intellectuals, and civil society activists, to the extent they existed in the desolated country. And when the agreement broke down, it retained that vision and attempted to give it flesh. The absence of a government provides lawyers and diplomats with a handle for isolating the Somali case as a precedent for the armed promotion of democracy under SC auspices. But that peculiar contextual feature relates only to the authorization of intervention. It does not limit the precedential force of the Security Council's post-intervention blessing for a contested idea of democracy.

The UNOSOM II phase of the Somali case is an instance of an SC-authorized and Secretary-General-administered pro-democracy operation. Haiti exemplifies an operation authorized by the Council but executed by an *ad hoc* coalition of states.[50] For its own contextual reasons, it too is susceptible to close confinement as a precedent for pro-democracy interventions. In that respect, the main contextual feature is consent to the intervention from the universally recognized albeit exiled and powerless government of the country. Since for international law purposes intervention has generally been defined as forced entry, one can fairly argue that this was not even a case of intervention. The difficulty with that position is that except in cases of external aggression, until very recently claimants effectively exercising the functions of government have generally been treated as the sole voice and agent of the state even if they came to power by unconstitutional means. Traditionally, most scholars and government leaders alike treated the means by which a *de facto* government achieved power as an internal matter irrelevant to the relations of states.[51]

Haiti and Sierra Leone

As the absence of a government helped secure China's acquiescence to the Somalia expedition, the presence of a government seeking foreign assistance helped China distinguish the Haiti case from one involving SC authorization of the use of force within a country against the will of its government and for the purpose of affecting its domestic practices and institutions. Haiti's greatest precedential importance is twofold: it supports the proposition that the violent overthrow of an elected government can constitute a "threat to the peace" for purposes of the jurisdictional criteria of Chapter VII; and it is a precedent for individual nations and intergovernmental organizations to treat as a legal nullity the *de facto* power that has overthrown a democratically elected government, at least where its election was observed and confirmed by respected international monitors.[52]

At this point it is unclear whether, in the discourse that constructs international norms, some effort will ultimately be made to limit the Haiti precedent to its regional context. The western hemisphere and Europe are the two areas where all or virtually all states have banded together and formally established democratic government as a condition of legitimate rule and of active membership in regional organizations. This entails non-recognition of "governments" that violate constitutional order in assuming power and, most clearly in the case of the OAS, a commitment to consider active means of displacing such governments.[53] International law has long recognized the capacity of states to construct special legal regimes for themselves that are binding on the parties to them so long as the special rules and principles and underlying policies are consistent with overriding universal norms. So China or other countries could in future argue that in treating the exiled government of Jean-Bertrand Aristide as the sole voice of the Haitian state, the SC simply deferred to the established right of states to establish special standards among themselves for the recognition of governments and so it did not set a universally applicable precedent.

With some other regional and trans-regional associations of states beginning to move down the path blazed by European and western-hemisphere countries, that view of SC action in the case of Haiti should prove progressively less persuasive. As Roland Rich recently noted, the Pacific Islands Forum and the British Commonwealth of Nations have put in place mechanisms similar to those of the OAS for discouraging coups and reversing those that occur.[54] While the Organization of African Unity did not adopt specific mechanisms at its 1999 and 2000 summits, it formally condemned the overthrow of elected governments and refused to invite representatives of the *de facto* authorities in states where it had recently occurred. But OAU behaviour also illustrates a problematic aspect of an emphasis on constitutional forms. While rejecting "putschists", it welcomed President Mugabe of Zimbabwe despite his violent assaults on civil liberties, the rule of law, and the political opposition, all of which facilitated his re-election and appear designed to do the same into the indefinite future.[55]

In any event, putting a regional spin on Haiti became more difficult in the wake of SC action in the case of Sierra Leone where the Council, again acting under Chapter VII, demanded that "the military junta take immediate steps to relinquish power in Sierra Leone and make way for the restoration of the democratically elected Government and a return to constitutional order".[56] The OAU has not yet equated legitimacy with democratically conducted and impartial elections. In other words, there is in Africa no special legal regime. So the demand for democratic restoration could be fairly taken to imply that the overthrow of an elected regime is something approaching an international crime.

Claims on behalf of an emerging norm of democracy or "democratic entitlement" do not rest only on the practice of the United Nations in Somalia, Haiti, and Sierra Leone (plus regional practice and UN and regional texts of one sort or another). Claimants invoke the entire body of peace operations over the past two decades – Namibia, Cambodia, Angola, Bosnia, and so on – noting that in every one of them the United Nations has made elections leading to the establishment of democratic government an integral part of its mission and in some cases its predetermined culmination.[57] Must we construe this practice as implying UN recognition of democracy as a legally privileged political arrangement? Not necessarily. While it is susceptible to that construction, UN practice also could be construed more modestly as imputing to democracy the character of a very useful, perhaps even indispensable, tool in the context of intrastate conflict for the reshaping of violent competition for power into less destructive forms. Moreover, if the practice is to be conscripted as proof of democracy's normative value (rather than its practical utility), is the content of that value clear? In some cases – Mozambique is one example – the agreement supervised by UN military and civilian personnel provided for majority rule, that is for winner-take-all elections, "all" being, of course, limited by the new constitutional arrangements.[58] In others – Angola is an example – the losing élite was guaranteed a substantial place in post-election governance of the country.[59] How much can we reduce the power-allocating consequences of electoral victory before we conclude that the democratic forms lack meaningful substance?

The proper roles of the United Nations

Through its technical assistance programmes, its electoral monitoring, and its peace operations, as well as through the norm-building declarations of its various organs, the United Nations is already engaged in the now almost quotidian business of democracy promotion. Norm-making aside, engagement in these forms is largely uncontroversial because it relies either on the initiative of the concerned member state (technical assistance and monitoring) or on the instrumental value of democratic forms for maintaining or restoring peace in violently divided countries. Potential controversy has also been avoided most of the time by the UN's flexibility in defining democracy, more precisely by not insisting in particular cases on any single contested conception. Somalia, as noted above, appears as an exception to that generalization.

This does not imply that the United Nations has been satisfied with democratic forms utterly without democratic content. In peace operations, democracy has at a minimum meant elections with a plurality of parties able to participate in an environment free of gross limits on speech and association. But the belligerent internal parties have generally played the dominant role in deciding how much elections should decide and on the institutional character of the post-conflict constitutional system.

As described above, the United Nations has episodically gone beyond this uncontested terrain. It has launched or legitimated or at least become associated with coercive efforts to construct or re-establish democratic political order. The question is whether and how to consolidate these precedents into a coherent doctrine which, over time, can and should command near universal support. The author does not believe coherence is likely if one looks only at the UN's engagement with coercive activities in defence of democracy. For they are a mere subset, and not necessarily an analytically useful one, of coercion in general. Individual states, *ad hoc* coalitions, regional agencies, and treaty-based trans-regional organizations, as well as the United Nations itself, episodically employ coercive means for a number of different and often mixed ends in contexts each necessarily unique in its full detail albeit similar in some important ones. A coherent doctrine will sort past, present, and imaginable cases into analytically useful and morally coherent categories shaped by a general idea of the conditions of legitimate coercion and also of the UN's role in clarifying, developing, and applying the rules and principles through which the idea acquires operational form.

Neither the Secretary-General, as head of the permanent civil service and arguably endowed with a certain autonomous authority to safeguard the institution's normative integrity, nor the Security Council, much less the General Assembly, has *consistently* claimed and attempted to make good a role of singular pre-eminence for the United Nations in the governance of coercion. Since 1945 various states and sub-global associations of states have episodically employed coercion for reasons other than self-defence against an armed attack.[60] In some cases they have sought UN authorization, either before or after the fact. In some cases the United Nations has appraised their behaviour without an invitation. In other words, review and appraisal has been episodic and, where it has occurred, the institutional voice has been less than consistent and clear – which is to be expected, since it is far more like an agora than a government. Nevertheless, as the earlier discussion of the general law of coercion attempted to suggest, in part by implication, its debates and decisions have helped to clarify the points of consensus and dissensus about the parameters of legitimate coercion.

Setting standards and judging their invocation

If the past is prologue, as to some degree it always is, states, whether individually or in association with others, will episodically employ militarized coercion to affect the domestic policies, the allocation of public goods, and/or the political arrangements of other states. Among the likely catalysts of action are gross violations of human rights and threats to and opportunities for the promotion of democratic government. The acts and omissions of the United Nations are likely to influence the incidence and intensity of the interventions anticipated, and will undoubtedly influence perceptions of the United Nations and therefore its authority. It is difficult to believe that an entirely extemporized response by the UN's organs to each incident will enhance that authority. For it is bound to result in a themeless, seemingly arbitrary mosaic. The most elemental rule of justice is "treat like cases alike". Institutions and politicians may claim that every case is so complicated as to be a one-off phenomenon. But that claim will and should fail. The generality of concerned people should spontaneously recognize, in light of the principles and purposes of the United Nations, decisive similarities among groups of cases.[61] If the United Nations were to treat members of each group differently, it would be inviting disrespect.

The Secretary-General and his associates are the guardians of the founding vision and the continuing mission of the United Nations. Among the tasks that therefore devolve upon them is to promote behaviour by the institution's organs that promises to maintain, even to strengthen, its moral authority. They must therefore attempt to illuminate for the UN's political organs the challenges they will face in the realm of intervention, and also to encourage development of a procedural and substantive framework for responding to cases as they arise. Such a framework would, of course, help to determine whether and how they arise. One approach to this task would be an informal memorandum from the office of the Secretary-General sketching the practice of coercive intervention over the past several decades, noting the consensus and points of contention among countries and scholars, and then structuring alternative normative *and* policy-driven frameworks for the consideration of the Security Council or of members states generally, upon which they would be encouraged to comment. Or it might simply circulate memoranda prepared by various think-tanks and groups of scholars.

Perhaps the most basic procedural issue for the United Nations is whether it should attempt to operationalize the role arguably assigned to it by the Charter scheme of world order, the role of monitor and judge of all transnational coercive activity, above all activity that involves the threat of force. Either the Security Council or the General Assembly has the authority, for instance, to formulate rules relevant to activity that threatens the political independence or territorial integrity of member states or a breach of the peace. Either could, for instance, clarify the contested issue of whether interventions by regional or subregional organizations – to protect or restore constitutional government, or end gross violations of fundamental rights, or punish an allegedly terrorist regime, or abort the clandestine production of weapons of mass destruction – require authorization in advance from the Security Council.

On balance, it would be unwise for the United Nations to assume the responsibility for judging every case of militarized intervention. It lacks the fact-finding capacity and the requisite degree of consensus about the full range of relevant norms. Moreover, normative, institutional, and material differences among regions mean that policies and practices that would be deeply threatening to international values and security in one region may enhance them in another. Yet UN organs will tend towards a one-size-fits-all approach, particularly when issuing abstract opinions rather than wrestling with individual cases.

This judgement, whether wise or flawed, about the prudence of the UN's imposing on itself the role of universal and ubiquitous judge is perfectly consistent with the earlier observation that the organization should try to develop a normative framework that will help structure decisions in the cases that concerned member states or the Secretary-General bring to either the SC or the GA for review. This can be accomplished by informal dialogue structured by the SG and perhaps initiated by the circulation of proposals from external bodies. As a possible contribution to that scenario the following propositions can be offered relating to the appropriate normative parameters of militarized coercion to protect and further democratic government.

• The United Nations should normally refuse to seat representatives of persons or parties exercising effective control of a member state in cases where they have overthrown a government elected in internationally monitored and certified elections. Representatives of the elected government should continue to occupy its seat.[62]

• Among the member states of treaty regimes that have made democratic government a condition of participation, intervention at the request of an elected government or pursuant to the regime's procedures in order to defend or restore a government elected in an internationally monitored and certified process is presumptively legitimate and should not be deemed an "enforcement action" under Article 53 of the Charter. Of course the SC retains its overriding jurisdiction to determine whether, under all the circumstances, intervention constitutes aggression or a threat to the peace. It might so decide if it found that the treaty regime was itself the result of coercive pressure in violation of the Charter or the elected government had been coerced into giving the invitation. If the exiled *de jure* government (or members of the treaty regime in the event the legal head of state and his colleagues have been disabled) should seek UN authorization for military operations, as in the case of Haiti, it should be given, again subject to the caveats previously specified.

Comment: In theory, the hypothesized treaty regime could be a mutual protection society of semi-authoritarian regimes which closely control the electoral process and in various other ways inhibit effective participation in governance by the majority of the population. Certainly one might have so described the Organization of American States at the time of its founding. The likelihood of this occurring today under conditions of vastly greater transparency and an international civil society of unprecedented influence and presence is much reduced. The treaty regime might also cloak efforts by a regionally (or subregionally) dominant state to impose satellite status on its neighbours.

- Requests for SC authorization of military intervention to establish or restore elected governments that are not members of pro-democracy treaty regimes should be denied unless they are incidental to a request based primarily on the occurrence in the target state of crimes against humanity or, as in the Somali case, a humanitarian crisis resulting from the collapse of political order.

  Comment: This proposal reflects what the author believes to be the extant value hierarchy of the generality of UN member states. Even states with authoritarian governments have conceded, at least implicitly, that intervention to prevent genocide, other forms of mass slaughter, and ethnic cleansing may be justified. Together with the first proposal above, this one can be seen as part of a compromise between states that recognize a democratic entitlement and those that still do not. Giving priority to violations of personal security rights can also be justified on epistemological and institutional grounds. Whether massive violation of personal security rights is occurring is purely a question of fact. Whether an elected government has been removed because it had itself undermined the constitutional order (as occurred in Peru during the Fujimori ascendancy) or created a national emergency by gross incompetence or massive corruption or had been suborned by private interests or foreign governments can be a complex question of fact, interpretation, and definition of democratic governance.

- Military intervention to overthrow a widely recognized unelected government not engaged in crimes against humanity should continue to be characterized as simple "aggression".

- In peace operations and other complex emergencies, the United Nations should continue to treat democratic governance as the only plausible basis for a sustainable politics in conflicted societies, while recognizing that the particular form of democracy must be shaped primarily by the indigenous parties with a view to mitigating the risk of internal conflict.

- Both the Human Rights Commission and the Human Rights Committee should continue exploring and seeking to elaborate the operational content of democratic governance.
- Since the Commission has already recognized that countries can and should evolve toward deeper and more developed forms of democracy, either it or the UN High Commissioner for Human Rights should develop criteria for measuring progressive development.

Despite the clear language of the Universal Declaration and the ICCPR, important member states and some scholars insist that multi-party competition for the people's vote is not the only legitimate form of government. Echoing the English conservative thinker Edmund Burke's indictment of the French Revolution and its theoretical foundations,[63] they argue that governmental forms evolve from specific historical circumstances as ways of dealing with the universal difficulties of maintaining that degree of order required for economic growth, social welfare, and personal security. In addition, some claim that, at least in certain circumstances, multi-party competition catalyses dangerous ethnic competition or otherwise threatens that sense of common nationhood necessary for civic peace and the efficient production of other public goods. Finally, some opponents of the democratic entitlement insist, again echoing not very ancient European predecessors of both the far right and left, that democratic government simply conceals élite rule.[64]

Defenders of alternative forms of rule do not, however, form a common front. For instance, the "divine rights" claims of the Saudi monarchy seem wholly inconsistent with elections and an individual human right to participate in government. The Chinese can at least argue that office is open to all on the basis of merit (although most high office also requires Communist Party membership) and that their system allows for varied forms of participation, albeit not elections except at the village level (with some possibility of expansion).

Resolutions of UN organs during the past decade have cut back the grounds available to advocates of other political forms while allowing temporal space for evolution toward democracy and conceding that democracy can assume forms that will vary considerably from one other. On balance the normative tide still seems to flow in favour of the democratic entitlement. One could say that the terrain is still contested, but opponents are falling back.

Another contest is being waged within the democratic movement over its content. It is now generally accepted that democracy entails more than periodic multi-party elections; it also requires a liberal society in the sense of a substantial measure of protection for rights of association, expression, and conscience. More uncertain is the degree to which the democratic entitlement requires that ordinary individuals actually be able to influence decisions affecting their life chances. Another point of unresolved tension occurs where majority preferences clash with the claims of national minorities and indigenous groups. With respect to democracy's internal tensions, the United Nations is but one among many forums where the contest will continue.

Notes

1. Since 1945 more than 80 territories that had formerly been governed under UN trusteeship agreements have gained independence from their colonizers and joined the United Nations.
2. "Declaration on the Granting of Independence to Colonial Countries and Peoples", Art. 1, adopted by the UN General Assembly on 14 December 1960, Res. 1514 (XV).
3. GA Res. 2145, UN GAOR, 21st Session, Supp. No. 16, UN Doc. A/6316 (1966).
4. See, for example, Henkin, Louis, Richard Crawford, Oscar Schachter, and Hans Smit. 1993. *International Law*, 3rd edn. St Paul, MN: West Publishing, Ch. 9.
5. For example, when President Clinton began discussing the possibility of invading Haiti, he gave the following reasons: Haiti was in the US backyard, Haiti had been used as a staging area for drugs bound for the USA, Haiti was the only western-hemisphere country where military leaders had seized power from a democratically elected leader, several thousand US nationals lived in Haiti and 1 million Haitian Americans lived in the USA, and continued military rule could result in massive refugee flows to the USA. Murphy, Sean. 1996. *Humanitarian Intervention: The United Nations in an Evolving World Order*. Philadelphia, PA: University of Pennsylvania Press.
6. "List of Electoral Democracies", World Forum on Democracy, January 2000, available at www.fordemocracy.net/electoral.shtml.
7. SC Res. 282, UN SCOR, 25th Session, 1549th Meeting, UN Doc. S/INF/25 (1970).
8. Rhodesia's Unilateral Declaration of Independence provoked a UN resolution permitting Britain to use military force. See SC Res. 253, UN SCOR, 23rd Session, 1428th Meeting, UN Doc. S/RES/253 (1968). As Thomas Franck notes, "It is no longer arguable that the United Nations cannot exert pressure against governments that oppress their own peoples by egregious racism, denials of self-determination and suppression of freedom of expression. That litany is being augmented by new sins: refusals to permit demonstrably free elections or to implement their results." Franck, Thomas. 1992. "The emerging right to democratic governance", *American Journal of International Law*, Vol. 86, No. 1.
9. Universal Declaration of Human Rights, 10 December 1948, GA Res. 217A(III). The abstaining states were Byelorussian SSR, Czechoslovakia, Poland, Saudi Arabia, Ukrainian SSR, Union of South Africa, the USSR, and Yugoslavia. *The Universal Declaration of Human Rights: A Magna Carta for All Humanity*, available on the web page of the UN Office of the High Commissioner for Human Rights at www.unhchr.ch/udhr/miscinfo/carta.htm.
10. The economist Joseph Schumpeter's seminal definition of democracy. Schumpeter, Joseph. 1942. *Capitalism, Socialism and Democracy*. New York: Harper.
11. UN General Assembly resolution entitled "Enhancing the Effectiveness of the Principle

of Periodic and Genuine Elections", GA Res. 45/150, UN GAOR, 45th Session, Supp. No. 1, UN Doc. A/45/1 (1991).

12. CHR Res. 2000/47, 25 April.

13. *Ibid.*

14. King Fahd of Saudi Arabia defended his country's refusal to allow democratization by appealing to "our Islamic beliefs that constitute a complete and fully-integrated system", maintaining that democracies were not suited to his region or to the "unique qualities" of the Saudi people.

15. See Larry Diamond for an exploration of efforts at democratization and the governments' response in China, Taiwan, and Hong Kong. Diamond, Larry (ed.). 2001. *Elections and Democracy in Greater China*. Stanford, CA: Stanford University Press.

16. Chen. Yizi. 1998. "The road from socialism", *Journal of Democracy*, Vol. 9, No. 1.

17. Gittings, John. 2002. "China's new elite abandons workers", *The Guardian*, 15 November.

18. From conversations between the author and senior Ugandan government officials in March 1994 when the author was assisting in the drafting of Uganda's new constitution.

19. See Diamond, Larry. 1996. "Democracy in Latin America: Degrees, illusions, and directions for consolidation", in Tom Farer (ed.) *Beyond Sovereignty*. Baltimore: Johns Hopkins University Press.

20. For a discussion of transitional democracies operating in the "grey zone" see Carothers, Thomas. 2002. "The end of the transition paradigm", *Journal of Democracy*, Vol. 13, No. 1.

21. Article 2(1): "Each State Party to the present Covenant undertakes to take steps, individually and through international assistance and co-operation, especially economic and technical with a view to achieving progressively the full realization of the rights recognized in the present Covenant ..."

22. CHR Res. 2001/36, 23 April.

23. *Ibid.*

24. Diamond, note 19 above.

25. *Ibid.*

26. Pastor, Robert A. 1998. "Mediating elections", *Journal of Democracy*, Vol. 9, No. 1.

27. Vienna Declaration and Programme of Action, General Assembly Distr. GENERAL A/CONF.157/23, 12 July 1993, available at www.hri.ca/vienna+5/vdpa.shtml.

28. See for example the General Assembly's "Uniting for Peace" resolution, GA Res. 377(v), UN GAOR (1950).

29. "UN Sanctions against Rhodesia – Hearings Before the Senate Comm. on Foreign Relations", 92nd Congress, 1st Session (1971) (statement of Dean Acheson). But see also McDougal, Myers S. and W. Michael Reisman. 1986. "Rhodesia and the United Nations: The lawfulness of international concern", *American Journal of International Law*, Vol. 62, No. 1.

30. For an analysis of the precedents and arguments, see Farer, Tom. 2003. "Humanitarian intervention before and after 9/11: Legality and legitimacy", in J. L. Holzgrefe and Robert O. Keohane (eds) *Humanitarian Intervention, Ethical, Legal and Political Dilemmas*. Cambridge: Cambridge University Press; Franck, Thomas M. 2003. "Interpretation and change in the law of humanitarian intervention", in J. L. Holzgrefe and Robert O. Keohane (eds) *Humanitarian Intervention, Ethical, Legal and Political Dilemmas*. Cambridge: Cambridge University Press; Stromseth, Jane. 2003. "Humanitarian intervention: Incremental change versus codification", in J. L. Holzgrefe and Robert O. Keohane (eds) *Humanitarian Intervention, Ethical, Legal and Political Dilemmas*. Cambridge: Cambridge University Press

31. Reisman, W. Michael. 2000. "Unilateral action and the transformation of the world

constitutive process: The special problem of humanitarian intervention", *European Journal of International Law*, Vol. 11, No. 1.

32. See, generally, Farer, Tom. 1993. "The role of regional collective security arrangements", in Thomas G. Weiss (ed.) *Collective Security in a Changing World*. Boulder, CO: Lynne Rienner.

33. The USA justified its invasion of Panama to the OAS on the grounds that it was restoring democracy by ousting Noriega. The OAS voted overwhelmingly to condemn the invasion. OEA/ser. G/P/RES.534 (800/89) corr. 1 (1989).

34. Eleven members of the Security Council were against the US intervention in Grenada but were unable to pass a resolution against it due to US opposition. See Boyle, Francis A., Abram Chayes, Isaak Dore, Richard Falk, Martin Feinrider, C. Clyde Ferguson Jr, J. David Fine, Keith Nunes, and Burns Weston. 1984. "International lawlessness in Grenada", *American Journal of International Law*, Vol. 78, No. 1.

35. GA Res. 38/7 (1983) condemned the military intervention as a "flagrant violation of international law and the independence, sovereignty and territorial integrity" of Grenada, and called for an "immediate cessation of the armed intervention and the immediate withdrawal of the foreign troops".

36. Murphy, note 5 above.

37. *Ibid.*, citing the US statement in support of the ECOWAS intervention in UN Doc. S./PV.3138 (1992).

38. See Doswald-Beck, Louise. 1985. "The legal validity of military intervention by invitation of the government", *British Yearbook of International Law*, Vol. 56.

39. Hall, William Edward. 1884. *A Treatise on International Law*. Oxford: Clarendon Press.

40. Chesterman, Simon, Tom Farer, and Timothy Sisk. 2000. "Competing claims, self-determination, security and the United Nations", Occasional Paper, International Peace Academy, Vail, CO.

41. For a discussion on the validity of intervention pacts and the conditions under which a state can revoke its consent to intervention, see Wippman, David. 1995. "Treaty-based intervention: Who can say no?", *University of Chicago Law Review*, Vol. 62. See also Farer, Tom. 1988. "The United States as guarantor of democracy in the Caribbean Basin: Is there a legal way?", *Human Rights Quarterly*, Vol. 10, No. 2.

42. Murphy, note 5 above.

43. The leaders of the Organization of Eastern Caribbean States supported the US intervention. In justifying the intervention, US Secretary of State George Schultz stated "What kind of country would we be if we refused to help small but steadfast democratic countries in our neighborhood to defend themselves against the threat of this kind of tyranny and lawlessness?" Murphy, note 5 above.

44. See Farer, note 41 above.

45. The OAS strongly condemned the invasion as a violation of international law and demanded the withdrawal of all invasion forces.

46. The discussion of the Somali case rests largely on the author's experience as legal adviser to Admiral Jonathan Howe, the special representative of the Secretary-General, and as the executor of the Security Council's demand for an investigation into the initial attacks on UN forces. The author's report was delivered to the Office of the Secretary-General in August 1993 and an executive summary was disseminated to the Council. For a discussion of the Somalia intervention, see Murphy, note 5 above.

47. SC Res. 794, UN SCOR, 47th Session, 3145th Meeting, UN Doc. S/RES/794 (1992). This resolution empowered a US-led coalition, the Unified Task Force (UNITAF), to use "all necessary means to establish as soon as possible a secure environment for humanitarian relief operations in Somalia".

48. SC Res. 814, UN SCOR, 48th Session, 3188th Meeting, UN Doc. S/Res/814 (1993).

49. See Murphy, note 5 above.
50. On 31 July 1994 the United Nations specifically authorized military intervention in Haiti. SC Res. 940, UN SCOR, 49th Session, 3413th Meeting, UN Doc. S/Res/940 (1994). Following the passage of SC Res. 940, the USA entered into agreements with several Caribbean countries, including Antigua and Barbuda, Barbados, Belize, Jamaica, and Trinidad and Tobago, to provide non-combatant forces to be used following the US invasion. Murphy, note 5 above.
51. See for example Marek, Krystyna. 1968. "Identity and continuity of states", *Public International Law*, Vol. 59. Yet the last decade has seen a proliferation of articles exploring the right of states to intervene in support of the emerging norm of democratic governance; but see Franck, note 8 above.
52. The United Nations authorized intervention into Haiti by relying primarily on its authority to maintain international peace and security pursuant to Chapter VII of the UN Charter. See SC Res. 940, note 50 above, authorizing "Member States to use all necessary means to facilitate" the restoration of the Aristide government.
53. Second Summit of the Americas, Santiago Declaration, 19 April 1998.
54. Rich, Roland. 2001. "Bringing democracy into international law", *Journal of Democracy*, Vol. 12, No. 3.
55. See Agence France-Presse. 1999. "OAU summit closes with calls for democracy, dignity", Agence France-Presse, 14 July.
56. SC Res. 1132, UN SCOR, 51st Session, 3822nd Meeting, para. 1, UN Doc. S/RES/1132 (1997).
57. See for example Franck, note 8 above.
58. Ratner, Steven R. 1999. "New democracies, old atrocities: An inquiry in international law", *Georgetown Law Journal*, Vol. 87.
59. Cornwell, Richard and Jakkie Potgieter. 1998. "Angola – Endgame or stalemate?", Occasional Paper No. 30. Pretoria: Institute for Security Studies, April.
60. Farer, note 30 above; Franck, note 30 above; Stromseth, note 30 above. See also Farer, Tom. 1993. "A paradigm of legitimate intervention", in Lori Fisler Damrosch (ed.) *Enforcing Restraint: Collective Intervention in Internal Conflicts*. Washington, DC: Council on Foreign Relations.
61. The US-led intervention in Iraq probably makes this proposition appear rather Panglossian. We may be entering an era of profound divisions among the leading states about when intervention is justified.
62. The exception would be the case where a democratically elected government violates constitutional restraints and establishes an autocracy.
63. See Burke, Edmund. 1790. *Reflections on the French Revolution*, edited by Conor Cruise O'Brien. Bloomington, IN: Viking Press.
64. Pan, Wei. 2003. "Toward a consolitive rule of law regime in China", *Journal of Contemporary China*, Vol. 1, No. 34.

3

Crafting Security Council mandates

Roland Rich

By entrusting a collective institution with safeguarding peace among nations, the States Members of the United Nations have indeed taken a decisive step towards the establishment of a true constitution of the international community. Chapter VII of the Charter is the key element of that constitution.[1]

Article 39 of the UN Charter, the first Article in Chapter VII, states that "the Security Council shall determine the existence of any threat to the peace, breach of the peace, or act of aggression and shall make recommendations, or decide what measures shall be taken ... to maintain or restore international peace and security". In discharging this responsibility, the Security Council has vast powers.[2] Its ability to employ those powers turns on the political will of the international community as represented by the membership of the Council. In half a century of practice the Council has been through periods when it was unable to form the necessary will to take action and other periods when the options open to the Council appeared limitless.[3] In the Cold War years, the common denominator for action was a very narrow field hardly extending beyond the fight against apartheid. In the immediate post-Cold War years the Council took it upon itself to tackle problems as varied as humanitarian disasters in the Horn of Africa, state-sponsored attacks on civil aviation, the establishment of international criminal courts, imposing peace conditions, organizing national elections, reinstating elected national leaders, and undertaking humanitarian interventions.[4]

In adopting resolutions mandating action, the Security Council is acting at times as both an executive and a legislature.[5] It is a decision-making body deciding on enforcement actions, peacekeeping missions, the imposition of sanctions, or steps towards state-building. The decisions are couched in terminology that has a critical bearing on the particular action. The terminology to devise limits on actions, assign roles to various international actors, and furnish the UN Secretariat with its mandate is contained in the resolutions adopted by the Council and their accompanying documents. Just as the Council combines both executive and legislative decision-making elements, so does the terminology in its resolutions flow from both political and quasi-legal considerations.

The purpose of this chapter is to examine the way Security Council resolutions are crafted, in particular in relation to the democratization mandates laid down by the Council. This will require an examination of the body of work accomplished by the Council in this field as well as an examination of the development of the terminology employed and the process of arriving at that terminology.

The breadth of action

The volume of work of the Council in recent years suggests that the key developments in this regard have taken place since the end of the Cold War. In the 43 years between 1946 and 1989, 646 resolutions were passed by the Council at the rate of about 15 a year. In the following 13 years to 2002, the Council passed a further 808 resolutions at the rate of about 62 a year, or four times the annual volume of work.

In the past decade the complexity of the Council's work has also increased. Sanctions regimes have become more sophisticated, at times targeting non-state actors and occasionally dealing with individuals' criminal responsibility. The interdiction regimes have also become "smarter", often focusing on arms embargoes but also incorporating difficult features such as the oil-for-food rules in the Iraqi sanctions regime[6] or freezing of government funds in the Libyan sanctions regime.[7] The most difficult and ambitious development in the Council's work has been its attempts at state-building. Since the first attempt outside the trusteeship system at taking responsibility for a territory and its people in the case of Namibia in the late 1970s, which itself only entered the implementation stage at the end of the Cold War, the Council has spent the last decade grappling with a score of situations on four continents while attempting to build or rebuild states traumatized by war, genocide, or foreign occupation.

While each of the situations is clearly *sui generis* flowing from their unique combinations of history and geography, the common aspect of the UN's work in these situations is the multiplicity of objectives to be achieved. Whereas the few arms embargoes of the Cold War years basically required UN member states to undertake not to trade arms with the country or entity the subject of the embargo, the recent interventions require the United Nations itself to take the front-line role. That role may incorporate an interdiction regime, but is likely to include many other aspects. There is often a requirement for monitoring the implementation of a peace agreement, including separation of forces agreements, cantonment, and storage of weapons. There may also be a complicated logistical process of food delivery in a humanitarian emergency. The security situation may not be fully resolved at the time of the UN intervention, thus requiring a strong military component. To these complicated logistical exercises one must also often add a difficult sociological exercise of capacity-building for institutions to take over key governance activities. And one of the most common and visible of these governance activities is the holding of elections, at times in the form of an act of self-determination and at times as a means of determining the political choice to govern the country as a critical initial step in the state-building process. The multiple objectives are expressed in a mandate and the mandate is part of or authorized by the key Security Council resolution triggering an intervention.

Table 3.1 lists the "state-building" situations the Council has faced. The single resolution listed for each situation is perhaps open to misinterpretation. The Council often returned repeatedly to the various situations to consider developments and debate options. The resolutions listed are the first or key mandates for state-building in each case. Where two resolutions are listed, the Council significantly altered or extended the mandate. The Secretary-General's reports listed in the table on page 65 are the documents before the Council when considering the intervention. This chapter will draw mainly on these examples to examine the democratization element in those mandates.

Law or politics?

Straddling the executive and legislative divide, the resolutions of the Security Council tend to be the product of both law and politics. The Council is the ultimate political organ of the United Nations. Its very composition and voting method are designed to reflect a certain world order and to accommodate a certain global balance of power.[8] One of

Table 3.1 Mandates containing democratization or state-building aspects

Situation	Mandate	Year	SG's report
Namibia	SCR431 and SCR435	1978	S/12636
Namibia – implementation	SCR632	1989	S/20412
Western Sahara	SCR690	1991	S/22464
El Salvador	SCR693 and SCR832	1991/1993	S/22494
Croatia	SCR743	1992	S/23592
Cambodia	SCR745	1992	S/23613
Angola	SCR747	1992	S/23671
Mozambique	SCR797	1992	S/24982
Somalia	SCR814	1993	S/25354
Liberia	SCR866 and SCR1020	1993	S/26422
		1995	S/1995/881
Haiti	SCR867	1993	S/26480, S/26352
Rwanda	SCR997	1995	S/1995/457
Bosnia-Herzegovina	SCR1035	1995	S/1995/1031
Croatia-Eastern Slavonia	SCR1037	1996	S/1995/1028
Angola – consolidation	SCR1118	1997	S/1997/438
Central African Republic	SCR1159 and SCR1230	1998	S/1998/148
		1999	S/1999/98
Sierra Leone	SCR1181	1998	S/1998/486
Kosovo	SCR1244	1999	
East Timor	SCR1272 and SCR1410	1999	S/1999/1024
		2002	S/2002/432
Congo (DRC)	SCR1291	2000	S/2000/30
Afghanistan	SCR1378	2001	

the great challenges facing the Council is that the changing nature of the world order in the post-Cold War era is raising fundamental political questions about the composition and voting methods of the Council. It comes as little surprise that the Council would employ political solutions in its decision-making.[9]

At the same time, the Council is aware that there is a need for a certain level of consistency in its work. While not bound by any concept of legal precedent, the Council's will nevertheless needs to be conveyed by recourse to terminology that should have clear meaning to both the parties involved in the situation and the implementers of the decision. This calls for great care in the terminology employed and for use of processes analogous to those used by law-making bodies.

The result is a hybrid system of law and politics. At times the identical formulation is used to convey the identical decision, but at other times fine distinctions are employed in terminology, either to distinguish the resulting decision from previous ones or simply to hint at a certain result where the necessary political will may not be present.

Some formulations are necessary to trigger certain effects. The Council will invariably utilize the term "acting under Chapter VII of the Charter" or refer to certain Articles of Chapter VII where it wishes its decision to have mandatory effect.[10] Because the Charter arms the Council with this power only in certain circumstances, the resolution has a recitation of one of the three broad triggering circumstances: a threat to the peace, a breach of the peace, or an act of aggression.[11] The formulation most commonly used is a determination that certain developments constitute "a threat to international peace and security". This formulation covers the broadest situations and requires less by way of supporting argumentation than does a determination that there has been a breach of the peace. However, where the breach of the peace is glaring, as in Iraq's invasion of Kuwait, the Council did employ the language of "breach of the peace".[12] The Council has never determined in its resolutions that there has been an "act of aggression". This is probably because the concept of "breach of the peace" is sufficiently broad to cover an "act of aggression", and also because the exact definition of an act of aggression is not fully clear even though a 1974 General Assembly resolution attempted to settle a definition of aggression.[13]

The legal power of a phrase in a Council resolution and the politics behind that phrase were never better demonstrated than in the crafting of Resolution 678 of 29 November 1990, which authorized the use of force against Iraq. Yet the resolution did not actually use the term "use of force"; instead it employed the phrase "all means necessary". Noted journalist Bob Woodward has described the process of arriving at this phrase in detail.[14] The terminology of the draft resolution was the subject of over 200 meetings held by Secretary of State James Baker with foreign ministers and heads of state, but the key phrase was finally agreed upon in a meeting with Soviet Foreign Minister Eduard Shevardnadze, who initially rejected recourse to the term "use of force". While the Soviet leadership accepted the concept of using force to evict Saddam Hussein from Kuwait, they preferred to employ a euphemism to authorize it. Five different formulations were tried before the "all necessary means" language was finalized. To cement the meaning of the phrase, it was agreed that Baker, in his coincidental role as rotating chair of the Council in November 1990, would describe the intent of the phrase to include the use of force. If there were no disagreement, this would make the meaning of the phrase open to no other interpretation. Once the meaning of the phrase was accepted by the Council to authorize the use of force, it was used again on several subsequent occasions where this meaning was required.

The use of this language brings into stark relief the more equivocal language used in Resolution 1441 of 2003, where the threat against Iraq is contained in the phrase "it will face serious consequences". Whereas some leaders have argued that this is equivalent to an authorization of use of force,[15] it is noteworthy that the same process of examining the accompanying statements made by the US representative does not necessarily lead to this conclusion. In the US statement after the vote on UNSCR 1441, Ambassador Negroponte specifically accepted that the resolution contained "no 'hidden triggers' and no 'automaticity' with the use of force".[16]

This raises the question of the consistency of usage of language by the Council and what can be drawn from that usage. The evolution of language authorizing action is shown in Table 3.2,[17] which tends to reinforce the consistency of employment of the "all necessary means" language when the Council is authorizing use of force as compared to the situations when it is employing the "serious consequences" language. A possible

Table 3.2 The terminology of UN enforcement mandates

Situation	Resolution	Year	Authorizing terminology
Korea	83	1950	"assistance as may be necessary to repel the armed attack"
Rhodesia (sanctions)	221	1966	"the use of force if necessary"
Iraq	678	1990	"all necessary means"
Somalia	794	1992	"all necessary means"
Bosnia-Herzegovina	781 – no-fly zone	1992	"all measures necessary"
	836 – safe zones	1993	"necessary measures, including use of force"
	1031 – peace agreement	1995	"all necessary means"
Haiti	940	1994	"all necessary means"
Albania	1101	1997	"ensure the security and freedom of movement of the personnel of the force"
Central African Republic	1125 1136	1997 1997	"ensure the security and freedom of movement of their personnel"
Iraq	1154	1998	"any violation would have severest consequences"
East Timor	1272	1999	"all necessary measures to fulfil its mandate"
Iraq	1441	2003	"Iraq will face serious consequences"

distinction could be made whereby the "serious consequences" language is seen as threatening the use of force as opposed to authorizing it.

The political nature of the Council's decisions is quite clear. The use of accompanying statements to elaborate on the meaning of the resolution resembles the method of treaty interpretation whereby if the meaning of certain words cannot be understood through their ordinary and natural meaning, the records of the negotiating conference may be referred to as a guide to the meaning of the words under review.

Another example of the hybrid political and legal effect of Council resolutions can be found in the use of legal-sounding terms that have weighty political impact. Resolution 731 (1992) took measures to bring to justice the terrorists who destroyed a civilian aircraft over Lockerbie. The resolution directed its actions against Libya. A Libyan agent has subsequently been convicted for his involvement in the attack on the aircraft.[18] But the original resolution linked the action to Libya by noting that investigations "implicate officials of the Libyan Government". The resolution used this quasi-legal term to put political pressure on Libya to accept the eventual court proceedings that proved guilt beyond reasonable doubt.

Who holds the pen?

Mandates are normally written into Security Council resolutions. Upon adoption by the Council, the mandate provides the direction, guidelines, and limits of the mission the United Nations is undertaking. If adopted under Chapter VII of the Charter, as are most mandates having democratization as one of the key objectives,[19] the terms of the mandate become the critical words establishing the legality of the UN's subsequent actions. The question of who drafts the resolutions thus becomes an important element in determining objectives and intentions.

As with so many issues concerning the Security Council, it is necessary to draw a line between the Cold War and the post-Cold War work of the Council. It is only in the latter period that the Council could be said in any sense to be acting in a collegial fashion and thus using methodology appropriate to that method. Remnants of the Cold War methodology may remain in so far as China is concerned, because while insisting on being consulted closely, China does not engage as actively in the drafting process as the other permanent members.[20] Leaving aside therefore the dominant fissure of the Cold War era, the drafting process can be viewed in terms of a number of tensions within the Council's work methods.[21]

National or collective responsibility for drafting resolutions?

While the Council ultimately takes collective responsibility for its resolutions, the almost invariable practice is that responsibility for the first draft of that resolution falls to one country. This is for reasons both of politics and practicalities. Clearly drafting in committee is not an efficient method of work unless that committee has a coherent first draft before it. Politically, it is usually a delegation closely involved in the issues before the Council that will undertake the drafting process.

Political proximity to an issue might emerge through one or more of several factors. Proximity and membership of the same geographic group as the subject country or countries may often be the determining factor. A past or present alliance or other close relationship may be another factor determining which delegation will take responsibility for producing the first draft.

Given the continuing nature of many of the troubled situations before the Council, there has been an increasing tendency informally to designate a particular group of countries to oversee certain situations. These "contact groups" or "core groups" or simply "friends" maintain a close watch on the situation and when drafting work is required, designate one of their number to undertake it. The following comments draw on Teixeira, who lists 17 such contact groups currently operating in the Security Council.[22] Where the matter is of the highest political importance, such as was the case with Iraq before the 2003 war, the five permanent members consult among themselves. In certain regional situations the core group is constituted by a small group of most-interested countries whether or not they happen to be currently members of the Security Council. Accordingly, the East Timor "core group" comprises the USA, the UK, Portugal, Japan, Australia, and New Zealand, and the responsibility for preparing the first draft of Council resolutions and decisions falls on one or other of the two permanent members. Where one of the permanent members has a particular interest in a situation, such as Russia's interest in Abkhazia (Georgia), it plays the main role but four other countries – the USA, France, the UK, and Germany – have constituted themselves as "friends of the Secretary-General" and attempt to have a moderating influence on Moscow and Tbilisi.

The pragmatic nature of these arrangements can be seen in the fact that in relation to the long-standing issue of Western Sahara, although there is a "group of friends" comprising the USA, France, the UK, and Russia, the main influence including over the drafting process is exercised by the Secretary-General's special representative, James Baker, former US Secretary of State.

The result of these arrangements is to combine the necessity for collective engagement and responsibility with the efficiency of individual drafting of the base document.

P5 dominance or E10 influence?

An examination of the contact group process quickly demonstrates the dominant role of the permanent members (P5). One of the permanent members tends to take the lead role in virtually all the groups. The USA, for example, participates in 14 of the 17 groups. The dominance of the P5 is largely a function of the veto power they wield. Having a far more valuable vote than the elected members (E10) of the Council translates into far broader influence over decision-making.

But there are reasons beyond the veto. Security Council processes and politics are not easy to master. The issues are such that they involve not only diplomats but also ministers and heads of government or state. The E10 are placed in the role of enthusiastic amateurs when compared with the P5 hard-bitten professionals. The P5 have seen the elected members come and go and there is a natural tendency to concert more closely with fellow permanent members. The P5 therefore have the advantage of continuity, mastery over process, broad diplomatic networks on which to draw, and the capacity to exert political, economic, and military influence.

There is often resentment among the E10 over what certain members may see as the high-handedness of the P5.[23] The criticism usually is a variation on the problem of lack of consultation with the E10. The tendency to seek consensus decision within the Council tends to put a premium on the P5 reaching agreement first, with the E10 then falling into line. This tends to establish as the key decision-making issue whether any of the P5 is prepared to veto a resolution. Rarely is decision-making on resolutions dependent on the availability of the nine votes in favour required under Article 27 of the Charter. Yet the bitter debates concerning a second resolution on Iraq in 2003 turned at times on whether the USA and the UK could attract the nine votes necessary to force a veto from one or more of the other P5. In this tricky situation the E10 were far less comfortable, with Chile pleading to the P5 in effect to return to their normal hegemony over Security Council affairs.[24]

This episode demonstrates the essentiality of P5 involvement and concertation in the Security Council's affairs for the Security Council to be effective under current conditions. P5 dominance is a reflection of global politics, though it may not be a perfect reflection. It therefore stands to reason that the P5 will have the most decisive influence on the shape and text of the Council's resolutions and decisions, including their statebuilding and democratization mandates.

Is the UN Secretary-General an equal actor in the process?

Any discussion with senior figures in the UN Secretariat will elicit self-deprecating comments that the Secretary-General and his staff are the mere servants of the organization and that on matters of peace and security the Secretariat simply follows the instructions of the Security Council. This deference is politically understandable but does not reflect accurately on the relationship between the Secretariat and the Council.

It goes without saying that the Council and in particular its permanent members wield a level of political and military might which the Secretary-General and his handful of staff cannot in any way match. After all, while the General Assembly formally appoints the Secretary-General, it is the Council that nominates and has the decisive say in the appointment.[25] This is true of the original appointment and perhaps the permanent members have an even greater weight in the reappointment of the Secretary-General for a possible second and final term, after which they lose their influence through that power of reappointment. It is also true that the Secretary-General has no vote or veto in the Council and has no option but to accept the mandates handed down by the Council. The Charter nevertheless envisages that the Secretary-General is more than a mere servant of the members because he has been given the power independently to draw matters to the Security Council's attention.[26] Yet even in this case, the Charter suggests that the formal role is more that of a messenger than that of an actor in the political process.

But on this issue, reality belies formality.[27] Table 3.1 showing the 20 key democratization mandates contains a column on the relationship of the resolution to a report by the Secretary-General. In these 20 situations, 18 refer to such a report or reports. The reports do not normally flow from the Secretary-General's personal initiative. The Security Council usually requests them, but the baton is then clearly passed to the Secretariat to fashion recommendations to resolve the situation under review. The Secretariat's involvement may not always be as the principal external mediating force. But the presence of the Secretary-General or his representative either as principal mediator or as providing legitimacy to a regional or other mediating process is nevertheless critical to the eventual shape of the international response to the situation. The reports tend therefore to be a key means of shaping the Council's decision-making. In recent years the reports have become more detailed and constructive, to the point that in several resolutions the Security Council has considered it sufficient to approve the report and adopt its recommendations as the mandate for the intervention.[28]

Table 3.1 also notes two situations in which the mandate-setting resolution does not refer to a report by the Secretary-General – Resolutions

1244 and 1378 on Kosovo and Afghanistan respectively. In both cases the mandate is drawn from annexes to the resolution that are not UN reports. In the Kosovo case, the intervention was by NATO with the United Nations scrambling to keep up. The intervention was authorized by the Security Council retrospectively and the mandate flowed from previous political negotiations, in particular the Rambouillet Agreement. The United Nations played a legitimizing role rather than a leadership role, and the involvement of the Secretary-General in shaping events was less pronounced than in other cases under study. The Afghanistan case, however, while flowing from the UN-authorized use of force under the inherent right of self-defence in Article 51 of the Charter, also appears at first blush to be a case of minimal Secretariat involvement. The resolution, however, adopts a subtle means of allowing the situation in Afghanistan to progress through a transitional administration to a democratic form of governance. While this situation does not have a mandate-shaping report, it has a most influential special representative of the Secretary-General in the form of Lakhdar Brahimi playing a key role.

The Secretary-General is clearly a highly influential figure in the setting of mandates. He, his staff, and his special representatives can often play a critical role in conceptualizing the shape of the UN intervention, articulating it in reports, and quietly negotiating it through the Security Council. It would, however, be wrong to think of this process as separate from the deliberations of the Council. The Secretary-General does not work in a vacuum. Delegations keep in close touch with progress and offer their assessments and concerns as the process develops. While the Secretary-General's reports are his own, for which he must take responsibility, their substantive provisions have often already obtained the tacit approval of the key members of the Council.

Does the action take place in New York or in capitals?

It follows that much of the negotiation and drafting of mandates takes place in New York. This allows for a certain body of expertise to develop that can build on common experience. New York most often is the negotiating place for resolutions. At times, delegates in New York will have considerable latitude and discretion in this process. This is often a function of the size of the country and the time zone it is in. Many small countries serving a rare term as elected members of the Council have little option but to arm their representatives with considerable discretion to participate in the negotiating process within the scope of broad guidelines set by capitals. They often do not have the expertise, the experience, or sufficiently timely advice of the issues to do otherwise.

Foreign ministries of course wish to involve themselves as closely as possible in the issues, and the foreign ministries of the permanent members tend to be best placed to do so. While most countries adopt the practice of having the drafting of resolutions done by their delegations in New York, it can certainly be the case that where the resolution is being initiated by a certain country, the first draft will originate at headquarters rather than at the New York mission.

The time zone also comes into play. Washington and New York being in the same time zone allows far greater scope for involvement by the State Department, the National Security Council, or even the White House than for example by the Chinese Foreign Ministry, which is 12 hours ahead of New York.

Another key element is how politically sensitive the issue under consideration may be. As noted above, Secretary of State Baker negotiated the key terms of Resolution 678 in face-to-face talks with his Soviet counterpart. In the 2003 battle of wills as to whether there should be a new resolution enabling the use of force against Iraq, the key figures were heads of state and government, with diplomats in New York acting out parts in a play whose script had been written on the basis of phone calls and press releases at the highest levels of government.

Is there a mandate jurisprudence?

In many ways this is the critical question. Is there a coherent and iterative process that builds on the style and terminology of the previous resolutions to establish an understandable pattern? Is that pattern understandable to the implementers of the mandate? Is there a broad concept of precedence in mandate language? The answer to these questions would seem to be substantially in the positive.

One readily identifiable development is the growing complexity and detail of the mandates. The mandate given to the United Nations in Resolution 632 in 1989 was to "ensure conditions in Namibia which will allow the Namibian people to participate freely and without intimidation in the electoral process under the supervision and control of the United Nations leading to early independence of the Territory". The relative simplicity of the decolonization situation in Namibia lent itself to a relatively simple and understandable mandate with a definite objective of independence. Yet the rather vague injunction to the mandate implementers to "ensure conditions" that will allow the objective to be fulfilled would be progressively refined in future mandate-setting resolutions.

By 1997, dealing with neighbouring Angola with all its complications of internal rivalries and decades of foreign interference, the complexity of the mandate had increased remarkably. The Security Council adopted

Resolution 1118 establishing the UN Observer Mission in Angola and incorporating the mandate recommended by the Secretary-General. The mandate has 25 separate elements divided into five major areas. An indication of the complexity of the operation can be gleaned by noting the many different operative verbs shaping the mandate, including monitor, verify, promote, carry out, provide good offices, inspect, supervise, help develop, investigate, and serve as focal point. This is a quantum leap from the vague "ensure conditions will allow".

Another example of the increasing detail and complexity of the mandates can be found in the broadly analogous situations of the proposed self-determination referenda in Western Sahara and East Timor. Neither represented a traditional decolonization situation, both involved occupation by a neighbouring country rather than by a distant colonial overlord, and both situations were presented before the Security Council after considerable negotiations among the parties principal involving the Secretary-General. Yet in Resolution 690 in 1991, the Council referred to the apparent political agreement and the Secretary-General's report and then decided "to establish a United Nations Mission for the referendum in Western Sahara", elegant in its simplicity but avoiding many of the tough issues that have since dogged the process. Eight years later the Council was far more prescriptive. Resolution 1246 decided "to establish the United Nations Mission in East Timor to organize and conduct a popular consultation, scheduled for 8 August 1999, on the basis of a direct, secret and universal ballot, in order to ascertain whether the East Timorese people accept the proposed constitutional framework providing for a special autonomy within a unitary Republic of Indonesia or reject the proposed special autonomy for East Timor, leading to East Timor's separation from Indonesia ..."

A possible exception to the increasing complexity of mandates is the process being adopted in Afghanistan. The mandate is based on the assumption that the international community's role in the state-building process must be subservient to local efforts given the weak state/strong society dichotomy. The tactic is therefore to adopt the "small footprint" idea by setting out the broad goals but leaving considerable discretion as to means in the hands of the SG's special representative.

The shape of the mandate has also developed in the post-Cold War Security Council's work. From the single-sentence mandates in the Namibia and Western Sahara situations there appears to be an evolution in mandate drafting. Resolutions in the early to mid-1990s tended to spell out in greater detail the elements of the mandate. The security aspects were invariably spelled out first, followed by the technical assistance and humanitarian aspects of the mandate. A good example is Resolution 797 of 1992 establishing the UN Operation in Mozambique (ONUMOZ) and approving the mandate terms recommended by the Secretary-General, which comprised six elements: four significant security-related tasks, followed by the task to "provide technical assistance and monitor the entire electoral process", and completed by the task to coordinate humanitarian assistance.

A similar pattern can be seen in 1993 with the revised mandate of the UN Mission in Haiti (UNMIH), where Resolution 867 sets out the security elements of the mandate first. But an important development was the specific separation of the military and civilian tasks of the mandate. The security assistance was to be provided by UNMIH while the civilian assistance was to be the responsibility of the International Civilian Mission in Haiti (MICIVIH). This pattern of separating the different aspects of the mandate into its component parts was a practical innovation that assisted the implementers to discharge their specific responsibilities.

By the time the Security Council was authorizing large interventions, such as those in Bosnia-Herzegovina in 1995 and in Eastern Slavonia in Croatia in 1996, it had become normal practice to separate the military and civilian tasks of mandates. The practice was also followed in Resolution 1181 establishing UNOMSIL in Sierra Leone, where the military and civilian components of the mandate were clearly distinguished.

The pattern of compartmentalizing mandates was greatly refined in Resolution 1118 of 1997, which incorporated the Secretary-General's recommended mandate comprising five elements: political aspects, police matters, human rights issues, military aspects, and humanitarian aspects. A further refinement can be seen in Resolution 1291 of 2000, extending the mandate of the UN Organization Mission in the Democratic Republic of Congo (MONUC), which specifically lists, in operative paragraph 4, the seven elements of the civilian mission as human rights, humanitarian affairs, public information, child protection, political affairs, medical support, and administrative support.

The process of refinement with each mandate, building on the experience and learning of the previous mandates, amounts to a body of jurisprudence for both mandate drafters and implementers. That process does not equate to a formula that must be slavishly adhered to. Every situation will invariably present particular problems and issues that will require specific mandate language and formulations. The MONUC mandate provides a good example of a task calibrated to a particular situation. It does not fall back on the common injunction to hold free and fair elections, but instead focuses on the preliminary task of state-building by requiring close cooperation with the "facilitator of national dialogue" foreshadowed by the 1999 Lusaka cease-fire agreement. The human rights objective is also carefully worded to give priority focus to vulnerable groups such as women, children, and demobilized child soldiers.

As with any political process, faults can be found. The mandates can at times be seen as exercises in political expediency rather than the implementation of universal principles. A dominant underlying theme in the mandates, expressed openly in the early mandates and more subtly in later mandates, is a concern to keep down costs. The impact can be seen in both the size of the intervention and its duration. There is accordingly a growing sophistication in the drafting of democratization and nation-building mandates by the Security Council, reflecting the body of practice that has been developed and incorporating the lessons learned from previous interventions.

Mandate terminology

In examining the terminology used in mandates one is also struck by a consistency of language. As noted above, there is a necessary repetition in the verbs used to describe the action. Many mandates require monitoring and verification. Many require support for local capacity-building. Others require the implementers to advise, support, or assist local processes in various fields. The repeated use of the verbs facilitates better understanding of the scope of the particular mandate.

Yet the crafting of mandate language is certainly a far more involved process than one of cut-and-paste from previous resolutions. The art is to find a mandate that fits and that is achievable. In searching for the right terminology, the first instinct, particularly of the international lawyers involved in the drafting process both in New York and in capitals, is to find a formulation that has meaning based on a certain use in the past. For generalists or geographic experts involved it is also often a question of settling upon a term that has worked in the past, that has been used by the other members of the Council in previous resolutions, and that has been previously approved by political leaders.

An examination of the core group of mandates demonstrates that below the general similarities there are significant variations. Resolution 1244 on Kosovo simply requires that one of the responsibilities of the international civilian presence shall be "protecting and promoting human rights". Resolution 1181 on Sierra Leone required the civilian element to "report violations of international humanitarian law and human rights". Resolution 866 of 1993 on Liberia requires a "report on any major violations of international humanitarian law". Resolution 1118 on Angola contains three human rights objectives: contribute to the promotion of human rights, help develop capacity, and "investigate adequately allegations of abuses and initiate appropriate action". The use of the term "adequately" is a reflection of the difficulty of taking action on the ground and a concession of the limits of the UN's reach. An example of the specificity of the mandate provisions on human rights can be found in Resolution 1020, which required UNOMIL in Liberia "to assist local human rights groups in raising voluntary contributions for training and logistic support".

Similarly fine-tuned formulations may be found in the mandates dealing with electoral matters. The mandates in the early 1990s were relatively simple, requiring the United Nations, as did Resolution 797 of 1992 concerning Mozambique, "to provide technical assistance and monitor the entire electoral process". In Liberia, Resolution 1020 shared the task of observing and verifying the election results with the then Organization for African Unity and the Economic Community of West African States. But in relation to the Central African Republic, Resolution 1230 of 1999 described MINURCA's mandate in the electoral field as restricted to playing "a supportive role". In Eastern Slavonia, on the other hand, the United Nations was required to organize the elections and certify the results; while in East Timor, conscious of the various devices employed by Indonesia over the years, Resolution 1246 spelled out in clear detail that "a direct, secret and universal ballot" was required for the act of self-determination.

Perhaps the most difficult aspect of crafting Security Council resolutions is the articulation of the political result being sought. When that result is clear, as in the Namibian decolonization situation or the East Timor case after its clear decision in the act of self-determination, the Council can confidently work towards independence and democratic governance. In Haiti it was assistance to the legitimate constitutional authority, and the Security Council expressly stated in Resolution 940 (1994) "that the goal of the international community remains the restoration of democracy in Haiti and the prompt return of the legitimately elected President". In relation to Sierra Leone the major demand made by the Security Council in Resolution 1132 (1997) was "that the military junta take immediate steps to relinquish power in Sierra Leone and make way for the restoration of the democratically elected Government and a return to constitutional order". But in other cases where the people are still engaged in a form of state-building, the terms require more careful elaboration. In relation to the Democratic Republic of Congo, the objective is national dialogue. In Somalia it was to rehabilitate national institutions and promote national reconciliation. At times the best that can be achieved at a particular moment is to establish a process towards a final goal of democratic governance. In Afghanistan that process is based on the establishment of an interim authority that has guidelines on how it is to operate. But when the objective is unclear or unknown, as in the case of Kosovo, the terminology cannot hide the confusion and the goal of "substantial autonomy" becomes more of a hindrance than a help to the implementers of the mandate.[29]

Problems with mandates

The foregoing account of the way democratization and state-building mandates are drafted looks at only one aspect of a far larger issue. The crafting of the mandate is an important part of the process, but it is not in itself decisive to the success of an intervention. The importance of the mandate is, nevertheless, beyond question.

Then Secretary-General Boutros Boutros-Ghali in his *Agenda for Peace*[30] and its companion agendas for development and democracy offered "a comprehensive vision through which global problems might be more effectively met by global solutions".[31] In relation to the large UN interventions, he notes that:

the basic conditions for success remain unchanged: a clear and practicable mandate; the cooperation of the parties in implementing that mandate; the continuing support of the Security Council; the readiness of Member States to contribute the military, police and civilian personnel, including specialists, required; effective United Nations command at Headquarters and in the field; and adequate financial and logistic support.

Thus a clear and practical mandate was seen as one of six basic requirements for success. The other five requirements are very weighty. They encompass large issues of politics and implementation. Yet the political and implementation issues have both direct and indirect impacts on the crafting of mandate language.

One of the political problems concerns the actions of other parties. Mandates are constructed based on certain premises. One of those premises is the coherence of the political agreement negotiated by the disputing parties. If the agreements are negotiated in bad faith, or are beyond the ability of the signatories to implement, or are overtaken by subsequent events, the mandate that flows from them may be inappropriate. Many of the major UN interventions are built on the foundations of a peace agreement (Table 3.3).

One can point to examples of problems with mandates caused by problematic underlying agreements. The timetables and tasks assigned to MINURSO turned out to be unachievable because of continuing disagreement between the parties. UNTAC performed its mandated tasks, but the refusal of Hun Sen to accept defeat in the elections and the for-

Table 3.3 UN interventions built on the foundations of peace agreements

Intervention	Country	Agreement
MINURSO	Western Sahara	UN Settlement Proposals 1988
UNTAC	Cambodia	Paris Agreement 1991
ONUSAL	El Salvador	Mexico Agreements 1991
ONUMOZ	Mozambique	Rome Agreement 1992
UNOMIL	Liberia	Further to Cotonou Agreement 1993
MONUA	Angola	Lusaka Protocol 1994
MINURCA	Central African Republic	Further to Bangui Agreement 1997
UNAMET	East Timor	New York Agreement 1999
UNAMSIL	Sierra Leone	Lome Peace Agreement 1999
MONUC	Democratic Republic of Congo	Lusaka Cease-fire Agreement 1999

mation of an unworkable coalition government would leave basic political problems unresolved. UNAMET successfully conducted the self-determination ballot but its limited mandate did not foresee or prepare for the subsequent violence intended to vitiate the result of the vote.

In *Agenda for Peace*, Boutros-Ghali points specifically to problems with mandates that could in themselves trigger the lapse of the agreement by the feuding parties:

There are three aspects of recent mandates that, in particular, have led peace-keeping operations to forfeit the consent of the parties, to behave in a way that was perceived to be partial and/or to use force other than in self-defence. These have been the tasks of protecting humanitarian operations during continuing warfare, protecting civilian populations in designated safe areas and pressing the parties to achieve national reconciliation at a pace faster than they were ready to accept. The cases of Somalia and Bosnia and Herzegovina are instructive in this respect.[32]

Another situation where the UN's mandate may be hostage to the politics of outside forces is where the principal outside political force is not the United Nations itself but another country or regional group. The best example of this is the Kosovo operation. The United Nations was constantly playing catch-up, first in the process leading to the Rambouillet Accords and then after the humanitarian intervention by NATO forces. It is a telling fact that the documents establishing the political context on which the mandate of UNMIK is based in Resolution 1244 are annexes to the resolution drawn from negotiations conducted outside the United Nations. In such circumstances the United Nations had no choice but to accept an unusual mandate requiring uncertain provisional steps "pending a political solution".

Other problems with mandates have been highlighted by the Brahimi Report.[33] A basic premise of the report is "the pivotal importance of clear, credible and adequately resourced Security Council mandates", and it notes that "most [UN failures] occurred because the Security Council and the Member States crafted and supported ambiguous, inconsistent and under-funded mandates". The Brahimi Report refers to some of the political problems noted above, including the problem of implementing mandates developed elsewhere, but it also highlights other serious problems.

One such problem is the Secretariat recommending mandates it thinks the Security Council wishes to implement rather than mandates it thinks it is in a position to fulfil. This can occur because of the apparent urgency to reach a compromise formulation making it expedient to paper over the anticipated problems. These compromises can often lead to vague and ambiguous formulations that are difficult to implement and may thus compromise the integrity of the operation. Formulations such as an instruction "to promote a climate of confidence"[34] or "establishing an environment conducive to the organization of free and fair elections"[35] are too vague to be of much service to the implementers on the ground.

Mandates need to be clear and practical, but the political process of their drafting may lead to inconsistent obligations. The UNMIK operation in Kosovo provides an example. Resolution 1244 contains a mandate requiring a raft of differing and slightly contradictory functions: the provision of transitional administration by UNMIK; the establishment of provisional self-governing democratic institutions for autonomous self-government; a general injunction to work towards substantial autonomy and meaningful self-administration; and facilitating a political process designed to determine Kosovo's political status as long as it is in line with the Rambouillet Accords. No wonder the head of mission confessed to being confused.[36]

Ambiguity and inconsistency can be and often are cured by sensitive management of the situation by those on the ground, but under-resourced operations are far more difficult to cure. The problem of funding shortfalls is largely based on a decade-long dispute between the USA and the United Nations over the American contribution to the peacekeeping budget.[37] In view of the UN's activism in the 1990s, the peacekeeping budget blew out to be two or three times the size of the regular budget. UN members have argued that the cost of the privileged situation of the permanent members is that they must pay a larger percentage share of the peacekeeping budget. The US share was 31 per cent for the peacekeeping budget as compared to 25 per cent for the regular budget. As part of the US pressure to renegotiate these percentages,[38] large parts of the assessed contributions were withheld, leading to a US debt to the United Nations that at one point almost led to the possibility of a loss of the US vote in the General Assembly under Article 19 of the Charter. The dispute has been largely resolved with the UN decision to lower the US assessed share to 27 per cent of the peacekeeping budget and 22 per cent of the regular budget. But in the period of the UN's state-building activism the lack of funds largely due to US withholdings had a deleterious effect on peacekeeping operations. The lack of funds also had an impact on mandates, with drafters having to limit the scope of UN responsibilities to meet the available funds. The most notorious example was the inability of the inadequate peacekeeping force in Bosnia-Herzegovina to protect "safe areas". The mandate only asked the peacekeepers to assess threat levels because the Security Council was not prepared to accept the cost of the 30,000-strong force requested by the Secretary-General which would have allowed for a broader mandate to protect civilian populations.[39]

Inaction or half-hearted actions flowing from concerns about the cost of implementing mandates undermine the legitimacy of the UN interventions and thus have a corrosive impact on their effectiveness. Clearly funding is not unlimited for such interventions, but at the very least the UN efforts should not be undercut by nations wishing to prove a political point through the withholding of their assessed contributions.

Appraising mandates

Having described the alchemy through which mandates are forged and having analysed problematic aspects of mandates, how can one conclude the study and appraise the process? One obvious difficulty is that of selectivity. By focusing on the interventions shaped by mandates, those situations that fall outside the realm of the possible in international politics also fall outside the appraisal process. So appraising mandates tells us nothing about the fate of Chechnya or self-determination for Kurdish people or the future of Tibet.

Focusing on the interventions themselves poses further problems of appraisal. Is an intervention successful because fighting stopped or cease-fires were maintained? This is often the media interpretation of events and thus a key component in shaping public perceptions. But the fundamental question of the health of the polity that is the subject of the intervention remains unanswered if we look simply at the cessation of hostilities. Measuring state-building is a difficult medium- to long-term venture. Perhaps the best political measurement is the satisfaction with the UN intervention by the parties principal, including not only the leaders and factions within the polity but also the key actors in the international community such as the permanent members, the troop and civilian staff contributors, and the neighbouring countries. It is perhaps on this basis that the 1995 *Agenda for Peace* claimed that in most cases the interventions have been "conspicuously successful", with Namibia, Angola, El Salvador, Cambodia, and Mozambique drawing particular praise. Many commentators would agree with this general comment.[40]

The success of an intervention tells us that the clear and practical mandate was well suited to the result being sought. But the success of the intervention is also due to the five other factors said to be critical: the cooperation of the parties in implementing that mandate; the continuing support of the Security Council; the readiness of member states to contribute the military, police, and civilian personnel, including specialists, required; effective UN command at headquarters and in the field; and adequate financial and logistic support. So the mandate is only one part of the formula.

Within the process of judging the intervention as a whole, mandates need to be appraised on their clarity and practicality. A workable mandate will comprise mainly action tasks that are simply described for the benefit of both the implementers and the subjects. Many of these tasks will be measurable in terms of performance, cost, and timeliness. A workable mandate will avoid vague compromise words that paper over essential differences and thus leave the dilemma unresolved and in the hands of the implementers. A workable mandate will have direction and closure. The end point may not always be predictable, but the direction should be clear and a point should be ascertainable where the emergency intervention ends and the regular processes of development assistance take over. A workable mandate will have a defined division of labour. This may be based on subject matter, on geographical area, or on organizational competence. One of the avoidable problems referred to in *Agenda for Peace* concerns difficulties with coordination arising from the various specific mandates decreed for the agencies by discrete intergovernmental bodies. The United Nations has the responsibility to coordinate its various inputs into a coherent effort.

It is open from the foregoing analysis to conclude that the UN process of developing mandates for democratization and state-building purposes has improved with practice. Mistakes have clearly been made, but they have contributed to the learning and drafting process. It would be unrealistic to demand that the vagaries of international politics be somehow eliminated from the process of decision-making and formulation of mandates. The power of the permanent members can be seen as a way of channelling *realpolitik* into the decision-making process. For that reason alone, it would be futile to demand consistency. Interventions that have a direct impact on one of the permanent members will not be treated in the same way as the more remote situations.

To what extent should democratization be a priority in the mandate? The problem with asking this question is that democratization competes with the re-establishment of security and the provision of humanitarian aid as the three major thrusts of mandates. There can hardly be a process of democratization without a generally secure environment, and humanitarian aid in an emergency situation is clearly a priority for the subject peoples. The better way of posing the question is to ask whether sufficient priority is being given to the democratization process. That is a valid question because without a democratization process it is unlikely that the polity can ultimately achieve a form of governance that will encourage reconciliation and favour long-term recovery socially and economically.

The reply, inevitably, is yes and no. Yes, democratization has found a place in the UN's rhetoric and in its mandates. Indeed, even delegates from non-democratic countries happily accept the inclusion in mandates of provisions for free and fair elections and support for civil society. Mandates have become more sophisticated and the UN's response is improving with experience. There have been significant achievements in half-a-dozen difficult situations and a willingness to build on these processes in the future.

But there is also a negative response. The problem is one of maintaining focus. Democratization is not achieved by putting out fires, nor is it established by a single transition election; it is a long-term process requiring the patience to endure setbacks and to accept the slow pace of reform. Each new crisis faced by the United Nations naturally detracts attention from the smoky ruins of the last fire.[41] The funds required for the long haul are often inadequate and the benefits gained initially are put at risk.

A mandate can therefore only *begin* a process of democratization. It can put some of the basic foundations in place and set a certain direction. Thereafter the process of democratic transition and consolidation is in the hands of many actors and political forces. No more should be asked of the UN interventions in the field.

Notes

1. Tomuschat, Christian. 1997. "International law as the constitution of mankind", in *International Law Commission International Law on the Eve of the Twenty-first Century.* New York: United Nations.

2. Caron comments on the irony of dealing with a suddenly effective Security Council and the legitimacy of that power. Caron, David D. 1993. "The legitimacy of the collective authority of the Security Council", *American Journal of International Law*, Vol. 87, No. 4.

3. Chopra, Jarat. 1998. "United Nations peace maintenance", in Martin Ira Glasser (ed.) *The United Nations at Work*. Westport: Praeger.

4. See Sato, Tetsuo. 2001. "The legitimacy of Security Council activities under Chapter VII of the UN Charter after the end of the Cold War", in Jean-Marc Coicaud and Veijo Heiskanen (eds) *The Legitimacy of International Organizations*. Tokyo: United Nations University Press.

5. Though Schachter notes that the United Nations was never conceived as a legislative body, the mandate terminology tends to have a legislative effect. Schachter, Oscar. 1994. "United Nations law", *American Journal of International Law*, Vol. 88, No. 1.

6. UNSCR 706 (1991).

7. UNSCR 883 (1993).

8. As Paul Reuter noted, "extremely subtle voting rules are not the best way of achieving a delicate equilibrium". Reuter, Paul. 1958. *International Institutions*. London: Allen and Unwin.

9. A useful discussion on perceptions of fairness in the Council's work can be found in Franck, Thomas M. 1995. *Fairness in International Law and Institutions*. Oxford: Oxford University Press, particularly Ch. 7, "The bona fides of power: Security Council and threats to the peace".

10. Chesterman, Simon. 2001. *Just War or Just Peace*. Oxford: Oxford University Press, Ch. 4 and appendices.

11. Security Council action is not contingent upon which of the three heads of power is invoked. McDougal, Myers and Florentino Feliciano. 1994. *The International Law of War: Transnational Coercion and World Public Order*. New Haven: New Haven Press.

12. UNSCR 660 (1990).

13. UNGA Res. 3314 (XXIX).

14. Woodward, Bob. 1991. *The Commanders*. New York: Pocket Star Books.

15. Australian Prime Minister John Howard argued that it "self-evidently meant the use of military force". ABC Radio, 25 February 2003.

16. UN Press Release SC/7564 of 8 November 2002.

17. Based on Conte, Alex. 2003. "Bush v Iraq: A critical analysis of the Iraqi conflict", paper presented at the Eleventh Annual Conference of the Australian and New Zealand Society of International Law, 4–6 July, Wellington, New Zealand.

18. A three-judge panel found Abdel Basett Ali Al-Megrahi, a former Libyan intelligence officer, guilty of murder and sentenced him to life in prison. CNN.com, 1 February 2001.

19. But note the difficult impact of having the UNTAC operation under Chapter VI, whereby all parties including the Khmer Rouge knew that force could only be used in self-defence. Brown, Frederick. 1998. "Cambodia's rocky venture in democracy", in Krishna Kumar (ed.) *Postconflict Elections, Democratization and International Assistance*. Boulder, CO: Lynne Rienner.

20. From the veto of Bangladeshi membership of the United Nations in 1972 to the veto in 1999 of the continuation of UNPREDEP in Macedonia, China has allowed narrow bilateral issues to influence its voting pattern, though both actions were subsequently allowed to proceed.

21. The following comments are based on interviews with officials dealing with Security Council matters from the foreign ministries of some permanent members in March and April 2003, as well as discussions with officers of the UN Secretariat in September 2002.

22. Teixeira, Pascal. 2002. "Le Conseil de sécurité a l'aube du XXIème siècle", UNIDIR/2002/7. Geneva: UNIDIR.

23. Mahbubani, Kishore. 2004. "The permanent and elected members of the Council: A complex relationship", in David M. Malone (ed.) *The United Nations Security Council.* Boulder: Lynne Rienner.

24. Chesterman, Simon and David Malone. 2003. "The Security Council feels the heat", *International Herald Tribune,* 26 February. Chilean intervention in the Security Council debate of 7 March 2003 is noted in Security Council Press Release SC/7682.

25. Article 97, UN Charter.

26. Article 99, UN Charter.

27. Ben Dhia, Abdelaziz. 1998. "Le rôle du Secrétaire Général des Nations Unies en matière de maintien de la paix et de la sécurité internationales", in *Boutros Boutros-Ghali Amicorum Discipulomrumque Liber.* Brussels: Emile Brulant.

28. A good example is the establishment of MONUA under Resolution 1118, where the operative article simply adopts Chapter VII of the Secretary-General's report.

29. The Secretary-General's first special representative to Kosovo, Bernard Kouchner, is quoted as saying he read Resolution 1244 twice every morning and still had no idea what "substantial autonomy" meant. See Chesterman, Simon. 2001. *Kosovo in Limbo: State-Building and "Substantial Autonomy".* New York: International Peace Academy.

30. UN Doc. A/47/277 – S/24111, "*An Agenda for Peace,* preventive diplomacy, peacemaking and peacekeeping. Report of the Secretary-General pursuant to the statement adopted by the Summit Meeting of the Security Council on 31 January 1992", 17 June 1992.

31. Hamburg, David and Karen Ballentine. 1998. "Boutros-Ghali's *Agenda for Peace*: The foundation for a renewed United Nations", in *Boutros Boutros-Ghali Amicorum Discipulomrumque Liber.* Brussels: Emile Brulant

32. UN Doc. A/47/277 – S/24111, note 30 above.

33. "Report of the Panel on United Nations Peace Operations – A far-reaching report by an independent panel", UN Doc. A/55/305 – S/2000/809, www.un.org/peace/reports/peace_operations/.

34. UNSCR 1118 (1997), drawing on the Secretary-General's Report S/1997/438.

35. UNSCR 867 (1993), drawing on the Secretary-General's Reports S/26480 and S/26352.

36. See note 29 above.

37. See Better World Campaign Factsheets, www.betterworldfund.org/factsheets/o_21559.shtml.

38. Reducing peacekeeping costs became a formal policy through Presidential Decision Directive 25 signed by President Clinton on 5 May 1994 and released to the public in unclassified form on 22 February 1996 by the White House. See www.fas.org/irp/offdocs/pdd25.htm.

39. Sato, note 4 above.

40. Considerable support can be found in the analysis of the UN-supervised elections in El Salvador and Mozambique in Baloyra, Enrique. 1998. "El Salvador: From reactionary despoticism to partidoctratia", in Krishna Kumar (ed.) *Postconflict Elections, Democratization and International Assistance.* Boulder, CO: Lynne Rienner; Turner, J. Michael, Sue Nelson, and Kimberly Mahling-Clerk. 1998. "Mozambique's vote for democratic governance", in Krishna Kumar (ed.) *Postconflict Elections, Democratization and International Assistance.* Boulder, CO: Lynne Rienner. More nuanced assessments are made in relation to Cambodia and Angola in Brown, note 19 above; Ottaway, Marina. 1998. "Angola's failed elections", in Krishna Kumar (ed.) *Postconflict Elections, Democratization and International Assistance.* Boulder, CO: Lynne Rienner.

41. Moeller, Susan D. 1999. *Compassion Fatigue – How the Media Sell Disease, Famine, War and Death.* New York: Routledge.

4

Building democracy through benevolent autocracy: Consultation and accountability in UN transitional administrations

Simon Chesterman

The UN Security Council resolution that established the UN Interim Administration Mission in Kosovo (UNMIK) authorized the Secretary-General to establish an international civilian presence to govern the territory.[1] In its first regulation, UNMIK asserted plenary powers: "All legislative and executive authority with respect to Kosovo, including the administration of the judiciary, is vested in UNMIK and is exercised by the Special Representative of the Secretary-General." The special representative (SRSG) was further empowered to appoint or remove any person to or from positions within the civil administration, including judges. Beneath its brief text, UNMIK Regulation No. 1999/1 bore the signature "Dr Bernard Kouchner, Special Representative of the Secretary-General".[2]

The governance of post-conflict territories by the United Nations embodies a central policy dilemma: how does one help a population prepare for democratic governance and the rule of law by imposing a form of benevolent autocracy? And to what extent should the transitional administration itself should be bound by the principles that it seeks to encourage in the local population? Three years into the mission, the Ombudsperson established by the Organization for Security and Cooperation in Europe (OSCE) to monitor, protect, and promote human rights in Kosovo published a damning report on UNMIK's record on both fronts:

UNMIK is not structured according to democratic principles, does not function in accordance with the rule of law, and does not respect important international human rights norms. The people of Kosovo are therefore deprived of protection of their basic rights and freedoms three years after the end of the conflict by the very entity set up to guarantee them.[3]

This tension between the means and the ends of transitional administration highlights key differences between recent UN operations and colonial or military occupation. The trusteeship system (and the mandates system before it) imposed minimal constraints on colonial powers to consult with or respect the human rights of subject peoples. Similarly, military occupation of the form seen in the aftermath of the Second World War put the rights of the local population a considerable distance below the military and political objectives of the occupation. Territories administered by the United Nations, by contrast, have typically enjoyed virtually the entire corpus of human rights law. This would, in theory, include the emerging right to democratic governance.

As the Ombudsperson's report quoted above makes clear, however, practice has not always followed theory. The present chapter will explore this tension by considering the related questions of consultation and accountability. The first section looks at the different forms of consultation with local populations that have evolved in the various operations – a necessary precursor to the transfer of some or all power to local actors that has generally taken place through the staging of elections. (Elections themselves will not be considered here; they are the subject of other chapters.) The second section then examines whether a transitional administration itself can or should be held accountable for its actions in either a legal or a political sense.

Consultation with local actors

It is commonly assumed that the collapse of state structures, whether through defeat by an external power or as a result of internal chaos, leads to a vacuum of political power. This is rarely the case. The mechanisms through which political power are exercised may become less formalized or consistent, but basic questions of how best to ensure the physical and economic security of oneself and one's dependants do not simply disappear when the institutions of the state break down. Non-state actors in such situations frequently exercise varying degrees of political power over local populations, at times providing basic social services from education to medical care. Even where para-statal actors exist as parasites on local populations, political life goes on.[4]

The question of whether and how to engage such non-state actors in a peace process has long exercised both writers on and practitioners of conflict resolution. Recognition of groups accused of war crimes as legitimate political actors – such as the Khmer Rouge in Cambodia and the Rebel United Front (RUF) in Sierra Leone – remains controversial. At the same time, the United Nations has been curiously reluctant to engage with religious organizations, such as the Catholic Church in East Timor. In this section, the focus will be limited to the question of consultation with local actors in circumstances where the United Nations or another international actor (such as the Office of the High Representative in Bosnia) has assumed some or all governmental powers for a sustained period in Bosnia, Eastern Slavonia, Kosovo, and East Timor. The three cases from the Balkans (where elections have dominated the political landscape) will be discussed briefly before turning to a more detailed consideration of the evolution of appointed consultative mechanisms in East Timor.

Consultation in the Balkans

When authorizing the UN Transitional Administration for Eastern Slavonia, the Security Council requested the Secretary-General to appoint a transitional administrator "in consultation with the parties and with the Security Council".[5] This must be read in the context of Croatian President Franjo Tudjman's demand that a US general be appointed head of the UN operation, and the importance of ensuring Tudjman's and Yugoslav President Slobodan Milosevic's commitment to the peaceful transfer of Eastern Slavonia from Serb to Croat control.[6] In Kosovo, consultation in the appointment of the SRSG was only required with the Council itself.[7] In Bosnia, which was not placed under the control of the United Nations, other political constraints were at work. In particular, there was an implicit agreement among the guarantors at Dayton that the "high representative" would always be European, that one chief deputy was likely to be German and another American, and that the OSCE head of mission would always be American.[8]

Appointment of the transitional administrator is, of course, only the first of a great many decisions that are made in the course of such an operation. Neither the mission in Eastern Slavonia nor that in Kosovo included in its mandate an obligation to consult more generally with local actors. This may be contrasted with the mandate for East Timor, which stressed the need for UNTAET to "consult and cooperate closely with the East Timorese people".[9] Here it is noteworthy that senior UN staff in New York had a more restrictive view of the role of the early transitional administrations than they ultimately assumed. In particular, the UN legal counsel later lamented the fact that these bodies had become "legislative factories", assuming for themselves governing powers beyond the temporary caretaker role initially envisaged.[10]

Bosnia-Herzegovina

The problems attendant to rule by decree are most evident in Bosnia, where inconsistencies between the local and international political élites on occasion degenerated into farce. As part of the efforts to undermine the leadership of Serb nationalist Radovan Karadzic, the high representative in July 1997 supported Republika Srpska (RS) President Biljana Plavsic's dissolution of the RS National Assembly, then controlled by Karadzic's SDS party. The high representative went so far as to overrule a decision by the RS Constitutional Court that her action was unconstitutional, on the basis that the court's decision was a consequence of political pressures. Such faith in Plavsic may have been overstated – she was later indicted herself by the Hague Tribunal for genocide and pleaded guilty to one count of crimes against humanity.[11]

Under the Dayton Accords, the high representative was established to "facilitate" efforts by the parties and to mobilize and coordinate the activities of the many organizations and agencies involved in the civilian aspects of the peace settlement.[12] The high representative was also granted "final authority in theatre" to interpret the accords as they applied to the civilian implementation of the peace settlement.[13] Two years into the operation, the Peace Implementation Council at a summit in Bonn welcomed Carlos Westendorp's intention to use these powers "to facilitate the resolution of any difficulties" in implementing the mandate – in particular, his power to make "binding decisions" and to take "actions against persons holding public office or officials ... who are found by the High Representative to be in violation of legal commitments made under the Peace Agreement or the terms for its implementation".[14] From March 1998 until November 2002, the different high representatives dismissed, suspended, or banned from public office 100 elected officials at all levels of government – including a former Prime Minister of the Bosnian Federation (Edhem Bicakcic), a President of Republika Srpska (Nikola Poplasen), and a member of the Bosnian presidency (Ante Jelavic).[15]

The exercise of these "Bonn powers" has been criticized both for individual cases and the broader message that it sends to local parties. The justification for Poplasen's dismissal, for example, was his refusal to accept as prime minister a moderate candidate who had majority support from the RS National Assembly and was favoured by Western powers.[16] More generally, the accretion of these powers marked a reversal of moves towards self-governance. This was driven by Western frustration at the slow pace of implementation on the political side and the fact that nationalist parties by late 1996 had consolidated their control both politically and demographically.[17] That this was only 12 months after an ethnic war that had lasted more than three years led some to argue that these deadlines had less to do with Bosnia than with the domestic concerns of the intervening powers.[18] By 2000 the situation was characterized by the International Crisis Group as a paradoxical combination of a flawed democracy and a semi-international protectorate in which the international community often appeared reluctant to use its powers effectively.[19] In October 2002, Bosnians elected to power the same nationalist parties that had torn their country apart in the first place.[20] However the means employed in Bosnia are evaluated, the ends of a peaceful and multi-ethnic Bosnia do not appear to have been achieved.

Eastern Slavonia

The UN Transitional Administration for Eastern Slavonia (UNTAES) enjoyed, by contrast, a relatively simple mandate: the peaceful reintegration into Croatia of its last Serb-held territory after a period of UN administration. Once Presidents Tudjman and Milosevic had accepted that political framework – albeit grudgingly and for different reasons – this guaranteed much of the local support necessary for implementation. Nevertheless, UNTAES stressed the need to enlist the "cooperation" of local Serbs and Croats. Joint implementation committees (JICs) were established on various issues as a means of providing a forum for the two parties, though SRSG Jacques Paul Klein retained the power to remove obstructive individuals from office – a power that was threatened and, on occasion, used against "intransigent" local actors.[21]

UNTAES is now generally regarded as a success, though this had less to do with the consent of local parties than the prior agreement of the relevant external actors. In addition to the clarity (and relative simplicity) of the mandate, other key factors were the unity of command over civilian and military components, the threat of credible military force through NATO, and the strength of Klein's personal leadership. Rather than local ownership, then, UNTAES stands as an example of the importance of a strong and unified international presence.

Kosovo

Kosovo avoided Bosnia's hydra-headed structure, but the territory was politically stillborn. Security Council Resolution 1244 (1999) authorized an international civil presence in Kosovo, but it was laced with compromise language necessary to achieve consensus in New York. In the end, the resolution stated that UNMIK was to provide:

an *interim administration* for Kosovo under which the people of Kosovo can enjoy *substantial autonomy within the Federal Republic of Yugoslavia*, and which will provide *transitional administration* while establishing and overseeing the development of *provisional democratic self-governing institutions* to ensure conditions for a peaceful and normal life for all inhabitants of Kosovo.[22]

This created a near-impossible mandate on the ground. Some UN officials reported that Kouchner, head of the mission from July 1999 until January 2001, claimed to read the text of Resolution 1244 twice every morning and still have no idea what "substantial autonomy" meant.[23]

A second lesson from Bosnia was avoiding a commitment to early elections. Instead, Kosovo was governed by UNMIK while structures were established through which Kosovar representatives could "advise" it. The only quasi-governmental body that included Kosovars was, for some time, the Kosovo Transitional Council (KTC). Intended to represent the main ethnic and political groups, it was designed to "provide [the SRSG] with advice, be a sounding board for proposed decisions and help to elicit support for those decisions among all major political groups".[24] From February 2000, the Joint Interim Administrative Structure (JIAS) began to replace the parallel structures that had for some years collected revenue and provided some public services. The executive board of the JIAS was the Interim Administrative Council (IAC), comprising the three Kosovar Albanian political leaders who were parties to the Rambouillet Accords of June 1999 (Rexhep Qosja, Ibrahim Rugova, and Hashim Thaçi), a Kosovar Serb, and four representatives of UNMIK. The IAC was empowered to make recommendations to the SRSG, who could either accept these or advise in writing within seven days of "the reasons for his differing decision".[25]

No one was under the illusion that these bodies wielded any actual power. In the wake of the October 2000 regime change in Belgrade, Serbia increased cooperation with UNMIK, suggesting that some sort of autonomy arrangement might be possible within a reconstituted Federal Republic of Yugoslavia. This caused anxiety within the Albanian population, but it seems highly unlikely that Kosovo will ever again be placed under the direct jurisdiction of Belgrade. Most Kosovar Albanians look eagerly towards joining Europe – and are encouraged to do so, not least through the adoption of the euro in January 2002 to replace the German mark. Full membership of the European Union is unlikely anytime soon, of course. The most likely scenario is that Kosovo will remain an international protectorate of ambiguous status for some years to come.

In the course of drafting the constitutional framework for provisional self-government, adopted in May 2001, these tensions put UNMIK officials in the odd position of having to resist Albanian attempts to include reference to the "will of the people". Such a concept remains controversial in Kosovo precisely because the one thing that excites all parties – the final status of Kosovo – is the issue on which senior UN staff must officially profess not to have an opinion. It was nevertheless clear that Kouchner favoured independence, while his successor Hans Haekkerup held a more conservative interpretation of his mandate. Speaking in June 2001, Haekkerup said that a decision on the future status of Kosovo required a level of "political maturity" and readiness to compromise that the parties had not yet attained.[26] The constitutional framework was specifically designed to force such compromises. A seven-member presidency of the Assembly was given control over procedure; it includes two members from each of the top two parties, one from the third party, plus one representative from the Kosovo Serb community and one from a non-Serb minority group (comprising the Roma, Ashkali, Egyptian, Bosniac, Turkish, and Gorani communities). The government must include at least one Serb and one non-Serb minority representative in ministerial positions. The framework also provides for the appointment of a president of the Assembly, a prime minister, and, more controversially, a president of Kosovo.[27]

These structures reflect the fact that politics in Kosovo continues to be fought strictly along ethnic lines. With the exception of the conflation of the Roma, Ashkali, and Egyptian communities (comprising a total of perhaps 3 per cent of Kosovo's population), every active political party in Kosovo remains ethnically "pure". No one talks of reconciliation in Kosovo – on the second anniversary of UNMIK's arrival in Kosovo, Haekkerup observed that the hatred that fuels inter-ethnic violence "does not seem much diminished".[28] "A time will come for reconciliation between Albanians and Serbs," observed Fatmir Sejdiu, former general secretary of the Democratic League of Kosovo (IDK). "But not yet."[29]

Quite apart from the implicit acceptance of ethnic politics, however, UNMIK's stated hopes of inter- and intra-community compromise are not supported by the process that led to adoption of the framework. None of the local participants agreed to the text as finally adopted – a "compromise" that had to be forced on them by Haekkerup.

Consultation in East Timor

In contrast to the missions in Bosnia and Kosovo, East Timor had a uniquely clear political end point. The outcome of independence was never really questioned after the transitional administration was established,[30] but the timing and the manner in which power was to be exercised in the meantime soon became controversial. This was manifested both in the different forms of consultation attempted in the first two years of the mission and in the process through which a constitution was ultimately adopted prior to independence.[31]

Experimentation and resignation

The widespread assumption that East Timor in late 1999 was a political and economic vacuum was perhaps half true. Even before the vote to separate from Indonesia, East Timor was one of the poorest parts of the archipelago; in the violence that followed, the formal economy simply ceased to function. Unemployment through the transitional administration period remained at around 80 per cent, with much economic activity being parasitic on the temporary market for expatriate food and entertainment. Politically, however, the situation was and remained more complex.

Certainly, East Timor exhibited an atypical form of political life. As the territory prepared for its first elections in August 2001, many ordinary Timorese expressed doubts about the need for political parties. This stemmed from the view that divisions between the Revolutionary Front of Independent East Timor (Fretilin) and Timorese Democratic Union (UDT) parties in 1974–1975 were exploited by Indonesia and facilitated its invasion and subsequent annexation. Significantly, Xanana Gusmão, who later became East Timor's first president, was not formally associated with any political party. He was president of the National Council of Timorese Resistance (CNRT), an umbrella organization of groups that opposed Indonesia's occupation, but repeatedly stated that this was not a political party and that it would not run in the elections. The CNRT was eventually dissolved in June 2001. The CNRT's status was important because it was the vehicle through which UNTAET haltingly attempted to carry out its mandate to consult with the Timorese population. From soon after UNTAET's deployment, the CNRT was regarded as representing the Timorese people, giving enormous political sway to its leadership – arguably at the expense of other sections of the population. The questionably representative nature of the CNRT was reflected in its August 2000 decision to adopt Portuguese as the official language of East Timor, a language understood by fewer than 10 per cent of the population and by virtually no one under 30.[32] This was compounded when Fretilin broke from the CNRT in the same month, coinciding with a proliferation of smaller parties.

The flip side of the perceived lack of political sophistication among the Timorese was that many of the expatriates working for UNTAET and the 70-odd international non-governmental organizations (NGOs) tended to treat the Timorese political system as a *tabula rasa*. This attitude led to the first significant civic education initiative proposed by the United

Nations being rejected by the Timorese. A letter from Timorese NGOs to the director of political affairs, Peter Galbraith, complained of inadequate consultation in the development of the project, and the fact that the vast majority of the $8 million budget was earmarked for the salaries of international staff. This approach greatly underestimated the interest and capacity of Timorese actors to play an active role in civic education. Following changes of personnel and the formation of a steering committee with substantial local representation, Timorese civil society returned to the table in January 2001.

Many of these problems were referable to a contradiction within Security Council Resolution 1272 (1999). It established UNTAET in order to give the East Timorese eventual control over their embryonic country, stressing the need for UNTAET to "consult and cooperate closely with the East Timorese people".[33] At the same time, however, UNTAET followed the Kosovo model of concentrating all political power in the United Nations and the SRSG,[34] while endowing the administration with all the institutional and bureaucratic baggage that the United Nations carries.

The failure to elaborate on the meaning of "consult and cooperate closely" gave UNTAET considerable latitude in its interpretation of the mandate. The initial approach was to establish a non-elected council, with representatives of UNTAET and local political factions. Created in December 1999, the 15-member National Consultative Council (NCC) was a purely advisory body, but in practice it reviewed (and endorsed) all UNTAET regulations.[35] Nevertheless, as the situation in East Timor became more stable, there were calls for wider and more direct participation in political life.

On 5 April 2000 Sergio Vieira de Mello, the Brazilian SRSG and transitional administrator, announced the appointment of Timorese deputy district administrators to operate under the 13 international district administrators. In addition, new district advisory councils would be established. These were to have "broad participation of representatives of political parties, the Church, women and youth groups". In particular, the SRSG noted, "We wish to establish advisory councils in the districts that are representative of the East Timorese civil society more than was possible in the NCC." In addition, he announced that proceedings of the NCC, which had been criticized by some as overly secretive, would be opened to representatives of NGOs and of FALINTIL.[36]

The criticisms of UNTAET in Dili were echoed and amplified in the districts, where district administrators complained of their exclusion from policy decisions. In a letter to deputy SRSG and head of UN administration Jean-Christian Cady, they warned that the appointment of deputy district administrators might exacerbate the problem if it was not accompanied by meaningful reform in the decision-making process:

These high-level posts might satisfy the international community's demand for involvement but will not increase our authority at a local level if the process is not handled correctly. Unless it is part of a broader integration strategy it is likely to be perceived as tokenism.[37]

Weeks earlier, the head of district administration, Jarat Chopra, had resigned in a very public disagreement with senior UNTAET staff.[38]

As the SRSG later acknowledged at the national congress of the CNRT, more radical reform was needed:

UNTAET consulted on major policy issues, but in the end it retained all the responsibility for the design and execution of policy. What is more, the NCC came under increasing scrutiny for not being representative enough of East Timorese society, and not transparent enough in its deliberations. Faced as we were with our own difficulties in the establishment of this mission, we did not, we could not involve the Timorese at large as much as they were entitled to.[39]

In May 2000 the SRSG presented two options to Timorese leaders. The first model was a "technocratic model", by which the administration would be fully staffed with East Timorese, so a fully national civil service would be in place at independence. The second was a "political model", whereby East Timorese people would also share responsibility for government in coalition with UNTAET and hold several portfolios in the interim government. He explained that the latter option was a mixed blessing, as those East Timorese would also share UNTAET's role as a "punching bag".[40]

The latter model was chosen, and the National Council (NC) was established by a regulation passed on 14 July 2000. Importantly, the transitional administrator did not chair the NC and its membership was exclusively East Timorese (though all appointed by the transitional administrator). Its 33 (later 36) members comprised representatives of the CNRT and other parties, together with representatives from the Church, women's and youth organizations, NGOs, professional and labour organizations, the farming and business community, and Timor's 13 districts.[41] On the same day, a "Cabinet of the Transitional Government in East Timor" was established.[42] Of the eight posts initially established, four were assigned to East Timorese (internal administration, infrastructure, economic affairs, and social affairs) and four to international staff (police and emergency services, political affairs, justice, and finance).

In October 2000 the NC was expanded to 36 members and José Ramos-Horta was sworn in as Cabinet member for foreign affairs.[43]

The selection of the new representatives of East Timor continued to reflect UNTAET's reliance on the CNRT in general and on Gusmão in particular. This was most evident in the selection of the four Timorese Cabinet members – essentially chosen by Gusmão – which was seen by some as reflecting political allegiances established in 1975 rather than representing the interests of the Timorese in 2000. Two positions went to Fretilin (Ana Pessoa and Mari Alkatiri), one to the UDT (João Carrascalão), and one to the Catholic Church (Fr Filomeno Jacob).

Soon after establishing the NC, UNTAET announced at a daily press briefing that the East Timorese Transitional Administration (ETTA) had replaced UNTAET's governance and public administration (GPA) pillar, and that ETTA should now be referred to as a "government".[44] (UNTAET had originally been established with three components or pillars: governance and public administration, humanitarian assistance and emergency rehabilitation, and military.[45]) The idea, as senior UNTAET officials later explained, was that UNTAET should eventually be regarded as a UN assistance mission to ETTA. This was sometimes described as a "co-government" approach, in contrast to the earlier "two-track" approach.[46] Such an arrangement could only ever be theoretical, as the SRSG retained ultimate power, but it represented a decisive shift in thinking less than one year into the mission.

With the benefit of hindsight, UNTAET officials later described the early attempts at consultation as "confused at best", and as leading to justified criticism on the part of the East Timorese. Capacity-building and preparation for government were originally seen as a requiring a "bottom-up" creation of an East Timorese civil service, with minor consultation at senior levels. The inadequacy of that consultation, combined with the failure to achieve significant headway in "Timorizing" the civil service, led to pressure to reform UNTAET's structure.[47] Unlike the NCC, which was generally presented with draft regulations for approval, the National Council had power to initiate, modify, and recommend draft regulations; to amend regulations; and to call Cabinet members before it to answer questions regarding their respective functions.[48]

Nevertheless, these powers did not reflect the reality of governance in East Timor – at least, not to the satisfaction of the Timorese. Gusmão expressed the collective frustration by October 2000 in the following terms:

We are not interested in a legacy of cars and laws, nor are we interested in a legacy of development plans for the future designed by [people] other than East Timorese.

We are not interested in inheriting an economic rationale which leaves out the social and political complexity of East Timorese reality. Nor do we wish to inherit the heavy decision-making and project implementation mechanisms in which the role of the East Timorese is to give their consent as observers rather than the active players we should start to be.[49]

The Timorese Cabinet members shared these sentiments; in December 2000 they threatened to resign. In a letter to the SRSG, the Timorese Cabinet members (excluding José Ramos-Horta, who was out of East Timor at the time) complained of being "used as a justification for the delays and the confusion in a process which is outside our control. The East Timorese Cabinet members are caricatures of ministers in a government of a banana republic. They have no power, no duties, no resources to function adequately."[50]

The threat of resignation was used frequently as a political tool in East Timor. The Cabinet members' threat came soon after Gusmão himself threatened to resign from his position as speaker of the NC. Earlier that year, in the August 2000 CNRT congress, both Gusmão and Ramos-Horta resigned twice, only to be reinstated. Gusmão resigned once again from the NC in March 2001. In the absence of real political power, resignation – essentially an attempt to challenge UNTAET's legitimacy by undermining its claims to be consulting effectively – was the most effective means of expressing frustration and trying to bring about change.

A constitution for Timor-Leste

The most concrete political legacy that UNTAET will leave East Timor is likely to be its constitution. In debates on this question in early 2001, frequent analogies were made with Fiji and the USA. Fiji was presented as an example of a country with a serviceable constitution that was nevertheless regarded as imposed by foreigners and therefore of dubious local relevance; these factors were cited during a coup there in May 2000. The USA – in particular the controversial election in November 2000 of George W. Bush as its forty-third president – was cited as proof that it does not matter how flawed a constitutional procedure is or how dubious the results to which it gives rise: provided that the citizens feel ownership of the constitution itself (or are at least apathetic to the issue) they will accept it.[51]

UNTAET officials stated repeatedly that they had no intention of involving themselves directly in the drafting process. UNTAET did, however, organize the vote for the Constituent Assembly and remained committed to a "perfect election". These positions reflected competing and potentially inconsistent obligations. On the one hand, the United Nations was committed to disseminating the values enshrined in the UN

Charter and other treaties: the promotion of democracy, freedom of association, and the rule of law. On the other, the choice of political system
that was adopted had to lie with the Timorese themselves. In discussions
on a draft regulation on political parties, for example, UNTAET resisted
a push to exclude parties that had opposed Timor's independence. It was
quite possible that an elected Constituent Assembly would impose a
similar requirement in the constitution, however, and it was far from
clear what, if anything, UNTAET could do to prevent this.

A related problem was the possibility that East Timor would become
a one-party state. Fretilin was always certain to win an overwhelming
majority of the vote in the August 2001 elections – estimates ranged up to
90 per cent – and there were fears that it would then impose whatever
constitution and legislative programme it wanted. Senior UNTAET staff
confessed that they regarded such an outcome as undesirable, but were
reserved as to what they should (or could) do to avoid it. As a start, they
encouraged the Timorese to adopt a mixed voting system with proportional representation in the hope that smaller parties would be represented in the process. Fretilin eventually won 55 of 88 seats.

Procedural difficulties also arose. The elected Constituent Assembly
was tasked with drafting and adopting a constitution, which it did on 22
March 2002. The Assembly then transformed itself into the first legislature prior to presidential elections, held in April. But two of the most
contentious questions for a constitution are how the legislature is elected,
and what powers it holds *vis-à-vis* the other organs of government. The
process followed in East Timor presumed a consensus on at least the
voting method before the Assembly could be elected, and mandated that
legislature-in-waiting to define the scope of its own powers.

At the same time, some UNTAET staff warned of "worrying authoritarian tendencies" within the Timorese leadership. Locally organized
civic education programmes were sometimes likened to propaganda
campaigns. "I have grave doubts that anything democratic will come out
of this," observed one senior international official. "Look at Cambodia:
everyone regards it as a success but it was an utter disaster – look who
we put in power!"[52] The *Jakarta Post* ran a story on these lines bearing
a title of fulsome irony for an Indonesian paper: "The new Timor: A
Xanana republic?"[53] Gusmão railed against such criticisms in his 2001
New Year's speech, deriding those who "spout forth points of view ... in
a remote-control-style". He went on to draw what he saw as broader
lessons from East Timor's engagement with the international community:

We are witnessing another phenomenon in East Timor; that of an obsessive acculturation to standards that hundreds of international experts try to convey to
the East Timorese, who are hungry for values: democracy (many of those who

teach us never practised it in their own countries because they became UN staff members); human rights (many of those who remind us of them forget the situation in their own countries); gender (many of the women who attend the workshops know that in their countries this issue is no example for others); NGOs (numerous NGOs live off the aid "business" to poor countries); youth (all those who remind us of this issue know that in their countries most of the youth are unemployed) ...

It might sound as though I am speaking against these noble values of democratic participation. I do not mind if it happens in the democratic minds of people. What seems to be absurd is that we absorb standards just to pretend we look like a democratic society and please our masters of independence. What concerns me is the non-critical absorption of (universal) standards given the current stage of the historic process we are building.[54]

This bears interesting similarities to the "Asian values" arguments of the 1990s, when South-East Asian leaders (and some Western commentators) defended authoritarian political systems on the basis of their alleged effectiveness in promoting economic success. Few UN staff felt comfortable even discussing the idea that good governance might not always be coterminous with multi-party democracy. For its part, of course, UNTAET could hardly lay claim to democratic legitimacy. Vieira de Mello held absolute power in East Timor at the pleasure of the UN Security Council, whose composition continues to reflect the balance of power at the end of the Second World War. Neither he nor his staff was accountable in any direct way to the Timorese population, an issue that is discussed in the next section.

Criticism of the Timorese leadership's style was not limited to expatriates, however. Aderito de Jesus Soares, of the Timorese Jurists Association, spoke of the need to change the "culture of command" in Timorese political life that developed within a clandestine resistance.[55] Other Timorese NGOs have also been critical of the closed nature of Timorese political processes. The greatest point of leverage for the international community will be Timor's continued reliance on development assistance over the coming years, and so it is highly unlikely that independent East Timor will be overtly draconian. There is, however, a real danger that Timorese civil society will become regarded as simply a channel for aid rather than as a legitimate part of political life.[56]

Consultation and responsibility

Transitional administrations are generally created to help a population achieve some form of political transformation – most obviously from conflict to peace, but also from informal to formal political structures. In order to oversee such a transformation effectively and to ensure its durability, it is essential that the local population have a stake in the creation of these structures and in the process by which power is transferred. Consultation is also important for the day-to-day governance of the territory. But final authority remains with the international presence and it is misleading to imply otherwise. If the local population had the military and economic wherewithal to provide for their security and economic development then a transitional administration would not have been created. Where a transitional administration is created, its role is – or should be – precisely to undertake military, economic, and political tasks that are beyond existing local capacities.

These issues are quite distinct from the basic question of whether it is appropriate or possible to drive such a transformation from above. Nor is this intended to suggest that ownership is unimportant. As the UN operation in Afghanistan shows, it is possible (though difficult) to ground a post-conflict political transformation on local ownership and a light international presence.[57] It is disingenuous, however, to assert that a successful transitional administration requires both centralized control in the hands of a well-resourced SRSG *and* ownership on the part of the local population. As Bosnia demonstrates, handing over power prematurely can be highly destabilizing – not least when it has to be taken back. In Kosovo, the ambiguity of the territory's final status continues to prevent the transfer of meaningful power. Eastern Slavonia shows that consent of local parties may be less important than the clarity of the broader political settlement. In East Timor, by contrast, UNTAET was more clearly exercising power held on trust for the Timorese – once the threat to peace and security diminished, the primary obligation was to prepare the country for its independence.

What linked these otherwise disparate situations was the decision to create a temporary authority under international auspices with virtually unlimited powers. Such operations are not without historical precedent – most relevantly in the mandates and trusteeship systems of the League of Nations and the United Nations, as well as the military occupations following the First and Second World Wars. Whereas these earlier examples were transparently premised on the military superiority of the colonial or occupying power, however, this reality is now sometimes seen as politically unpalatable and therefore masked behind the language of ownership. This is a mistake. Ownership may well be the end of the transitional administration, but by definition it is not the means. This does not mean that meaningful power should not be transferred swiftly to local hands, or that local actors should not be engaged in meaningful consultative mechanisms. Rather, it means that such transfers should be seen as the incremental completion of the administration's mandate. This in turn suggests that power should generally be transferred from the bottom up, and that it should be clear what the relative capacity of the local and international institutions will be. Kosovo fails on the latter aspect; Bosnia fails on both.

Premature discussion of ownership may also overshadow the capacity-building aspect of a transitional administration. In East Timor, for example, talk of "Timorization" was sometimes conflated with ownership. Attention was therefore given to the appointment of local staff without focusing on the training that would enable them to do their jobs. The lack of skilled local workers was initially addressed by importing international staff (of varying quality and interest) who, it was assumed, would not only be able to fulfil civilian functions in the transitional administration but to train Timorese staff to do the same. Doing a job and training another person to do it are, however, quite distinct skills. The result, as UNTAET officials later acknowledged, was that Timorese staff did less on-the-job training than they did standing around and watching.[58]

Such considerations are quite separate from barriers particular to the United Nations that have emerged in this context. Most importantly, East Timor's experiment with the ETTA structure ran into bureaucratic difficulties when it was suggested that international staff should work directly under Timorese managers. There was great unwillingness to submit to such oversight, which might have entailed Timorese officials completing field evaluation reports for mission staff, with consequences for subsequent mission placements and promotions. This reflected the reality that the United Nations was not operating under the control of the embryonic Timorese institutions, but also raised squarely the question of to whom these international staff are accountable for their performance in the governance of such post-conflict territories.

Accountability of international actors

The administrations in Eastern Slavonia, Kosovo, and East Timor derived their legal authority primarily from resolutions of the Security Council, which in turn finds its legitimacy in the UN Charter, a document that is the closest thing to a constitution for the current international order. In other situations, such as Bosnia, the high representative derives his authority from a treaty signed by interested parties that delegated power to the new body. Still other situations, such as the post-war occupation of Germany and Japan, took place under conditions of unconditional surrender to a victorious army or armies.

The latter two circumstances are necessarily *sui generis*, though international humanitarian law does prescribe some basic principles for belligerent military occupation. For example, the 1907 Hague Regulations state that an occupying power must respect the laws in force in the country "unless absolutely prevented".[59] This was elaborated in the Geneva Conventions of 1949, which constrain the ability of an occupying power to alter laws or the status of public officials.[60] This is, of course, somewhat at odds with the administrations being considered in this chapter, where the entire purpose of temporary occupation is radically to change the political structures in the occupied territory. This section will focus on the first situation, where an administration receives a mandate from the Security Council, with particular reference to the more expansive operations in Kosovo and East Timor. In both territories sweeping powers were delegated to the SRSG, who literally became "the law".

There are a number of distinct reasons for establishing checks on the exercise of such power. The most obvious is that decisions might be made that do not take local interests into account. Those mechanisms that might address such concerns have been considered in the previous section on consultation. As indicated, these have largely been seen as sources of advice rather than genuine partnership, but the legitimacy that even non-binding consultations bring to the transitional administration can be used against it, in the manner that resignation was in East Timor. A second reason is the danger that power might be abused in a criminal fashion. Manifestly dictatorial or corrupt acts on the part of the SRSG would, presumably, lead to dismissal by the Secretary-General or action by the Security Council. In the case of individual criminal acts by those representing the United Nations (prominently including crimes of sexual violence), this raises questions of personal immunity that are beyond the scope of the present work. (Similarly, it will not be possible to examine the extent to which non-governmental organizations can and should be held accountable for their actions.)

Of particular interest in this section are two further aspects of accountability that are relevant to these operations. The first is the balance that a transitional administration strikes between responding to legitimate security threats and its obligation to protect and promote human rights. Here the failure to acknowledge the military basis for transitional administration – combined with the enthusiastic promulgation of human rights norms as the law of the land – has led to situations such as that in Kosovo where UNMIK has been sharply criticized for its failure to embrace the norms it bears primary responsibility for espousing. This leads to the second concern, which is that a transitional administration exercising power in a manner that contradicts principles intended to bind future local regimes – such as democratic principles, the rule of law, separation of powers, respect for human rights – may actually harm the prospects of good governance in the longer term.

Existing mechanisms

The only mechanisms available in Kosovo or East Timor whereby a member of the local population could challenge decisions or actions by UNMIK or UNTAET have been those created by the administrations themselves. An ombudsperson was created in each territory, while East Timor had an additional check on the management of donor funds through the Office of the Inspector General.

Ombudsperson in Kosovo

Kosovo's Ombudsperson was established by the OSCE on 21 November 2000. The office is intended to "promote and protect the rights and free-doms of individuals and legal entities and ensure that all persons in Ko-sovo are able to exercise effectively the human rights and fundamental freedoms safeguarded by international human rights standards, in partic-ular the European Convention on Human Rights and its Protocols and the International Covenant on Civil and Political Rights". It was to act independently and without charge. The Ombudsperson has wide juris-diction to receive and investigate complaints from any person in Kosovo concerning human rights violations and actions constituting an abuse of authority by UNMIK or any emerging central or local institution. This jurisdiction is limited to cases within Kosovo arising after 30 June 2000, and excludes cases involving the NATO-led Kosovo Force (KFOR) and disputes between UNMIK and its staff. During or following an inves-tigation, the Ombudsperson's powers are essentially limited to making recommendations, including recommendations that disciplinary or crimi-nal proceedings be instituted against a person. If the officials concerned do not take appropriate measures within a reasonable time, the Om-budsperson may draw the SRSG's attention to the matter or make a public statement.[61]

By July 2002 approximately 3,500 people had contacted the Ombuds-person, with 590 formal applications being lodged. Most concerned property issues (such governmental takings of or damage to property, and difficulties in gaining access to property), employment issues (such as discriminatory recruitment practices and unjust dismissals), fair-trial issues, and impunity issues (governmental failures to investigate or pros-ecute crimes). Slightly more than half of these applications were rejected on formal grounds. The Ombudsperson also opened 24 investigations on his own initiative. Many complaints were received against KFOR; these were forwarded to KFOR for its consideration. The Ombudsperson also released five "special reports". These reports addressed immunities of KFOR and UNMIK in their institutional capacities; the applicable law and primacy of human rights instruments; two aspects of deprivations of liberty under "executive orders"; and the registration of contracts for the sale of real-estate property.[62]

The fact that UNMIK will remain in control of Kosovo for the foreseeable future raises particular questions about how it should govern. Within the UNMIK structure there is an increasing tension between those who regard respect for human rights and the rule of law as central to the institution-building aspect of UNMIK's mandate, and those who see this as secondary to the overriding concerns of peace and security. This is epitomized in the different approaches taken to the detention of persons under executive orders.

The OSCE and the Ombudsperson in Kosovo have both issued reports criticizing UNMIK's practice of holding arrested individuals in detention for extended periods of time before being brought before a judicial authority, and of extended detention prior to trial. Persons have also been held in continued detention despite a lawful order by a judicial authority to release them, including orders by a panel of international judges. The OSCE reports, for example, that a judge ordered the release of Shaban Beqiri and Xhemal Sejdiu in November 1999, but that they were nevertheless held in detention by order of the commander of KFOR (a COMKFOR "hold") until July 2000 and were brought to court in handcuffs.[63] COMKFOR argued that its power to detain derives from Resolution 1244, which gives KFOR the responsibility of "ensuring public safety and order until the international civil presence can take responsibility for this task".[64] Two years into the mission, UNMIK officials argued that Kosovo still ranked as an "internationally-recognized emergency". And, in such circumstances, "international human rights standards accept the need for special measures that, in the wider interests of security, and under prescribed legal conditions, allow authorities to respond to the findings of intelligence that are not able to be presented to the court system".[65] Human rights law does provide for derogation from particular norms, including the right to a fair trial, but this is generally limited to a time of "war or other public emergency threatening the life of the nation" and there must be some form of official notification of this situation.[66] No such notification was offered in Kosovo – due largely to political reservations against admitting that Kosovo even two years after UNMIK arrived remained a "public emergency". Rather, the view was taken that a Chapter VII resolution adopted by the Security Council absolves a UN operation from certain human rights obligations.[67]

Following criticism by the Ombudsperson, as well as international human rights organizations such as Human Rights Watch[68] and Amnesty International,[69] a detention review commission of international experts was established by UNMIK in August 2001 to make final decisions on the legality of administrative detentions.[70] The commission approved extension of the detentions of three men held in connection with the bombing of a bus in which 11 Serbs were killed until 19 December 2001 – a few weeks after Kosovo's first provincial elections – ruling that "there are reasonable grounds to suspect that each of the detained persons has committed a criminal act". At the end of that period, the three-month mandate of the commission had not been renewed; in its absence, the Kosovo Supreme Court ordered the release of the three detainees.[71] The last person held under an executive order, Afrim Zeqiri, was released by a judge on bail in early February 2002 after approximately 20 months in detention.

One of the ironies of the current situation is that many of those who argue in favour of greater respect for human rights now argue implicitly that there should have been *less* respect for human rights at the start of the operation. Specifically, many international staff attribute some of the ongoing difficulties in establishing the rule of law in Kosovo to failures to assert such principles robustly in the first weeks and months of the operation.

Ombudsperson in East Timor

In East Timor, an Ombudsperson was appointed in September 2000 but only became operational around May 2001 – and even then without an UNTAET regulation establishing the mandate of the office. The Ombudsperson engaged in some formal enquiries but was more limited in scope than Kosovo's Ombudsperson, lacking both the mandate to investigate human rights and the institutional support of being part of an organization like the OSCE. The office was generally seen as ineffective.

Office of the Inspector General in East Timor

A second body in East Timor, with no counterpart in Kosovo, was the Office of the Inspector General. Formally established in November 2000,[72] this body emerged from a demand by the CNRT to establish a Timorese body to verify the use of funds from the World Bank-administered Trust Fund for East Timor (TFET). It operated under an interim mandate given by the SRSG in January 2001, and released reports on issues such as misappropriation of fuel, the purchase of faulty computers, the purchase of school furniture, the rehabilitation of markets, the use of funds in the Department of Justice, and the employment of teachers at "phantom schools". Much of the Inspector General's time, however, was spent on more general dissemination activities – producing pamphlets on nepotism, collusion, bribery, and so on. The effectiveness of this position as a watchdog was therefore limited.

Do as I say, not as I do

From the rationales for accountability described earlier, it is clear that the mechanisms created in both Kosovo and East Timor regarded accountability as relevant in terms of the possibility of misuse of power. At the same time, it is also clear that this has been regarded first and foremost as a political rather than a legal problem. Thus the Ombudsperson in Kosovo has a broad mandate to address human rights violations, but no capacity to enforce its decisions. In the most egregious case of deprivation of liberty, change came as a result of political pressure from the Ombudsperson together with human rights organizations.

In East Timor the relative engagement of the Timorese population, together with a secure environment and a clear political future, have combined to mean that the lack of a fully functioning ombudsperson has not been the subject of widespread criticism. In addition, UNTAET's Human Rights Unit provided a further channel for complaints against the transitional administration. Local concern for good governance of the territory is reflected in the successful Timorese push to establish an Office of the Inspector General, though his mandate was limited to East Timor Transitional Administration (ETTA) activities and later diverted towards uncontroversial activities such as dissemination rather than investigations.

In neither situation has the contradiction between what the transitional administration says and what it does been seen as a significant problem. This was less of a concern in East Timor, where the high level of cooperation between the SRSG and the Timorese leadership meant that no regulation proposed by the National Council was vetoed by the SRSG. In addition, East Timor was on track for independence, which it successfully attained in May 2002. In Kosovo, a combination of legitimate security concerns and the ambiguity of Kosovo's future appear to have led senior UNMIK officials to view the rule of law as a barrier rather than a bedrock for their activities. The issue of executive detention is the most obvious example of this, with senior officials defending the policy on the basis that Kosovo continued to be in a state of emergency, while being unprepared to articulate this publicly for fear that it might reflect badly on the mission.

It is beyond the scope of this chapter to say what impact this has had on the behaviour of local political actors. Certainly, it is Kosovo's ambiguous political future and ongoing security threats that provide the main hurdle to fully functioning government. But as a sustainable political arrangement is sought for the territory, more significant powers are going to have to be exercised to local actors. As that happens, the inconsistencies between what Kosovo's administrators say and what they do may become more important.

Other forms of accountability

In addition to the absence of formal accountability provisions available to local populations, any attempt to establish alternative routes for criticism must deal with the UN culture of generally trusting the perspective of those in the field. Each of the missions considered here has been under an obligation to submit reports to the Security Council: UNTAES was initially requested to report monthly to the Council;[73] UNMIK was to report "at regular intervals", which tended to mean once every three months;[74] and UNTAET had to report every six months, though it generally did so with greater frequency.[75] Reports to the Council are generally taken at face value, however, unless grand political issues or budgetary questions animate discussion. This may be contrasted with the manner in which reports were solicited from administering powers under the trusteeship system, including provision for a questionnaire to be drafted by the Trusteeship Council and allowing it to accept petitions from inhabitants.[76]

Reactivation of the Trusteeship Council itself as an oversight body has been suggested in this context – most prominently by the International Commission on Intervention and State Sovereignty. Its report, *The Responsibility to Protect*, stated that a "constructive adaptation" of Chapter XII of the UN Charter might provide useful guidelines for the behaviour of administering authorities.[77] For it to provide more than guidance would require a Charter amendment, however, as Article 78 explicitly prevents the trusteeship system from applying to territories that have become members of the United Nations.[78] In any case, the direct associations with colonialism would be politically prohibitive. Nevertheless, there is no reason in principle why petitions might not be submitted directly to the Security Council or a committee constituted by it. The simplest mechanism to establish would be a transitional administration committee, modelled on the sanctions committees that oversee the Council's imposition of sanctions regimes. In 1999 the Council began to appoint independent investigative panels to provide the leverage of public exposure while maintaining the distance necessary to continued quiet diplomacy on the ground.[79]

Other alternatives, such as directly petitioning the Secretary-General or the General Assembly, would be unlikely to add much. The Secretary-General necessarily places considerable trust in his special representative and would be unlikely to second-guess him or her, while the Assembly is constrained from making recommendations on situations where the Council is playing an active role.[80]

Conclusion

The apparent contradiction between the means and the ends of transitional administration stems in large part from a reluctance to acknowledge the military force that gives it legitimacy. It is simply misleading to suggest that the international presence in Eastern Slavonia, Bosnia-Herzegovina, Kosovo, or East Timor depended in any meaningful way on local consent or "ownership". Consent of the local population marks the most promising exit strategy of the transitional administration, mediated through some form of democratic process that establishes a sustainable political framework. But it is not the starting point. What becomes crucial, therefore, is clarity as to how a temporary military occupation is to begin the process of transferring political control to local hands. This political trajectory will generally be laid out before the mission is established on the ground, however, which partly explains the paralysis of the operation in Kosovo and the ongoing difficulties in Bosnia.

As a consequence, accountability of international actors will necessarily be limited during the opening phases of an operation. Nevertheless, once the political trajectory towards normalization of the political environment has begun, creating mechanisms by which the international presence may be held accountable can both encourage the emergence of an indigenous human rights and rule-of-law discourse as well as improving the day-to-day governance of the territory. The failure to do so – or an actual or apprehended reversal of the political trajectory towards self-governance – will lead to frustration and suspicion on the part of local actors.

The resistance to comparisons between recent transitional administrations and the trusteeship system or military occupation is suggestive of a broader uncertainty as to the appropriateness of imposing good governance by force of arms. And yet most such operations are properly seen as the extension of a military intervention by outside powers precisely to overthrow malevolent or non-existent governance. Reconciling this tension between the means and the ends of transitional administration is the most delicate political task of any such operation; how this takes place may also have the most lasting effect on the development of political culture in the territory under benevolent autocracy.

Notes

1. SC Res. 1244, 10 June 1999, para. 10.
2. UNMIK Regulation 1999/1, 25 July 1999, "On the Authority of the Interim Administration in Kosovo", s. 1.
3. Ombudsperson Institution in Kosovo, *Second Annual Report 2001–2002*, 10 July 2002, available at www.ombudspersonkosovo.org.
4. See, for example, Zahar, Marie-Joëlle. 2001. "Protégés, clients, cannon fodder: Civil-militia relations in internal conflicts", in Simon Chesterman (ed.) *Civilians in War*. Boulder, CO: Lynne Rienner.
5. SC Res. 1037, 15 January 1996, para, 2.
6. Confidential interviews.
7. SC Res. 1244, note 1 above, para. 6. In East Timor the Council merely welcomed the intention of the Secretary-General to appoint a special representative: SC Res. 1272, 25 October 1999, para. 6.
8. Cousens, Elizabeth M. and Charles K. Cater. 2001. *Toward Peace in Bosnia: Implementing the Dayton Accords*. Boulder, CO: Lynne Rienner.
9. SC Res. 1272, note 7 above, para. 8.
10. Interview with Hans Corell, New York, 3 December 2002.
11. International Criminal Tribunal for the Former Yugoslavia, Case No IT-00-40-I, Indictment, 3 April 2000. In a plea agreement filed on 30 September 2002, Plavsic agreed to plead guilty to a violation of Article 5(h) of the Statute of the International Tribunal (persecutions on political, racial, and religious grounds), in exchange for which the prosecutor agreed to dismiss the remaining counts in the indictment.
12. General Framework Agreement for Peace in Bosnia and Herzegovina, Bosnia and Herzegovina-Croatia-Federal Republic of Yugoslavia, 14 December 1995, UN Doc. S/1995/999, Annex 10, Art. 1(2).
13. *Ibid.*, Annex 10, Art. 5.
14. Conclusions of the Peace Implementation Conference, Bonn, 9–10 December 1997, available at www.oscebih.org/essentials/pdf/bonn_peace_implementation_council_eng.pdf, para XI(2).
15. Office of the High Representative, "High Representative's Decisions by Topic, Removals and Suspensions", available at www.ohr.int/decisions/removalssdec. By year, the number of persons removed or suspended were as follows: 1998–7; 1999–32; 2000–28; 2001–14; January–November 2002–21.
16. Office of the High Representative, "Decision removing Mr Nikola Poplasen from the Office of President of Republika Srpska, Sarajevo, 5 March 1999", available at www.ohr.int/decisions/removalssdec.
17. Cousens and Cater, note 8 above.
18. See, for example, Chandler, David. 1999. *Bosnia: Faking Democracy After Dayton*. London: Pluto Press.
19. International Crisis Group. 2000. *Bosnia's November Elections: Dayton Stumbles*, ICG Balkans Report No. 104. Sarajevo/Brussels: ICG, 18 December, available at www.crisisweb.org.
20. *Washington Post.* 2002. "After the war", *Washington Post*, 12 November.
21. "Report of the Secretary-General on the United Nations Transitional Administration for Eastern Slavonia, Baranja and Western Sirmium", UN Doc. S/1996/705, 28 August 1996, para. 5; Department of Peacekeeping Operations. 1999. *Comprehensive Report on Lessons Learned from the United Nations Transitional Administration for Eastern Slavonia*. New York: DPKO, 9 December, available at www.un.org/Depts/dpko/lessons/untaes.htm, paras 29–31.

22. SC Res. 1244, note 1 above, para. 10 (emphasis added).
23. Confidential interviews.
24. "Report of the Secretary-General on the United Nations Interim Administration Mission in Kosovo", UN Doc. S/1999/779, 12 July 1999, available at www.un.org/Docs/sc/reports/1999/s1999779.htm, para. 20.
25. UNMIK Regulation 2000/1, 14 January 2000, "On the Kosovo Joint Administrative Structure".
26. Haekkerup, Hans. 2001. "UNMIK at Two Years", speech delivered at UNMIK Headquarters, Pristina, Kosovo, 13 June
27. UNMIK Regulation 2001/9, 15 May 2001, "Constitutional Framework for Provisional Self-Government".
28. Haekkerup, note 26 above.
29. Interview with Fatmir Sejdiu, Pristina, 26 June 2001.
30. In the popular consultation held on 30 August 1999, the East Timorese were asked to vote on the following question: "Do you accept the proposed special autonomy for East Timor within the unitary state of the Republic of Indonesia, or do you reject the proposed special autonomy for East Timor, leading to East Timor's separation from Indonesia?" Seventy-eight per cent voted for independence. See Martin, Ian. 2001. *Self-Determination in East Timor: The United Nations, the Ballot, and International Intervention*, International Peace Academy Occasional Paper Series. Boulder, CO: Lynne Rienner.
31. See further Chesterman, Simon. 2002. "East Timor in transition: Self-determination, state-building and the United Nations", *International Peacekeeping*, Vol. 9, No. 1. This section draws on some passages from that text.
32. Outcomes of the CNRT National Congress, 21–30 August 2000 (English version), Commission III, Recommendation B(4)(c), adopted by the National Congress 362-0-3. Senior Timorese leaders have been the strongest advocates of Portuguese. The key reason that is generally presented concerns the identity of East Timor, a geographical anomaly bound together only by its history of Portuguese (as opposed to Dutch) colonialism. Other reasons advanced concern the importance of good relations with lusophone countries (notably Portugal and Brazil), as well as the connection that Portugal grants into the European Union (and away from dependence on Asia – particularly Indonesia). In addition, Portuguese is said to support the development of Tetum, whereas Bahasa Indonesia would "kill" it. Finally, there is an emotional resentment on the part of many (mostly older) Timorese to the imposition of Bahasa Indonesia during Indonesian occupation.
33. SC Res. 1272, note 7 above, para. 8.
34. *Ibid.*, para. 1.
35. UNTAET Regulation No. 1999/2. See "Report of the Secretary-General on the United Nations Transitional Administration in East Timor", UN Doc S/2000/53, 26 January 2000, para. 4.
36. Press briefing by SRSG Sergio Vieira de Mello, Dili, 5 April 2000.
37. Dodd, Mark. 2000. "UN peace mission at war with itself", *Sydney Morning Herald*, 13 May.
38. Dodd, Mark. 2000. "UN staff battle over independence policy", *Sydney Morning Herald*, 13 March.
39. Address of SRSG Sergio Vieira de Mello to the National Congress of the CNRT, Dili, 21 August 2000.
40. "Security Council Briefed by Sergio Vieira de Mello, Special Representative for East Timor", UN Doc SC/6882, 27 June 2000.
41. UNTAET Regulation No. 2000/24, "On the Establishment of a National Council", 14 July 2000, para. 3.2.

42. UNTAET Regulation No. 2000/23, "On the Establishment of the Cabinet of the Transitional Government in East Timor", 14 July 2000.
43. "Report of the Secretary-General on the United Nations Transitional Administration in East Timor (for the period 27 July 2000 to 16 January 2001)", UN Doc S/2001/42, 16 January 2001, para. 9.
44. UNTAET daily briefing, 8 August 2000.
45. SC Res. 1272, note 7 above, para. 3.
46. Beauvais, Joel C. 2001. "Benevolent despotism: A critique of UN state-building in East Timor", *New York Journal of International Law and Politics*, Vol. 3.
47. Confidential interviews.
48. UNTAET Regulation No. 2000/24, note 41 above, para. 2.1.
49. Dodd, Mark. 2000. "Give us a say, urges Gusmão", *The Age*, 10 October.
50. Dood, Mark. 2000. "Give us a free hand or we quit, leaders say", *Sydney Morning Herald*, 5 December.
51. For example, the analogy was made by Galbraith, a US citizen, in public consultations on the constitutional timetable held in Dili in January 2001.
52. Confidential interviews.
53. Kingsbury, Damien. 2000. "The new Timor: A Xanana republic?", *Jakarta Post*, 16 December.
54. Jose "Kay Rala Xanana" Gusmão. 2000. "New Year's Message: The right to live in peace and harmony", Dili, 31 December.
55. Interview with Aderito de Jesus Soares, Dili, 15 January 2001.
56. Cf. Chopra, Jarat. 2002. "Building state failure in East Timor", *Development and Change*, Vol. 33.
57. Chesterman, Simon. 2002. "Walking softly in Afghanistan: The future of UN state-building", *Survival*, Vol. 44, No. 3.
58. Confidential interviews.
59. Convention (IV), "Respecting the Laws and Customs of War on Land and Its Annex: Regulations Concerning the Laws and Customs of War on Land", The Hague, 18 October 1907, available at www.icrc.org/ihl, Art. 43.
60. "Convention Relative to the Protection of Civilian Persons in Time of War" (Fourth Geneva Convention), Geneva, 12 August 1949, available at www.icrc.org/ihl, Arts 54 and 64.
61. UNMIK Regulation No 2000/38, 30 June 2000, "On the Establishment of the Ombudsperson Institution in Kosovo". The Ombudsperson Institution was formally inaugurated on 21 November 2000: see Ombudsperson Institution in Kosovo, *First Annual Report 2000–2001*, 18 July 2001, available at www.ombudspersonkosovo.org.
62. Ombudsperson Institution in Kosovo, *First Annual Report, ibid.*; Ombudsperson Institution in Kosovo, *Second Annual Report*, note 3 above.
63. OSCE, Kosovo, "Review of the Criminal Justice System (February–July 2000)", available at www.osce.org/kosovo; Ombudsperson Institution in Kosovo, Special Report No. 3, "On the Conformity of Deprivations of Liberty Under 'Executive Orders' with Recognized International Standards", 29 July 2001, available at www.ombudspersonkosovo.org.
64. SC Res. 1244, note 1 above, para. 9(d).
65. *UNMIK News*. 2001. "UNMIK refutes allegations of judicial bias and lack of strategy", *UNMIK News*, Pristina, 25 June.
66. See European Convention on Human Rights, Art. 15; International Covenant on Civil and Political Rights, Art. 4.
67. Confidential interviews.
68. Human Rights Watch. 2002. *World Report 2002*. New York: Human Rights Watch.
69. Amnesty International press release, 21 February 2001.

70. UNMIK Regulation 2001/18, 25 August 2001, "On the Establishment of a Detention Review Commission for Extra-Judicial Detentions Based on Executive Orders".
71. Qirezi, Arben. 2002. "Kosovo: Court overturns Haekkerup detention orders", *IWPR Balkan Crisis Report*, No. 308, 11 January; UNMIK press release, 19 December 2001.
72. UNTAET Regulation No. 2000/34, 16 November 2000, "On Appropriations (No. 2)"; S/2001/42, para. 38.
73. SC Res. 1037, 15 January 1996, para. 4. The renewal of its mandate saw this reduced to requiring a report every three to four months: SC Res. 1079, 15 November 1996, para. 6.
74. SC Res. 1244, note 1 above, para. 20.
75. SC Res. 1272, note 7 above, para. 18.
76. UN Charter, Arts 87–88.
77. International Commission on Intervention and State Sovereignty. 2001. *The Responsibility to Protect*. Ottawa: International Development Research Centre, available at www.iciss.gc.ca, paras 5.22–5.24.
78. UN Charter, Art. 78.
79. See Cortright, David and George A. Lopez. 2002. *Sanctions and the Search for Security: Challenges to UN Action*, International Peace Academy project. Boulder, CO: Lynne Rienner.
80. UN Charter, Art. 12(1).

5

Elections in post-conflict societies

Benjamin Reilly

Elections have become an integral element of many UN peacekeeping missions over the past decade. The reason for this is clear: the focus of most UN missions has shifted from one of pure peace-building to one of state rebuilding or, in some cases like East Timor, state creation. In such cases, elections provide an inescapable means for jump-starting a new post-conflict political order; for stimulating the development of democratic politics; for choosing representatives; for forming governments; and for conferring legitimacy upon the new political order. They also provide a clear signal that legitimate domestic authority has been returned – and hence that the role of the international community may be coming to an end. For all of these reasons, elections have become a central part of many UN peacekeeping missions. In addition, electoral assistance outside peacekeeping missions has become something of a growth industry since the fall of the Berlin Wall and the "third wave" of democratization have led to a threefold increase in the number of putatively democratic governments around the globe.

Despite this, there has been a considerable variation in the relative success of elections in meeting the broader goals of democratization from country to country and case to case. In some cases, such as Namibia and Mozambique, elections clearly played a vital role in making a decisive break with the past. In others, such as Angola, flawed elections created more problems than they solved. In Haiti administrative inefficiencies undermined the credibility of the broader electoral process. By contrast, in Cambodia technically successful electoral processes were soon over-whelmed by the realities of power politics. And in Bosnia premature elections helped to kick-start the façade of democratic politics, but also helped nationalist parties cement an early grip on political power. While this mistake has been avoided in Kosovo and East Timor, it is still to be seen how elections influence the process of peace-building in these post-conflict societies, and in other cases like Afghanistan.

What is clear, however, is that in any UN mission the holding of elec-tions forces critical political choices to be made. Elections represent a key step in a broader process of building political institutions and legit-imate government. Elections influence to what extent the internal politics of fragile new states become stabilized, whether the new political dis-pensation comes to be viewed as legitimate, and how the rhythm of peaceful democratic politics can evolve and become sustainable. Varia-tions in electoral procedures can also play a key role in determining whether the locus of political competition evolves along extremist or centrist lines, and in the development of fractionalized versus broad-based political parties.

There are three main areas of variation in electoral processes which influence the shape of post-conflict politics in most countries. First, there is the question of timing: should post-conflict elections be held as early as possible, so as to fast-track the process of establishing a new regime? Or should they be postponed until peaceful political routines and issues have been able to come to prominence? Second, there are the mechanics of elections themselves. Who runs the elections? How are voters enrolled? What electoral formula is used? And so on. Third, there is the often un-derestimated issue of the effect of the elections on political parties. Es-pecially in cases of weak civil society, political parties are the key link between masses and élites, and play an absolutely crucial role in building a sustainable democratic polity. Hence, the interaction between parties and the electoral process is itself crucial. Are the political parties contest-ing the election narrow, personalized, sectarian, or ethnically exclusive entities, using the political process to pursue their wartime objectives? Or are they broad, multi-ethnic, programmatic organizations with real links to the community? And how can the former be discouraged and the latter promoted?

More generally, there is the overarching issue of under what circum-stances elections help to build a new democratic order, and under what circumstances they can undermine democracy and pave the way for a re-turn to conflict. As one survey of post-conflict elections notes, the high expectations often put on post-conflict elections tend to be accompanied by a weakness in the preconditions for their success: "most war-torn societies lack the political climate, social and economic stability, institutional infrastructure, and even political will to mount successful elections".[1] There is also a deeper issue: while elections are an essential step in building a functioning democracy, ill-timed, badly designed, or poorly run elections can actually undermine the broader process of democratization. This overarching theme is the subject of this chapter.

Timing

As a starting point, the issue of election timing is a crucial – and underappreciated – variable in election planning. Issues of timing also directly affect administrative choices, electoral system designs, and the way political parties form. In some cases, timing demands – particularly the need to hold a quick election – have influenced the choice of electoral laws, and these have affected not just the party system but also the broader incentives presented to political actors as part of the election process. This was the case in Angola's abortive 1992 presidential elections, held under the Bicesse Accord aimed at stopping Angola's long-running civil war. The major parties contesting the election were the political wings of two former liberation-movements-turned-armies: the governing MPLA, led by President Eduardo Dos Santos, and UNITA, led by Jonas Savimbi. Due to the extraordinary nature of the election (the first ever held in Angola) and severe timing pressures, a hastily drafted electoral law was enacted which included, as part of the presidential election, a run-off between the top two candidates if no one gained a majority in the first round of voting.

This choice of formula had two impacts: first, it precluded any possibility of power-sharing between the two main combatants, as the election itself could only be won by one candidate. Second, it provided an escape hatch for parties weakly committed to the process, which could get an indication of their support levels after the first round of voting. When Savimbi realized after the first round that he was unlikely to win the election, he rejected the election and went back to war. The issues of timing and electoral system choice thus impacted directly on the overall failure of the Bicesse peace process in Angola. Of course, it is possible that this may have occurred anyway. But the design of the electoral system clearly presented strategic opportunities for candidates to remove themselves from the contest – an incentive that would have been lesser under a different set of institutional rules.

Such events may suggest that democracy itself is part of the problem in such highly fraught situations, and that post-conflict situations are too fragile to be exposed to the competitive pressures of the electoral process. But this oft-heard critique ignores several factors. First, elections can be purposively designed to encourage not winner-takes-all outcomes, but the sharing of power between groups. Indeed, many would argue that some form of power-sharing is a primary requirement in post-conflict situations. Second, critics of elections as instruments of democratization often ignore the real need to construct a legitimate governing authority in post-conflict circumstances. Not least because so many of today's conflicts take place within states, the overarching challenge of many UN missions is to build or rebuild a sustainable democratic state that can function without direct international involvement. Elections are a crucial element in achieving this. State-building is a priority issue for UN missions in Afghanistan, Kosovo, and East Timor, for example, where the UN missions are confronted with the challenges of attempting to build functioning democracies in societies only recently ravaged by violent conflict.

One valid criticism of elections in post-conflict scenarios, however, is that if held too early they can undermine the nascent democratic order. This has been a fundamental problem of many UN-supervised elections: they have been held too soon and too quickly after peace has been restored. In fact, over the last decade UN peacekeeping missions appear to have developed a kind of standard operating procedure. Once a minimum level of peace has been obtained (which does not necessarily mean a full cease-fire agreement), and a basic level of infrastructure is in place, the next step is usually to hold some kind of elections – often within a year or two of the start of the mission – followed by a rapid hand-over to the newly elected authorities and an even more rapid departure of UN troops and personnel. This results in pressure to hold elections as quickly as possible, regardless of whether existing social conditions are conducive to the cut and thrust of open electoral politics or not.

But if held too early, elections in fragile situations can easily undermine the longer-term challenge of building a sustainable democracy. Elections in conflictual situations can act as catalysts for the development of parties and other organizations which are primarily (and often solely) vehicles to assist local élites in gaining access to governing power. They can promote a focus on regional, rather than national, issues. They can serve to place in positions of elected authority leaders committed to exclusionary visions of the country – leaders who are, in many cases, the very same ones who started or fought the conflict in the first place. This generals-to-politicians transformation has been a recurring problem in the Balkans, where nationalist parties and élites have attempted to use the political process to continue to press their sectarian aims. Early elections also tend to elicit more extreme reactions from voters than an election held after a period of state rebuilding. This is one of the perverse realities of post-conflict elections: the *sine qua non* of the democratic process, elections, can also be its undoing.

This appears to be one area where there has been some genuine learning over time by the United Nations. In contrast to Bosnia, Angola, and a range of other rushed elections, in Kosovo, East Timor, and now Afghanistan pressure to hold instant national elections has been resisted. Instead, a two-year period of political development has been used to prepare the ground for elections as part of the much longer process of democratization. In both Kosovo and East Timor, relatively peaceful national elections were held in the second half of 2001. In Afghanistan, the two-year time-frame is being used again. Although questions remain as to whether even two years is time enough, there is now little doubt about the benefits of this more gradual approach.

Election timing also has other implications. For example, timing considerations impact directly on the shape of the political party system. A major goal in democracy-building should be the creation of parties which are broad-based, have strong links to local communities, and campaign on a national platform. But in post-conflict situations many political parties are not broad-based vehicles for presenting competing policy and ideological platforms, but rather narrowly focused, personalized, élite cartels. In other cases, political movement are often merely thinly disguised variants of the armies which fought in the original conflicts, as exemplified in Bosnia by the growth of nationalist parties like the (Croat) HDZ, (Serb) SDS, and (Bosniac) SDA, respectively. This problem also afflicts former liberation movements, such as East Timor's Fretilin or the Kosovo Liberation Army, which attempt to transform themselves into mainstream political organizations. Either way, holding elections too early in the transition period can have the perverse effect of stymieing the development of more aggregative and programmatic political parties – institutions which are now widely accepted to be important facilitating agents for successful democratization.

A second issue is the coordination of election timing with sub-national elections, and hence the degree of coordination between local and national-level élites. Some scholars argue that in a new democracy holding national elections before regional elections generates incentives for the creation of national, rather than regional, political parties – and hence that the ideal process of election timing is to start at the national level first and then work one's way down.[2] Others, such as Diamond, believe that simultaneous national and local elections "can facilitate the mutual dependence of regional and national leaders. The more posts that are filled at the regional and local level ... the greater the incentive for regional politicians to coordinate their election activities by developing an integrated party system."[3] This was the situation at Indonesia's 1999 elections, with identical party-based ballots being presented to voters at simultaneous elections for national, provincial, and local assemblies, which greatly strengthened the nascent party system.

In recent years, however, standard UN practice has been to start at the local level: rather than leading with national elections, the preferred approach has been to hold local or municipal elections first, allowing steps towards democratization to be taken gradually. This approach is particularly suited to "state-building" elections, which can help develop party politics from the ground up, as in East Timor and Kosovo. In Afghanistan, the Lloya Jirga election process facilitated by the United Nations in 2002 can be seen as performing a similar function. The relative success of these cases suggests that national elections do not necessarily always have to be held before local ones. In general, the comparative evidence indicates that local elections should come first and that a "bottom-up" approach to electoral timing is probably the best way to encourage the development of party politics and to inculcate voters in the routines of electoral politics.

A final timing constraint comes not from the domestic realm but from the approach taken by the international community. International policy-makers have often viewed elections as a convenient punctuation point in a peacekeeping mission, which cannot just usher in a new government but also provide a convenient exit point for international involvement. Thus Cambodia's exemplary 1993 election, the culmination of the biggest UN peacekeeping mission to date, was followed by a rapid departure of the United Nations and other international forces from Cambodia – a departure which did little to translate the results of an exemplary electoral process into solidifying a fragile new polity. Soon after, a "coup" by the "second" prime minister, Hun Sen, against the most popular elected party, FUNCINPEC, saw Cambodia return to its familiar politics of intimidation and authoritarian rule. Elsewhere, rushed elections (for example, in Liberia) with little in the way of broader political support have undermined the legitimacy of the election process, creating further problems for future democracy-building efforts.

There are, however, powerful pressures, both domestically and internationally, for early elections to occur as part of the process of state rebuilding in post-conflict societies. For one thing, given the risk-averse nature of the international community when it comes to peacekeeping commitments, such elections can (as noted above) provide a clear "exit strategy" for international involvement. But supporting the difficult process of transforming a poor, traumatized, and war-ravaged society into a well-functioning democracy requires more than the presence of a few hundred UN officials for 18 months, with an election at the end. It means, quite simply, being prepared to invest substantial time and money in an open-ended process of social and political development. With the exception of the Balkans, which benefit from their location in Europe (and where observers are talking about an international presence in the region for *decades*), there are few post-conflict societies anywhere in the world where international actors have the inclination to pursue such an open-ended strategy. In most cases, the roving eye of the international media and the governments of major Western states moves on to other, more fashionable, issues.

A second-best alternative to such open-ended commitment is not to rush into immediate elections following a peace deal, but rather to encourage local involvement for a few years until some of the basic elements of a pluralistic party system and a functioning state have been established. This was the approach taken by the United Nations in both East Timor and Kosovo, where local leadership forums have been introduced *without* an electoral process. In East Timor, for example, the United Nations developed the National Consultative Council, made up of representatives of East Timor's government-in-waiting, into a form of unelected legislature which included representatives of youth, church, and women's groups. In Kosovo, as noted earlier, national elections were postponed in favour of municipal polls, where the stakes are lower and the responsibilities of elected officials were focused on service delivery rather than national issues. In both cases the evidence suggests that, by involving local actors in the process of governing while lengthening the transition to full-blown national elections, a more mature and responsible form of party politics has begun to be developed. This approach has much to recommend it for future operations.

Electoral mechanics

The mechanics of the electoral process can have a profound – and often profoundly misunderstood – impact on the success or failure of post-conflict democratization. Electoral mechanics can be divided into two main areas: the electoral *system* – that is, the formula by which votes are converted into seats, including the way ballot papers are laid out and the structure of electoral districts – and the electoral *administration* – such as the electoral management body, the provisions for voter registration, boundary delimitation, and the like. Between them, these two areas comprise some of the most important variables influencing the success or failure of post-conflict elections, and indeed democratization more generally.

While electoral systems have attracted a voluminous academic literature, issues of electoral administration remain under-studied by scholars and underrated in general in terms of their effect on post-conflict polities. Voter registration, for example, is a perennial area of concern, not least because nearly all post-conflict elections take place in an environment where basic census and other records are missing. The construction of a comprehensive register of voters is thus often a first step in the bureaucratic process of state-building. It is also often an enormously time-consuming, logistically challenging, and resource-intensive process: in Cambodia, for example, the voter registration period took almost a full year before the election and demanded huge amounts of time, personnel, and money. Because electoral districts and polling places are often drawn and allocated on the basis of voter registration records, this process usually impacts on these areas too.

However, probably the most important administrative decision concerns the composition of the body managing the elections, and specifically whether the elections are run by the government of the day or some form of independent electoral commission is established, and whether such a body is comprised of political parties or non-partisan civil servants. The worldwide trend is definitely towards independent electoral commissions staffed by non-partisan civil servants; indeed, since the world's largest democracy, India, adopted this model at independence it was been widely adopted around the world. However, the influence of the USA is important here, as the US form of electoral administration is based around political appointees and party representatives. Many post-conflict democracies, particularly in Latin America, have adopted this model. Rafael Lopez-Pintor argues that, when there is no better tradition or an existing body of widely respected independent civil servants, a party-based electoral authority may be the only realistic choice.[4]

However, despite some success cases, the comparative evidence (and, after the Florida debacle at the 2000 presidential elections, that of the USA itself) suggests that, in general, independent commissions run by apolitical civil servants are to be preferred to those comprised of political parties. Party-based commissions have an almost inevitable tendency to split along party lines. In Haiti, for example, the Provisional Electoral Council was made up of representatives of the political parties, but was also deeply divided along party lines, and internal mistrust and divisions prevented it from working efficiently.[5] In Cambodia, by contrast, a non-partisan electoral commission was widely seen as one of the outstanding elements of the entire UN mission. Non-partisan commissions were also a prominent and successful part of UN missions in Namibia and East Timor.

The dangers of using party-based electoral administrations was graphically demonstrated by Indonesia's transitional elections in 1998. Amid the flowering of new political movements that often accompanies a democratic opening, a requirement that both the government and opposition political parties must be represented on the General Elections Commission (KPU) resulted in a deadlocked and unwieldy body of no less than 53 persons, most of them party representatives (including some individuals who were also candidates for the election). The result was that, during the preparation for one of the most important transitional elections of the 1990s, the body charged with running the elections, the KPU, became almost completely dysfunctional, being deeply divided along party lines and unable to take even basic decisions (at one stage, fist fights broke out between different members of the commission). After the elections, which were administratively flawed, the Indonesians moved quickly to discard the party-based KPU and replace it with a much smaller, non-partisan body of 11 non-party and non-government representatives.

Electoral processes also need to be sustainable. While the United Nations plays an important "vector" role in spreading new practices and technologies, there is a distinction between the ideal electoral technology and the capacity of a recipient country to handle that technology in a sustainable manner. A number of internationally financed and run elections over the past decade have introduced a level of electoral technology which was clearly unsustainable by the host country, and could not be replicated in their second, locally run, elections. Cambodia and Mozambique both fall into this category. Highly expensive levels of basic equipment and staffing are a common problem; an over-reliance on sophisticated information technology more suited to a first-world country than a third-world one is another (a typical example is the use of computerized electoral rolls in countries where electric power is unreliable). Building a *sustainable* electoral administration needs to be the overriding aim in such situations, even where this means using more basic technology or equipment. Similarly, donors need to think hard about the relative merits of funding expensive one-off international election observation missions (sometimes known as "electoral tourism") versus the longer-term benefits of directly supporting the domestic electoral administration and local observer groups. The latter is less glamorous but usually has a much greater pay-off in actually assisting the consolidation of a new democracy.

While these and other issues of electoral administration continue to receive inadequate attention, the design of electoral systems, by contrast, has long been recognized as one of the most important institutional choices for any political system. Electoral systems can be purposively designed to achieve particular outcomes, and serve to structure the arena of political competition, including the party system. The great potential of electoral system design for influencing political behaviour is thus that it can reward particular types of behaviour and place constraints on others. This is why electoral system design has been seized upon by many scholars as one of the chief levers of constitutional engineering to be used in mitigating conflict within divided societies.[6] As Lijphart notes, "If one wants to change the nature of a particular democracy, the electoral system is likely to be the most suitable and effective instrument for doing so."[7] As well as their suitability for engineering, electoral rules also serve to structure the arena of political competition during election campaigns. This has important behavioural consequences for both voters and candidates. Because elections represent a primary arena of political competition in many new democracies, and different strategies of cooperation or antagonism between the players can increase or decrease their prospects for success, the electoral system is a key mechanism in shaping wider political practices, and can have an effect far beyond the elections themselves.

Electoral systems also have a direct impact upon politics in societies divided along ethnic, religious, ideological, or other lines. Donald Horowitz, for example, argues that "the electoral system is by far the most powerful lever of constitutional engineering for accommodation and harmony in severely divided societies, as indeed it is a powerful tool for many other purposes".[8] Arend Lijphart says that "the electoral system has long been recognized as probably the most powerful instrument for shaping the political system".[9] Timothy Sisk writes that electoral systems "play an important role in 'engineering' the results of democratic voting, and along with other institutional choices can have a profound impact on the nature of political parties and the general character of democracy".[10] Beyond this consensus on the importance of electoral systems, however, there is profound disagreement among theorists as to which electoral systems are most appropriate for divided societies.

Two schools of thought predominate. The scholarly orthodoxy has long argued that some form of proportional representation (PR) is all but essential if democracy is to survive the travails of deep-rooted divisions. For example, Arthur Lewis's study of the failure of post-colonial democracy in countries such as Ghana, Nigeria, and Sierra Leone in the late 1950s and 1960s prompted him to argue that divided societies need PR to "give minorities adequate representation, discourage parochialism, and force moderation on the political parties".[11] Such arguments foreshadowed, in part, the electoral recommendations of "consociational" approaches to managing ethnic cleavages in divided societies, which emphasize the need for divided societies to develop mechanisms for élite power-sharing if democracy is to be maintained. In terms of electoral systems, consociationalists argue that some form of proportional representation is all but essential for divided societies, as this enables all politically significant ethnic groups, including minorities, to form ethnically based parties. Their prescriptions for electoral system design often focus on the need for party-list PR, usually in large districts. This is based on the tendency of PR to produce multi-party systems, and hence multi-party parliaments, in which all significant segments of the population can be represented, and on the empirical relationship between proportional electoral rules and "oversized" or grand coalition governments, which are a fundamental feature of the power-sharing approach on which con-sociationalism is based. The use of large, multi-member electoral districts is particularly favoured because it maximizes proportionality and hence the prospects of multiple parties in parliaments, which can then form the basis of an cross-ethnic government coalition.[12] PR election rules are thus important of themselves – because they are likely to facilitate pro-portional parliamentary representation of all groups – and also an im-portant component of wider consociational prescriptions that emphasize the need for grand coalitions, group autonomy, and minority veto powers.

In contrast to this orthodoxy, an alternative approach sometimes typi-fied as "centripetalism" maintains that the best way to mitigate the de-structive effects of ethnicity in divided societies is not simply to replicate existing ethnic divisions in the legislature, but rather to utilize electoral systems that encourage cooperation and accommodation between rival groups, and therefore work to break down the salience of ethnicity rather than foster its representation in parliament.[13] Drawing on theories of bargaining and cooperation, centripetalism advocates institutional de-signs which encourage opportunities for dialogue and negotiation be-tween opposing political forces in the context of electoral competition. By privileging cooperative campaign strategies with increased prospects of electoral success, candidates representing competing (and sometimes violently opposed) interests are presented with incentives to negotiate for reciprocal support, creating an "arena of bargaining" where vote-trading arrangements can be discussed.[14]

Centripetalist approaches advocate the use of electoral rules which encourage "vote-pooling" and "preference swapping" in order to en-courage inter-ethnic bargaining and promote accommodative behaviour. At the core of this approach is the need to make politicians reciprocally dependent on the votes of members of groups other than their own.[15] The most reliable way of achieving this aim, according to proponents of the centripetal approach, is to offer sufficient electoral incentives for campaigning politicians to court voter support across ethnic lines. For example, some electoral models – such as preferential systems like the alternative vote (in Fiji) or the single transferable vote (Northern Ire-land) – permit (or even require) voters to declare not only their first choice of candidate on a ballot, but also their second, third, and subsequent choices amongst all candidates standing. Parties that succeed in negotiating preference-trading agreements for reciprocal support with other parties will be rewarded, thus strengthening moderate voices and the political centre. This gives them strong institutional incentives both to engage in face-to-face dialogue with their opponents and to negotiate on broader policy issues than purely vote-seeking ones. The overall effect is thus to reorient electoral politics away from a rigid zero-sum game to a more fluid, complex, and potentially positive-sum contest. The success of "pro-peace" forces at Northern Ireland's breakthrough 1998 election was dependent to a significant extent on such vote transfers towards the moderate middle and away from extremists. Fiji's transitional 1999 election also utilized centripetal procedures, as did the transitional 1990 election in Estonia. Sri Lanka and Papua New Guinea are other examples of countries in which centripetal electoral systems have or will be used.

Regardless of whether consociational or centripetal approaches (or some mixture of the two) are favoured, there is widespread agreement amongst many scholars that some type of power-sharing government featuring all significant groups is an essential part of democracy-building in divided societies. In particular, multi-ethnic coalitions are favoured by both consociationalist and centripetalists as desirable institutions for divided societies. This form of the power-sharing model is most often associated with proportional elections, as PR is the surest way of guaranteeing fair results and minority representation. Lewis, for example, argues that "one of the advantages of proportional representation is that it tends to promote coalition government".[16] Yet the comparative evidence from many cases suggests that power-sharing has been less stable and less in evidence in post-conflict elections than many scholars would have predicted. In most cases, moreover, proportional elections have resulted in majority rule: Namibia, Mozambique, and Liberia are all examples of this. In each case, however, the largest party would probably have won an even greater majority had alternative institutional designs been employed.

It is instructive to note that almost all of the major transitional elections conducted in recent years, including those held under UN auspices, have utilized some form of PR. In fact, transitional elections in Namibia (1989), Nicaragua (1990), Cambodia (1993), South Africa (1994), Mozambique (1994), Liberia (1997), Bosnia (1996, 1998, 2000), Kosovo (2001), and East Timor (2001) were all conducted under proportional representation rules. In particular, the simplest form of proportional representation – party-list PR – appears to have become the *de facto* norm of UN parliamentary elections. The November 2001 elections in Kosovo, for example, used a national-list PR system to elect the 120-

member central assembly. In presidential systems this has usually been combined with some form of run-off election for the presidency. Only Haiti in 1995, which used a run-off system for its parliamentary elections, has deviated from the PR norm (and there, as in Angola, the record of this system was mixed, to say the least: in Haiti, as in Angola, some losing candidates trailing after the first round of voting chose to boycott the second round, thus undermining the legitimacy of the process as a whole).

As would be expected from their widespread use, PR systems have many advantages for transitional elections in new democracies: they are fair, transparent, and provide a clear correlation between votes cast in the election and seats won in parliament. By bringing minorities into the process and fairly representing all significant political parties in the new legislature, regardless of the extent or distribution of their support base, PR is often seen as an integral element for creating an inclusive and legitimate post-authoritarian regime. But the adoption of such systems for post-conflict elections has usually been dictated more by administrative concerns, such as the need to avoid demarcating individual electoral districts and producing separate ballot papers for each district, than these wider political issues. Indeed, in many post-conflict elections national PR systems are the only feasible way to hold an election quickly, as a uniform national ballot can be used, no electoral districts need be demarcated, and the process of voter registration, vote counting, and the calculation of results is consequently simplified. In Liberia in 1997, for example, population displacement and the lack of accurate census data led to the abandonment of the old system of single-member majoritarian constituencies in favour of a proportional system with a single national constituency.

However, national PR systems also have some disadvantages, as they provide no geographic link between voters and their representatives, and thus create difficulties in terms of political accountability and responsiveness between elected politicians and the electorate. In addition, many new democracies – particularly those in agrarian societies – have much higher demands for constituency service at the local level than they do for representation of all shades of ideological opinion in the legislature. It has therefore increasingly been argued in Namibia, South Africa, Cambodia, and elsewhere that the proportional systems used at the first transitional elections should be modified to encourage a higher degree of *geographic accountability* – such as by having members of parliament represent territorially defined districts and service the needs of a constituency. A popular choice in recent years has been for "mixed" electoral systems, in which part of the legislature is elected on a national level by proportional representation and some is elected at a local level from single-member districts, so that both proportionality and accountability are maximized. For example, the August 2001 elections for East Timor's 88-member constituent assembly used a mixed system, with 75 of the assembly's seats elected on a nationwide basis by proportional representation and 13 seats (one for each district) elected by first-past-the-post.

There are also variations within PR systems that need to be considered. For example, the precise kind of PR formula used can influence the extent to which minor parties are represented, or major parties are advantaged. In Cambodia, the use of a "Hare" divisor at the provincial level, rather than a "largest remainder" system nationwide, had a major political effect: minor parties which would have gained seats had one national constituency been used fell short, while the two major parties – the Cambodian People's Party and FUNCINPEC – both gained "seat bonuses" as a result of these (apparently minor) system choices. Overall, an additional 10 parties would have gained representation had the election been held on a national rather than a provincial basis.[17] In Namibia, by contrast, a highly proportional national PR system was introduced: with no legal thresholds in place, a party needed less than 1 per cent of the vote to gain election.

As such cases suggest, it is impossible to divorce the shape of the party system, and prospects for post-election power-sharing, from the design of the electoral system. All three are mutually entwined to a large extent. For example, different types of electoral formula can encourage or retard different types of party constellations, and can also influence the extent to which post-conflict parties are broad-based and moderate entities, drawing cross-communal support, or whether they are (as in Bosnia) merely former armies in a new guise – wolves in sheep's clothing. Proportional representation, while fairly representing all views, can also enable small extremist parties to gain crucial footholds in power. In support of this contention, some comparative studies have found that smaller "district magnitude" – the number of members elected from each electoral district – is the crucial institutional variable in blocking the rise of "fringe" or extremist parties and encouraging the development of a broad-based party system, suggesting that less proportional systems are to be preferred.[18]

Other technical considerations can also have major implications. Take the case of designing list PR systems for ethnically divided societies: because such systems can utilize one standard national ballot paper and do not require electoral districts to be drawn or voter rolls to be demarcated on a geographical basis, they are by far the simplest system for electoral administrators – and, arguably, voters – facing first-time elections in new democracies. But in places like Bosnia, the application of PR has also been seen to undermine the process of democratization by disengaging politicians from voters and, worse, permitting the development of hard-line nationalist political parties which can achieve electoral success by making narrow, sectarian appeals to their core ethno-political base. Indeed, recent Bosnian elections have served to emphasize that under such conditions the surest route to electoral victory under PR is to play the ethnic card – with disastrous consequences for the longer-term process of democratization.

Because of these concerns, the most recent Bosnian elections, in November 2000, therefore utilized an "open-list" PR system, in which voters could choose not just between parties but also between candidates within parties, with the expectation that this would encourage greater identification with and responsiveness from elected politicians. But – as any scholar familiar with the use of the same system in the deeply ethnically torn country of Sri Lanka could have advised – this was a risky move in a divided society where ethnic affiliation remains the primary basis of voter choice. In Sri Lanka, parties that have attempted to field a multi-ethnic candidate list have found that such "open lists" can undermine, rather than promote, multi-ethnic government: Sinhalese voters will, if given the chance, deliberately move Tamil candidates placed in a winnable position on a party list to a lower position. This may well be a problem which could have afflicted major parties in South Africa as well, had not the electoral system used been a "closed" list which allowed major parties such as the ANC and the NP to place ethnic minorities and women high on their party list. In Bosnia, the 2000 elections saw a wave of victories for extremist parties and candidates, a wave of victories that the "permissive" open-list PR electoral system only served to encourage, as it contained no real incentives for inter-ethnic cooperation or moderation.

Political parties and power-sharing

Transitional democracies, particularly those moving from a deep-rooted conflict situation, typically have a greater need for inclusiveness and a lower threshold for the robust rhetoric of adversarial politics than their established counterparts. Similarly, the stable political environments of most Western countries, where two or three main parties can often reasonably expect regular periods in office via alternation of power or shifting governing coalitions, are very different from the type of zero-sum politics which so often characterizes divided societies. This is one of the reasons that "winner-take-all" electoral systems like first-past-the-post have so often been identified as a contributor to the breakdown of democracy in the developing world: because such systems tend to lock out minorities from parliamentary representation they can, in situations of ethnically based parties, easily lead to the total dominance of one ethnic group over all others.[19] Democracy, under these circumstances, can quickly become a situation of permanent inclusion and exclusion, a zero-sum game with frightening results.

But there are also distinctive elements of political parties in post-conflict situations that appear to transcend institutional considerations. Because of the underdeveloped and deeply divided nature of most post-conflict societies, elections often have the effect of highlighting societal fault-lines and hence laying bare very deep social divisions. In such circumstances, the easiest way to mobilize voter support at election time is often to appeal to the very same insecurities that generated the original conflict. This means that parties have a strong incentive to "play the ethnic card" or to take hard-line positions on key identity-related issues, with predictable consequences for the wider process of democratization. Post-communist elections in Yugoslavia in the early 1990s, for example, resulted in the victory of extremist nationalist parties committed to (and achieving) the break-up of the federation. The 1993 elections in Burundi, which were supposed to elect a power-sharing government, instead mobilized population groups along ethnic lines and served as a catalyst for ethnic genocide a few months later. Similarly, Bosnia's 1996 and 1998 elections effectively served as ethnic censuses, with parties campaigning on ethnic lines and voters reacting to heightened perceptions of ethnic insecurity by electing hard-line nationalists to power, greatly undermining the process of democracy-building.

For this reason, scholars and policy-makers alike have frequently identified the need to build broad-based, cross-regional, and multi-ethnic political parties in fragile multi-ethnic states, particularly those susceptible to separatist appeals. Horowitz, for example, has consistently advocated the need for broad multi-ethnic parties or coalitions of parties as a key facilitating factor in avoiding ethnic conflict.[20] Similarly, Huntington argues that fractionalized and ethnically or regionally exclusive party systems are extremely damaging for democratic prospects and are, consequently, found widely in the failed democracies of the third world.[21] A 26-nation study of democracy in developing countries concluded that "a system of two or a few parties, with broad social and ideological bases, may be conducive to stable democracy".[22] Diamond sums up the prevailing view of many scholars, arguing that "political parties remain important if not essential instruments for representing political constituencies and interests, aggregating demands and preferences, recruiting and socializing new candidates for office, organizing the electoral competition for power, crafting policy alternatives, setting the policy-making agenda, forming effective governments, and integrating groups and individuals into the democratic process".[23] By contrast, under the conditions of "polarized pluralism", featuring competition between extremist movements, the logic of elections changes from one of convergence on median policy positions to one of extreme divergence.[24] Politics becomes a centrifugal game. Such fragmented party constellations are empirically much more likely to experience violence and the breakdown of democracy than more moderate multi-partism based on a few "catch-all" political parties.[25]

For this reason, there is an increasing focus in the policy world – which has yet to be adequately digested by scholars – on the need to build broad-based, programmatic political parties in new democracies, and to avoid the narrow, personalized, and sectarian parties and party systems that have undermined so many new democracies. Particularly in societies split along ethnic lines, cross-regional and multi-ethnic parties that compete for the centre ground appear to be a – and perhaps the – crucial determinant of broader democratic consolidation and peace-building. For this reason, new democracies around the globe have, over the past few years, experimented with a unusual array of institutional approaches to encourage the development of sustainable political parties and party systems.

There are several ways of doing this. First, *party rules* governing the formation, registration, and campaigning of political parties can be enacted which encourage parties to be cross-regional and cross-ethnic in their composition. This was the approached used successfully at Indonesia's transitional 1999 elections, where to qualify to compete in the election political parties must have established a branch structure in more than half of Indonesia's 27 provinces, and within each of these provinces must also have established branches in over half of all regions and municipalities. The Indonesian drafters stated clearly that their aim was to discourage political groups based on ethnicity or region which could form the basis of secessionist claims, and to encourage the development of broad-based organizations campaigning on a national platform.[26] The results from the 1999 election were encouraging for these expectations, as the main electoral contest did indeed appear to take place between three large cross-regional parties, and the level of ethnic violence associated with the elections was much lower than had been feared (although it appears to be rising again in the post-election period). Variations on this approach have also been used in several other Asian and West African countries.

Second, *electoral systems* can be designed to enable voters to rank-order choices between candidates ("preferential voting"), a process which has been shown to help sustain centrist parties. This was the approach used at Northern Ireland's break-though 1998 "Good Friday agreement" elections, which utilized a single-transferable-vote form of electoral system which enabled voters to indicate secondary choices on their ballot. Analyses of these elections have found that the use of a transferable ballot enabled "pro-peace" Republican and Unionist voters to give their first vote to their communal party, but to transfer their "secondary" votes to pro-agreement non-sectarian parties (thus advantaging the "moderate middle" of non-ethnic parties). Vote transfers overwhelmingly flowed from sectarian parties on both sides towards the pro-agreement but non-sectarian middle.[27] Pro-agreement parties on both sides of the sectarian divide benefited from such vote transfers, which – among other things – were ultimately crucial in converting a bare "anti-agreement" Unionist voter majority into a bare "pro-agreement" Unionist parliamentary majority. Evans and O'Leary, for example, conclude that the principal reason that a workable assembly emerged from the 1998 elections "was the adoption, or re-adoption, of the single transferable vote ... voters' lower-order preferences kept the Assembly on-track by reducing the numbers of seats that the anti-Agreement unionist parties won in the election".[28]

Third, *distribution requirements* can be enacted which require parties or individual candidates to garner specified support levels from across different regions, rather than just their own. The best-known example of this type of cross-regional engineering has been in Nigeria. Nigeria's February 1999 presidential elections which swept Olesegun Obasanjo to power took place under laws which contained a so-called "distribution requirement": instead of the usual majority vote requirement, successful candidates had to obtain not just a majority of the vote, but also not less than one-quarter of the vote cast in at least two-thirds of the states of the federation. The intention behind this kind of distribution requirement – first introduced in 1979 and since adopted in two other African countries as well – was to ensure that the winning candidate gained cross-ethnic support across the country rather than just in one part. Again, a primary aim was to counter the fissiparious secessionist tendencies that may have been unleashed by the electoral process under different rules. From the 1999 presidential election, the preliminary evidence is encouraging: Obasanjo ran on a cross-ethnic platform and in fact gained greater votes outside his own region than within it (precisely because, it appears, he campaigned on a cross-regional multi-ethnic platform).

Fourth, the "rules of the game" can be constructed in such a way as to encourage, or require, parties to put forward *multi-ethnic lists of candidates*, thus encouraging multi-ethnicity *within* parties. In countries as varied as Lebanon, Singapore, and South Africa, the "rules of the game" encourage parties to present multi-ethnic candidate lists to the voters. In Lebanon, for example, election is dependent, at a practical level, on being part of a mixed list of candidates representing different religious groups. In most cases candidates must compete for election against other members of their own group. Electors choosing between party lists must thus make their choice on the basis of criteria other than ethnicity. In Singapore, most MPs are elected from multi-member districts known as "group representative constituencies", which each return between three and six members from a single list of party or individual candidates. Of the candidates on each party or group list, at least one must be a member of the Malay, Indian, or some other minority community. Moving from a compulsory to a voluntary model of multi-ethnic candidate lists, the closed-list proportional representation system used in South Africa's 1994 elections enabled the major political parties voluntarily to adopt a multi-ethnic candidate composition – thus enabling the major "black" party, the ANC, to place white and coloured members at winnable places on their candidate list.

Finally, *external interventions* can be used to try to stimulate the development of a meaningful party system where none exists. In Kosovo, for example, the OSCE has devoted substantial resources to introducing a network of "political party service centres", which are intended to support the territory's nascent political groupings and provide them with logistical and material assistance and, by implication, move them towards becoming functioning, policy-oriented political parties rather than the narrow and personalized vehicles for ethnic extremists that were evident in Bosnia. The party service centres aim to help strengthen the organizational capacity of Kosovo's political parties, and to assist them develop their policy platforms and prepare for election campaigns. They have a particular focus on assisting parties that have demonstrated they are viable and have a popular mandate. In Papua New Guinea, which has a weak and fragmented party system that has destabilized executive government, a new law to tries to strengthen the party system by encouraging newly elected MPs to build stable coalitions in parliament, and granting the resulting "parliamentary parties" monetary and administrative support. The laws also provide for a by-election if an MP votes against his or her own party leader in a parliamentary confidence vote. Both the Kosovo and Papua New Guinea approaches can be seen as "top-down" inducements to organize and build sustainable parties.

Conclusion

Over the course of the 1990s, elections came to be seen not just as a means of choosing representatives and changing governments, but as a form of conflict resolution. While there is no doubt that well-designed and implemented elections *can* play this role, this "quick-fix" approach to elections in post-conflict situations has created more problems than it has solved. There have been many elections, often conducted at the behest of the international community, which only served to inflame and politicize the root causes of conflict.

Democratization is a long-term process of social and political development, not a short-term event run by or for the international community. The impact that external interventions can have on democratization – particularly in post-conflict situations – is largely limited to the design and construction of hardy institutions; the provision of adequate security and infrastructure conditions; a modest input into the norms and routines of a first election; and assistance with election monitoring. Beyond that, democracy is a domestic game, and its longer-term outcomes are very much the preserve of local actors and conditions. International interventions are crucial in putting in place the short-term conditions for a transition to democratic rule, but their longer-term impacts are necessarily limited.

Given this, the most important contribution that the international community can make is to help establish coherent and robust political institutions, rather than to engage in broader attempts at social engineering. Because institutions structure the routines of behaviour in which political actors engage, they are crucial elements, over the longer term, in helping to build a moderate and sustainable political culture in which routines of cooperation and accommodation come to be accepted as the norm rather than the exception. But such routines have to be allowed to develop organically within a facilitating institutional framework. The role for the United Nations and other external actors should ultimately be to make sure that such a framework is the best and most appropriate that can be devised. Such a limited focus is necessarily a modest endeavour – but a worthy one nonetheless.

Acknowledgements

Thanks to Ted Newman, Robin Ludwig, Roland Rich, and Laurence Whitehead for their helpful comments on earlier drafts of this chapter. The usual caveat applies.

Notes

1. Kumar, K. 1998. "Postconflict elections and international assistance", in K. Kumar (ed.) *Postconflict Elections, Democratization and International Assistance*. Boulder, CO: Lynne Rienner.

2. Linz, J. and A. Stepan. 1996. *Problems of Democratic Transition and Consolidation: Southern Europe, South America, and Post-communist Europe*. Baltimore: Johns Hopkins University Press.

3. Diamond, L. 1999. *Developing Democracy: Towards Consolidation*. Baltimore: Johns Hopkins University Press.

4. Lopez-Pintor, R. 1998. "Nicaragua's measured move to democracy", in K. Kumar (ed.) *Postconflict Elections, Democratization and International Assistance*. Boulder, CO: Lynne Rienner.

5. Nelson, S. 1998. "Haitian elections and the aftermath", in K. Kumar (ed.) *Postconflict Elections, Democratization and International Assistance*. Boulder, CO: Lynne Rienner.

6. There is a wide range of works on this subject. See Horowitz, D. L. 1991. *A Democratic South Africa? Constitutional Engineering in a Divided Society*. Berkeley: University of California Press; Lijphart, A. 1977. *Democracy in Plural Societies: A Comparative Exploration*. New Haven: Yale University Press; Lijphart, A. 1995. "Electoral systems", in S. M. Lipset (ed.) *The Encyclopedia of Democracy*. Washington, DC: Congressional Quarterly Press; Sartori, G. 1968. "Political development and political engineering", in J. D. Montgomery and A. O. Hirschman (eds) *Public Policy*, Vol. 17. Cambridge: Cambridge University Press; Sartori, G. 1994. *Comparative Constitutional Engineering: An Inquiry Into Structures, Incentives and Outcomes*. London: Macmillan; Reilly, B. 2001. *Democracy in Divided Societies: Electoral Engineering for Conflict Management*. Cambridge: Cambridge University Press; Reilly, B. and A. Reynolds. 1999. *Electoral Systems and Conflict in Divided Societies*. Washington, DC: National Research Council.

7. Lijphart 1995, *ibid.*

8. Horowitz, note 6 above

9. Lijphart, A. 1991. "The alternative vote: A realistic alternative for South Africa?", *Politikon*, Vol. 18, No. 2.

10. Sisk, T. 1993. "Choosing an electoral system: South Africa seeks new ground rules", *Journal of Democracy*, Vol. 4, No. 1.

11. Lewis, W. A. 1965. *Politics in West Africa*. London: George Allen and Unwin.

12. Lijphart, A. 1990. "Electoral systems, party systems and conflict management in segmented societies", in R. A. Schreirer (ed.) *Critical Choices for South Africa: An Agenda for the 1990s*. Cape Town: Oxford University Press.

13. Sisk, T. 1995. *Democratization in South Africa: The Elusive Social Contract*. Princeton: Princeton University Press; Reilly, note 6 above.

14. Reilly, *ibid.*

15. See Horowitz, D. L. 1985. *Ethnic Groups in Conflict*. Berkeley: University of California Press.

16. Lewis, note 11 above.

17. The author thanks Michael Maley for the data on this point.

18. Willey, J. 1998. "Institutional arrangements and the success of new parties in old democracies", *Political Studies*, Vol. 46, No. 3.

19. The classic argument on this remains Lewis, note 11 above.

20. See Horowitz, note 15 above; Horowitz, note 6 above.

21. See Huntington, Samuel P. 1991. *The Third Wave: Democratization in the Late Twentieth Century*. Norman: University of Oklahoma Press.

22. See Diamond, L., J. Linz, and S. M. Lipset. 1995. "Introduction: What makes for democracy?", in L. Diamond, J. Linz, and S. M. Lipset (eds) *Politics in Developing Countries: Comparing Experiences with Democracy*, 2nd edn. Boulder, CO: Lynne Rienner.

23. Diamond, L. 1997. "Introduction: In search of consolidation", in L. Diamond, M. F. Plattner, Y. Chu, and H. Tien (eds) *Consolidating the Third Wave Democracies*. Baltimore and London: Johns Hopkins University Press.

24. Sartori, Giovanni. 1976. *Parties and Party Systems*. Cambridge: Cambridge University Press.
25. See Powell, G. 1982. *Contemporary Democracies: Participation, Stability, and Violence*. Cambridge, MA: Harvard University Press.
26. McBeth, John. 1998. "Dawn of a new age", *Far Eastern Economic Review*, 17 September.
27. Reilly, note 6 above.
28. Evans, G. and B. O'Leary. 1999. "Northern Irish voters and the British-Irish agreement: Foundations of a stable consociational settlement?", paper presented at the American Political Science Association annual meeting, Atlanta, GA, September.

6

Democratization with the benefit of hindsight: The changing international components

Laurence Whitehead

Introduction

Twenty years ago democratic transitions were infrequent and their out-comes were uncertain.[1] In a bi-polar world the two dominant blocs generally promoted loyal protégés, and discouraged the security risks associated with democratic experimentation. Political democratization also raised anxieties about the stability of economic arrangements – as voters oscillated between left and right parties this might produce shifts between socialist and capitalist economic orientations. So democratization was plausibly viewed as an uncertain undertaking, one that would have to be internally driven, one that was potentially counterhegemonic and therefore most likely to succeed when domestic strategic interactions favoured agreement, and when external destabilizing pressures could be minimized. The relevant unit of analysis was thus the individual state (or national political regime), and attention was focused on those states that possessed sufficient internal autonomy to screen out international intrusions.

With 20 years of hindsight this panorama has been transformed. Today's assessments may be no better founded than those of the 1980s, but they rest on strikingly different background assumptions. Democratization is now more commonly viewed as the norm rather than the exception. Un-satisfactory outcomes are most often presented as temporary setbacks to a predetermined course. There has been an explosion of international political and economic incentives for states to qualify as democracies, and these external reinforcements are widely expected to "lock in" democratization processes in most or all properly administered states. Where such expectations are clearly being frustrated, the leaders of international opinion reach for such labels as "rogue states", "collapsed" or "failed" states, often as a pretext for encroachments on state sovereignty. There has been a proliferation of the use of coercion and intervention in the name of human rights and democracy, and transitional administrations that are supposed to help instil new democratic regimes. This radical shift in the outlook of international actors reflects the end of the bi-polar conflict and the discredit of socialist economic models. More recently it has been reinforced by a perception that Western-led security interests are best served by managing the risks of controlled democratization. Among currently influential neo-conservative circles Western-imposed democratization is justified by the need to avert the much greater risks of anti-democratic backlash and disorder that might otherwise prevail.

This radical shift in the international environment necessarily reconfigures the profile of current and prospective democratization processes, and therefore demands a reconsideration of earlier analytical assumptions. Topics for reassessment include the balance between the external and internal drivers of regime change; the privileged site of state sovereignty as the main locus of attention; the declining counterhegemonic potential of successful democratizations; the reduced economic options available to most new political democracies, whatever their electoral outcomes; the new emphasis on democracy as security rather than democracy as liberation; the need to evaluate the preferences (and indeed the strategic interests) of external controlling forces when explaining institutional design choices; the associated shift from a conception of democracy based on consent and local authenticity to one structured around control and even intrusion; the redirection of geographical focus towards both the Islamic world and the most fragile and vulnerable of states, and away from those regions of the world that initially stimulated transitology, regions where the internal supports for democratization are better developed; and the consequent appropriation of democratic discourse and rhetoric as justification for potentially neo-imperial initiatives that can now apparently be pursued unilaterally, without regard for countervailing responses.

If world politics has indeed been transformed over the last 20 years as indicated above, then it is hardly surprising if analytical models developed for an earlier era require a far-reaching rapid development of the object of study. If background conditions can change so fast it would be rash to assume that the hindsight of 2004 will prove more definitive than the attempted foresight of 1983.

A backward look, post-Iraq

According to the highest government officials in Washington and London, the post-invasion Karzai administration in Kabul is on the way to establishing a democratic Afghanistan, and the coalition of Western forces that have taken control of Iraq since the collapse of Saddam Hussein's government are also in the early stages of democratizing that country.[2] Influential figures in the Bush administration indicate that Iran, Syria, and Saudi Arabia, amongst others, should also voluntarily democratize or their rulers can expect to experience similar externally directed "regime change". For that matter, Myanmar (Burma), Cuba, North Korea, and various other undemocratic regimes are currently referred to as potential candidates for similar treatment. This is not just a peculiarity of the Bush administration, or a temporary response to the shade of the 11 September 2001 terrorist attacks. It is rather the culmination of a new trend in international politics that has been building momentum since the collapse of the Soviet bloc, if not before. Earlier milestones include the imposed democratization of the former German Democratic Republic; the US invasion of Panama to depose a dictator; the large-scale UN operation to democratize Cambodia; the internationally imposed settlement of ethnic conflict in Bosnia; the expulsion of Serb forces from Kosovo; and the eventual democratization of the post-Milosevic rump republic of Serbia. There was even a joint South Africa/Botswana military intervention in Lesotho in 1998 which constituted an interim political administration charged with paving the way for the (reportedly quite fair) electoral process of May 2002. In 1999 East Timor was detached from Indonesia and administered by the United Nations as a precursor to democratic elections and independence. What this brief review of recent examples of "imposed democratization" tells us is that this pattern of behaviour is longstanding, widespread, and has involved a wide array of international actors. In some cases the main focus really has been to democratize and then stand back; in other cases the rhetoric of democracy may conceal less worthy objectives and less satisfactory outcomes. But this is no flash in the pan. Old theories of democratization that screened out the international components, or that viewed external imposition and control as aberrant, need to be reassessed in the light of the evidence. Indeed, it might be justifiable to reverse the argument and regard external democracy promotion or imposition as the more normal or representative path to democratization, with internally led readjustments as the exception. Nothing in the recent record or in the present conjuncture indicates that this highly conditioned or coerced route to democratic transition is on the wane.

This panorama is very different from the picture that presented itself to the authors of the Wilson Center's "Transitions from Authoritarian Rule" project in the early 1980s.[3] At that time most of the available evidence seemed to warrant an almost exclusive focus on the strategic interactions between domestic power contenders and social groups within each national polity. In late Cold War conditions democratization could reasonably be viewed as a national process that was more or less the counterpart to "détente" at the international level. Parties with opposing histories and interests might agree to respect and be jointly bound by procedures that would limit their freedom of action but enhance their chances of security and cooperation. But this was an uncertain undertaking not likely to prove durable in all cases. The most favourable conditions were where the long-term political resources of the rival contenders were reasonably matched (so they could each harm the other in the absence of an agreement). The domestic political order had to be sufficiently robust and autonomous to offer reasonable incentives and assurances to the opposing forces. And their foreign backers had to be willing to stand back and tolerate an uncertain compromise rather than to escalate, promote proxy wars, or in other ways undermine the trust required for mutual confidence-building. The "transitions" studies focused on Southern Europe (Greece, Portugal, and Spain had all undergone intense ideological polarization as precursors to authoritarian rule – now international conditions favoured a reversal of this). Southern Europe was compared with Latin America – a more varied region, but again one in which the ideological polarization of the post-Cuba revolution period was in the process of reversal, thus favouring détente both internationally and internally. These were the only conditions in which it made sense to theorize about transitions from authoritarian rule in the early 1980s. But they were, as it turned out, exceptional conditions, and the resulting theoretical constructs reflected these limited and special circumstances.

Even in these spatially and temporally restricted conditions, more attention could have been devoted to the international dimensions of democratization. With hindsight, the Reagan administration's "rescue mission" in Grenada in October 1983 can be seen as a more significant precursor of future democratization experiences than was realized at the time. So the next section of this chapter recapitulates some recent arguments by the author concerning the role of regional and international factors in shaping the democratization processes of Southern and Eastern Europe and Latin America. The following section generalizes about the full range of democratizations since the 1970s, viewing them as long-term, open-ended processes that can be seen as containing five overlapping components. The chapter then concentrates on those more recent democratizations not contemplated in the Cold War years, and not covered previously. Moving away from these restrictive and relatively favourable settings, it focuses instead on the less favourable settings – those where state sovereignty has been interrupted or set aside, and where the so-called "international community" has been most assertive in imposing its priorities and its interpretation of how to achieve democratization. The concluding section attempts a stock-taking of the lessons to be learnt from this more coercive and interventionist set of episodes. It reviews eight headings where earlier analytical assumptions require reconsideration in the light of recent and current experience.

Reassessing the international dimensions: Europe and Latin America

International dimensions were screened out of the early democratization literature for three main reasons. There was inductive theorizing based on exemplary cases such as post-Franco Spain, the *abertura* in Brazil, and redemocratization in Peru, all of which seemed internally driven. Democratization was conceived as a regime change occurring in a given pre-existing national polity; therefore any external influence would only become operative if accepted and transmitted by domestic political actors. Moreover, democratization was viewed as a relatively short "transitional" interlude between two stable regimes, or configurations of élite accommodation – one hierarchical and authoritarian, the second pluralist and controlled by an independent electoral process. If the main focus of democratization studies was on the rewriting of the "rules of the game" so as to incorporate all electorally significant political actors, that was bound to direct the focus of analysis towards internal debates over representation and institutional design.

These three considerations all made sense at a time when the construction of a framework for comparative analysis of the political dimensions was being attempted for the first time, and on the basis of few examples. At that point it was essential to prioritize certain themes (such as élite recomposition, and the redesign of constitutions and electoral systems), and to agree on a basic vocabulary and framework of assumptions that would structure the comparisons. But the resulting neglect of external processes and international dynamics was, from the outset, a distortion of reality, and it tended to persist far too long in the face of mounting evidence that something crucial was being overlooked.

For example, the Spanish transition was preceded by those of Greece and Portugal, both of which were precipitated by military defeat in external wars. The internal dynamics of the Spanish transition were sharply influenced by a widespread concern to avoid the dangerous upheavals taking place in neighbouring Portugal. The Peruvian return to barracks occurred at a time of tension between Peru and Chile, when the threat of conflict with the Pinochet dictatorship reinforced Peru's need for a regime change to heal internal divisions and secure external support. The *abertura* in Brazil – the opening up of the political process and the lessening of the control of the military – was followed by the much more adventurist strategy of self-preservation adopted by the Argentine military, which culminated in the Falklands War and the resulting collapse into democracy. Thus, even in the early days, international dynamics required more attention than was recognized by much "transition' theorizing. This became still more obvious when the end of the Cold War brought about a swathe of democratizations in Central and Eastern Europe, and in parts of Africa, and when the pacification of war-torn Central America (carried out under UN auspices) also led to democratization experiments on that isthmus.

As such experiences accumulated they challenged the assumption that external influences would only become effective if channelled through fully constituted domestic political agencies. On the contrary, in the extreme case of East Germany democratization consisted of liquidating the separate state, adopting wholesale the institutions of the Federal Republic, and substituting West German political parties (and even leadership personnel) for those previously in control in the East. Although there was only one such extreme case of democratization-through-incorporation (a complete negation of the internal processes emphasized by the "transition" theorists), there were multiple instances of hybridity. For example, the democratization of the Baltic republics involved the restoration of national sovereignties that had been suppressed half a century before. Given the historical background it was controversial whether the Russian-speakers who had settled in these republics after their forced annexation must be recognized as full citizens and authentically "domestic" political actors. This had to be established through negotiation in the course of the democratization process, and could not be taken as given *ex ante*. In a similar way, in Nicaragua the ex-Contras returning from US-funded bases in Honduras were not automatically recognized as domestic political actors, nor were the Guatemalan guerrillas who returned from their bases in Mexico. In both cases international agreements backed by UN supervision were required to guarantee these transformations. All these examples brought into question the simplifying assumptions that underpinned the model of democratization as occurring in pre-established national polities.

The third, related, reason for downplaying international factors and influences was the assumption that democratization was a short interlude between two stable regimes. This worked well for Spain between Franco and King Juan Carlos, and for Uruguay between the military and the restored party system. But with hindsight we can see that such crisp and clear transitions from one coherent system of rule to another are the exception rather than the norm – especially if the transition is supposed to be towards the implantation of a high-quality and unconstrained democratic regime. Democratization in this sense may take decades rather than years (Brazil and Portugal); the outcome may be constrained by authoritarian enclaves (Chile, or in a different key Romania); the process may prove erratic (Nicaragua, Slovakia) or even reversible (Ecuador, Peru). In any case the "quality" of the democratic outcome may leave much to be desired for many years after the "transition" stage has passed (Bolivia, Bulgaria). In summary, it is increasingly recognized by policy-makers – and even by political scientists – that democratization has to be understood as a long-term, dynamic, and potentially open-ended process.[4] International organizations such as the OAS and the Council of Europe have been obliged to come to terms with this reality, which is also reflected in the tabulations of the increasing number of agencies which rank countries according to various dimensions of their democratic performance. As these examples suggest, the consequence of refocusing the comparative study of democratization on the long term, rather than on short-term transitions, is to widen the frame of debate. Questions of institutional design and representative procedures may perhaps be settled through domestic decision-making over a limited period of time. But broader questions of democratic accountability, rule-of-law observance and rights protection, anti-corruption enforcement, citizen security, and local democracy all take much longer and may require more international cooperation and support. On this wider view of what democratization must really involve, it becomes artificial to draw a sharp line between domestic and international dimensions of the process, and impossible to screen out all that is not strictly domestic.

Five overlapping components of democratization

On the assumption that democratization can best be understood as a complex, long-term, dynamic process with a relatively "open-ended" eventual outcome, it becomes possible to distinguish five overlapping components of that process, each of which can be separately theorized, analysed, and compared. These five are the regime transition; the institutional design of the new democracy; its social foundations; the normative basis of democratization; and the "creative destruction" arising from the exercise of popular sovereignty. Each of these components of democratization can be studied case by case on a national basis, and the countries can then be compared and ranked according to their performance under each heading. But, as indicated below, each of these five components can also be reanalysed from a regional and international perspective (which is the relevant concern here).

First, as already noted, the "transition" component focuses on the short term, and directs attention to the strategic interactions required for the negotiation of new more "institutional" and inclusionary rules of the game for determining élite circulation within a given national polity. This may be an élitist and procedurally minimalist conception of democracy, but even so experience shows that certain international dimensions of political action need to be incorporated into the analysis. The cohesion of the authoritarian coalition may be destabilized by the withdrawal of external support (as when the Carter administration brought pressure to bear on the Balaguer administration in the Dominican Republic in 1978; or when Gorbachov removed Soviet support from the Honecker regime in East Germany). More dramatically, external military defeat or public humiliation may precipitate the demise of an authoritarian regime (the Greek colonels in Cyprus, Galtieri in the South Atlantic, or Suharto humbled by the IMF). Once a transition has begun, the question of national boundaries may arise as one of the issues for internal negotiation and external recognition (as in the case of the Baltic republics, or Cyprus, or indeed Guatemala and its claims on Belize). For example, a key difficulty concerning the prospective democratization of Serbia is whether or not the resulting democracy would include either Kosovo or Montenegro.

Not infrequently regime transitions also bring into question preexisting security alliances, and thus stimulate strong reactions from treaty partners. Thus the democratization of Portugal and Greece brought their NATO attachments into doubt, whereas the democratization of Spain, and later of the Czech Republic, Hungary, and Poland, eventually expanded NATO, with consequences that were desired by some neighbours and feared by others. The democratization of Nicaragua resolved a security problem for the USA, whereas parallel regime changes in Haiti and Panama were not entirely so welcome in all parts of Washington. Still operating within a procedurally minimalist conception of democratic transition, other important international issues could concern whether or not to offer foreign exile and legal shelter to exiting authoritarian rulers (as Brazil has done for Paraguay's ex-dictator Stroessner); whether or not to provide election monitoring and subsequent economic assistance; and how far if at all the form and content of a transition can be prescribed from outside. (The US Congress has laid down a very detailed and precise blueprint for the transition it wishes to see in Cuba – so precise that the US executive would have little scope for discretion in reacting to any regime change that might be gestated from within the island.) A final lesson from experience concerns the fact that great powers can find authoritarian breakdowns difficult to anticipate, let alone to control. Thus Washington waited until the last possible minute before embracing the cause of democracy in the Philippines, and persisted too long in anticipating a democratic outcome in China after Tiananmen before reversing course and accepting communist rule.

The second component of democratization concerns institutional design. As the references to the Helms-Burton law in Cuba and the process of German reunification have already indicated, experience shows that under some circumstances external dictation may play a fundamental role in determining the new "rules of the game" adopted by an incipient democratic regime. The 10 new democracies which joined the European Union in 2004 are required to adopt 86,000 pages of Community law (the *"acquis communautaire"*), significant portions of which determine key rules of the game for the political process. Similarly, even Turkey, though not yet given a date for admission to the EU, finds itself required to rewrite fundamental parts of its constitutional system, not in response to any domestic balance of forces but in order to meet externally determined standards of democratic probity. In most of Latin America the degree of external prescription is considerably milder and there is far more tolerance of slippage, but even there too it would be mistaken to analyse processes of institutional design and democratic so-called "consolidation" as if these were solely the products of internal political choice. One has only to review the legal conditions attached to the Caribbean Basin Initiative, the monitoring activities of the OAS, and the case-load of the Inter-American Commission for Human Rights to glimpse the multiple channels of international encouragement, standard-setting, and conditionality that now contribute to the "crafting" of democratic institutional practices (both formal and informal) throughout the Americas. These patterns of mutual adjustment and liberal convergence will almost certainly continue to grow in importance as regional integration proceeds. As noted in several chapters earlier in this book, while in some favoured countries such international pressures and influences may set in motion "virtuous circles" of institutional reform and enhanced international recognition, they also have the potential to generate "vicious circles" of resistance and resentment among those countries that become classified as laggards. The examples of Haiti (in the Americas) and Albania (in Europe) suggest that this negative syndrome can also become self-reinforcing. In Afghanistan and Iraq the occupying forces risk being perceived as promoting schemes of institutional design (strong presidentialism in the first case, ethnic federalism in the second) that are selected because of their supposed advantages for the security of the West, rather than because of their domestic rationality or their local legitimacy.

A third component of democratization, conceived as a broad and open-ended long-term project, concerns the establishment of secure "social foundations" that can underpin a democratic political system. This large topic is typically considered in two distinct segments, although in principle they should be examined together. They are the so-called "civil society" foundations of democracy and the supposed "market economy" foundations. What should concern us here are the international factors that may contribute to – or detract from – these social foundations. Without entering into the complex debates on how such foundations may be constituted, and what channels may link them to political institutions and democratic outcomes, it may suffice to illustrate the issues by outlining the various roles played by churches and diasporas (as proxies for "civil society"), and by transnational corporations and trade agreements (as proxies for "market economy"). This should serve to demonstrate the significance of the international dimensions in both cases. The Catholic Church has very strong social support in much of Latin America and major parts of Europe. It played a crucial role in opposing communism in Poland, and in supporting the Solidarity movement that led democratization there. It also played a major role in various Latin American democratizations, notably in Chile and Guatemala. But it has also provided vital support to the Franco dictatorship in Spain, and its role in Croatia was at least equivocal. For the present purposes the key point is that whether strengthening democratic processes or impeding them, the Catholic Church was always both socially embedded and supranational in structure. The Vatican provided doctrinal guidance and hierarchical discipline that influenced the behaviour of key elements of civil society in many new democracies, both in Europe and in the Americas.[5] Similar points can be made about the role of international diasporas in influencing civil society in new democracies. Each diaspora has its own highly political distinctive outlook, and each is to some extent a reflection of the state of "civil society" in the country from which it emigrated. But in any case these different diasporas each exert a durable influence on the "social foundations" of democracy in their respective home countries. As with the Catholic Church, whether supportive or obstructive, these influences are highly significant and were clearly supranational. Therefore evaluations of "civil society" in new democracies should not overlook the importance of such international dimensions. Nor can the presumed "market economy" foundations of democratization be studied in a purely domestic idiom, when trade liberalization and foreign investment flows are rapidly reshaping the structure of business and the patterns of commercial life. Whether transnational corporations are viewed as agencies of modernization which thereby reinforce the foundations of democratic politics, or as concentrations of economic power beyond the reach of democratic accountability (good examples exist to support both hypotheses), it is undeniable that TNCs exert a durable influence in most new democracies, and that their strategies are shaped by international as well as domestic considerations.

Fourth, given this intermingling of internal and external influences and agencies, the normative principles regulating democratization can only emerge from deliberations that take place on an international scale. It was always the case that even the most apparently self-contained of democratic regimes were constructed on the basis of norms and values that originated and persisted in a wider world of ideas. In the recent and newer democracies of Europe and the Americas this is truer than ever, since the already existing "older" democracies of North America and Western Europe provided ready-made bodies of doctrine to reinforce their pragmatic appeal. Some analysts are deeply sceptical about the normative claims invoked to justify processes of democratization. They prefer interpretations founded on the rational calculation of self-interested actors, and view normative discourse, moral claims, and arguments based on notions of "democratic legitimation" as mere manipulation or self-deception.

However, this perspective cannot do justice to the multiple instances where a distinctively democratic morality and outlook has generated behaviour that can hardly be explained in terms of calculating self-interest. This refers not only to Nelson Mandela and Aun Sang Suu Kyi but to thousands of their anonymous followers, whose efforts and sacrifices were also necessary if these figureheads were to stay the course. In any case, the debate is not just about the motives of political actors, but more importantly about the principles on which a durable democratic regime would have to be based in order to differentiate itself from its authoritarian predecessors. The alternative interpretation views democracy as an ideal that can inspire sacrifice, and can help to resocialize polarized societies by promoting reconciliation and an ethic of tolerance. This view directs attention to such imperatives of civilized behaviour as the banning of torture, the repudiation of genocide, and the endorsement of fundamental human rights that should take precedence over any calculus of self-regarding advantage. It treats democracy as a system of values that favours dialogue and compromise over the domination of the weak by the strong. On this view when the strongest Western democracies engage in "preventive" war on the bases of doubtful intelligence, where they create legal "black holes" beyond the reach of the Geneva Convention (as in Guantanamo), and where they tighten security to the point that it threatens traditional rights of free expression, it may be questioned whether such practices should be marketed under the label of democracy promotion.

From this normative perspective it becomes possible to reinterpret the history (and therefore the collective identity) of nations and peoples to make it consistent with a future democratic project. It is only in terms of some such value postulates that one can secure consensus in favour of a durably self-limiting and accountable form of state organization. No doubt such claims can be overstated and misused, but without some normative basis of this kind it would be impossible to differentiate long-term, open-ended processes of democratization from all other varieties of historical process. From the standpoint of this volume what matters is that all such claims concerning rights and norms are inherently international. They can in no way be limited within the confines of any single national political system. In fact, as we have recently witnessed in the courts of Europe and subsequently of Latin America, neither genocide nor torture can any longer be sheltered by extra-territorial legal immunities. Going beyond the strictly legal procedures for promoting and upholding democratic norms, the open exchange of information across national boundaries has promoted the development of specialized communities of experts dedicated to the defence of specific values (Amnesty International on fair trials and true process, and the Inter-American Press Society (SIP) on press freedom, for example). Direct people-to-people transmission mechanisms (such as the ability to watch West German television on East German sets) may in some cases have been more powerful agencies of democratization than any government-directed initiatives. The development of information technology makes this all the more likely in the future. Admittedly these linkages could also have some negative consequences (generalizing ostensibly universal values that in fact serve the interests of "Western imperialism", according to some critics, threatening local cultural traditions according to others). The intention here is not to arbitrate on such debates, but only to stress that if democratization has a normative content then that necessarily reinforces the salience of international dimensions of the process.

Fifth, and finally, there is one more component of democratization that requires an airing if we are to view this as an open-ended process, and not simply the replication of static and established models of political representation. This concerns the ultimate arbiter of outcomes in a democratic process – the will of the electorate (or "popular sovereignty"). Certainly popular sovereignty is only democratic provided it is channelled through constitutional procedures that include "checks and balances" and rule-of-law protections for the rights of minorities. But in turn such procedures and guarantees are only democratic provided that ultimately they are subject to confirmation (or revision) by the people whose affairs they regulate. Analysts of democratization have tended to under-emphasize this point, perhaps because of their concern with strengthening fragile institutions and building social consensus around new and not yet entirely credible political regimes. It is an uncomfortable fact that previous authoritarian regimes may sometimes have reflected the popular will; and there is a risk that a focus on popular sovereignty issues could encourage forms of institutional design (plebiscites, write-in legislation, recall votes) that could bypass political parties and undermine representative democracy. There can be no doubt that the exercise of popular sovereignty is potentially unpredictable and destabilizing. It may reopen questions that most politicians in new democracies would prefer to leave closed. How exactly is the electorate defined and configured? How stable are its wants, how far does it acquiesce to what the "political class" has on offer? If dissatisfied, does it have any redress beyond the musical chairs of party competition?

These are foundational issues in the history of democracy, and so can hardly be omitted from any analysis of democratization viewed as a long-term and open-ended process. Just as capitalism can be viewed as an engine of "creative destruction" in a market economy, so popular sovereignty may be viewed as the functional equivalent for a political democracy. Moreover, recent experiences, such as the near eclipse of the political class in Venezuela, or its failure to "take" in the former East Germany, confirm that such issues arise in practice, and are not just theoretical. The leader of the failed Hungarian national democratic revolution of 1848, Lajos Kossuth, once summed up the meaning of democracy as "nothing about the people without the people". This is clearly not the precept upon which the current eastward enlargement of the European Union is founded, but it indicates why forms of democracy promotion through international convergence and integration that go too far in disregarding the sensitivities of national electorates are liable to backfire. There is a point where the claims of popular sovereignty tend to clash with democratization viewed as an international project. In principle frictions of this kind can be smoothed away by the creation of supranational forms of democratic representation and accountability (a directly elected European parliament, the Central American parliament, councils of ministers or presidential summits of leaders answerable to their national electorates). In practice, however, representative democracy at the international level tends to stretch the fiction of representation to its limit. If only the most cosmopolitan sectors of the political class have real access to the more international levels of decision-making they may become so out of touch with their national electorates that they risk a "popular sovereignty" backlash against integration or even convergence.

In summary, both theory and experience indicate that democratization must be viewed as a long-term, open-ended process. If so, its components include not only the well-studied topics of transition and institutional design, but also the broader and more elusive issues of social foundations, normative principles, and popular sovereignty. Each of these five components can be studied from the perspective of a single national polity, thereby highlighting the domestic aspects of democratization. But as we have seen, there are major international dimensions to all five components of democratization. A focus on processes of regional convergence and integration serves to highlight and clarify the major features of the Latin America and European democratizations that were initially downplayed or overlooked. The study of democratization in terms of region-wide convergence around shared norms and common institutional practices can help explain the timing and momentum of developments better than if purely national sequences are all that are considered. But recognition of the transformative power of international cooperation, convergence, and integration must not lead to denial of the continuing significance of large power inequalities between nations, and major impediments to the construction of supranational democratic identities. Hence any realistic analysis of democratization in these two regions must consider laggards as well as leaders, backlash as well as convergence.

International organizations and democracy promotion in unfavourable contexts

Since the richest, more powerful, and most secure nations of the world are now nearly all democracies, it has been possible to forge agreements between leading states in the international system which have extended "democratic conditionality" to a widening range of regional and functional groupings of states, thus pressing poor, weak, and insecure nations to conform to standards set by the group leaders. The idea that international organizations should attach a higher priority to democracy promotion than in the past is increasingly fashionable, at least in the West. This probably also reflects the increased proportion of member states in most such organizations that are, at least formally, now classified as "democracies", and that gain international prestige and even benefits from such a status. It also reflects the fact that some international organizations include commitments to democracy (or at least to some basic universal values concerning human rights and respect for international law) among their goals, or even requirements for membership. In addition, since the end of the Cold War, if not before, there has been a tendency to downgrade the claims of "national sovereignty" and "non-intervention", and to extend the scope attributed to shared international norms as arbitrators of the conduct of nations. (A good recent example would be the tightened standards that the EU is attempting to set for future participation in what used to be known as the Lomé Agreement, which will in future be designated the Cotonou Process.)

For some mixture of these reasons the international community has become increasingly committed to democracy promotion over the past decade or so, and these practices are become more institutionalized and perhaps more effective. Even before the end of the Cold War the five permanent members of the Security Council had come round to a more positive view of the possibilities for promoting political reform and regional conflict resolution through the UN system. The 1988 Namibia agreement provides the strongest evidence of this new trend. Since then, the forward momentum of this movement has been remarkable. Not only has it extended geographically to places where it had long seemed unlikely to reach (Bosnia, Haiti, Paraguay, East Timor); it has also broadened institutionally (it has become a more or less direct concern of the World Bank, NATO, the OSCE, and various international legal institutions); and a proliferating network of non-governmental organizations has emerged to reinforce and lock into place their pro-democracy commitments (the NED, IDEA, CAPEL, and various other national foundations, for example).

There is evidently an extremely wide and diverse range of international organizations that need to be considered. In some cases one can focus directly on the United Nations (say, with regard to El Salvador or Namibia). In others there are regional organizations within the UN framework that may become the main focus of our attention (the OAS in Peru and the OSCE in much of the post-Soviet bloc). But there are also international alliance structures outside the United Nations which may have a very important role to play in some democratizations (such as NATO in the Balkans and the EU and Visegrad countries, and the Commonwealth). Where economic incentives are the key there may be arrangements like the Lomé Agreement or the Caribbean Basin Initiative that play a crucial role. Sometimes there are lesser regional entities that pop up almost out of nowhere and acquire a sudden significance in relation to some particular crisis (such as the Organization of Eastern Caribbean States in the Grenada crisis). Then there are international organizations whose charters foreswear political commitment, but which nevertheless have recently appeared to tailor some of their decisions with a view to their impact on a certain variant of democratization (the international financial institutions, at the behest of their dominant shareholders, seem to have played such a role in Russia and Ukraine, for example). In addition, there is an ever-widening range of less official international organizations (those concerned with election monitoring, or the international protection of human rights, or the defence of press freedom, and so forth). There are also partisan international organizations (the Christian Democratic and Socialist Internationals, the ICFTU, etc.) which may take an active role in those countries where their affiliates are directly involved in transition politics. And there are all sorts of non-governmental pro-democracy international organizations, like Amnesty International, which may also figure in certain cases.

Of course all these disparate international entities need to be studied within an analytical framework that extends well beyond their separate institutional structures. Their impact will depend upon a broader set of norms and values concerning the appropriateness of democracy promotion in particular settings. This encompassing normative framework (which may include treaty commitments, legal instruments, economic incentives, and political dialogue as well as morally uplifting declaratory statements) is at best still under construction. It is recent, ambiguous, contested, and in many respects still untried.

Concerning the UN system, the legal basis for its involvement in democracy promotion can be traced back to Article 21 of the Universal Declaration of Human Rights (1948). Paragraph 3 reads "The will of the people shall be the basis of the authority of government; this will shall be expressed in periodic and genuine elections which shall be by universal and equal suffrage and shall be held by secret vote or by equivalent free voting procedures." Various regional institutions within the UN system reiterated this commitment, including the 1950 European Convention, the 1969 American Convention, and the 1981 African Charter on Human and People's Rights. But during the Cold War these declarations were frequently disregarded, not only by the Soviet bloc but also by the "non-aligned" movement, and indeed by many states within the so-called "free world". Non-intervention in the internal affairs of sovereign states was the doctrine usually invoked to block most UN initiatives that might have lent substance to the universal declaration. There were some exceptions to this general state of affairs, for example in certain regions where a local consensus in favour of democracy could be generated (Western Europe, and progressively after the mid-1980s Latin America). Also the UN system supported decolonization, which was often accompanied by at least one more or less democratic election; and it steadfastly opposed apartheid both in South Africa and in South-West Africa. In fact UN support for competitive elections in Namibia on the basis of universal suffrage was one of the most striking precursors of the shift toward democracy promotion as an international priority. It took shape before the dismantling of the Berlin Wall, with the United Nations supervising the 1989 Namibian elections that were the precursor to the recognition of independence in 1990. Like subsequent UN operations in Cambodia, El

Salvador, Mozambique, and elsewhere, a clear linkage was established between conflict resolution and democracy-building, and the Security Council authorized the Secretary-General to conduct these operations with both aims in mind.

More generally, since the end of the Cold War the Security Council has been much freer to authorize mandatory and coercive measures involving democracy promotion or imposition under Chapter VII of the UN Charter. (It is estimated that since 1990 the Security Council has invoked Chapter VII about 120 times, although this does not mean that "all necessary means" to restore the peace were authorized in every case.) The key point to note here is that democracy promotion is typically embedded in a broader set of conflict-resolution objectives, rather than pursued in isolation. There may well be a tension between the UN desire to terminate its peacemaking activities and withdraw its forces (which implies the early convening of an election, even though conditions for a durable democratization may not be present) and the goal of democracy-building. It is also important to note that the typical locus of such UN operations – generally very weak or even "failed" states – is neither the most representative nor the most propitious setting for democratization. At times the United Nations has also found itself drawn into democracy-promoting activities in states where the Security Council has not determined that there was any threat under Chapter VII (Kosovo, for example). In some cases the United Nations has felt obliged to terminate a democracy-promoting mission on the grounds that the local situation had become too unstable (such as Angola in 1999 and Haiti in 2000).

Another large and wide-ranging international organization with an active democracy-promotion programme is the 54-member Commonwealth. Unlike the United Nations, the Commonwealth has no charter. It traces its "democratic vocation" back to the rather vague Singapore Declaration of Commonwealth Principles of 1971 ("belief in human liberty and human rights, abhorrence of racial discrimination", etc.). The 1991 Harare Declaration gave this more substance by directly linking "full participation in the benefits of Commonwealth membership" to "willingness to adhere to democratic ideals". The 1995 Millbrook Action Programme proceeded to establish mechanisms for dealing effectively with violations of the Harare principles. For a brief interlude in 1999 (between the election of a democratic government in Nigeria and the overthrow of an elected government in Pakistan), for the first time in its history no member of the Commonwealth was subject to military rule. At the Durban summit of 2000 the Commonwealth heads of state applied the Millbrook principles, provisionally suspending the membership of Pakistan until democracy was restored. Islamabad was, however, allowed a two-year grace period before full suspension of membership and additional sanctions – a time limit that was to run out in October 2001. But of course September 2001 saved the Pakistan regime from that embarrassment. In June 2000 Fiji was also provisionally suspended from Commonwealth membership following the arrest of its democratically elected prime minister, but the Solomon Islands avoided suspension when the authority of its parliament was reasserted. Despite these public exercises in the exertion of peer-group pressure and some provision of technical assistance, it cannot be said that the Commonwealth's democracy-promotion activities have exerted more than a marginal influence in most target regimes.[6] Zimbabwe, for example, remains sheltered from outright condemnation because the South African government does not wish to aggravate relations with its northern neighbour. At the 1999 Durban summit India's Prime Minister Vajpayee resisted pressure for the toughening of Commonwealth rules on democracy and human rights malpractices. Despite these limitations the Secretary-General of the Commonwealth, Don McKinnon, proceeded in September 2000 to urge the United Nations to suspend from membership those states that found themselves subject to illegal government.

For democracy promotion to become a systematic component of the activities of major international organizations, it would be necessary to specify how success (or failure) is to be evaluated, and by whom. Admittedly there are some quite clear-cut instances where the outcome is beyond dispute. In Namibia, for example, the United Nations had a clear and long-standing commitment to the need for competitive elections on the basis of universal suffrage, and when that was achieved (largely through UN auspices) Namibia was both admitted to the international community as a sovereign state, and recognized and rewarded as a new democracy. (With 10 years' hindsight it may be necessary to question Namibia's democratic status, but by then the United Nations had discharged its essential responsibility and was no longer such a key player in guiding Namibian political affairs.) UN involvement in the democratization of El Salvador followed a similar trajectory, and is generally recognized as a comparable success. At the other extreme, there are also some equally clear-cut failures. At the end of 1947 the United Nations accepted the responsibility for organizing democratic elections throughout Korea as a preliminary to reunifying the country. No elections were held in the North, and those that took place in the South were clearly undemocratic. Nevertheless the United Nations accepted the southern results as valid, and Syngman Rhee became the first president of the Republic of Korea, claiming to represent all Korea. This UN failure paved the way to the Korean War, and the state of unresolved hostilities that divides the peninsula to this day.

However, most attempts at democracy promotion by international organizations fall somewhere in the grey area between these two extremes. Here the questions of how to evaluate outcomes, and who decides, become highly sensitive. If international organizations are left unencumbered to assess their own achievements, there is an evident risk that they will give themselves the benefit of the doubt and classify as success outcomes that on a more neutral reading would not deserve approbation. In other words, their standards of democratic performance are liable to be too low. This tendency is reinforced by the facts already noted – that not all their members are democracies, that their own internal procedures may be relatively undemocratic, and that too strong an insistence on high democratic standards may absorb scarce resources and require the sacrifice of other objectives to which they are also committed. Moreover, once an international organization has intervened to promote democracy it must concern itself with the prospects for an honourable withdrawal. So there may well be a conflict between the obligation to uphold high democratic standards and the desire for a quick exit route.

The Haitian example provides a vivid illustration of the potential long-term problems here. Assuming international organizations are in principle willing to engage in democracy promotion, and can agree on appropriate standards of evaluation, and are willing to accept the implied trade-offs against other objectives, and can marshal the necessary resources, it still remains an open question what methods and instruments of democracy promotion are appropriate for them. In general, and above all in the post-Cold War context, international opinion outside the USA tends to assume that political, legal, and diplomatic methods should be privileged, whereas the use of force, sanctions, or trusteeship procedures ought to be relegated to the status of a last resort. There are both practical and principled reasons why international organizations should hesitate to commit themselves to intrusive or coercive forms of democracy promotion. These require more resources and are more likely to strain the internal cohesion of the international community. Moreover, on theoretical grounds it is reasonable to argue that democracy must be built from within. In the absence of adequate domestic organization and support to sustain a democratization drive, international organizations are more likely to impose an artificial and transient appearance of a democratic regime than to implant an authentic and durable democracy. The downside of coerced democratization is particularly evident in Bosnia, where issues of criminality and problems over human rights violations have dogged the transitional administration, and where the international presence has become associated with the propagation of an artificial economy based on donor dependence, and where the long-term prospect could well turn out to be that irreconcilable hatreds flare up as badly as ever once the international presence is removed.

In practice, the territories most likely to attract UN involvement were among the least promising locations for democracy promotion (let alone democratic consolidation) that could be found in the entire globe. The UN Secretariat, far more than the Commonwealth or the European Union, has been the focus of a powerful process of negative selection. The societies that find themselves subject to transitional administration by the United Nations may be among the most deserving of all beneficiaries of democracy assistance, but they are also the most needy, the most problematic, and the least promising. The UN's competitors in the business of international democracy assistance have a head start, a substantially higher probability of being associated with a successful outcome, by virtue of the initial range of cases that come their way.

To invoke the language of "failed states" might be to exaggerate, but it would not be to invent. More concretely, the United Nations tends to find itself accumulating responsibilities for the operation of "transitional administrations" in jurisdictions where conventional state authority was absent, had been withdrawn, or had virtually broken down (Timor, Cambodia, Haiti, Kosovo, and also, for different reasons, Namibia). The crucial indicator of lost public authority in most of these jurisdictions was the absence of any organized protection of the population from generalized violence and the wholesale destruction of property. Thus the most critical component of UN activity was the establishment of an international authority geared to the creation of such protections. These were all cases where the traditional argument for non-intervention (the need to respect state sovereignty) had lost its force due to the palpable debility or perversity of the state authorities nominally in charge. The UN Secretariat was particularly well suited to dealing with such situations, in part because it would only act on instruction from the great majority of normally functioning states (entities which of course retained a strong interest in the principle of state sovereignty); in part because it possessed the capacity to deliver large-scale administrative and material resources at short notice; and in part because it could be relied upon not to turn a short-term intervention into a permanent occupation (as powerful individual states were wont to do). But there are also difficulties involved in accepting this particular division of labour. One is that there are always more jurisdictions that might qualify for the establishment of a transitional authority than cases where the United Nations has the necessary support and resources to act. A second is that if the United Nations is too easily drawn in this may create a perverse incentive – the interests likely to benefit from a UN intervention may be encouraged to precipitate the very collapse of public order that will bring it about. The third, most critical for the present purposes, is that it is not always so easy to craft a successful exit strategy as it is to become involved in the first place. This is where the issues of democracy promotion and democratization arise.

Even where local conditions are favourable, international consensus is strong, and adequate resources are provided, it is doubtful whether an international initiative can create a democratic regime. At best it can facilitate the creation of such a regime by independently constituted local actors and interests. More often than not international resources will run low before disagreement and conflict of interest between these local authors of democratization have been overcome. So such action involves the politics of the "second best". For example, it may be preferable to stabilize a semi-democratic regime that permits a timely exit rather than to hold out for impeccable democratic standards that cannot be attained before a UN mandate is exhausted. But there is a slippery slope here. Stabilizing a semi-democratic regime may be difficult to distinguish from stabilizing an undemocratic regime. New democracies may to some extent be inherently unstable, particularly as they seek to assert their new-found sovereignty in a world of states accustomed to the maintenance of local order by undemocratic means.

Since 11 September 2001 the international agenda has shifted, and the United Nations has become a critical arena in the West's new "war on terror". In this new context the notion of the United Nations taking responsibility for the administration of "failed states" that can only be restored to independence once they have been "democratized" has attracted new sources of support. It has also stirred up new sources of anxiety. In September 2002 Secretary-General Kofi Annan proclaimed the independence of East Timor and its entry into the United Nations as the 191st member state, following 32 months of direct rule by UNTAET (the UN Transitional Administration in East Timor). The new state faces many social, economic, and security dangers, and its status as a democracy could well be tested by future challenges, but overall the UN's role in Timor seems to confirm the organization's viability as an instrument of democratization. For some observers this experience is now viewed as an encouraging precedent for similar activities elsewhere – in Kosovo (although independence from Serbia remains a matter of contention), but perhaps also in Iraq following a possible Security-Council-sanctioned "regime change", and perhaps subsequently in various other locations where the existing anti-democratic state of affairs could lead to international intervention and the temporary suspension of formal sovereignty. The urgency of this proposition arises from the perception that weak or badly ruled states may be providing shelter and encouragement for the non-state terrorist groups that have recently become the prime focus of international security concerns. If so, such states may have to be subjected to external control, at least until they cease posing such dangers to the international community. But (with few exceptions) the advocates of this kind of pre-emptive suspension of sovereignty wish to dissociate themselves from accusations of practising traditional imperialism. Therefore they seek UN endorsement for their acts of intervention, and they hope to preserve a broad support coalition by acting within the loose framework of international law, and by pledging to restore sovereignty once these perceived security threats have been removed. Instead of permanent annexation by a single power (traditional imperialism), they aim for temporary occupation by an international organization representing all the main powers. But if these occupations are to be temporary then it is necessary to indicate before intervening what broad exit strategy is envisaged. UN-led experiments in democratization have thereby acquired a new and much wider political utility.

But if the assault of 11 September 2001 has elicited a new enthusiasm in some quarters for UN-led transitional administrations followed by democratization, this security-driven logic has also wakened new anxieties and sources of resistance in other parts of the international community. None of the permanent members of the UN Security Council needs to envisage a diminution of their sovereignty as a result of the new logic, since they all enjoy the right of veto over initiatives that might otherwise adversely affect them (for example in Chechnya, Tibet, Corsica, Guantanamo, or Gibraltar). But of course all those listed as "rogue states" are bound to take a much more critical view, and in addition quite a few other governments and currents of opinion will require considerable reassurance before they can overcome their hesitations about this new orthodoxy. Thus, most Arab and Islamic governments are bound to wonder about the selective application of this doctrine (even if they can be persuaded to accept its basic rationale). If the suspension of sovereignty can be justified on the grounds that a state is in violation of UN resolutions and poses a potential security threat to its neighbours, then why does this test not imply any limitation on the exercise of its sovereignty by Israel, if not within its own borders at least within the Occupied Territories, they are liable to ask. If the answer is that Israel is a democracy, and therefore its sovereignty is beyond question by the United Nations, then the sceptics may enquire about the status of Indonesia at the time of the UN's entry into Timor. Beyond the intricacies of such comparative debates the underlying concern is who decides on behalf of the international community when it is acceptable to suspend the sovereignty of a member state, and how much reliance can be placed on the objectivity of such decision-taking. Above all, when the new "war on terror" casts a shadow of suspicion over so many countries at the same time, how are the UN's priorities to be determined, and what redress is available in the event of misjudgement? Since a substantial proportion of the General Assembly consists of states that either do not qualify as democracies and/or do not exercise complete control over the security threats that may be lodged within their jurisdiction, this type of anxiety is potentially widespread.

Another area of anxiety concerns the dynamics of a UN transitional administration once an international intervention has been sanctioned and carried out. Cambodia, Namibia, and Timor all offer relative reassurance that – at least in the limited number of suitable cases – the process can be kept on track, and the outcome can be achieved with reasonable punctilio, at a bearable cost, and without adversely affecting the basic security of neighbouring states. But these were all "post-Cold War" episodes, and even that category contains some less reassuring experiences – in Angola, for example, or arguably in Kosovo. Afghanistan, by contrast, is the first of the new "war on terror" international interventions, and the implications of generalizing this type of operation are seen by the sceptics as considerably more troubling. The UN role in post-Taliban Afghanistan falls far short of the kind of "transitional administration" that provided it with a model for action in the 1990s, and in Iraq (for obvious reasons) the United Nations has been displaced by a much more one-sided US-led administration. Nevertheless, in Afghanistan it was the Security Council (acting on the advice of UN Special Representative for Afghanistan Lakhdar Brahimi) that convened a special meeting of Afghan representatives to devise a provisional administration and deploy an international security presence in the capital, following the previous government's flight from Kabul. It was also the Security Council that in December 2001 accepted a British offer to provide an international security assistance force for the capital (with a six-month time limit), and that endorsed the legitimacy of the new governing council under Hamid Karzai. So if the result is to bring peaceful and legitimate authority to post-intervention Afghanistan, and to remove the country as a source of instability and security threat to its neighbours and the world, the United Nations is entitled to receive some of the credit. But equally, if warlordism and narco-criminality prevail, if Afghanistan remains a "failed state", and if its neighbours continue to experience spill-over disturbance from its unresolved internal tensions, then the UN's pacifying and democratizing credentials will be impaired. At present the jury is still out on this question, but neighbours of Iraq, North Korea, and other "axis of evil" candidates for revocation of sovereignty by the Security Council are unlikely to find this precedent particularly reassuring.

Analytical conclusions

The second section of this chapter drew attention to the mounting evidence that the international components of most processes of democratization tend to be far more prominent that was recognized in the initial "transitions" literature. It explained this omission partly in terms of the distinctive temporal and spatial conditions limiting the evidence on which initial theorizing was based. But it also acknowledged that relevant indications had been "screened out" of consideration and ought to be reinstated. More important, it argued that over the subsequent 20 years there has occurred a radical shift in the international context shaping processes of democratization (a shift that is still ongoing). As a result there is a need to reassess and reconfigure earlier assumptions about the international components of democratization. The third section focused on the two regions that have provided the most favourable external environment for democratization: Europe and Latin America. Here the predominant international forces at work have been supportive and mutually reinforcing. Positive conditionality and value convergence have prevailed, although even in these settings it is possible to identify significant elements of sanction and imposition as well. The fifth section of the chapter turned to the growing number of democratic transitions being attempted under strong international supervision and control, in contexts that are far less favourable. It paid particular attention to various initiatives led by what is often termed "the international community" (the United Nations, the Commonwealth, the Cotonou Convention, etc.). But, of course, there is also a growing disposition to undertake more unilateral forms of intervention and political imposition, especially in the Islamic world following 11 September. The consequences of this new component of external democracy promotion are still highly uncertain, but are in any case unlikely to replicate previous patterns.

This concluding section reviews nine key analytical assumptions that seem to have guided earlier theorizing, and that may require reassessment in the light of current and prospective developments.

The balance between the external and internal drivers of regime change

Even when processes of democratization seem most strongly driven by internal factors, it is important to consider the external incentives, constraints, examples, and transmission mechanisms that can feed into the most crucial strategic interactions. Likewise, even when the most powerful rulers on earth proclaim their intention to bring about some specified variant of regime change in a hitherto sovereign independent polity, it is equally important to consider all the internal filters, adaptations, and re-interpretations through which this external fiat gets converted into a local outcome. Moreover, the barrier separating external from internal causal factors is never absolute (think of the problems of classifying the activities of the church, the media, and the diaspora communities, for example). And as globalization advances and state sovereignty retreats the permeability of this barrier increases. But in the end there is an overall judgement to be made about the appropriate balance of emphasis in the most typical cases of democratic transition. In the early 1980s that judgement heavily privileged the internal dimensions. Recent evidence and the arguments of this chapter indicate that this was an error. The external drivers often require at least as much attention as the internal dynamics. Both interact and may require assessment as an integral package.

State sovereignty as the privileged locus of attention

So far democratization has occurred almost exclusively at the level of the individual state. This is still essentially true, despite all the changes that are supposed to have reduced the salience of state organization. There is some scope for additional work on the democratization of regional communities of states (such as the EU), or the democratization of international organizations (such as the United Nations or the international financial institutions). There is also scope for more work on democratization of sub-national units, political parties, trade unions, and perhaps even the media or the markets. But if the state is not democratized these other "add-ons" are insecure and ineffective. If the state is democratized that provides the foundation for everything else. Of course, the state is not a ready-made and standardized container. Indeed, humanitarian intervention or the forceful impositions of democracy are often caused by the failure of the pre-existing state structure. But this key analytical point remains – in the absence of an effective state it is hardly possible to achieve a worthwhile democratic transition. Meaningful democratization must still include respect for, and promotion of, an important degree of state sovereignty.

The declining "counterhegemonic potential" of even successful democratizations

The democratizations of Greece and Portugal in the mid-1970s were clearly "counterhegemonic" developments, in that authoritarian regimes strongly aligned with one side in the Cold War were replaced by much more broad-based democratic regimes in which previously suppressed political voices were free to argue far greater independence from the old security alliances, more experimentation in terms of socio-economic reform, and more emphasis on popular aspirations as opposed to the courting of favour from external protectors. The democratizations of Chile and El Salvador also fit this mould, and parallel developments in Poland and Hungary achieved the same effect on the other side of the bi-polar divide. The transition in South Africa can also be viewed as coun-terhegemonic in this sense. Even the democratization of Taiwan can be viewed as an emancipatory step away from external dependencies. But since the early 1990s the structure of the international order has shifted. There is now a unipolar rather than a bi-polar security system. Interna-tional economic arrangements are more universal, rule-bound, and (cer-tainly for most new democracies) constraining than in the past. The scope for domestically driven policy experimentation is accordingly reduced. Where sovereign democratic rights are respected they are accompanied by powerful associated obligations and responsibilities. The voters of newly democratic Mexico and Turkey find their international options to be strongly limited, and even their internal socio-economic choices are hedged in by manifold external restrictions. As for the citizens of East Timor, or the voters of Kosovo, their room for manoeuvre is of course still more limited. This seems a major and durable change in the con-notations of democratization in the twenty-first century, as compared to earlier decades.

The reduced policy discretion available, whatever the electorate may wish

In mid-June 2003 the news agencies reported that the Director of the IMF, on a visit to Buenos Aires, had told the Argentine Congress that it must lift the current suspension on mortgage repossessions if it wished to secure further international economic assistance. The US ambassador in Bolivia has told the government there that it will receive no economic assistance if it eases up on its "zero-coca" policy. The aid community has told the government of Haiti that the resignation of a recently appointed chief of police precludes the disbursement of funds needed to permit some minimal degree of orderly public administration. These examples can be multiplied indefinitely. In each episode the livelihoods and eco-nomic security of substantial blocs of voters and citizens are directly imperilled by decisions taken from outside, by non-nationals with no democratic accountability to the groups affected. Democracy persists, in the sense that Argentines, Bolivians, Haitians, and the rest can periodi-cally choose their national authorities through competitive electoral con-tests. But once ensconced in their offices those national authorities have little – or perhaps no – say in the economic and social outcomes of most interest to their voters. To some extent it was always the case, at least in the poorest and most economically vulnerable of new democracies. But in current conditions this is much more visible, widespread, recurrent, and perhaps more damaging to democratic stability than in the past. It is another aspect of the democratization process that was perhaps underestimated by earlier generations of analysts. But with hindsight it cannot be missed.

The new emphasis on democracy as security, rather than democracy as liberation

Authoritarian regimes typically promise to strengthen security, and ask in exchange for heightened discipline and the reduction of personal freedoms. In reaction against such regimes, democratic transitions are typically associated with increased uncertainty, and perhaps even insecurity, compensated by a restoration of lost liberties. This exchange was a familiar feature of past democratizations, and it still has some currency even today. But, especially since 11 September 2001, the liberating dimension of regime change has been downgraded, replaced by a new emphasis on security. Electoral processes may still allow freedom of choice, access to information, and the right to organize and petition – all freedoms lacking under authoritarian rule. But the freedom to choose may be limited to a narrow range of safe alternatives; the information available may well be manipulated to serve the requirements of order and stability; and the right to organize and petition may be selective and incomplete. In the extreme case of Iraq it is hard to see how the occupying forces could contemplate anything but a highly controlled and filtered version of political representation. But this is only a strong version of tendencies observable elsewhere – in Cambodia, in Kosovo, in Japan, of course – but also in more reputable democracies as well, wherever the fear of terrorism and insecurity overwhelms the impulse for independence from officialdom. This leads on to the next point.

Institutional design choices may be substantially constrained by the preferences (or indeed the strategic interests) of the external democracy promoters

As democratic transitions proliferated during the 1980s and 1990s a new sub-field flourished within the political science community. Old debates about comparative constitutionalism and electoral system design were revisited and updated. The theoretical and empirical study of institutional design choices became more sophisticated and more technical. This shift may have reflected trends in the profession, but it also responded to the emerging opportunities for consultancy and policy prescription as leading Western governments marshalled expertise in the area of international democracy promotion. As the range of attempted democratizations spread deeper into post-Soviet and post-colonial regions the balance of emphasis shifted away from incremental adjustments to existing design principles. More scope emerged for *tabula rasa* re-engineering of complete national political systems. Thus the comparative politics of institutional design began to mimic accompanying Western practices in the area of economic transformation. Like the new cohort of macroeconomic advisers, a community of technical experts in the field of democratic political institution-building began to crystallize. On a strong version these Western experts might possess specialized knowledge capable of optimizing the prospects for democratic stability, or on a weaker version they could warn against common design errors. Throughout all this the underlying assumption remained that these design prescriptions were simply geared to the promotion of the institutional "rules of the game" most likely to consolidate a democratic regime and therefore to elicit durable domestic consent.

With the benefit of hindsight enough experience has now accumulated to permit a more critical evaluation of the scope and limitations of this type of analysis. In addition to the questions that might be raised concerning its theoretical assumptions and its methodological simplifications, recent experience indicates that where domestic forces and institutional traditions were weakest the resulting design choices may have emerged not exactly from technical advice within a *tabula rasa* context, but rather under constraints arising from the preferences and interests of the external democracy promoters.[7] (In some cases these preferences may be derived directly from their strategic interests, in others they may reflect intellectual fashions or national practices gestated in the West and then transferred unreflectively to these new settings.) Conspicuous examples include the West's desire for a centralized presidential regime based in Kabul (where external control over the incipiently "democratic" regime in Afghanistan is concentrated); and the West's resistance to a unified democratic process in Iraq (where it could be anticipated that a consistent assembly based on universal suffrage might seek to undo various of the *faits accompli* decided by the occupying forces). Detailed analysis of such cases is unlikely to uncover many instances of pure external imposition, unmediated by domestic interests and traditions, but the preferences of the external democracy promoters may override (or at least heavily constrain) such local input, and that in turn may substantially affect the stability and indeed the legitimacy of the resulting institutional system. If democratic institutions rest on a sense of local ownership ("authenticity") then the process by which they are constructed may be as critical as the technical content of their incentive structures.

This observation about institutional design choices illustrates a broader tendency, notably seen in the next point.

The shift from democracy as consent to democracy as control

Debates about democratization are also invariably about what kind of democracy is desired, or considered to be feasible. The early "transitions" literature, with its focus on strategic interactions between opposing currents of domestic opinion, privileged a version of democracy structured around the building of consent and the establishment of local credentials of political authenticity. This was a "dialogical" as well as a domestically oriented conception of democracy. But other more monolithic conceptions of democracy are also possible. Democracy can be conceived as the expression of a majority will to affirm collective values and silence discordant challengers. For example, in the early years of Spanish democracy the main innovation was that long-suppressed voices (communists, nationalists, republican sympathizers) were allowed their cacophonous expression. By contrast the democracy of the Aznar years celebrates national unity (against ETA, against immigrants, and against corrupt left-wingers). This shift from an emphasis on building consent to one of exerting control seems to be occurring not only within some new democracies, but within some old ones as well. And it occurs not only within individual countries, but also at the international level.

The redirection of international attention from fragile new democracies to threatening non-democracies

As recently as three years ago it was still possible to view the dominant trend in the post-Cold War as "liberal internationalism". From this standpoint the fragile new democracies of Asia, Africa, Europe, and Latin America represented the best hope for a safer and fairer world. It was therefore justified to channel resources and structure incentives so as to reinforce the direction of change in these new regimes, and to encourage their neighbours to move in the same direction. The enlargement of NATO and the EU represents the most ambitious of these initiatives, but the OAS, the Commonwealth, and others also seemed likely to reinforce this philosophy. The first signs of a reversal came before 11 September (notably with regard to the coup in Pakistan, but also, for example, in relation to the democratic movement in Zimbabwe). Since then the speed of the reversal has been remarkable. Efforts to lend international support to faltering democratic regimes outside Europe have lost all priority and momentum. Instead there has been a concerted drive to threaten and destabilize a selection of non-democratic regimes, notably in the Middle East but also more widely. The resulting reorientation of alliances and policy instruments has played havoc with the structure of expectations linked to liberal internationalism. The marginalization of the United Nations and the silencing of the Commonwealth are just two illustrations of this broader shift. How can the international community hope to uphold uniform high standards of human rights performance when at the same time it condones indefinite detentions without trial in Guantanamo Bay, for example? Whether this is a temporary retreat from the still-consensual values of the 1990s or some more systemic upheaval of the international order remains to be seen. But its implications for the comparative analysis of democratic transitions can hardly be disregarded.

Democratic discourse is being appropriated to rationalize neo-imperial projects of global restructuring

Such a stark concluding statement requires various qualifiers, of course. First, not everyone, even in the present Bush administration, endorses a single global strategy. Second, the events in Iraq and Afghanistan are too recent to provide a secure basis for any longer-term assessments. Third, even if Washington was united and even if these designs were proceeding smoothly, it is very questionable whether the USA has either the resources or the staying power to go much beyond what it has already accomplished. The neo-conservative vision to which this segment alludes is extraordinarily ambitious in scope, but also very sketchy in substance.

This chapter is only concerned with the international components of democratization, as they can be assessed with the benefit of hindsight. So it is not appropriate to speculate about the broader direction of world politics. All that can be said in conclusion is that the rhetoric of democracy and democratization has recently been appropriated to justify (or rationalize) strikingly unilateral and coercive policies that are far removed from what mainstream scholars in the field had anticipated. That is not to say that these developments were without precedent (Latin Americanists are well aware of the Dominican intervention of 1965, for example). Nor is it the case that policy-makers are acting in entire isolation from the available academic literature.[8] What can be said is that the international components of the subject matter are subject to rapid and indeed spectacular shifts over quite short periods of time. This scholarly analysis is therefore subject to periodic shocks from experiences and for that reason analytical models require regular re-evaluations.

Notes

1. This chapter has benefited from discussion at panels on "What Have We Learnt from Thirty Years of Transitions from Authoritarian Rule?" at the XIX World Congress of the International Political Science Association, Durban, South Africa, 30 June–4 July 2003.

2. This chapter went to press in January 2004. At this point Western occupying forces were planning to scale back gradually their presence in both countries. In Afghanistan an Islamic republic is envisaged with strong presidential powers, and a proposed presidential election in 2004 followed by parliamentary elections in 2005. Iraq has not so far established a comparable constitutional framework or electoral timetable.

3. See Schmitter, Philippe C., Laurence Whitehead, and Guillermo A. O'Donnell (eds). 1986. *Transitions from Authoritarian Rule: Latin America*. Baltimore: Johns Hopkins University Press; Schmitter, Philippe C. and Guillermo A. O'Donnell (eds). 1986. *Transitions from Authoritarian Rule: Tentative Conclusions About Uncertain Democracies*. Baltimore: Johns Hopkins University Press; O'Donnell, Guillermo A., Philippe C. Schmitter, and Laurence Whitehead (eds). 1986. *Transitions from Authoritarian Rule: Comparative Perspectives*. Baltimore: Johns Hopkins University Press; O'Donnell, Guillermo A., Philippe C. Schmitter, and Laurence Whitehead (eds). 1986. *Transitions from Authoritarian Rule: Southern Europe*. Baltimore: Johns Hopkins University Press.

4. A view the author has developed more fully elsewhere: Whitehead, Laurence. 2002. *Democratization: Theory and Experience*. Oxford: Oxford University Press.

5. Other Christian churches also influenced civil society in ways that extended beyond national boundaries, but in most cases this is harder to document. (The role of the Dutch Reform Church in first endorsing apartheid and later proclaiming it a sin deserves special mention, in particular since this debate linked democratic Holland with the Afrikaners of South Africa.)

6. The Commonwealth Secretariat is request-driven, meaning that assistance and intervention are not possible unless at the request of the government concerned. Thus, unpopular and non-democratic governments are able to keep the public spotlight away simply by not inviting the Commonwealth to, for example, observe elections. However, a high-level review group headed by President Mbeki is currently reviewing this, and the Secretariat is investigating the possibility of establishing an "early-warning system" to avert undemocratic practices, such as military takeovers.

7. Recent experience only confirms a long record of historical precedents, including such celebrated examples as the 1903 Platt Amendment to the Cuban Constitution, and many failed British attempts to export the "Westminster" system of democracy.

8. Readers of Tony Smith's Twentieth Century Trust volume have no grounds for surprise at the subsequent course of events. Smith, Tony. 1994. *America's Mission: The United States and the Worldwide Struggle for Democracy in the Twentieth Century*. Princeton: Princeton University Press.

Part II

Perspectives from the United Nations

7

The UN's electoral assistance: Challenges, accomplishments, prospects

Robin Ludwig

Since 1989 the United Nations has become an important source of international support and expertise in the conduct of democratic elections. Prior to that date the electoral experience of the organization was very limited, largely reflecting its activities in the field of decolonization. In that context, the United Nations was often called upon to supervise referenda related to questions of self-government that were organized in colonies and territories by the governing authorities or administrative powers. The United Nations had no mandate to assist with elections in sovereign states.

Article I of the UN Charter provides an important justification for the organization's decolonization activities. This article states that one of the obligations of the organization is to facilitate "friendly relations among nations based on respect for the principle of equal rights and self-determination of peoples". Referenda provided an effective and peaceful mechanism to help determine the will of "peoples".

The growth in the membership of the United Nations during the 1960s and 1970s provides the best evidence of the success of decolonization. During that 20-year period some 40 new members were admitted as they obtained independence. The total membership of the United Nations has now grown from 51 member states in 1945 to 191 member states with the admission of East Timor on 27 September 2002. All trust territories have attained self-governance or independence; only 16 non-self-governing territories remain.

In addition to decolonization, the ending of the Cold War brought dramatic changes to the agenda and composition of the organization. The United Nations was called upon to assume a new, more active role in peacemaking and conflict resolution. Growing international emphasis was also placed on its work in the promotion and protection of human rights. In December 1988 the General Assembly adopted Resolution 43/157 that emphasized the "significance of the Universal Declaration of Human Rights and the International Covenant on Civil and Political Rights, which establish that the authority to govern shall be based on the will of the people, as expressed in periodic and genuine elections". At the same time, international negotiations on a variety of long-term conflicts began to show signs of success. After years of civil war in several regions, the time was approaching when "the will of the people" might be expressed peacefully through the conduct of elections.

Beginning with the 1988 Protocols of Geneva and Brazzaville concerning the long-standing problem of Namibia, the next three years resulted in the signing of peace agreements related to conflicts in Angola, Cambodia, El Salvador, Mozambique, and Nicaragua. In each case the United Nations was requested to assist with the holding of elections. Although the organization had no history of assisting with elections in sovereign states, its international membership and neutrality made it a logical choice for undertaking such a sensitive task. Since that time, the demand for UN electoral assistance has continued and increased. The evolution of UN electoral assistance reflects two important changes: the more dynamic role assumed by the organization in peacemaking and conflict resolution since the end of the Cold War, and the growing support of member states for UN activities that promote greater respect for human rights throughout the world.

Origins of UN electoral assistance

The beginnings of UN electoral assistance were not uncontroversial. In General Assembly debates about the issue in the late 1980s and early 1990s, some member states expressed concern that the organization might begin to dictate what type of elections governments should hold and how they should be organized. Other member states worried about the possibility of UN interference in the internal affairs of states. The debates also included practical issues, such as where to locate an office related to electoral assistance – in the Department of Political Affairs at headquarters in New York or in the Office of the High Commissioner for Human Rights in Geneva.

The major political concerns of member states were ultimately allayed with the preparation of clear guidelines for the provision of electoral assistance. Particularly important was the proviso that electoral assistance would be provided only on the basis of an official written request from an appropriate government office. Regarding the physical location of a new office, a decision was made to establish a small unit in the Department of Political Affairs at UN headquarters in New York. This decision probably reflected the prevailing view of elections as a tool in conflict resolution.

Discussions related to electoral assistance were conducted over several years until 1991, when the General Assembly adopted Resolution 46/137, entitled "Enhancing the effectiveness of the principle of periodic and genuine elections". With this resolution, the General Assembly established an organizational structure for the provision of electoral assistance. The resolution called for the designation, by the Secretary-General, of a focal point for electoral assistance activities, and allocation of a small number of staff to assist the focal point in his or her functions. The staff would be responsible for assisting in the evaluation of requests for assistance; developing and maintaining a roster of international experts; establishing an institutional memory and building on electoral experience; and maintaining liaison with regional and other intergovernmental organizations in order to coordinate activities and avoid duplication of efforts. The resolution also called for the establishment of a voluntary trust fund for electoral assistance activities in order to ensure financing for member states wishing assistance.

Given the concerns expressed by member states as to how electoral assistance was to be provided, specific procedures and guidelines were established. These guidelines, although slightly modified based on practical experience, are essentially the same today as when they were originally conceived. Any member state wishing electoral assistance must submit a written request to the Secretary-General or the focal point for UN electoral assistance activities (currently the Under Secretary-General for Political Affairs). The request must be submitted at least four months prior to the date of elections; a longer lead-time is highly recommended. The lead-time is important in order to allow sufficient time for a background briefing by the political desk officer, conduct of a needs-assessment mission, recruitment of relevant experts, and provision of assistance in advance of the election. Without the necessary lead-time, assistance may not be feasible or its effectiveness seriously compromised. In such cases, the United Nations must generally inform the requesting state that it is not in a position to fulfil the request.

Needs-assessment missions

An essential and often highly sensitive first step in providing electoral assistance is the conduct of a needs-assessment mission (NAM). Although NAMs are a routine component of the initial evaluation process, their results are rarely predictable. These missions are often the first in-country contact between international election experts and government officials, and they require concrete and practical discussions of electoral needs, assumptions, and international standards. The NAM is responsible for answering two basic questions: is the requesting government sincere in its effort to organize and conduct credible elections, and if so, what type of assistance should the United Nations provide?

A basic concern for the United Nations is to ensure that the organization is not used to legitimize a substandard electoral process. One might argue, however, that the United Nations should assist particularly in cases where the validity of an election may be in doubt. This is true if a government demonstrates a desire and willingness to make changes that will contribute to a credible process. If such willingness is absent, assistance will be a waste of resources and send a message of international support when none is warranted.

Aside from a desire to receive a UN "stamp of approval" for an electoral process, some governments also consider a request for assistance as a means of obtaining international donor support and finances. In some of these cases, national officials are surprised by the extent of the discussions and assessment made by a NAM. Their assumption that a request for assistance and the hosting of a NAM will automatically result in a reward of international donor funding has frequently proven erroneous. In other cases, officials have requested assistance for a specific component of elections such as the budget, again with the goal of obtaining donor support, while insisting that important procedural elements such as freedom of the media or the vote count remain untouched. Their requests for assistance are often dropped when the NAM offers assistance for election components that they may not wish to change. Although all NAMs generally have the same basic format, their results may range from the provision of one or more types of UN assistance to no assistance and they may engender difficult and sensitive negotiations.

In a routine case, the focal point dispatches a NAM to the requesting country for approximately 10 days. Its objectives are to review the country's plans and infrastructure for elections, determine whether support exists within the country for a UN role, and determine how the United Nations might best be able to assist. The mission experts meet with representatives of government, the election commission, civil society, the media, political parties, and the international donor community. The UN Development Programme (UNDP) resident coordinator (RC) is normally their first contact in the country, and plays a critical supportive role not only in the conduct of the needs-assessment mission but also with any subsequent electoral assistance projects.

The NAM is normally composed of two experts (one staff member and one specialized consultant), and they submit a report and recommendations to the focal point upon returning to headquarters. On this basis, the focal point decides whether the United Nations will provide assistance, and, if so, what type. If the decision is positive, it triggers expert recruitment by the Electoral Assistance Division. In the field, the UNDP RC initiates coordination with international donors and relevant government offices.

In most cases, a NAM results in a decision to provide a specific type of assistance, such as poll-worker training, legal review, or advice on voter registration, and a corresponding project is formulated and implemented. However, the NAM may also be the end of the assistance process if the United Nations determines that assistance is not warranted or if the requesting government does not agree to what is offered. Needs-assessment missions, while routine components of the electoral assistance process, are by no means a simple technical evaluation.

Types of electoral assistance

Since the establishment of the Electoral Assistance Division, the types of electoral assistance available to member states have evolved considerably. In the early 1990s, most UN assistance involved the recruitment of hundreds of international election observers who worked for many months in the context of large peacekeeping operations. Over time, however, the United Nations began to seek means of providing assistance with less cost, greater organizational speed, and a less intrusive presence in the host country. The majority of requests for assistance are not related to peacekeeping or conflict resolution but to relatively peaceful transitions of leadership. In these cases, a more subtle presence is sufficient. The emphasis of UN assistance has always been to support the efforts of the requesting government as appropriate – not to highlight its own presence unless it serves a broader political purpose such as confidence-building.

Although election observation is the best-known and most visible form of assistance, technical assistance is requested most frequently. The trend toward technical assistance has become increasingly pronounced over the past eight years. Most recently, between August 2001 and July 2003, technical assistance was provided to 27 member states and one non-member state (Palestine). Support for international election observers was provided in only three cases: Cote d'Ivoire, Lesotho, and Nepal.

Beginning with the Namibian elections of 1989, the United Nations has offered six basic types of electoral assistance.

Supervision of elections

Election supervision is normally provided exclusively in the context of decolonization. This form of assistance was last provided in the context of Namibia's transition to independence in 1989–1990. Such assistance must be authorized by the Security Council or General Assembly, and a special representative of the Secretary-General (SRSG) is appointed to oversee the entire process. In the case of Namibia, Martti Ahtisaari of Finland was appointed SRSG and he worked closely with the Administrator-General (appointed by the government of South Africa) throughout the mission of the UN Transition Assistance Group (UNTAG) to ensure Namibia's orderly transition to independence.

The SRSG certified each stage of the electoral process, beginning with the pre-campaign political preparations, through voter registration and the final vote tabulation, to publication of the results. In such cases there is no sovereign state responsible for the process; as a result, UN observers follow and report on the activities of the ruling authority in organizing and conducting the process. Because of the historical and political context for Namibia's electoral process, international interest and support were extremely high. The United Nations provided almost a one-to-one ratio of international staff to election officials appointed by the Administrator-General. On election day, 1,753 UNTAG members, representing over 100 nationalities, supervised approximately 2,500 electoral officials appointed by the Administrator-General. Given the costs in terms of time and human and financial resources, such intensive international coverage of an election is unlikely to be repeated.

Verification of elections

Election verification was conducted most frequently in the early 1990s in response to specific electoral provisions in international peace accords; verification missions were usually one element in a larger UN peace-keeping operation. The concept of election observation became familiar to the general public based on news reports and interviews with UN election observers in Angola (1992), El Salvador (1994), Mozambique (1994), and Nicaragua (1990). Similar to election supervision, these operations also require approval by the Security Council or the General Assembly and the appointment of a special representative who certifies each step of the electoral process. This often begins with the drafting of an appropriate legal framework, and continues through registration, the election campaign, election day, and the final announcement of the vote count. In contrast to election supervision, UN verification missions take place in sovereign states and the role of UN observers is to verify the legitimacy of the process as conducted by the host government.

Organization and conduct

The United Nations has been directly responsible for organizing and conducting elections only twice: in Cambodia (1993) and in East Timor (1999–2002). Such assistance is extremely costly in terms of time and financial and human resources, since it requires the United Nations generally to assume the role of a sovereign state in planning and conducting the elections. In the case of Cambodia, the first electoral needs-assessment mission took place in late 1991. Elections "for a national constituent assembly were the focal point of the Paris Agreements". The 18-month mission ultimately involved some 15,500 international troops and 6,000 civilians to staff the $1.7 billion mission.[1] Similar to election supervision and verification, this type of assistance requires Security Council or General Assembly approval and a special representative is appointed. Unlike the previous two forms of assistance, the United Nations is directly responsible for planning and conducting the elections. In these cases, the organization does not observe elections, as this would create a conflict of interest. Observation in these cases is carried out by other regional, intergovernmental, or non-governmental organizations.

Coordination and support

In an effort to reduce the necessary lead-time and basic operational costs, the Electoral Assistance Division developed the coordination and support model for election observation. This innovation resulted in a less intrusive UN presence than is possible with a verification mission, since there is no SRSG appointed and no official certification of the process by the organization. No approval by the General Assembly or Security Council is needed, thereby saving several months in the set-up of the mission.

The basic function of the organization in these cases is to coordinate international observers provided by interested states at their own cost. For such missions, the United Nations establishes a small coordinating secretariat in the requesting country. The secretariat organizes briefings and debriefings for all observers, deployment plans, and logistical assistance, but the United Nations itself does not provide observers or issue statements on the electoral process. Instead, observers sent by interested states work together as a joint international observer group, sharing their observation reports and issuing a common statement after the announcement of the vote count. Since the observers leave the country shortly thereafter, they may be more inclined to make an honest statement regarding the elections knowing that they do not risk later repercussions for themselves, the local UN office, or their embassies. Coordination and support missions are less intrusive for the requesting country but allow comprehensive observer coverage – in terms of both time and geography. This is the most frequent form of observation now used by the United Nations.

Domestic observation

Support for domestic observation was introduced in Mexico in May 1994 at the request of the Mexican government. Elections were scheduled for 21 August and the United Nations assisted in training some 30,000 observers provided by 14 national non-governmental organizations. Such assistance is even less intrusive than the coordination and support model, since it involves observation by citizens of their own electoral process.

Domestic observation is not possible in every country, however, since it is relatively expensive and requires the availability of a large number of trained personnel, often members of respected non-governmental organizations. In Mexico domestic observers have participated in national elections since 1994 and, more recently, in state elections. Domestic observer groups have also participated in elections in several African and European states such as Kenya, Tanzania, and the former republic of Yugoslavia.

Technical assistance

Although least well known, technical assistance is the form most commonly requested by member states. Such assistance is tailored to the specific needs of the requesting member state and may include planning election logistics, electoral calendar and budget preparation, comparative advice on electoral systems and registration methods, computer applications, boundary delimitation, legal advice, poll-worker training, or civic education. Such assistance may require a few weeks or several months.

Several of these forms of assistance may be combined or provided sequentially. For example, in Malawi in 1992–1993 several technical missions were conducted prior to the 1993 referendum in order to advise the government on the timetable for the referendum and procedures for registration and voting. Although the primary task of the UN secretariat in Malawi was to coordinate the work of international observers, the government also requested the United Nations to assist in procuring referendum materials. As a further example of combined forms of assistance, the United Nations, at the request of the government of Mexico, conducted a technical review of the Mexican electoral system in 1994, while also preparing the domestic observers for their first observation of national elections.

International cooperation

Within the UN system, the Electoral Assistance Division cooperates most closely with the UNDP and the two organizations have issued a joint note of guidance that informs all member states and UNDP resident coordinators of the procedures for requesting UN electoral assistance. Because of its field presence, the UNDP is often the first point of contact for governments wishing to submit a request and the UNDP RC serves a critical role as field adviser and catalyst in the early stages of UN electoral assistance. Depending on the type of assistance required and its timing, the UNDP resident coordinator performs a variety of functions, including fund-raising and coordination of international project funds, project management, and negotiations with the host country. For long-term capacity- and institution-building, the UNDP takes a leading role.

Several additional UN offices also provide forms of electoral assistance. The Department of Economic and Social Affairs (DESA) is a sponsor, together with the UNDP, IDEA, and the International Foundation for Election Systems (IFES), of the Administration and Cost of Elections (ACE) project. The purpose of ACE is to give election administrators easy access to objective information and analysis of technical alternatives in election administration, processes, and costs. This information has been produced in a CD-ROM format and made available to all election administrators. DESA also provides on-site electoral advice to requesting member states.

The Office of the High Commissioner for Human Rights (OHCHR) has often been called upon to review legal frameworks for elections and advise on constitutional law, legislative reform, and human rights issues. During the preparations for and conduct of elections in some member states, the OHCHR has also taken on special human rights monitoring functions. That office has also been important in assisting with the design and enhancement of legal and judicial systems, processes, and institutions that are essential not only for credible elections, but for the effective functioning of democracy.

The UN Volunteers (UNV), a subprogramme of the UNDP, is an important partner in the provision of electoral assistance. Based on their international roster of volunteer specialists and fieldworkers, they have identified and recruited hundreds of staff for electoral missions in various parts of the world. UNVs have played an important role in election administration and observation, often in difficult conditions and with very little advance notice. UNVs have been critical to UN electoral operations in the Central African Republic, East Timor, Kosovo, and Nigeria. Most recently UNVs served as election observers for Madagascar's December 2002 legislative elections.

Although the United Nations began to assist with elections and electoral processes in the late 1980s and early 1990s, relatively few other intergovernmental organizations offered electoral assistance at that time. Over the past 12 years, however, a variety of intergovernmental and regional organizations have become active in this field, providing requesting states with more options and opportunities for meaningful and comprehensive support. The European Union, the Organization of American States (OAS), the Organization for Security and Cooperation in Europe (OSCE), and the Organization of la Francophonie (OIF) now offer various types of electoral assistance. The International Institute for Democracy and Electoral Assistance (IDEA), also an intergovernmental organization, was established in Stockholm in the early 1990s and is an important partner in research and the provision of electoral assistance.

Although the United Nations consults with these and other organizations on a regular basis, the general policy is to let the regional organization take the lead in providing assistance to countries within the region. In cases where two or more organizations do become involved, experience has shown the value of a clear delineation of functions. For example, the United Nations and the OAS have worked together effectively on several occasions in Haiti, allocating a technical assistance role to the United Nations and responsibility for international observation to the OAS. In other contexts, such as the 1998–1999 elections in Nigeria, the United Nations coordinated the deployment plans of observing organizations in order to ensure the broadest possible election coverage and avoid observer overlap.

Given the variety of electoral assistance organizations and institutions that now exist, election commissions have many potential sources of assistance. The United Nations continues to receive many requests (some 54 over the past two years), but often works in countries where other forms of assistance are already being provided by others. The challenges of coordinating assistance have clearly increased over the years and considerable time must be dedicated to discussions with other electoral assistance entities and with donors, particularly in the context of NAMs. Such coordination has encouraged discussion of common standards for activities such as election observation and legal codes, and has helped to ensure more effective and comprehensive assistance to requesting states.

Coordinating assistance for a specific election, however, is also quite different from coordinating post-election or other forms of assistance. When assisting with a specific election, the time available is finite and activities involved are relatively specific. In any country, only x number of ballots and x number of ballot boxes are required; there would be no purpose in a donor seeking to provide more. If the United Nations has been requested or mandated to coordinate international observers or electoral assistance, donors have tended to contribute towards a concerted international effort, with the UNDP leading resource mobilization efforts. The assistance activities that are needed can clearly be shared; poll-worker training may be provided by one donor and voter education by another within the broader umbrella of UN electoral assistance activities. Given the specific needs and time element of an election, donors tend to work together until the election has taken place.

Post-election assistance, however, is more difficult to coordinate. Often the government makes no specific requests since it considers elections a past priority until the next cycle begins. Without direction from the government, donors tend to bring in their own national experts to give advice, and this can often result in conflicting or duplicate activities by other donors. Since donors rather justifiably wish to receive recognition for their support, they are likely to arrange their assistance activities with the government on a bilateral basis. As a result, other donors may be unaware of their plans until they are being implemented. A further complication is the lack of a deadline and the potential for some post-election activities, such as civic education or support for the media, to continue for months or years. Without the unifying focus of a single election, the coordination of electoral assistance becomes more complicated and the role of the United Nations as the primary coordinator of assistance is less easily justified or accepted.

The growth in the number of willing international organizations capable of providing electoral assistance has been an important and rapid change over the past 10 years. Regional organizations have taken on a far more active role than was possible in the early 1990s, and national election administrators are finding many more sources of assistance than in the past. The challenge for the United Nations and its partners will be to expand and build upon their existing election expertise (for example, new applications of information technology) while ensuring that, together, they provide the best and most comprehensive assistance possible.

Learning from experience

One of the most important lessons of UN electoral experience over the past decade is the evolution of a more realistic view of the role that elections can play in the creation of democracy. In the early 1990s many in the international community believed that the successful conduct of an election would establish the basis for the growth of a viable democracy. Experience demonstrated, however, that although elections contribute substantially to democratization, elections alone are not enough. Without effective democratic institutions and processes, such as fair and effective legal systems, a free press, and transparency in government, the impact of one round of elections may be short-term and negligible. In the most unfortunate cases, elections may be used to validate and maintain an undemocratic *status quo*.

Over the past 14 years, UN electoral assistance activities have been oriented increasingly toward the creation of sustainability. The emphasis has shifted from elections as a political quick-fix to recognition that democratic development takes time. The past 50 years have shown that democratization is not necessarily a linear and upward progression in every country; in some cases, democratic progress has stagnated for years or regressed. Given the unprecedented number of countries currently engaged in this long-term process and the resources being allocated to democratization, the issue of sustainability is now being seriously addressed in the planning and design of most electoral assistance projects.

The problems of sustainability vary from one country to the next, but often reflect economic, political, or social factors or a combination of these. Based on UN experience, several of the more common obstacles in each of these categories can be highlighted. In some cases solutions have been found, particularly if the host government is committed to furthering the democratic process. In addressing other obstacles, the United Nations and its electoral assistance partners continue to explore new approaches and means of support.

Economic challenges

A common problem for governments engaged in democratization is a lack of financial resources. In the early 1990s, international donors often provided financial support for national elections since elections were considered an important event affecting the international relations of the country. In some cases, however, newly elected governments found that they lacked the financial resources to organize and conduct local elections, and in some cases found it difficult to obtain donor support since such elections were not considered to have an international dimension. Some donors expressed concern that support for such elections might be considered interference in the internal affairs of the state. Others, however, noted that local elections may be the best method for citizens to develop a sense of democracy and understanding of elections since the issues involved affect the community and voters may personally know the candidates.

A lack of readily available financial resources can also raise the cost of elections. In the past, many national budgets contained no budget line for the administration of elections and the ongoing maintenance and upgrading of the electoral system. As a result, each election involved the

recruitment and training of new staff, the conduct of a new national registration exercise, and a variety of expenses due to a lack of long-term
planning. (For example, several million ballots ordered four weeks before an election cost significantly more than ballots ordered with several
months' lead-time.)

A further difficulty encountered by many newly elected multi-party
governments is the demand for scarce resources from other sectors of
government. After the successful completion of elections, many new
governments find that government resources are urgently needed in sectors related to food, education, and health. In some cases a new distribution of government resources is required in order to fulfil promises
made during the election campaign. Continued expenditures on electoral
systems and processes often become a low priority in the mix of demands
facing a newly elected government.

For the international community and the United Nations, experience
has shown that substantial international funding of one election (such as
Cambodia in 1993) does not necessarily establish a permanent basis for
future elections. In some cases, donors request that equipment and materials provided for elections through a UN peacekeeping budget should
be returned after completion of the process. In addition, the international
personnel recruited to conduct an election often complete their assign-
ments with the announcement of the election results. Because of the focus on organizing and conducting the election, little attention is devoted
to capacity-building and improvements in its aftermath. While many
would argue that the price of elections is often minimal compared to the
human and financial price of war, better future planning could contribute
significantly to furthering democracy with reduced costs.

The international community can most easily provide assistance by
continuing its support after an election is held. Based on the working relationships and trust that have already been established, further assistance is most easily provided immediately after the elections in order to
establish a permanent election commission and administration. Lack of
consistent support may result in a loss of trained staff, unreliable maintenance of the established system, and downgrading of electoral issues
among the new priorities facing the government. The UNDP has been
particularly effective in providing long-term support for building permanent and effective electoral institutions and processes.

Political concerns

A variety of political factors can slow or hinder democratization. Similar
to conflicting needs for economic resources, new government officials
face competing demands for their attention and the establishment of po-

litical priorities. In this context, they simply may not consider the institutionalization of elections or democratization to be essential activities, particularly since they have recently won elections and a new round will not take place for several years. Without the political will and commitment of the government to continue the democratization process, progress can easily stall.

International donors sometimes face a difficult and sensitive situation in seeking to encourage new governments to continue their efforts towards democratization. Although they may express support and encouragement, they must avoid being viewed by the government as seeking to dictate what its priorities should be. At the same time, newly elected governments often lack clear priorities, particularly those necessary for achieving long-term goals, and may appreciate donor advice. The sensitive relationship between donor and host countries can be an important factor in whether democratization efforts continue or stagnate.

When considering the question of sustainability, past government practice may leave a significant legacy. Although many new governments were created after winning first-time multi-party elections, their predecessor administrations often remained in power for multiple terms, controlling the media and curbing a variety of political rights in order to ensure their continued rule. For some leaders the desire to remain in power, despite a successful democratic election and a break from the abuses of past regimes, provides a strong impetus for the suspension of democratic practice when the term limits have been reached.

The most difficult cases for international donors are those in which an incumbent government is systematically dismantling the institutions and mechanisms of democratic governance while requesting international assistance with elections. The NAM becomes very sensitive in these cases. Although the United Nations avoids assisting with pro-forma, non-democratic elections, arguments are sometimes made that, without a UN presence, the opposition will become violent, unrest will spread, and the country (and potentially the region) will be destabilized. In such cases, the organization may offer minimal assistance for a technical component of the electoral process (such as media advice or poll-worker training). Coordination of observers and election observation will not be offered in order to avoid having to issue a statement on the conduct of the elections.

The true dilemma for the United Nations and others in such cases is whether to provide any assistance at all for elections that are clearly not competitive. Some argue that it is important to provide international support for national groups and institutions which are seeking to further democracy, such as the election commission or the media. Such assistance may contribute to an improved security situation in the short term and provide leverage for additional negotiations with the government. Others argue that any form of assistance will associate the organization with election fraud, betray established guidelines for providing assistance, and, most serious for the long term, demonstrate to voters that the international community is willing to collude in supporting a flawed process. From this perspective, no assistance is considered warranted and the government should be isolated until its leadership returns to a more genuinely democratic path.

In considering both arguments, awareness of international standards for elections is essential. Since the conditions and context for each election differ, international standards provide a starting point for the assessments made by a NAM. Ultimately, when a decision is made to assist or not to assist, the decision reflects an awareness of the specific electoral situation and a difficult political calculation as to how, at the least, to prevent further deterioration of the situation and, at best, to encourage positive actions toward greater democracy.

Donors play an important role in encouraging governments to continue the democratization process. In this context, donors may offer continuing assistance and, together, may provide comprehensive and long-term support. They must, however, ensure that their assistance does not overlap or duplicate the assistance offered by other donors. International donors must also be consistent in their focus on democratization as a priority activity. If international donors lose interest in elections and democratization following the successful conduct of an election, governments may easily focus on other issues.

Social issues

For citizens in many countries, voting and democracy remain relatively unfamiliar concepts. Although the introduction of elections and multiparty politics has been welcomed by voters in many countries, many citizens actually have a very limited understanding of these ideas and the values behind them. Long-term civic education programmes and encouragement of popular participation in political life are major priorities for many new democracies.

In focus group studies conducted by the National Democratic Institute (NDI) in Malawi in the 1990s, researchers found that there was no word for "democracy" in Chichewa, the local language. They also found that many Malawians were suspicious of the concept of multi-partyism, particularly after more 30 years of single-party rule. One focus group participant noted that there "was room for only one bull in the kraal; otherwise they fight". Malawians also spoke of the more traditional means of solving disputes, which involved sitting under a banyan tree with the tribal chiefs and discussing a problem until an agreed solution was found. The idea that different political parties, representing opposing views, might work together in parliament was difficult for them to accept. There was considerable concern that multi-partyism would lead to violence and instability.[2]

In addition to a lack of democratic tradition and experience, many new democracies have large percentages of illiterate voters. Since the concept of a viable democracy is generally premised on the existence of an informed and engaged populace, these newly democratic nations lack an important component for one of the fundamental pillars for success. In countries such as the Gambia, Mozambique, or Côte d'Ivoire, political discussion is based largely on personalities and family and ethnic distinctions rather than on policy issues and professional performance. The media, which often find it difficult to survive financially, report primarily on news in the capital and major cities where more literate populations reside. Rural populations may receive little or no news and often have limited understanding of how government works and the role of their representative in parliament.

During a series of focus group interviews conducted in Cambodia in 1995, NDI researchers found that many Cambodians had relatively little interest in democracy, its freedoms, or its responsibilities. Participants in their discussions stated that they rarely discussed politics, indicated that they had no role in the creation of a democratic Cambodia, and trusted that the United Nations would return in order to ensure that future elections would be conducted fairly.[3] Their lack of interest and understanding provided international election assistance organizations with useful insight into the challenges that exist in seeking to generate an informed and activist voting public.

The United Nations has been exploring a variety of approaches to civic education and the encouragement of greater popular participation in politics. A project of particular note is under way in Nigeria and may serve as a useful model for others. As a follow-up to the national elections of 1997–1998, a series of civic education forums has been organized on selected topics in order to enable participants to engage in constructive dialogue with a view to evaluating the democratic process and prioritizing democracy-related themes for specific activities. The forums have addressed topics such as "citizenship, gender, and participation in the electoral process and governance" and "enabling environment and constitutionalism in Nigeria". Representatives from some 50 national non-governmental organizations (NGOs) and government agencies participated in each forum. Based on donor funding, seed money was provided to NGOs for relevant project proposals that would result in practical implementation of ideas discussed in the forums.

The international community might also direct attention to a review of legal instruments, many of which were drafted in the early 1990s in great haste due to the impetus at the time to proceed quickly in organizing and conducting multi-party elections. In some cases, the constitution and/or election laws do not necessarily accurately reflect the traditional legal assumptions and values of the country. The incidence of amendments and revisions may suggest a need to revisit these fundamental legal instruments in order to ensure that they truly reflect the essential legal norms and principles of the country.

Looking to the future

The number of requests for electoral assistance received by the United Nations since 1989 provides telling evidence of the desire and appreciation of member states for electoral assistance. The growth of UN activity in this field over 14 years marks a significant change in the priorities of the organization and its member states as well as an evolution in the broader beliefs of the international community regarding concepts of human rights and governance around the world.

Since 1989, the international community has come to realize that the holding of an election is no guarantee of a democratic future. Although elections were frequently considered by many in the international community as an exit strategy (and still are by some), experience has shown that a hasty and general withdrawal of international assistance following elections often results in significant loss in terms of resources, knowledge, and political momentum to establish essential institutions for the future. The need for post-election assistance and support aimed at capacity-building and the strengthening of electoral institutions and processes became clear.

Based on its recognition that conditions prior to, during, and following elections must be conducive to a credible process, the General Assembly approved a resolution in 1994 (A/RES/48/131) in which it recommended that "the United Nations, in order to ensure the continuation and consolidation of the democratization process in member states requesting assistance, provide assistance before and after elections have taken place...." One year later, the General Assembly amended the title of the relevant resolution to read: "Strengthening the role of the United Nations in enhancing the effectiveness of the principle of periodic and genuine elections *and the promotion of democratization*." These two resolutions, together with the Vienna Declaration and Programme of Action adopted by the World Conference on Human Rights on 25 June 1993, opened the door for more comprehensive and longer-term efforts by the organization to assist its member states in developing democratic institutions and practices.

The early cases of electoral assistance, such as Cambodia, Mozambique, and Nicaragua, where elections were a component of international peacemaking/peace-building, have generally led to successful transitions from violent conflict to peaceful resolution of disputes through the political process. Since that time, the broader process of democratization in these countries has begun and will continue for many years to come. Future efforts will focus on technical assistance, in areas such as the building of permanent electoral institutions, creation of viable political parties, development of responsible and open media, and encouragement of an informed and active civil society. Despite the difficulties and costs involved, few would argue for a return to the violence and destruction of the early, pre-election, 1990s.

In many countries, several cycles of elections have been conducted successfully over the past decade and the holding of regular and periodic elections has become an accepted component of national political life. Voters have developed confidence in the abilities of their national election administrations to conduct legitimate elections. As a consequence, the need for the confidence-building presence of international observers is declining and demand for more sophisticated and specific forms of technical assistance is growing. Technical assistance will continue to be the most sought-after form of assistance for the foreseeable future.

Despite the predominance of requests for technical assistance, the United Nations will continue to face major challenges that entail elections – alone and as components of larger peacekeeping operations. From that perspective, past successes, as well as disappointments such as Angola and Haiti, have contributed to more realistic and practical planning for future involvements. For peacekeeping missions that include an electoral component, Angola and other missions have led to careful review and assessment of political and logistical feasibility, timing, and sequencing of the various mission components. Future major missions will benefit from their predecessors.

UN electoral assistance has evolved significantly since the organization's supervision of the 1989 Namibian elections. The field is dynamic and changing rapidly, based on new and growing demands from member states and the trust they have placed in the organization's integrity and effectiveness. The decisions of the General Assembly, first in 1991 and later in 1994 and 1995, to encourage not only the provision of electoral assistance but also democratization mark important milestones, not only in the brief history of UN electoral assistance activities, but in the larger and ongoing evolution of the international political and human rights agenda.

Notes

1. United Nations. 1995. *The United Nations and Cambodia (1991–1995)*. New York: United Nations.
2. National Democratic Institute. 1994. *The Nation is the People*. Washington, DC: NDI.
3. National Democratic Institute. 1996. *Public Attitudes Toward Democracy in Cambodia: A Focus Group Study*. Washington, DC: NDI.

8

UN democracy promotion: Comparative advantages and constraints

Edward Newman

National governance is intrinsically linked to human rights, welfare, and the provision of public goods. It is increasingly accepted that governance is also linked to security among and within states. Democratic governance is the benchmark of good governance, and perhaps even the "fundamental standard of political legitimacy in the current era".[1] Moreover, democracy has become a significant, although contested, international norm as value judgements regarding governance are increasingly embedded in international politics and institutions. In line with this, a broad and multifaceted range of democracy promotion and assistance activities – directly or indirectly – underscores the policies and activities of many states and non-state entities. The promotion of "good governance" – whatever the definition – figures prominently in the official policies of many states, particularly their overseas aid programmes. In the regional context, many organizations or arrangements have long had standards of good governance and democracy that apply to their membership. International non-governmental organizations and foundations have also played an important role in supporting democratic aspirations and institutions. The idea of democratic governance also underpins much of the contemporary work of the United Nations. Indeed, the founding of the United Nations, in addition to being an alliance against aggression in the Second World War, was premised upon the belief that stable, peaceful conditions within states underpin peaceful and stable relations between states.

A number of questions are raised by the subject of democracy promotion and assistance. Can "external" international actors – such as hegemonic states, global organizations, regional organizations, financial institutions, and NGOs – have a decisive, substantial, and enduring impact upon domestic transition and democratization? In other words, can external actors bring democracy where there has been no democracy? Alternatively, can assistance programmes only have a positive impact where the society in question is already moving towards democracy anyway? Are top-down government assistance programmes the most effective, or those that work with civil society and non-governmental groups? What are the motives and interests of the actors who assist or promote democracy? Has the promotion of democracy in post-conflict and divided societies had a significant role in conflict settlement and reconciliation? Or can electoral processes exacerbate ethnic/religious differences, and even encourage new outbreaks of conflict? What values or models of democracy do external agents such as the United Nations or the USA bring with them to the democratization process? Are "international standards" of democracy and democratization sensitive to indigenous traditions and authority structures? This chapter will identify and explore a range of issues related to democracy assistance, and attempt to identify the comparative advantages that the United Nations has, or could have, in this area.

Democracy assistance and promotion: The normative foundation

There is a growing consensus, based upon empirical research and evolving political norms, that democratic governance is a human right, that it is conducive to sound development and stable, plural societies, and that it correlates to peaceful relations between and within societies (although democratic *transition* can increase instability). In some circles this has become an article of faith:

Countries that govern themselves in a truly democratic fashion do not go to war with one another. They do not aggress against their neighbors to aggrandize themselves or glorify their leaders. Democratic governments do not ethnically "cleanse" their own populations, and they are much less likely to face ethnic insurgency. Democracies do not sponsor terrorism against one another. They do not build weapons of mass destruction to use on or to threaten one another. Democratic countries form more reliable, open, and enduring trading partnerships. In the long run they offer better and more stable climates for investment. They are more environmentally responsible because they must answer to their own citizens, who organize to protest the destruction of their environments. They are better bets to honor international treaties since they value legal obligations and because their openness makes it much more difficult to breach agreements in secret. Precisely because, within their own borders, they respect competition, civil liberties, property rights, and the rule of law, democracies are the only reliable foundation on which a new world order of international security and prosperity can be built.[2]

Whilst this may contain some empirically questionable assertions, it reflects the confidence of liberal democratic thought at the turn of the century. Since the terrorist attacks in the USA on 11 September 2001, the issue has gained renewed urgency. Recent experience of Afghanistan has shown how corrupt, unstable, ineffective, and repressive governance was a source of misery for millions in that country: human rights, development, and education (amongst other things) all ranked around the worst in the world. At the same time, such an environment can also be a breeding ground for violent grievance and terrorism, the effects of which have a far wider impact upon international peace and security. The September 2001 terrorist attacks underlined the relationship between security and governance. Terrorism finds fertile ground in undemocratic and conflict-torn societies: the promotion of democracy must now also be seen as a part of the quest for international peace and security. Democracy – both in theory and practice – is not perfect, but it is nevertheless becoming a settled ideal of political organization.[3]

Actors, activities, and tools of democracy promotion and assistance

The range of democracy assistance activities is wide. It covers organizing, conducting, and validating elections; developing civil society and political parties; bolstering the rule of law, judicial institutions, and security; strengthening accountability, oversight, and transparency; enhancing legislative training and effectiveness; and civic education, public awareness, and the media. In a broader sense, this field also involves assistance in economic governance and development, which is fundamentally important to democratic development, although not always seen directly as democracy assistance. In terms of approaches, bottom-up democracy promotion and assistance focuses on strengthening civil society and public awareness and developing local capacity. It is often implemented through local and international non-government actors. In contrast, top-down assistance is implemented through governments and concentrates more on formal institutions and processes.

A range of actors is involved in democracy assistance, and they all reflect particular characteristics and bring particular qualities to the field.[4] Individual state governments, regional organizations, global international organizations, public and private foundations, and NGOs have all made their mark. Government assistance represents perhaps the largest sector of assistance in financial terms.[5] The tools most commonly used include aid assistance targeted at enhancing the democratic qualities of processes and institutions within the target country. It is generally partisan – it is in support not only of processes but also of particular political outcomes. It can be endowed with comparatively large resources: financial, human, and sometimes even military. It is closely tied to perceptions of national interest relating to strategic, economic, and ideological outlooks. It can be tied to domestic party politics and political agendas in the donor country, and thus influenced by changes in the party of government, political priorities, and the nature of political leadership and sometimes personalities. Unilateral national democracy assistance is comparatively less likely to be even-handed and detached from vested interests in terms of the choice of recipient states and the choice of the political interests that benefit from assistance. In its content, volume, and where it is directed, it is generally tied to the political agenda and perceived interests of the donor.

US democracy promotion, the largest of all actors in budgetary terms, has been interpreted in a number of different ways: a practical and sincere policy that reflects the US historical commitment to democracy and liberalism; a façade designed to mask US hegemony; and a manifestation of Western cultural imperialism. John Ikenberry argues that US democracy promotion "reflects a pragmatic, evolving, and sophisticated understanding of how to create a stable international political order and a congenial security environment". The motivation is simple: "the United States is better able to pursue its interests, reduce security threats in its environment, and foster a stable political order when other states – particularly the major great powers – are democracies rather than non-democracies".[6] William Robinson presents a quite different interpretation. He argues that US democracy promotion is in reality a project to pre-empt more radical forms of governance taking root in developing countries whilst extending US hegemony and economic interests. As he puts it, this is "signaling new forms of transnational control accompanying the rise of global capitalism" – albeit consensual means of control rather than coercive ones.[7] Thus, "what US policymakers mean by 'democracy promotion' is the promotion of polyarchy. Polyarchy refers to a system in which a small group actually rules and mass participation in decision-making is confined to leadership choice in elections carefully managed by competing elites."[8]

Regional organizations are notable for promoting democracy through the development of norms and laws relating to governance. The tools here are characteristically legal and political, although democracy aid is also involved. In some cases democratic governance applies to their membership. The European Union is "founded on the principles of liberty, democracy, respect for human rights and fundamental freedoms, and the rule of law"; member states that do not uphold these standards in the eyes of their peers are subject to sanctions, including suspension from membership.[9] An open democracy is clearly an explicit condition for membership. The OSCE and the Western European Union are similarly explicitly active in supporting and promoting democracy, both as a condition of membership and in terms of external activities and policies.

The Organization of American States developed the American Convention on Human Rights in the 1970s and its Inter-America Commission on Human Rights has played a significant role in human rights and good governance in the region. The OAS's 1991 Santiago Declaration committed the region's governments to support any elected regime threatened by hostile forces. Subsequent to this, the Washington Protocol provides for the expulsion of a state from the OAS in the event of the overthrow of a democratically elected regime, and the Managua Protocol commits members to promoting democratic consolidation and preventing democratic regression. Whilst the impact of this has been mixed, it nevertheless contributes to an "evolving regime of democracy protection" in the region.[10] A further contribution to these norms is provided by the commitment of the South American regional trade treaty, Mercosur, to suspend the participation of any member in the event of a military coup.

Even in regions where transnational political networks are not as deep nor institutionalized – such as Africa and Asia – there is a gradual coalescing of political norms that have implications for governance within states in the context of regional groupings. Some regional arrangements are much less effective in promoting democracy: the Association of South-East Asian Nations, for example, continues to reflect the preoccupation with sovereignty and opposition to interference. Other regional arrangements, such as the Southern African Development Community, the African Union, and the South Asian Association for Regional Cooperation, are also limited in their democracy assistance and promotion efforts as a result of historical and political differences amongst members.

NGOs and foundations, some of which have support from governments – such as the National Endowment for Democracy, the Westminster Foundation for Democracy, and Germany's *stiftungen* (foundations)[11] – find their niche in track-two and bottom-up democracy assistance. This can involve funding pro-democracy civil society actors in transitional societies, organizing exchanges of democratic leaders, providing expertise for institution-building, encouraging accountability and transparency by conducting informal oversight and scrutiny, and funding local projects aimed at strengthening democratic processes. However, large international NGOs and foundations are sometimes called upon to play a more substantive and direct role in democracy assistance by observing and validating elections, advising governments, and assisting in building institutions. The tools at the disposal of NGOs and foundations are financial and technical assistance.

The United Nations, amongst the international organizations, has a unique role in democracy promotion, assistance, and facilitation; according to one observer, it is the "international agent for democratization".[12] Whilst the Charter is based upon the sovereign state, "We the peoples" implies that the people's will should lie behind that sovereignty. The Charter commits its signatories to "faith in fundamental human rights, in the dignity and worth of the human person, in the equal rights of men and women and of nations large and small". Amongst the purposes of the United Nations are the promotion of the principle of equal rights and self-determination of peoples, and human rights and fundamental freedoms for all without discrimination "as to race, sex, language or religion". More explicitly, the Universal Declaration of Human Rights of 1948 expresses the UN's mandate for the promotion of democracy. It reaffirms that all persons are born "free and equal in dignity and rights", and that all persons have a right to "take part in the government of his country, directly or through freely chosen representatives". Most explicitly, "The will of the people shall be the basis of the authority of government; this will shall be expressed in periodic and genuine elections which shall be by universal and equal suffrage and shall be held by secret vote or by equivalent free voting procedures." Subsequent legal instruments have codified this further.[13]

It is important to emphasize that, whilst these legal instruments promoted certain norms that implied some form of democracy within states, they did not yet imply an international norm of democracy promotion. State sovereignty and non-intervention into domestic affairs were emphasized in all such instruments, underscored by Article 2(7) of the UN Charter. Democracy was promoted as a vague principle to be addressed at the national level; international consideration was considered too sensitive, especially during the ideological fervour of the Cold War and at a time when newly independent countries were not eager to compromise their hard-won sovereignty by international scrutiny of their domestic processes of governance. The end of the Cold War opened up political space. The changing context appeared to have brought an increased opportunity to address human rights issues at the international level, and a growing acceptance of a wider conception of peace and security. The end of the Cold War also challenged structural and global notions of international security and saw a shift in attitudes from a paradigm of national security to one of "human security" that sees issues of governance *within* states as of direct relevance to peace and security *between* states, and thus a legitimate issue of international relations. General Assembly Resolution 43/157 of 8 December 1988 reaffirmed the right to take part in the government of one's country, and the establishment of the UN-sponsored International Conferences of New or Restored Democracies set in motion a debate. Following the second conference the General Assembly requested the Secretary-General to prepare a report to study "the ways and mechanisms in which the UN system could support the efforts of governments to promote and consolidate new or restored democracies".[14]

The culmination of the UN's deliberation of the consequences and prospects for democracy and democratization was the Secretary-General's report *An Agenda for Democratization*.[15] Simultaneously, there were mounting requests by numerous governments for assistance in building the institutions of democracy. Yet the idea of highlighting and conceptualizing the UN's role in the process of democracy and democratization was a "risky business", given the preoccupation with state sovereignty and connotations of intervention that might be implied; many in the United Nations clearly did not see this as being within the authority of the international civil service.[16]

This whole changing context – and most notably the evolving transnational conditionalities and inputs upon "domestic" politics – has challenged the established meaning of democracy: for one observer, "Regional and global interconnectedness contests the traditional national resolutions of the central questions of democratic theory and practice."[17] The classical democratic questions are premised upon a fairly homogeneous, delineated, national political community, where politics has the state as its terms of reference. The evolution of democracy has brought into question this notion of political community, national identity, citizenship, and representation.

The United Nations and democracy assistance and promotion: Comparative advantages and disadvantages

The United Nations has a number of hypothetical comparative advantages and disadvantages in its democracy-assistance activities. On the practical side, the United Nations has a network of governance programmes throughout the developing world through the UNDP residential offices, which form a natural "lead agency" function for democracy assistance activities. The United Nations is also an important – although not necessarily always successful – international actor for organizing security and peacekeeping in post-conflict societies; when governance/democracy issues are a component of conflict settlement or peace-building, the United Nations often takes a leadership role as a part of its overarching responsibilities.

Apart from its practical capacity, the United Nations has universally recognized legitimacy. It is the embodiment of human rights norms and values. It works generally only on the basis of consent by the country requesting assistance, and it has a clear mandate to promote peace and good governance. It is also helpful that the United Nations can directly assist elections at the request of states without raising tensions with state sovereignty. Moreover, the United Nations does not work with a universal template, is generally sensitive to local context, and is not driven by a "national" vision/agenda (in contrast, for example, to US democracy promotion). Its legitimacy also derives from the perception that there is less likelihood of mixed or ulterior motives behind UN democracy assistance compared with national efforts. If there is less likelihood of competing economic/strategic interests compared with national democracy promotion efforts, there is in theory less "selectivity" in the countries in which it becomes involved. Thus, the relevant UN units will receive and act upon any request for assistance in strengthening democratic processes, as long as the practical conditions and timeframe are satisfactory. In addition, the United Nations is relatively accountable and transparent. Apart from exceptional Chapter VII enforcement actions, the United Nations is involved in target countries at the request of the host sovereign authority and must provide a full account of its activities.

It is also possible to generalize potential comparative disadvantages. The United Nations has a small budget compared to national government efforts, and this certainly applies to electoral assistance. Indeed, the size of the Electoral Assistance Division within the Department of Political Affairs seems modest when compared to the tasks expected of them (although much of their work is done by consultants). Some democracy assistance missions are smaller and shorter than would be considered necessary for the task, and UN staff would readily accept that expectations from such missions must remain modest. Partly as a result of this, it could also be suggested that the UN's knowledge of the local context is often not as thorough as other actors involved in democracy assistance and promotion. Even the resident UNDP offices in most countries cannot match the local knowledge and intelligence of, for example, the US diplomatic presence. In addition there are political limitations to what the United Nations can do and thus what it can achieve, in accordance with the UN's structure as an intergovernmental organization. The United Nations generally has to work through governments. It cannot independently engage in grass-roots democracy promotion or assist NGO's. Nor can it directly support a political opposition actor, even if the political opposition is "more democratic" than the government. The United Nations – and certainly not UN Secretariat staff members – cannot generally criticize governments and states apart from by the decision of a representative organ such as the General

Assembly or the Security Council. None of these limitations applies in a formal sense to national democracy promotion efforts or the work of NGOs. Even regional organizations are increasingly able to censure and discipline members that violate norms relating to democratic governance. Generally, the United Nations is thus sensitive to sovereign prerogatives and the norm of non-intervention. It works at the request of governments rather than democracy *per se*, although certain standards are of course applied. As a condition of this, the United Nations has little power or authority (except in exceptional circumstances) to respond forcefully to backsliding. For example, in the case of Cambodia, after the coup in 1997 the UN Security Council issued a statement condemning the violence, but this statement did not blame any party and avoided calling the situation a coup.

UN democracy promotion: Themes and challenges

The span of UN activities in this field is vast, ranging from technical assistance in drafting and implementing election laws to nation-building on the basis of democratic governance.[18] The range of issues the United Nations must grapple with in undertaking this demanding work is also vast. It must respect Article 2(7) of the Charter – which prohibits interference in matters within the domestic jurisdiction of states – while also taking leadership on behalf of the international community and upholding basic human rights. Its work must be based on the concept of state sovereignty but be motivated by the high normative ideals set by the United Nations. Its rules of engagement are based on a Charter written in the midst of the Second World War, while it works in a post-Cold War world where some of the Westphalian premises are beginning to erode. The remainder of this chapter will raise a number of questions and controversies often associated with democracy assistance and democracy promotion. It will apply these debates in particular to the activities of the United Nations with consideration to the organization's comparative advantages and disadvantages.

Can external actors such as the United Nations have an enduring impact upon the political trajectory of a society?

Arguably, "there are no blueprints for building democracy or for assisting those seeking to do so. We are still years away from identifying, let alone prescribing, 'best practices' in this area."[19] Yet even while appreciating the uniqueness of different situations, we must understand the importance and value of learning lessons. Learning lessons assumes that we can establish propositions – in this case regarding the best ways of assisting democracy – on the basis of experience and observation. Thus, certain variables – such as the nature of civil society, level of ethnic homogeneity, level of cooperation of political élites, social and economic standards, and timing of elections – can be considered to be key explanatory or causal variables across different cases. On this basis, best practices can be established.

The conventional "political science" approach to democracy and democratization focuses upon domestic, indigenous variables without much attention to international actors or forces. According to this approach polities and politics are conditioned by the historical, cultural, power, and socio-economic dynamics of a particular community, usually delineated by territory.[20] Democracy, representation, accountability, consent – the most fundamental sources of political legitimacy – are concepts that have meaning in a contractual relationship between the government and the governed within a state. Yet in reality we know that transnational processes, international organizations, and the free flow of information have inevitably had a bearing on "national" political systems, sometimes with dramatic effect. International norms relating to governance and human rights at the regional and global levels have played a significant role in political outcomes and opportunities.[21]

Nevertheless, the relationship between domestic and international factors in democratization processes is complex and unclear.[22] It is uncertain "what factors cause liberal democracies to emerge and thrive and how manipulable these factors are by outside actors".[23] The effectiveness of international democracy promotion and assistance is debatable. Are there pre-conditions for democracy – be they social, economic, cultural, geographic – and if there are, are external actors able to instil or alter such variables? The existing democracy promotion literature is on balance cautious of big claims. Thomas Carothers observes the limited accomplishments and emphasizes the inherent limitations of democracy assistance: "democracy aid generally does not have major effects on the political direction of recipient countries. The effects of democracy programs are usually modestly positive, sometimes negligible, and occasionally negative."[24] He concludes that "democracy programs are at best a secondary influence because they do not have a decisive impact on the conditions of society that largely determine a country's political trajectory – the charter and alignment of the main political forces; the degree of concentration of economic power; the political traditions, expectations, and values of the citizenry; and the presence or absence of powerful antidemocratic elements".[25] So, for example, Lao Mong Hay argues that "perhaps the greatest obstacle to democracy in Cambodia is the anti-democratic behavior of the nation's political élite. However history, culture, and a low level of socio-economic development are also obstacles – though not insurmountable – to building a democratic political culture."[26] Carothers similarly argues that "Haiti was and remains a remarkably difficult place to try to build democracy, due to its catastrophic economic situation and ragged socio-political history".[27]

It is reasonable to suggest that people everywhere have an inherent desire to have at least some control over their lives. Participation in the organization of their communities would therefore seem to be a fairly universal, if latent, human desire. If the United Nations is facilitating this process, then it is quite possible for the organization to have a decisive impact in helping a society move forward. If the conditions are not ready then the positive impact is likely to be much less, and even minimal. The modest progress towards consolidated democracy in many of the countries that the United Nations has been involved in would seem to support this conclusion.[28] If the underlying social and economic variables are critical, how should the UN's democracy promotion efforts be designed and implemented? How should our expectations of outcomes be conditioned?

The role of the United Nations in this debate, given its particular characteristics, has a number of dimensions. Firstly, the organization has tended to be mostly involved in the lesser-developed countries and in those with the most challenging political situations (compared, for example, with actors involved in promoting democracy primarily in 'transitional' regions such as Eastern Europe). This is partly the reason why the record, in terms of having a substantial impact on building democracy, has been modest: the task has been so formidable. Secondly, local conditions and circumstances ultimately determine if a society embraces democratic forms of governance – and not an external actor. This is a fact that applies to all actors involved in democracy assistance and promotion. However, given the political constraints that the United Nations works under (alluded to above), the organization has been involved in societies where the local conditions and political élites have not been well disposed to democratic transition or consolidation. Thus, the United Nations may be invited to be involved in societies that are not ripe for meaningful democratic progress – sometimes by disingenuous political élites who may wish to legitimize their rule. Yet the United Nations generally has to accept a request; it has to approach a situation in good faith, even if it turns out to be an impossible situation.

Do international assistance activities promote democratic processes that are sustainable?

Democratic processes can be expensive; and it is important that the systems and processes which international entities support in developing countries are not beyond the means of such countries. There have been concerns that international democracy assistance is donor-led and donor-dependent, that it ignores the issues of affordability and long-term sustainability, "putting in place organizations, institutions, and processes that poor countries are unable to finance on their own, sometimes undermining more sustainable alternatives".[29] If international democracy assistance programs can be overly 'top-down', donor driven and pre-occupied with elections, then the corollary of this is that more emphasis should be attached to more modest bottom-up, demand-driven assistance. The United Nations works ultimately through governments, often on elaborate and expensive "top-down" democracy projects, and sometimes involving large numbers of international staff in high-profile one-off elections. Follow-on elections do not always meet the same standards. Therefore, the United Nations would seem to be (partially) vulnerable to the criticism that it does not promote sustainable practices and that it does not have much impact at the grass-roots level. This could apply in the most high-profile cases – such as Cambodia in 1993 – and with respect to the electoral assistance activities of the United Nations. This is partly because it works on the basis of specific elections, and the resources it can employ are often tied to political circumstances which can change from one year to the next. In terms of electoral activities, the United Nations cannot make a multi-year commitment to the deepening of democratic norms and practices, independently of other factors. However, the broad range of UN democracy-related activities involves many other governance sectors and programmes aimed at and including civil society, non-governmental organizations, and cross-party actors. It would therefore be wrong to conclude that the United Nations is restricted to unsustainable or excessively top-down electoral exercises.

Do international actors engaged in democracy assistance and promotion apply or impose a particular model of democracy?

It would not be surprising if the different actors involved in democracy assistance and promotion approached their work with different ideological and normative premises. Whilst democracy is rule for and by the people, there are clearly different emphases in its application, and these differences are reflected in the doctrine and practice of actors involved in democracy promotion. The USA's democracy promotion has a clear agenda, for example.[30] Ideologically, it reflects a commitment to liberal democracy, free market economics, and formal democratic procedures, rather than welfare outcomes. It also clearly reflects a commitment to US economic and strategic interests. Countries outside the US sphere of interest are less likely to receive assistance than those within, and the decision on which political actors receive assistance reflects the nature of their relationship with the USA. This is not the promotion of a "level playing field"; it intentionally privileges certain political ideas and actors above others for both pragmatic and ideological reasons. Other national democracy promotion programmes – such as those of West European states – also have their own agenda.

In theory, the United Nations is free from such an overtly ideological approach. The UN's *Agenda for Democratization* stated that "it is not for the United Nations to offer a model of democratization or democracy or to promote democracy in a specific case. Indeed, to do so could be counter-productive to the process of democratization that, in order to take root and to flourish, must derive from the society itself. Each society must be able to choose the form, pace and character of its democratization process."[31] The UN's approach is sensitive to cultural difference as well as being, generally, politically impartial. The United Nations pursues its work with a view to building the capacity of communities to develop their own forms of participation and collective decision-making, in the context of indigenous social conditions.

Yet no form of intervention – even if it is welcomed with open arms – is value-free. All substantial forms of intervention have an impact upon the future of a political community – if not, there would be no point in undertaking them. The whole concepts of "national" representation, equality, individual rights of citizenship, and secular and accountable forms of civil authority are premised upon the liberal vein of democracy. In some settings this is a departure from traditional – including familial, clan, religious – structures of authority, even if it is not "imposed". Is democracy based upon universal equality, secular political authority, and individual rights – however sensitively applied – congruent with all cultures and religions? Some argue otherwise: "the liberal principle of individuation and other liberal ideas are culturally and historically specific. As such a political system based on them cannot claim universal validity."[32]

The United Nations has a number of characteristics that seem to place it aside from other actors engaged with democracy promotion and assistance. In theory, political analysts are more likely to view the UN's assistance as impartial to local political dynamics. The United Nations generally becomes involved at the request of the host government and is very sensitive to issues of sovereignty and jurisdiction. At the same time, the involvement of the organization is conditional upon certain standards that are supposed to insulate it from exploitation and manipulation by the host government. Far from imposing or promoting a particular form of democracy, one might say that the United Nations is more likely to be overly even-handed and uninvolved.

How does the background of a particular country (its experience of democracy or otherwise) have a bearing upon the UN's success? How does (and how should) this background of experiences with democracy condition the UN's input?

Clearly the background of a society has a strong bearing upon the success of an external actor that is attempting to promote or assist democracy. Societies with a history of pluralism and democracy, with a strong civil society and developed civil institutions, and a sense of nation, even if interrupted by a period of conflict, are more likely to benefit from democracy assistance and promotion. Societies with little democratic tradition, with a weaker or oppressed civil society, will have greater difficulty embracing the ethos of democracy. A further, and more sensitive, issue is the level of socio-economic development, and whether there are foundational prerequisites for the existence of democracy. A key concern here is whether the UN involvement is timed and structured to take these foundational issues into consideration, rather than just reacting to short-term democratic impulses. Ignoring social and economic issues threatens the effectiveness of promoting democracy. Yet to engage in such issues brings the United Nations into controversial territory – making judgements about whether the people are "ready" for democracy, and whether democracy should be balanced against other priority areas such as development and stability. The decision for the United Nations to be involved and the timing of this would appear to be based less upon a scientific judgement of criteria or conditions, but on political factors.

In the electoral field the success of the United Nations would appear to be dependent upon local conditions. The organization essentially provides a technical service and cannot – and does not attempt to – fundamentally change society. Given the small size of the Electoral Assistance Division of the UN Department of Political Affairs, it is not possible to have experts on every possible situation that they are called to assess and possibly become involved in. They therefore apply a fairly standard set of approaches to every situation, without in-depth intelligence. However, in the broader governance assistance work of the United Nations, the UN units involved – such as the UNDP – do reflect real expertise through networks of residential in-country missions.

Does democracy assistance and promotion alter the nature of political community, or the political, social, or cultural dynamics of the recipient state?

The issue of impact is one of the most difficult questions relating to democracy promotion and assistance. Even analysts who are supportive of democracy assistance are cautious about its impact. But aside from the rather academic question of long-term impact there are more immediate problems related to managing the local political situation inside a target state. UN actors and the international community in general are faced with a sensitive decision in assisting democracy in certain circumstances. Most people in this field would recognize that it is not simply the process that matters, but also the results. Ideally, the process will marginalize militants and encourage pluralism and inclusive politics. However, this implies that external actors involved in promoting and assisting democracy should "push" the process in a certain direction in order to favour certain outcomes, which runs counter to the principle of a "level playing field".

In Bosnia the high representative and other international actors have gone to lengths to promote electoral outcomes which they thought represented the best chance of promoting the international agenda, in some cases using methods that would be considered unacceptable elsewhere or even in themselves "undemocratic". This has included the dismissal of officials judged to be counter to the aims of the operation, reconciliation, or democracy.[33] Indeed, under the Dayton Accords, the high representative was established to "facilitate" efforts by the parties and to mobilize and coordinate the activities of the many organizations and agencies involved in the civilian aspects of the peace settlement. The high representative was also granted "final authority" to interpret the accords as they applied to the civilian implementation of the peace settlement. From March 1998 to November 2002, the different high representatives dismissed, suspended, or banned from public office 100 elected officials at all levels of government – including a former prime minister of the Bosnian Federation, a president of Republika Srpska, and a member of the Bosnian presidency.[34] Similarly, the issue of consultation raises similar dilemmas, in terms of the local political actors who are given access to the process.

The United Nations can be in a difficult position as it deals with local political actors, some of whom may have dubious democratic credentials. It must, in principle, approach any situation with the objective of supporting a level playing field. It must also engage all major political actors as a matter of necessity. In practice, however, it must guide the process towards positive outcomes when it can.

Can democracy be in tension with other demands or public goods in post-conflict societies?

There is often pressure from the international community to move towards democracy in the countries in which the United Nations is involved. However, there is evidence that this can be in tension with other values or public goods – such as peace-building, reconciliation, efficient provision of public services, perhaps even economic reconstruction – especially in conflict and post-conflict situations. Early or ill-timed elections in post-conflict or delicate political situations can be hazardous – as experience of Angola and Burundi demonstrates.[35] They can exacerbate existing tensions and result in support for nationalists or for patterns of voting that reflect wartime allegiances, as in Bosnia.[36] On the other hand, it could be said that encouraging local parties to accept responsibility for their own futures earlier is necessary. In addition, it could be argued that democracy can weaken militant forces, as candidates opposed to reconciliation and integration might be seen as obstacles to the delivery of international aid.[37] Yet surely a tight and inflexible deadline for 'democracy' can be unhelpful: how then to balance the impulse and pressure for democracy with local sensitivities?

Amongst the actors involved in democracy assistance and promotion the United Nations can certainly find itself in the position of supporting various activities which may not all be perfectly complementary, especially in post-conflict societies. For example, the democracy that Burundi experienced – including the elections of 1993 – did little to help society. Indeed, elections may well have played a role in the ensuing instability and violence because they exacerbated an atmosphere of divisive political competition in a tense social environment. Ahmedou Ould-Abdallah served as the UN Secretary-General's special representative for Burundi between 1993 and 1995. He reflected that "majority rule simply could not be sustained given the realities of Burundi's political and security situation", and "in many African countries the introduction of democracy should be allied with a ten- to twenty-year transitional period of constitutional power sharing. Democratic habits and traditions are not formed overnight."[38] In other situations there has been pressure to organize and hold elections – sometimes as the end point of the international community's involvement in a conflicted society – when a longer-term commitment that does not necessarily include early elections might be more appropriate. The United Nations must sometimes accept the remit when circumstances are far from ideal, or even untenable. The result can be less than favourable, as in Angola in 1992 or in Bosnia in 2002, where "Bosnians elected to power the same nationalist parties that had torn their country apart in the first place".[39]

Concluding observations

The United Nations – mainly through the UN Development Programme and on a lesser level the Electoral Assistance Division of the Department of Political Affairs – has had a modestly successful although not dramatic impact upon the countries in which it has assisted democracy and democratization. Whilst Freedom House's assessments present a mixed picture for the countries in which the United Nations has been involved, it is important to consider the enormous tasks that the United Nations confronted in most of these countries. If we consider the cases where the United Nations has had a major electoral or democracy assistance role – Cambodia, Bosnia, Western Sahara, Angola, El Salvador, Eritrea, Haiti, Mozambique, Nicaragua, South Africa, Liberia, Kosovo, East Timor – the record is not wholly positive. The extent to which durable institutions have been created in some of these cases is questionable. The quality of democracy – accountability, transparency in political decision-making, an ethos of participation and inclusion, and a constructive civil society – is also questionable. In some cases these elements are completely absent, in the context of violence, nationalist/ethnic extremism, and corruption. The 1993 electoral process in Cambodia was a huge undertaking and largely successful. However, a volatile post-election power-sharing arrangement collapsed within a few years. In 1997 Second Prime Minister Hun Sen's Cambodian People's Party ousted First Prime Minister Prince Norodom Ranariddh and drove many senior government officials and members of parliament into exile. With the 1998 election, which promised a return to democracy, the country regressed into familiar patterns of intimidation and violence. The Freedom House annual assessment of democracy, assigning countries "free", "partly free", or "not free" by averaging their political rights and civil liberties ratings, has assessed Cambodia "not free" consistently in recent years, and according to its end-of-the-century survey, a "restricted democratic practice".[40]

In most cases the United Nations can only facilitate progress when local conditions are conducive to this. When conditions are not, or when the UN's approach is not entirely appropriate for the nature of local conditions, success is unlikely. Angola provides an illustration of this. The September 1992 election should have brought some 17 years of conflict to an end. With apparent Soviet and US consensus, the role of the United Nations was to monitor the elections and the other elements of the accord. However, the number of personnel assigned to the country was widely felt to be inadequate to help to organize the elections in time and promote confidence in the whole process. Another problem was the nature of the election, which was largely "winner takes all" – not an appropriate framework for national reconciliation after so many years of conflict and no experience of democracy. In addition, the United Nations had not insisted on thorough demobilization and disarmament, so both sides had the means to take up arms if the outcome of the election did not suit. The UN Secretariat also had to work within the confines of a number of other political pressures that were beyond its control. After the elections the country returned to civil war. Freedom House assessed Angola "not free" throughout the 1990s, apart from "partially free" in 1991–1992. Its end-of-the-century survey assessed Angola as "authoritarian".

Huntington's study of "third-wave" democracies found that by the late 1980s external observers had become a "familiar and indispensable presence" in almost all transitional elections.[41] Yet the major democracy assistance operations most clearly demonstrate the limitations of outside parties attempting to install democracy through elections. UN assistance is effective when applied to situations where a tradition of democracy is already ingrained, even if latent, where a certain level of social stability exists, and where facilitation and confidence-building are necessary to ensure trust and validation. In major operations in divided or post-conflict societies UN involvement seems fruitful only when a convergence of forces – both within the society and internationally – coalesce around a democratic future and accept the new rules of the game. Such a convergence was not present for Angola in 1992, but was for Mozambique. The social and economic context, and the policies and attitudes of powerful local and external actors, are the decisive factors, rather than the presence of the United Nations. For the UN to play a fruitful role in the facilitation or channeling of democratic convergence it must apply policies and electoral activities that are sensitive to the local context and given sufficient material support. Is "facilitation" of democracy a decisive role? Given that facilitation is only successful in the context of democratic convergence, it may be logical to suggest that the UN role is not decisive. Yet even when convergence does occur, democracy does not necessarily take root as a result of inadequate capacity and institutions, lack of trust, and lack of resources. This is where the United Nations can have an enduring impact, yet always contingent upon variables beyond its sphere of influence.

Notes

1. Held, David. 1996. *Models of Democracy*, 2nd edn. Cambridge: Polity Press.
2. Diamond, Larry. 1995. "Promoting Democracy in the 1990s: Actors and Instruments, Issues and Imperatives", a report to the Carnegie Commission on Preventing Deadly Conflict. Carnegie Corporation of New York, December.
3. See Inoguchi, Takashi, Edward Newman, and John Keane (eds). 1998. *The Changing Nature of Democracy*. Tokyo: United Nations University Press.
4. See Burnell, Peter (ed.). 2000. *Democracy Assistance: International Co-operation for Democratization*. London: Frank Cass.
5. For example, the USAID's four "democracy sectors" are rule of law, elections, civil society, and governance. The 2003 budget allocation for democracy promotion/conflict prevention is $200 million ($80 million more than in 2002).

6. Ikenberry, John. 2000. "America's liberal grand strategy: Democracy and national security in the post-war era", in Michael Cox, John Ikenberry, and Takashi Inoguchi (eds) *American Democracy Promotion: Impulses, Strategies, and Impacts*. Oxford: Oxford University Press.

7. Robinson, William. 2000. "Promoting capitalist polyarchy: The case of Latin America", in Michael Cox, John Ikenberry, and Takashi Inoguchi (eds) *American Democracy Promotion: Impulses, Strategies, and Impacts*. Oxford: Oxford University Press.

8. *Ibid.*

9. Treaty on European Union (consolidated version incorporating the changes made by the Treaty of Amsterdam), signed on 2 October 1997, Arts 6 and 7. See Pridham, Geoffrey, Eric Herring, and George Sanford (eds). 1994. *Building Democracy? The International Dimension of Democratisation in Eastern Europe*. London: Leicester University Press.

10. Eguizabal, Cristina. 2000. "Latin American foreign policies and human rights", in David P. Forsythe (ed.) *Human Rights and Comparative Foreign Policy*. Tokyo: United Nations University Press. See Farer, Tom (ed.). 1996. *Beyond Sovereignty. Collectively Defending Democracy in the Americas*. Baltimore: Johns Hopkins University Press.

11. Hearn, Julie. 1999. *Foreign Aid, Democratisation and Civil Society in Africa: A Study of South Africa, Ghana and Uganda*, IDS Discussion Papers No. 368. Brighton: University of Sussex.

12. Joyner, Christopher C. 2001. "The United Nations and democracy", *Global Governance*, Vol. 5, No. 3. See also Newman, Edward. 2001. "(Re)building political society: The UN and democratization", in Edward Newman and Oliver P. Richmond (eds) *The United Nations and Human Security*. Basingstoke: Palgrave.

13. See Rich, Roland. 2001. "Bringing democracy into international law", *Journal of Democracy*, Vol. 12, No. 3.

14. GA Res. 49/30, 7 December 1994.

15. The report was presented to the General Assembly on 20 December 1996 (A/51/761) as "Support by the United Nations system of the efforts of Governments to promote and consolidate new or restored democracies", a supplement to two previous reports on democratization.

16. Boutros-Ghali, Boutros. 1999. *Unvanquished. A US-UN Saga*. New York: Random House.

17. Held, note 1 above.

18. See Ludwig, Robin. 2001. "Letting the People Decide: The Evolution of United Nations Electoral Assistance", ACUNS Occasional Paper, Yale University.

19. Gyimah-Boadi, E. 1999. "The cost of doing nothing", *Journal of Democracy*, Vol. 10, No. 4.

20. See Lipset, Seymour Martin. 1959. "Some social requisites of democracy: Economic developments and political legitimacy", *American Political Science Review*, Vol. 53, No. 1; Lipset, Seymour Martin. 1963. *Political Man: The Social Basis of Politics*. Garden City, NY: Anchor Books; Lipset, Seymour Martin. 1994. "The social requisites of democracy revisited", *American Sociological Review*, Vol. 59, February; Moore, Barrington. 1967. *The Social Origins of Dictatorship and Democracy*. Boston, MA: Beacon Press; Dahl, Robert A. 1971. *Polyarchy: Participation and Opposition*. New Haven: Yale University Press.

21. See Rich, note 13 above.

22. See Whitehead, Laurence (ed.). 1996. *The International Dimensions of Democratization. Europe and the Americas*. Oxford: Oxford University Press.

23. Rose, Gideon. 2000. "Democracy promotion and American foreign policy – A review essay", *International Security*, Vol. 25, No. 3.

24. Carothers, Thomas. 1999. *Aiding Democracy Abroad: The Learning Curve*. Washington,

DC: Carnegie Endowment for International Peace. See also Youngs, Richard. 2001. *The European Union and the Promotion of Democracy. Europe's Mediterranean and Asian Policies.* Oxford: Oxford University Press; Burnell, Peter. 2000. "Democracy assistance: The state of the discourse", in Peter Burnell (ed.) *Democracy Assistance: International Co-operation for Democratization.* London: Frank Cass – "generally speaking democracy assistance is neither a necessary nor a sufficient condition for a democratic opening or for building democracy, although it could come close to being essential in some countries Outsiders lend support to a process that is locally driven."

25. Carothers, *ibid.*

26. Hay, Lao Mong. 1998. "Building democracy in Cambodia: Problems and prospects", in Frederick Z. Brown and David G. Timberman (eds) *Cambodia and the International Community: The Quest for Peace, Development and Democracy.* Singapore: Asia Society, Institute of Southeast Asian Studies. For an in-depth study see Peou, Sorpong. 2000. *Intervention and Change in Cambodia: Towards Democracy?* London: Macmillan; Peou, Sorpong. 1997. *Conflict Neutralization in the Cambodia War: From Battlefield to Ballot-Box.* Oxford: Oxford University Press.

27. Carothers, Thomas. 2000. *The Clinton Record on Democracy Promotion*, Carnegie Endowment for International Peace. New York: Carnegie Foundation.

28. For example, while not an infallible judge, Freedom House's assessments present a mixed picture for the countries in which the United Nations has been involved. In the "Freedom in the World Country Ratings 1972–2001", of the 70 countries in which the UN Electoral Assistance Division and the UNDP had had some form of involvement at some time over the 1990s, 13 were judged as "free", 40 "partially free", and 17 "not free" in 2001.

29. Ottaway, Marina and Theresa Chung. 1999. "Debating democracy assistance. Toward a new paradigm", *Journal of Democracy*, Vol. 10, No. 4. "Assistance has driven up the cost of democracy for many countries. Donors have encouraged expensive practices and institutions, but they will not finance them forever."

30. Carothers, note 24 above; Cox, Michael, John Ikenberry, and Takashi Inoguchi (eds). 2000. *American Democracy Promotion: Impulses, Strategies, and Impacts.* Oxford: Oxford University Press.

31. Boutros-Ghali, Boutros. 1996. *An Agenda for Democratization.* New York: United Nations.

32. Parakh, Bhikhu. 1993. "The cultural particularity of liberal democracy", in David Held (ed.) *Prospects for Democracy: North, South, East, West.* Cambridge: Polity Press.

33. See for example Caplan, Richard. 2002. *A New Trusteeship? The International Administration of War-torn Territories*, Adelphi Paper 341. London: International Institute for Strategic Studies.

34. Simon Chesterman, Ch. 4 in this volume.

35. Ould-Abdallah, Ahmedou. 2000. *Burundi on the Brink 1993–1995. A UN Special Envoy Reflects on Preventive Diplomacy.* Washington, DC: USIP Press.

36. See Pugh, Michael. 2001. "Elections and 'protectorate democracy' in south-east Europe", in Edward Newman and Oliver P. Richmond (eds) *The United Nations and Human Security.* Basingstoke: Palgrave.

37. Caplan, note 33 above.

38. Ould-Abdallah, note 35 above.

39. Chesterman, note 34 above.

40. Freedom House. 1999. *Democracy's Century: A Survey of Global Political Change in the 20th Century.* New York: Freedom House.

41. Huntington, Samuel P. 1991. *The Third Wave. Democratization in the Late Twentieth Century.* Norman: University of Oklahoma Press.

9

UNDP experience in long-term democracy assistance

Richard Ponzio

In earlier times there were lengthy discussions on whether one country or another was yet "fit for democracy". This changed only recently, with the recognition that the question was itself wrong-headed: a country does not have to be judged fit for democracy, rather is has to become fit through democracy. This is a truly momentous change.[1]

The last two decades of the twentieth century witnessed a historic shift in the global spread of democracy.[2] Of 147 countries with data, 121 – with 68 per cent of the world's people – had some or all of the elements of formal democracy in 2000.[3] This compares with only 54 countries, with 46 per cent of the world's people, in 1980. Since then 81 countries have taken significant steps in democratization while six have regressed.[4] Slowly recognizing the value of strengthening democratic institutions and processes to achieve broad socio-economic and political objectives in member countries, several bodies within the UN system today seek actively to reinforce national democratic efforts through technical and financial assistance. This chapter turns attention to the UN Development Programme's recent experience with long-term democracy assistance initiatives.

Along with the Office of the High Commissioner for Human Rights, the UN Office for Project Services, the UN Development Fund for Women, the UN Volunteers, the UN Capital Development Fund, the UN Centre for Human Settlements, and the UN Secretariat departments dealing with political affairs, economic and social affairs, and peace-keeping, the UNDP made the promotion of democratic governance a core operational activity in the 1990s. From support for electoral management bodies and parliaments to facilitating constitutional reforms and decentralization processes, the UNDP's approach to democracy assistance can be labelled primarily as "long-term" and "developmental", giving primacy to building indigenous governing capacity. This often stands in marked contrast with – but may be complementary to – short-term interventions associated mainly with political efforts to stabilize a country and build the foundations for recovery and peace. Consequently, the UNDP's contributions to democracy-building rarely capture significant media coverage and public interest, in a manner comparable to that received, for example, by many UN electoral assistance missions in post-conflict environments.

Following a short review of the evolution of the UNDP's involvement in long-term democracy assistance, the chapter will raise the following research questions in scrutinizing two distinct types of UNDP engagement, namely electoral systems support and assistance to legislative bodies.

- What is the UNDP's record in building indigenous capacity within formal and informal democratic institutions?
- To what extent is it possible to draw conclusions and "best practices" from limited experience in different contexts?

In examining these questions, the chapter will help the larger study on "The UN's Role in Democratization" address the broader and more complicated question:

- Does the UN system, through agencies such as the UNDP, have a decisive and enduring impact upon democratization in a country?

On the whole, the UNDP can be characterized as a relative newcomer to the field of democracy assistance with far to travel on the learning curve. Although the agency's long-term developmental perspective and close relations to a host country position it to make marked contributions, mixed performance on the ground, donor dependency, and the high-risk nature of aiding democracy (particularly in post-conflict environments) combine to caution those initiating new projects. In addition to reflecting on the above queries, the concluding section shares some critical observations about emerging areas of UNDP democratic capacity-building, including support for organizations and government institutions dealing with human rights, media and corporate accountability, local governance strengthening, access to justice, civilian oversight of the security sector, and improving the status of women and minorities in politics. It also comments on the need for greater theoretical and empirical work on the relationship between international organizations and democratization.

Evolution of UNDP involvement in democracy assistance

As discussed earlier in this volume, the United Nations entered the frontier of democracy assistance during the great era of decolonization of the 1960s and 1970s. Following its creation in 1966, the UNDP began slowly to provide financial and technical assistance to small-scale electoral projects. With the Cold War at its height in the 1970s and early 1980s and the movement to centralize resources and power in many newly independent states, the UNDP and other international organizations were often precluded from other forms of democracy assistance, such as strengthening legislative bodies, promoting access to justice and human rights, and supporting decentralization and strong local governance. Instead, the UNDP's early governance work primarily concentrated in the less politically sensitive areas of public administration support and civil service reform.

Various strands of the new political economy of the 1970s and 1980s (public-choice theory, rent-seeking behaviour, directly unproductive profit-seeking activities, and the new institutional economics[5]) greatly influenced the crafting of governance assistance priorities preoccupied with creating efficient institutions and rules that seek to promote markets and ensure that public services are managed effectively. Creating the conditions for sound economic management then became paramount to other governance considerations, such as expanding space for civic participation and ensuring access to justice for the poor and marginalized.[6]

Initially cast in the late 1980s and early 1990s as facilitating economic liberalization, today's "good governance" debate shifted steadily in the past decade towards improving and reforming the functioning of democratic institutions. The UNDP and a growing number of external development actors now afford as much attention to the "deepening of democracy" and establishing active, creative leadership roles for non-state actors as to traditional governance priorities such as contract enforcement and the reduction of transaction costs. What triggered this change? For one thing, renewed support for democracy, the rule of law, and the protection of basic human freedoms in the post-Cold War era weakened the arguments of "minimalist state" proponents. At the same time, the democratic resurgence in many countries brought growing numbers of leaders in line with basic norms of accountability and transparency.

Beginning in the early 1990s, the UN Development Programme started to move beyond traditional public sector management concerns and modest decentralization programmes to dealing with sensitive governance areas such as human rights, electoral management bodies, legislative support, and judicial and constitutional reform. From 1997, total UNDP allocations for programmes in support of democratic governing institutions were US$70,406,184 in 1997, $178,585,586 in 1998, and

$363,604,761 in 1999.[7] Responding to the growth in transitional democracies, the electoral assistance role played by the UNDP in the last decade has, in particular, served as a key entry point for undertaking a "new generation" of governance projects. Some key factors contributing to the UN Development Programme's growing involvement in policy and institutional strengthening include the lowering of ideological tensions since the end of the Cold War; the emerging consensus among donors and within programme countries on the need for certain economic and now political reforms; the heightened flows of information from information and communications technology advances; and the frustrations with – and consequent decreases in – traditional forms of development assistance.[8]

In recent years the UNDP has emerged as a major provider of policy advice and capacity-development technical assistance in the area of democratic governance (see Table 9.1). The UNDP's annual report of 2001 reconfirms the agency's heightened "assistance to countries managing democratic transitions through the coordination of donor support to electoral processes, the facilitation of national dialogue and support to promote civil society participation in political reform".[9] By far the greatest share of estimated country-level programme expenditure in 2001 from combined donor/local resources was delivered in the areas of governance, amounting to US$801 million or 45 per cent of total UNDP programme expenditure.[10] The development agency views its role as an

Table 9.1 UNDP sections involved in the "practice" of democratic governance

Research and policy guidance	Information clearing-house/coordination	Programme country operations
Democratic Governance Group/Bureau for Development Policy	Regional bureaux and regional governance programmes (e.g. PARAGON in Asia and Gold in the Pacific)	Operations/democratic governance technical specialists in 166 countries
Oslo Governance Centre/Bureau for Development Policy	Subregional resource facilities SURFs	Partnerships with OHCHR, UNOPS, UNIFEM, UNCDF, UNV, UNCHS, and UN Secretariat
Bureau for Crisis Prevention and Recovery	Bureau for Crisis Prevention and Recovery	
Human Development Report Office and Office of Development Studies	Democratic governance e-mail network and website	

agent of change and a trusted partner of national governments that can broker dialogue on sensitive issues of democratic governance with all actors – state, civil society, private sector, and other donors.

Besides on-the-ground, project- or institution-specific democracy assistance, over the past decade the UNDP has helped to prepare more than 270 regional, national, and subnational human development reports that addressed democratic-governance-related issues as integral dimensions of human development. Through disaggregated data analysis and ambitious governance reform recommendations, the reports serve as a catalytic tool for informed decision-making by policy-makers in diverse regions. The global *Human Development Report 2002,* on the theme "Deepening democracy in a fragmented world", placed political reforms and democracy assistance squarely at the centre of the UNDP's poverty reduction efforts.[11] Together with UNDP country advisory services, the human development reports are pressuring "good governance" proponents to reorient their priorities from the exigencies of economic growth and efficiency to those governance policies and institutions that best promote greater freedom, genuine day-to-day citizen participation, and sustainable human development. It is on these fundamental points that governance thinking within the UNDP and the broader UN system – and the policy prescriptions and programming that follow – challenges the conventional wisdom of the international financial institutions.

A brief survey and analysis of the UNDP's democratic assistance interventions in the areas of electoral and legislative support are summarized in the subsequent sections of this chapter. Whilst far from exhaustive, the following assessment will help to address the questions raised earlier about the UNDP's long-term democracy work and its capacity for making a difference in people's lives. Performance varies from country to country and from intervention to intervention. As with arguably all actors entering the burgeoning field of external democracy assistance, considerable room for improvement remains and progress rarely proceeds in a linear fashion. If the UNDP heeds the hard lessons from its own experience as well as others, it can begin to respond effectively to the all-out sceptics of democracy aid and overcome the obstacles and poor planning that contributed to past failures.

Long-term support for elections and electoral management bodies

Free and fair elections sustain the political legitimacy of democratic governments.[12] They are prerequisites for the establishment of strong governing institutions and good governance – which are, in turn, prerequisites for poverty alleviation and sustaining human development. As a result, the UN Development Programme has expanded its role, over the past decade, in supporting the state institution(s) charged with overseeing and managing electoral processes as a significant component of the organization's democratic institution-building activities.

The United Nations began its involvement in electoral assistance during the 1960s and 1970s when the Trusteeship Council assisted with the observation or supervision of some 30 plebiscites, referenda, and elections in various parts of the world. Between 1976 and 1990, the UNDP financed several small projects that provided electoral assistance on specific technical aspects of electoral processes and on the establishment of infrastructure necessary to conduct elections.

Since 1992, the UN Electoral Assistance Division's (EAD) response to increased requests for electoral assistance has relied extensively on the UNDP's financial and personnel resources. The UNDP's permanent field presence has proved a *sine qua non* for UN electoral assistance, as UNDP resident representatives/resident coordinators and staff provided established relationships with government, bilateral donors, non-governmental organizations, and political parties, logistical infrastructure, country knowledge, and financial resources for assistance. EAD staff normally contributed technical and political advice, but remained in-country for only brief periods.

From 1991 to 1999, the United Nations received requests for electoral assistance from 89 countries. The UNDP assisted 68 of those countries, including 40 in Africa, 13 in Latin America and the Caribbean, eight in Asia, five in Europe and the Commonwealth of Independent States, and two in Arab states (see Table 9.2). The Democratic Governance Group, part of the UNDP's Bureau for Development Policy, is the focal point within the UNDP for electoral assistance. Its electoral activities include liaising with EAD, managing global programmes for electoral assistance, conducting research on ways in which electoral bodies can be developed into permanent and sustainable governing institutions, and providing technical assistance in designing country-anchored capacity-development programmes. In the latter part of the 1990s, the UNDP started providing long-term democratic development assistance, as part of a broader governance support agenda.

Principal areas of UNDP electoral support

A study in 2000 on recent UNDP electoral support experience found a number of types of assistance from 10 country case studies (Table 9.3).[13] Increasingly, the UNDP invests technical and financial resources in independent electoral management bodies (EMBs) in order to promote

Table 9.2 List of countries where the UNDP provided assistance, 1991–1999

Albania	Mexico
Angola	Mozambique
Argentina	Namibia
Armenia	Nicaragua
Bangladesh	Niger
Benin	Nigeria
Brazil	Pakistan
Burkina Faso	Panama
Burundi	Paraguay
Cambodia	Peru
Central African Republic	Philippines
Chad	Romania
Colombia	Rwanda
Comoros	Sierra Leone
Republic of Congo	South Africa
Djibouti	Suriname
El Salvador	Togo
Equatorial Guinea	Uganda
Eritrea	Tanzania
Ethiopia	Yemen
Gabon	Zambia
Gambia	Zimbabwe
Ghana	
Guinea	**Total: 60**
Guinea Bissau	
Guyana	Reports and minor assistance
Haiti	
Honduras	Algeria
Indonesia	Cameroon
Kenya	Democratic Republic of Congo
Kyrgyzstan	Cote d'Ivoire
Lesotho	Nepal
Liberia	Senegal
Macedonia	Seychelles
Madagascar	Uzbekistan
Malawi	**Total: 8**
Mali	
Mauritius	*Sum total: 68*

political stability and build long-term capacity for the professional organization of elections. This new approach is partly in response to the diminished need for direct hands-on involvement of international electoral experts.[14] Although many countries continue to depend on financial and in-kind material assistance for elections from the international community, international experts are serving increasingly as "advisors or

Table 9.3 UNDP's electoral support: Matrix of 10 country case studies

Types of assistance	Case study countries*							
	Bangladesh (1997–present)	Brazil (1993–1994)	Cambodia (1998)	Kyrgyzstan (1995)	Guyana (1997)	Indonesia (1999)	Malawi (1993–1994)	Mozambique (1999)
Coordination of technical assistance	✓	✓	✓	✓	✓	✓	✓	✓
Supporting electoral management bodies	✓	✓		✓	✓	✓	✓	✓
Coordination and logistical support of international observers (with EAD assistance)			✓	✓	✓	✓		✓
Computerization of voter registry	✓	✓						✓
Voter and civic education	✓		✓	✓			✓	✓
Coordination of donor or government funds		✓	✓	✓	✓	✓	✓	✓
Training of election officials	✓	✓				✓		✓
Support to subnational elections	✓							
Longer-term capacity-building of election officials	✓			✓				✓

*These activities reflect major and minor interventions

215

technical specialists supporting initiatives and activities managed directly and fully by national EMBs"[15].

Long-term electoral capacity-development support: The case of Bangladesh

Following years of military rule in Bangladesh, elections in 1986 and 1988 that were boycotted by the opposition, and widespread political unrest promoted by a broad-based movement, power was handed over to a caretaker government 1990; it then proceeded to organize general elections in February 1991. Political instability, however, continued after the election, and 15 by-elections were held between 1991 and 1992. After yet a further deterioration in the political situation, a caretaker government was formed and oversaw the next parliamentary election in June 1996, in a tight timeframe of 90 days. The election was viewed to be relatively free, fair, and peaceful by international and national observers, and voter turnout rose to 73 per cent, compared with 40 per cent in 1991.

Following a request from the government of Bangladesh in April 1996, the UNDP provided extensive support to Bangladesh's 1996 parliamentary election, including training police officials, providing voters with relevant information on the electoral process, and assisting the co-ordination of international election observers.[16] The UNDP's immediate support activities underscored the long-term needs of the country's Election Commission. Consequently, the UNDP was encouraged by the government to formulate what became the project titled "Strengthening the Election Commission for Improvement in the Electoral Process".

With a budget of US$10 million for the period 1997–2001, the project sought to help the Election Commission strengthen democratic electoral processes in Bangladesh. More concretely, it aimed to develop capacity at three different levels: the Election Commission (by improving management capacity, the voter registration system, and the electoral database); election officials with duties at local levels (by strengthening the Election Training Institute); and the electorate (through voter education and civic awareness activities). In designing the project, it was envisioned that 400,000 polling officials and 370,200 polling agents, domestic election observers, and members of the Electoral Enquiry Committee would be trained through Bangladesh's Election Training Institute, thus strengthening the performance of several partners involved in organizing an election.

Results of the project

As a result of the project, progress was reported in the following areas.
• The Election Commission utilized project resources to train and prepare information support materials for the municipal elections in

February 1999. Project funds were used for similar purposes during the *union parishad* elections, the city corporation elections, and the by-elections in 1997.

- The project undertook a needs assessment for the Election Commission, including the procurement, implementation, and operationalization of a nationwide electoral database and 84 district databases.
- The Electoral Training Institute organized a comprehensive training programme for electoral officials at all levels of government.
- A long-term media-based programme for civic awareness on electoral issues through ADAB (an association of NGOs) was initiated.
- The project supported the development of electoral standards manuals for use by election officials during future elections.

Long-term democratic institution-building

The specific development objective of the project was to assist Bangladesh's Election Commission in institutionalizing an efficient and transparent electoral system. Taking a broader perspective, the project was seen as an important input into the government's efforts to strengthen the democratic process in Bangladesh, so that all future elections – including by-elections, local elections, national parliamentary elections, and presidential elections – are conducted in a free and fair manner that maximizes full citizen participation. The success of UNDP-supported interventions in the preparation of elections contributed to the development of a broader UNDP governance programme (including a US$5.5 million parliamentary strengthening programme and a comprehensive local governance programme). The UNDP was further invited to facilitate dialogue among settlers and an indigenous ethnic group in Bangladesh's Chittagong Hill Tracts, following more than two decades of conflict over land rights.

Some lessons learned from the UNDP's experience in electoral support

While each country setting poses unique challenges, some global lessons can be gleaned from UNDP successes and failures in election-related activities since the 1970s.

- The UNDP's emerging comparative advantage, among a myriad of electoral assistance providers, lies in helping countries establish independent and permanent electoral bodies through long-term institutional capacity development. Besides basic training in the management of electoral systems, this includes support for legal reform, institutional restructuring, improving professional development programmes, and strengthening public information and outreach capacity, resource management, and sustainability programmes. Support for elections in Bangladesh, Mozambique, and Kyrgyztan in the 1990s led to long-term programmes that facilitated the development of electoral management bodies.

- This leads on to the question of who manages elections. Elections are organized by independent electoral commissions in 77 countries. In 43 countries elections are conducted by the government, under the supervision of an independent electoral authority. In 28 countries, elections are run exclusively by the executive branch.[17]

- Electoral assistance has provided the UNDP and the UN system with a strategic entry point for broader, long-term democratic governance programming. Successful elections are critical to establishing political legitimacy within countries seeking to make a transition towards democracy away from more authoritarian (and sometimes violent) rule. By supporting recent elections in Indonesia, Mozambique, Bangladesh, Sierra Leone, and Nigeria (albeit in a limited role), the UNDP cultivated the relationships required to support governance reform efforts in sensitive areas such as human rights, decentralization, and judicial and media independence. Successful elections and strategic governance support measures rarely translate quickly into more accountable and open governing institutions, as acutely manifested through the UNDP's struggling efforts in Sierra Leone and Nigeria.

- Effective civic and voter education programmes, both prior to and following an election, help expand democratic participation. As illustrated by the UNDP's sponsorship of national democratization gatherings prior to Malawi's 1994 general election, and the post-election civic education strategies supported by the UNDP in Cambodia, Bangladesh, Indonesia, and Kyrgyzstan, awareness-raising programmes encourage people to influence governing institutions, defend their rights by holding representatives and government officials accountable, and contribute to society through civic actions. On the other hand, several UNDP civic and voter education programmes failed to raise people's consciousness by providing inappropriate and even irrelevant information to citizens.

- Regarding UNDP support for the conduct of elections, donor coordination and resource mobilization are UNDP services that are sometimes essential to the preparation of an election. Multi-party elections are highly complex and expensive undertakings that often require a sophisticated electoral capacity and level of resources beyond the reach of many developing countries. By facilitating donor coordination (as expressed, to varying degrees of success, in the cases of Kyrgyzstan 1995, Malawi 1994, Mozambique 1994 and 1999, Indonesia 1999, Guyana 1997, and Yemen 1996), the UNDP plays a central role in mobilizing foreign assistance, including among non-resident donors.

- In terms of elections and costs, the lowest-cost elections (in US$), at around $1 to $3 per elector, are held in countries with a long electoral experience, such as the USA and most Western European countries. Other recorded examples include Chile ($1.2), Costa Rica ($1.8), and Brazil ($2.3) in Latin America; Botswana ($2.7) and Kenya ($1.8) in Africa; India ($1) and Pakistan ($0.5) in Asia; and Australia ($3.2). At the other extreme, elections held as part of broader UN peacekeeping operations, as could be expected, are the most costly.[18]
- The UNDP provides valuable support for the implementation of technical assistance programmes for elections. The technical assistance can range from comprehensive assistance covering all aspects of an election, as in Mozambique in 1994 and 1999, to targeted assistance, such as a civic education campaign or the computerization of the voter registry, as in Brazil in 1994. The UNDP provides some element of support – from coordinating logistics and a coherent donor approach to advising on general policy issues – to the implementation of technical assistance in virtually every electoral support project.

Strengthening legislative bodies and promoting democratic reforms

By giving the electorate a voice on critical public policy issues and by serving as a counterweight to other major institutions of governance, legislatures are essential to the functioning of healthy democracies. Many people often assume that parliamentarians only make laws. By virtue of their law-making functions, however, parliamentarians are required to oversee and when necessary challenge government actions. The three core functions of a legislature – law-making, oversight, and representation – serve then as the foundation of parliamentary democracy. Helping parliamentarians understand and fully utilize these powers and functions of their legislature is the fundamental purpose of external legislative assistance.

As the proportion of democratically elected governments rose in the 1990s, the number of requests for international assistance to strengthen parliaments increased significantly.[19] The UNDP, along with other aid agencies, responded to the growing demand for technical assistance in this area by making legislative assistance a core component of the agency's democratic governance work. It seeks to meet the demand to improve parliamentary performance through training programmes, research projects, seminars, and related activities that fall under the heading of "capacity-building initiatives".

Whereas in 1994 only six UNDP projects supported the legislative process or the strengthening of parliament directly, by 2001 some 40

country offices reported on programmes to strengthen legislative capacity.[20] From this group, 12 country programmes support legislative
outreach to citizens, and 15 programmes are focused on reforming organization procedures, structures, and rules. Legislative development is
a key priority for the UNDP in Africa, where parliaments are being
strengthened in 20 countries, followed by the Asia-Pacific region with
nine legislative programmes. Often initiated in fragile states recovering
from acute periods of violent conflict, many legislative assistance activities face innumerable obstacles, ranging from scarce resources and a
limited culture of accountability to high levels of mistrust and intimidation between opposition groups and the government.

Principle areas of UNDP legislative support

Legislatures have requested UNDP assistance principally in the areas of
capacity-building for legislators and staff, as well as for institutional development (the operation and functioning of the legislature itself). Other
areas of UNDP legislative assistance are outlined in Table 9.4.[21] With
rare exception, the UNDP does not, in general, provide political party
training – a growth area for some development agencies.

Legislative assistance can take the form of, *inter alia*, drafting rules of
procedure, conducting orientation programmes, strengthening the functioning of committees, providing equipment and training for transcrip-
tion, training in legislative drafting, and funding for consultations on the
budget or constitutional reform. Requests for assistance come directly
from the legislature, and both the legislators and staff are normally the
direct beneficiaries of UNDP support. A study in 2001 on recent UNDP
legislative support experience found the various types of project beneficiaries from nine country case studies (Figure 9.1).[22]

The UNDP's 2001 *Results-Oriented Annual Report* claims that in the
year 2000 two-thirds of the annual targets for UNDP support to parliamentary structures, systems, and processes were reached.[23] Examples
of the results achieved included orientation progammes for parliamentarians, the facilitation of policy dialogue on parliamentary reform among
development partners, and an improvement in internal information flows
through the timely production of parliamentary records. It should be
noted that measuring progress in the area of parliamentary support raises
several legitimate concerns, including attributional issues and an inevitable reliance on subjective, perception-based indicators. Moreover,
unrealistic short-term targets should be avoided given the long-term developmental nature of parliamentary assistance – where democratic reforms require years if not decades, rather than weeks and months, to take
root.

Table 9.4 Categories of UNDP legislative assistance

Capacity-building for legislators and legislative staff	Training of members and/or staff on issues related to their functions, roles, and responsibilities as well as professional skills development.
Institutional development	The process of strengthening the internal organization of a legislature through modernization of entities, systems, and processes.
Constituency relations	Increasing/improving legislatures' interactions with their constituents and the public in general, as well as raising the profile of the legislature.
Legislative policy development	Assistance that touches on the substance of legislation or country policy.
Gender initiatives	Activities whose key aim is to affect the gender balance in political leadership and/or highlight or impact on the legislature's role in reviewing and passing gender-sensitive legislation.
Working with civil society	Activities that focus on actors outside of the legislature (researchers, civil society organizations, and the media) who directly interact with and impact on the legislature and the legislative process.
Political party training	Activities conducted directly with party members and leaders that focus on strengthening the party's internal structures and processes, which may in turn affect their transparency and efficiency in the legislature.
Promotion of human development	This includes support for legislative committee policy deliberations and research on poverty issues, gender mainstreaming, and budget allocations.
Constitutional reform	Technical assistance (to legislatures, constitutional committees, or commissions) on drafting, amending, or creating laws and documents that make up and affect a country's constitution.

Cognizant of the shortcomings in gauging success, sufficient evidence suggests that varying degrees of parliamentary reform emerged from strategic interventions in restructuring parliamentary committees, affording new competencies for the "timely review of reports, consideration of bills, passing of laws and amendments, public hearings, and legislation to strengthen legislative functions".[24] More recently, ambitious UNDP

	Reform committees	Entire legislature	Legislature staff	Provincial offices	Donor coordination
Bangladesh		●	●		●
Ethiopia		●	●		
Haiti		●	●		
Lao PDR		●	●	●	
Mozambique	●	●	●	●	●
Peru		●	●		
Viet Nam		●	●		●
Yemen		●	●		
Zimbabwe	●	●	●		

Figure 9.1 Beneficiaries from recent UNDP legislative assistance programmes

programmes have sought to support legislative bodies in decentralizing authority and resources through legal reforms (Niger, Pakistan, and Sierra Leone) and constitutional reform in a post-conflict setting (Solomon Islands).

Facilitating decentralized, democratic governance in Niger

After decades of military rule, Niger elected a civilian president and new 83-member parliament (the National Assembly) in late 1999.[25] Immediately, the National Assembly sought ways to redress its limitations and consolidate the process of transition to democratic civilian rule. In response to a formal request by the National Assembly, the UNDP initiated in April 2001 – in close collaboration with the National Democratic Institute for International Affairs (NDI) – a project titled "Improving the Capacity and Outreach of the National Assembly". The project sought to increase the level of national debate in the consideration of new laws through the building of capacity among members of the assembly (known as "deputies") to participate more effectively in the legislative process, better exercise oversight and control of the executive branch, and increase opportunities for citizen access and input to the consolidation of the democratic process ongoing in Niger.[26]

Initially the project was designed to deliver technical support through seminars and working sessions with deputies and to provide direct technical advisory services. However, the approach was soon adapted in response to requests from legislators to leverage technical expertise in the process of reviewing draft decentralization laws, including the organization of 30 public hearings across the country that reached over 15,000 people.

The request for the project's support in facilitating public consultations on forthcoming decentralization legislation was viewed as part of an institutional strategy to increase both the representative and the legislative capacity of the deputies. The project team agreed to support the highly complex and inherently risky decentralization process, interpreting it as an opportunity to practise legislative analysis, oversight functions, and "learning by doing" about how to engage in public consultations. It also had practical links to the budget process, since decentralization implied significant changes in the allocation of resources. The speaker of the Nigar National Assembly commented:

By virtue of our approach, we also demonstrated democracy. We argued, we compromised, and we worked with citizens to find solutions to decentralization at the commune level.

Among the positive outcomes from the public consultation process was a perceived improvement in the accessibility of deputies to civil society, and more specifically their constituents, on issues of national relevance. Deputies surveyed noted that the public consultations afforded them a new way of looking at the role of committees and heightened their respect for rules and procedures, while increasing transparency in the legislative process.[27] Utilizing the decentralization laws as the cornerstone of a public consultation process further allowed for the practical demonstration of the role of the deputies in law-making, oversight, and the conduct of their representational roles. By rising above partisan positions to discuss the proposed decentralization legislation openly, the deputies instilled public confidence in the National Assembly. They sent important democratic signals, reinforcing the transition from military to civilian governance.

After numerous debates and proposed amendments following the consultations, the National Assembly passed a comprehensive decentralization plan in May 2002. Substantively amending the bill on the transfer of authority 15 times, as well as a bill delimiting 265 newly created communes, the National Assembly fully exercised its constitutional independence in the process *vis-à-vis* the executive.[28] In 2003 local officials elected to manage the communes were able to make decisions previously under the purview of government ministries based in the capital.

To be sure, the favourable initial outcomes from recent assistance in Niger will be tested by the ongoing implementation phase of the decentralization plan. Within the National Assembly itself, several obstacles continue to limit the legislature's ability to play its constitutional role fully, such as the poor administration of legislative scheduling and human resources. Moreover, the question of sustainability arises in terms of the costs to continue in the future, as well as the transient nature of deputies – some of whom may not be re-elected to continue the precedent-setting process and retain the institutional memory of the benefits of the process.[29]

Some lessons learned from the UNDP's experience in legislative assistance

Thomas Carothers has described legislative assistance as "the area of democracy assistance that most often falls short of its goals".[30] When leaders are serious about reforming state institutions, however, the UNDP's legislative aid can help make possible significant improvements. Some valuable lessons from UNDP experience which will help to maximize the likelihood of achieving programming goals include the following.

- As demonstrated in most of the country cases cited in Figure 9.1, external agents must seek and maintain support for their legislative assistance projects from all political parties represented in the legislature and other key societal actors to ensure both high impact and long-term sustainability. For example, multi-partisan reform or modernization committees should be formed to ensure that ownership of the legislative development process remains with national institutions, rather than individuals or their political parties. Failing to build broad-based and high-level political support could lead to frequent bottlenecks and improper implementation of the projects, particularly when power changes hands in a legislature.
- The timing of legislative projects is critical. Many interventions by the UNDP immediately follow the inauguration of a new parliament, as shown in the Bangladesh and Mozambique cases. A well-timed legislative support project can benefit from widespread post-electoral enthusiasm for democratic development, especially when elections mark a critical milestone in a peace process. To the extent possible, near-term project-supported reforms should be solidified during the course of a parliamentary sitting to avoid setbacks and possible reversals caused by sudden dramatic changes in the composition of the parliament following an election.
- UNDP coordination with other legislative assistance providers is essential, as illustrated in the case of Niger. Given the multiple types of legislative support, the need for long-term commitment, and the costs involved, coordination among donors is as necessary in the provision of legislative assistance as in other areas of governance support. The UNDP may be well placed to assume the politically sensitive tasks associated with pooling resources for common strategic interventions and avoiding duplication. However, experience suggests that few bilateral agencies and NGOs providing legislative assistance welcome coordi-

nation from the UNDP or other bodies – this is particularly true for regional hegemons with their own political agenda in a recipient country.

- Public consultations build trust in the work of parliaments and deepen democracy. As demonstrated by UNDP-facilitated constitutional reform consultations held in 2003 across all nine provinces of the Solomon Islands, citizen consultations garner substantive interest in and strengthen respect for parliament as a legitimate governing institution – an achievement of heightened significance in post-conflict settings mired by deep-seated mistrust and animosity. When budgets for individual parliamentary outreach are limited, nationally supported public consultations offer politicians a chance to reach out to civil society groups, to seek citizen inputs into law-making and constitutional drafting processes, and even rise above partisan positions and party loyalties.[31]
- Part of the UNDP's value-added is through the recognition that legislative assistance is a long-term process requiring a long-term commitment. Taking a long-term development approach to legislative support, external assistance can contribute to and monitor the normally slow evolution of the legislature as it seeks to cope with new national challenges and assert its political influence. Following an extensive parliamentary needs assessment in 2001 in the conflict-ridden Solomon Islands, the UNDP convened in September 2002 a parliamentary strengthening and skills-building seminar for all members of parliament. Although participation was at times limited – particularly among newer members and those with strong links to militia groups, the seminar's communiqué established guidelines for reform that are currently reflected in the drafting instructions for a new national constitution.

A newcomer to democracy assistance with a long-term perspective

The widening and deepening of democracy in some 81 new countries over the past two decades was accompanied by the growing involvement of many international organizations in democracy promotion activities. While the existing literature on the relationship between international organizations and democratization is rich in detailed case studies, there are no cross-national empirical studies suggesting the conditions under which the relationship may hold.[32] Through a survey of selected UNDP democracy promotion activities during the past decade, this chapter has sought to contribute to an analysis of the UN's democratization efforts within countries, given the importance of the subject to international relations, comparative politics, policy-makers, and development practitioners.

Whilst the UN Development Programme has started to establish a role in the area of long-term democracy assistance, it must continue to adapt and address directly certain recurring constraints. The study highlights that these include uneven political commitment to democratic reforms; the modest visibility of certain initiatives; the application of sometimes inappropriate democratic models in client countries; and lack of national unity in which to embed and deepen democracy. External actors such as the UNDP can only succeed when favourable domestic circumstances exist for democratic change within a programme country. Domestic leadership with a strong political support base is crucial if technical assistance in the area of democracy promotion is to be leveraged and the desired results realized – a purely technical approach to democracy assistance will fail unless political obstacles are confronted. Further, as illustrated by the country cases and various lessons cited in this chapter, no single blueprint for democratic change exists when external actors seek to assist political and institutional reforms. Each case will require the application of an inclusive developmental approach that is tailor-made to the specific needs of a country.

The need to apply situation-specific democratic assistance strategies becomes more pronounced in crisis and post-conflict situations. Many argue that strengthening the institutions and culture of democratic governance is essential to ensuring that voices are heard in a peace process, and that a long-term, sustainable course is charted for the resolution of once-irreconcilable differences. Others view the introduction of democratic approaches in war-torn societies as naive and potentially threatening to advancing the goals of peace and stability, particularly when overall governing capacity is weak. All too often, external agencies such as the UNDP fail to examine carefully the potential trade-offs and inherent tension between near-term peace-building and democracy-building activities. The complications that arise were amply demonstrated in UNDP efforts (however well-intentioned) to establish new parliaments in the post-conflict transitional administrations of Rwanda and the Republic of Congo (while meeting some initial success in East Timor). In this volume, Benjamin Reilly describes the severe consequences of international support for flawed elections in Angola and Haiti, and arguably premature elections in Bosnia.

Acting as a substantive adviser, facilitator, and catalyst, the UNDP can be characterized as trying to reinforce, give greater legitimacy to, and build capacity over the long haul within the "champions of democratic governance", particularly civic actors that play increasingly a pivotal role in establishing democratic foundations. For example, the cases of Bangladesh and Niger examined in this chapter suggest that sustained UNDP inputs toward strengthening political institutions can empower progressive actors willing to assume risks for democratic change. Public consultations, designed in collaboration with political party representatives, can be a particularly effective tool for augmenting parliament's representative role. International agencies, however, would be ill-advised to drive a national or subnational process of democratization; to do so would undermine any indigenous democratic institutional arrangements from taking root. Although in-country experience varies, UNDP field operations exhibit a strong understanding and respect for local cultural and social conditions in the organization of self-governance democracy support programmes. This characteristic of many UNDP interventions derives from a long-term developmental approach which emphasizes the creation of sound institutional frameworks that allow for diverse political representation and transparent opportunities for public inputs.

In addition to the democracy promotion activities referenced in this chapter, emerging areas of UNDP technical assistance include support for organizations and government institutions dealing with human rights, media and corporate accountability, strengthening local governance, access to justice, civilian oversight of the security sector, and the status of women and minorities in politics. Interventions in these sensitive areas of political development are built increasingly into the external assistance strategies for post-conflict and transitional societies. They are, by their very nature, high-risk activities, subject to often volatile political conditions within a country and largely dependent on building strong "constituencies for change" around a particular reform effort.

It is important that the UNDP and other development agencies undertake a holistic, integrated approach to their democracy assistance activities. Electoral processes shape the character of parliament and vice versa. Similarly, strong media, judicial, and parliamentary oversight of the security sector are vital in the transition from authoritarian to democratic civilian rule. Considerable research is now required to ascertain the national and community impact achieved in these disparate sectors of UNDP democracy assistance, and how they can better work together in concert to strengthen governance.

Within the UN system and the wider international development community, the UN Development Programme seeks recognition for its democratic governance policy advice and institutional-strengthening activities, especially in areas that bring political elements into economic and social development. Besides overcoming institutional and bureaucratic constraints to address the broader issues of democratization, the UNDP, as a relatively small international organization, can only enhance its influence in this arena through a strategic commitment to building trusted partnerships within a country – rather than relying on conditionality. Tackling major development challenges in a long-term, sustainable manner requires strong, enduring relationships on several levels, whether within a country or in cooperation with outside actors. Solid partnerships, built on shared experience and appropriate technical advice, remain the bedrock upon which future UNDP democracy assistance will succeed or falter.

Notes

1. Tanzi, Vito, Ke-young Chu, and Sanjeev Gupta (eds). 1999. *Economic Policy and Equity*. Washington, DC: International Monetary Fund.
2. See, for instance, Huntington, Samuel P. 1991. *The Third Wave: Democratization in the Late Twentieth Century*. Norman: University of Oklahoma Press; UNDP. 2002. *Human Development Report 2002*. Oxford: Oxford University Press.
3. *Human Development Report 2002* calculations based on Polity IV. 2002. "Political Regime Characteristics and Transitions, 1800–2000", www.bsos.umd.edu/cidcm/inscr/polity/index.htm.
4. *Ibid.*
5. Some of the pioneers of this rich debate included Anthony Downs, Mancur Olson, James Buchanan, Gordon Tullock, and Douglass North. See Findlay, Ronald. 1991. "The new political economy: Its explanatory power for LDCs", in Gerald M. Meier (ed.) *Politics and Policy Making in Developing Countries*. San Francisco: ICS Press.
6. For example, while the *World Development Report 1997* on "The state in a changing world" gives comprehensive coverage to a range of governance issues, including decentralization and reducing corruption, the fundamental reforms and implementation strategies advanced are economic in character and, for the poorest countries, an extension of the structural adjustment policies initiated in the early 1980s. World Bank. 1997. *World Development Report 1997*. Oxford: Oxford University Press.
7. UNDP Division of Information Management and Analysis, 2000.
8. Drawn from remarks made by Thomas Carothers at the UNDP Global Resident Representatives meeting in Glen Cove, New York in March 2000.
9. UNDP. 2001. *Results-Oriented Annual Report 2001*. New York: UNDP.
10. *Ibid.* Some 90 (out of 166) programme countries reported democracy assistance interventions in the year 2000, in wide-ranging areas such as decentralization, judicial and legal reforms, and improving state-citizen relations. The UNDP claims distinction through its work on democratic governance by representing "political neutrality and support for UN values with a capacity development mandate embodied in a long-term approach to assistance and partnerships for capacity-development". UNDP. 2001. *Background on Thematic Trust Fund for Democratic Governance*. New York: UNDP.
11. UNDP, note 2 above.
12. For this chapter, elections are characterized by, *inter alia*, open registration procedures, secure and secret ballots, universal access to voting sites, the independence of supervisory bodies, and freedom of expression and association.
13. Di Rosa, Lisa and Richard Ponzio. 2000. *UNDP Electoral Support Retrospective: Ten Years of Experience*. New York: UNDP.
14. López-Pintor, Rafael. 2000. *Electoral Management Bodies as Institutions of Governance*. New York: UNDP.
15. *Ibid.* Historical trends now indicate that better prospects for free, fair, and effective elections exist where electoral bodies are not only independent from the executive branch, but also can rely on a permanent professional staff. This enables the commission to develop experience and expertise in basic planning and cost-effective techniques.

16. The UNDP's input contributed to the free and fair manner in which the election was conducted, the creation of mass voter awareness that resulted in a high voter turnout – especially among women voters – and the institutionalization of democratic electoral processes in Bangladesh. The heavy turnout was attributed, in part, to an extensive UNDP-supported voter education programme which produced posters, leaflets, copies of the election code of conduct, short films, folk shows, and a range of television and radio discussion programmes.
17. López-Pintor, note 14 above.
18. *Ibid.*
19. Statement by the UNDP administrator, Mark Malloch Brown, at the Pacific Regional Conference on Governance for Parliamentarians, Fiji, 27–31 March 2000.
20. UNDP Management Development and Governance Division. 1997. *Report on UNDP-Assisted Governance Projects Approved in 1994–1995*. New York: UNDP; UNDP, note 9 above.
21. Adapted from UNDP MagNet Website, http://magnet.undp.org/, *Parliamentary Assistance Technical Note*, July 2000.
22. UNDP. 2001. *UNDP Legislative Assistance Retrospective*. New York: UNDP.
23. UNDP, note 9 above.
24. *Ibid.*
25. Niger experienced a brief non-military interlude from 1993 to 1995 following democratic elections.
26. UNDP. 2002. *Review of "Improving the Capacity and Outreach of the National Assembly" Project in Niger*. New York: UNDP.
27. *Ibid.*
28. National Democratic Institute for International Affairs. 2002. "Niger: Strengthening the Legislative Process", proposal to the UNDP.
29. UNDP, note 26 above.
30. Carothers, Thomas. 1999. *Aiding Democracy Abroad*. Washington, DC: Carnegie Endowment for International Peace.
31. According to a detailed review of the "Improving the Capacity and Outreach of the National Assembly" project in Niger, "The public consultations demonstrated democracy in action, increasing the accessibility of parliamentarians, opening up the work of the parliament to the people, increasing the transparency of the parliament and parliamentarians, and facilitating a broad process of civic education." UNDP, note 26 above.
32. A noteworthy contribution, however, that analyses systematically the democratization-IO link is Pevehouse, Jon. 2002. "Democracy from the outside-in? International organizations and democratization", *International Organization*, Vol. 56, No. 3.

Part III

Case studies

10

Decolonization and democratization: The United Nations and Namibia's transition to democracy

Henning Melber

The mediated and controlled decolonization processes of Southern Africa towards the end of the twentieth century brought with them fundamental socio-political changes in many of the societies concerned. The UN intervention as a part of the solution for the dispute concerning South-West Africa/Namibia in 1989–1990 led directly led to a transfer of power. The transition to independence negotiated and implemented for Namibia under the initiative of the United Nations was a process of controlled change which finally resulted in changed control.[1] Effective social transformation can be a long and drawn-out process at best. The same applies to profound changes of political culture in societies in transition towards the establishment and consolidation of democracy. Indeed, there are lasting structural and psychological effects resulting from the colonial legacy, which continue to have an influence during the post-colonial era of social transformation.[2] This chapter explores the role played by the United Nations in contributing to a democratic post-colonial political order. It seeks to assess and draw conclusions on the extent to which the direct intervention by the United Nations provided a suitable environment for the introduction of a sustainable democratic political culture, and to what extent such an endeavour was constrained to limited success by both external and internal factors.[3]

A trust betrayed

Most parts of the territory of the Republic of Namibia were declared a protectorate of imperial Germany in 1884. "German South-West Africa" lasted for 30 years. During this period it was transformed into a settler-dominated society under foreign rule characterized by strict racial segregation. The structures imposed involved the violent subjugation of the local population which had lasting effects far beyond the actual period of German rule.[4] After the First World War the former German colony was declared a C-mandate, with far-reaching authority transferred upon the mandatory power. The trusteeship was executed on behalf of the British Crown by the Union of South Africa. With the end of the League of Nations (originally in charge of supervising the trusteeships) and the subsequent establishment of the United Nations, a long-lasting dispute emerged between the world body and its founding member South Africa. The future of the country, including the administrative and legal responsibilities and its status in terms of international law and self-determination, became one of the most prominent and genuine cases of internationally negotiated decolonization for most of the second half of the twentieth century.

The "winds of change" brought about the decolonization of most African countries by the late 1960s. This contributed towards a diversified composition of the family of sovereign states within the United Nations, which in turn had an impact on the discourse in the international policy arena. The emergence of independent African states and the establishment of the Organization of African Unity as well as the Non-Aligned Movement contributed markedly towards shifts in policy issues. These included the change of perception of unsolved decolonization conflicts like the case of Namibia. The 1960s therefore brought to an end the silent tolerance of the continued occupation of the territory by neighbouring South Africa in defiance of the authority and responsibility claimed by the United Nations.

The dispute turned into open conflict and demanded recognition in the context of international law.[5] The United Nations assumed full responsibility to remain seized with the matter for more than two decades in both the General Assembly and the Security Council. Namibia turned into a genuine and singular case of UN concern, manifested also by the creation of the UN Council for Namibia[6] and the UN Institute for Namibia. The liberation movement – in a process of formation during the 1950s and established since 1960 as the South-West African Peoples Organization (SWAPO of Namibia) – subsequently achieved unique status. As a result of intensive diplomacy it was – with the overwhelming support of the non-aligned countries and the Eastern bloc – acknowledged by the General Assembly as the only legitimate agency of the Namibian people[7] and obtained formal observer status to the UN bodies. Notwithstanding this considerable diplomatic success, however, the polarized situation of super-power rivalry prolonged the transition process to Namibian independence despite several far-reaching resolutions and diplomatic initiatives until the late 1980s, when UN Security Council Resolution 435 (1978) was finally implemented more than a decade after its adoption.[8]

The United Nations as multi-level broker

Until Namibian independence the United Nations played a crucial if not decisive role, culminating in the establishment of the United Nations Transitional Assistance Group (UNTAG) with supervisory powers for the transition of Namibia to an internationally accepted sovereign state under UN Security Council Resolution 435 (1978). The UN system can hence be considered as a midwife to the Republic of Namibia, proclaimed on 21 March 1990. The democratic political system established as the framework for the governing of this society has hence been shaped to a considerable extent both directly and indirectly by the United Nations and its agencies involved in the process. These agencies, however, were in themselves by no means a sign of homogeneity or uniformity. UN positions and policies on Namibia were represented in different ways, be it through the most radical support for SWAPO as expressed in the General Assembly resolutions, the role assumed by the UN Council for Namibia as an institution acting on behalf of a generally assumed Namibian interest otherwise not represented, or in the far more controversial (non-)decisions taken by the Security Council (and in particular the role of its permanent Western members). The Western Contact Group emerged during 1977 to overcome a stalemate in terms of geostrategic interests generally, and with regard to Southern Africa and Namibia in particular, as an attempt to prevent further isolation of the Western Security Council members over controversial issues related to the South African apartheid regime. At the same time its institutionalization was a visible indication of the existing differences on how to approach a lasting and acceptable solution to the Namibia problem. The initiative tried with intensive shuttle diplomacy (including proximity talks in decisive stages) to negotiate a compromise between the direct opponents (SWAPO and South Africa). The immediate result was reflected in Security Council Resolution 435 (1978). But the blueprint was followed by further negotiations on details as well as on more substantive issues. Consequently, and for a number of other reasons related to political changes in some of the countries (in particular the Africa policy emerging under the Reagan administration), this resolution failed to achieve implementation for years to come.

The subsequent policies through most of the 1980s were a reflection of continued negotiated compromise between the different power blocs and their global policy interests, while the battle over the occupied territory of Namibia continued politically, diplomatically, and militarily. Hence, it would be erroneous to assume that there has been one binding UN position on the Namibia conflict ever since the issue emerged. Instead, the United Nations created the forum to negotiate the decolonization process and ultimately to secure its implementation. This process lasted more than a quarter of a century and finally brought to an end more than 100 years of foreign occupation of the territory. In its course, it was accompanied by the articulation of different and at times conflicting political approaches from several social forces operating in a local Namibian, a regional Southern African, and a wider global context.

In the light of this complexity the United Nations was more of a conflict mediator and power broker seeking to reconcile the various interests operating also within its own structures. The overall goal of most if not all parties might have been to correct the existing anachronism of a trust betrayed towards the end of a century which had since the 1950s witnessed the era of successive formal independence for the African colonies. But the views on how to achieve this goal for Namibia differed considerably. With Namibian sovereignty in 1990 and – as a more or less direct result thereof – the subsequent democratic elections in South Africa during 1994, the era of European colonialism on the African continent was brought to an end. It would be a premature conclusion, however, to assume that this went hand in hand with the firm establishment and consolidation of democracy. As is argued below, independence and democracy are by no means identical. It was independence for Namibia which guided the UN intervention in the first place. Democracy figured at best as a complementary issue only.

Decolonization and democracy

SWAPO's armed liberation struggle, launched in the mid-1960s, had a major impact on the further course of decolonization. But Namibian independence was also the achievement of the international community, which after the Cold War period managed to end lengthy and complicated diplomatic negotiations first and foremost dominated by the strategic interests of the two power blocs. The internationally negotiated settlement ultimately resulted in a transition towards independence with a decisive degree of UN involvement based on the – though delayed –

implementation of Resolution 435 (1978). It paved the way for a legitimate government led by the previous liberation movement SWAPO.

The goal of the struggle was political independence in a sovereign state under a government representing the majority of the people so far excluded from full participation in society. The power of definition concerning the future post-colonial system was exercised during this process mainly by the national liberation movement. It voiced "the will of the people" in interaction with the international players. The struggle included exile politics and international diplomacy as relevant components. Dobell proposes that "Namibia provides a particularly fascinating case study of the gradual dismantling of a century of colonial rule, and its ultimate replacement – through democratic means, and monitored by external powers – by a movement which, some would argue, had in certain respects come to resemble the forces against which it had originally struggled."[9]

With reference to some of the contributions to the four-volume study entitled *Transitions from Authoritarian Rule*,[10] she suggests that there are three especially pertinent paths to democracy applicable to the Namibian case, namely "a) externally monitored installation; b) redemocratization initiated from within an authoritarian regime; and c) elements of the 'party pact' model".[11] While the term "redemocratization" might be misleading to the extent that it implies there would have been a political system of democracy in Namibia before (which is doubtful), the different components do offer a valid framework for analysis. In the context of this chapter, the emphasis lies on the first element of an externally monitored installation, with particular reference to the role of the United Nations. It has been by far the most important aspect in the process towards establishing a political system in post-colonial Namibia. The "externally monitored installation" model describes, as Dobell summarizes further, "cases in which an authoritarian regime is defeated by foreign democratic powers, which then 'play a major role in the formulation and installation of the democratic regime'".[12]

Dobell's study has the merit to show the relevance of translating these general theoretical reflections into the socio-political reality of the Namibian case, but a word of caution seems justified. The all-too-often-assumed (though not by Dobell herself) equation that liberation from the illegal occupation of Namibia by a colonial minority regime would imply more or less automatically the installation of a democratic system is misleading. The agenda was first and foremost shaped by the goal to establish a formally legitimate and internationally recognized sovereign Namibian state. By implication the expectation might have been among many of the forces involved that this requires the establishment and consolidation of democracy as a lasting political system. Explicit evidence for this, however, remains scarce and scattered. Throughout the 1970s and 1980s the liberation struggle was understood and perceived foremost as the right to self-determination of the Namibian population. Once achieved, the task to formulate and adopt further specifications was left to those policy-makers who emerged as representatives of the Namibian people. It was therefore not democratization which was the priority on the agenda for Namibia, but decolonization.[13] From a logical point of view this is an understandable approach, since there is no democracy under colonialism, hence only a decolonization process provides the necessary framework for democratization. Both can be and have been achieved to some extent in a parallel process at the same time. But it is important to note that the goals are neither identical nor necessarily congruent.

Evidence of this is offered in the case of Namibia, for which the mandate implemented by UNTAG under UN Security Council Resolution 435 (1978) provided for the supervision of free and fair general elections for a constitutive assembly. All parties registered were competing for votes under the transitional authority composed jointly by the South African administrator-general and the UN special representative. Those in competition, on the other side, were not operating from a basis of equal opportunities. While the one side (South African allies) could benefit from massive support from the colonial power, the other side (SWAPO) had the privilege of being the only recognized representative of the Namibian people internationally and received considerable assistance on the basis of this status. The possibility of similar (not to mention equal) support for other forces not aligned to either of the two sides was basically eliminated by the factual constraints. Martti Ahtisaari, previously head of the UN Council for Namibia and as UNTAG special representative counterpart to the South African administrator-general during 1989/1990, summarized the intrinsic contradiction of this constellation in a later interview:

I don't think it was the most democratic way of going about it but I think the justification for that was to concentrate the efforts *vis-à-vis* the occupying power. That was the fact which we had to deal with. But it obviously didn't make life easier and the solution of the problem either. Because in the end, I think, the mere armed struggle would never have solved the problem; and if you go for a democratic solution, then you have to give everybody the chance to participate and agree conditions so that they would be starting on a fairly equal basis.

As a result, he continued to argue, the political forces not affiliated to SWAPO "were eliminated from that political opportunity and that of course diminished plurality and complicated matters".[14]

The United Nations was, as argued above, more a power broker in the transition to internationally accepted independence than an agency promoting democracy as its priority. That the transition took place under conditions of free and fair general elections following democratic rules secured a necessary legitimacy to the outcome and contributed decisively to the general acceptance. To that extent democracy in practice offered some essential ingredients to the success of the decolonization process, which resulted in an internationally legitimized transfer of political power.

The midwife role of UNTAG

As a shock to most if not all observers, the actual implementation phase of Resolution 435 (1978) started with a massacre committed in cold blood. On 1 April 1989, when the plan became effective, several hundred SWAPO combatants gathered in northern Namibia were attacked by South African troops. Caught by complete surprise, they were liquidated without any meaningful defence efforts.[15] The justification for this mass execution was that they were accused of having invaded an area outside their originally confined (Angolan) bases in violation of the cease-fire agreement. South Africa claimed, on the basis of reconnaissance evidence, insurgents of the People's Liberation Army of Namibia (PLAN) had sneaked into Namibia to create the impression that they had been occupying bases inside the country. While SWAPO still officially denies that the PLAN fighters had been ordered only a few days earlier to move into Namibian territory, and vigorously refutes any other interpretation,[16] serious evidence points in a different direction.[17] Whatever the case, hundreds of young men caught by surprise had to pay the highest price and sacrificed their lives on a battlefield that was no longer supposed to exist. This certainly marked one of the darkest hours in the history of UN involvement in Namibian decolonization at a time when it was about to bring the conflict to a long-overdue end.

While the process was almost derailed as a result of these events, the subsequent solution to the incident actually put the implementation process not only back on track but reassured the political will among the relevant parties and stakeholders to bring the transitional period through the agreed stages to a successful end. Ahtisaari summarized in retrospective, the "tragic death of these people served that purpose that it reinforced the process finally".[18] At the same time, it highlighted the in-built dilemma between peacemaking and peacekeeping as part of a UN mandate of this kind. Despite this frustrating and sobering overture, however, the degree of violence was considerably (and decisively) reduced from mid-April onwards, though "law and order" under UN supervision in the continued presence of South African army contingents remained a relative matter. While a few more incidents showed the continued precarious situation, it was on the other hand a major achievement to limit physical violence to its actual levels in the further course of the process.

UNTAG had to maintain a precarious balance throughout, to underline the claim of being a neutral facilitator during the implementation process. The unfortunate events following 1 April ironically created, from the South African point of view, more confidence and trust in the honesty of UNTAG's way of handling the mandate. UNTAG continued to seek compromises with both parties in the conflict – South Africa and its local allies as well as SWAPO. The South African administrator-general, who officially remained the ultimate authority during the transition process, got away with a number of tactical tricks on procedural matters which were clearly seeking to favour the local allies. The liberation movement benefited from some goodwill in the process of an UNTAG fact-finding mission investigating in Angola accusations of human rights violations by SWAPO. The case was made by groups of "ex-detainees", who were returning after imprisonment and torture by their own liberation movement in camps in southern Angola, claiming that many more people were still missing. It might be questioned, given the number of occasions where the UNTAG authorities acted with flaws, if this was an honest brokerage in the true sense. But it was certainly an effective way of keeping all parties on board and making them ultimately honour the procedures and their results.

Despite all criticism raised during the transitional period with regard to the occasional lack of direct presence of UNTAG military or civilian personnel at various places in the vast country, the overall result can ultimately be considered to be better than originally expected by most. The figures presented by UNTAG at the end of its involvement displayed a massive investment into maintaining relative stability and an environment conducive to basically free and fair elections. On average there were during the period 6,700 members of UNTAG from a total of 109 countries in Namibia (4,300 of them in the military component, 1,500 as police monitors, and 900 as the civilian component). During the actual week of elections (7–11 November 1989) UNTAG presence peaked with 7,900 members. The total costs of the UNTAG operations amounted to some US$373.4 million. UNTAG had established a total of 42 district centres and 48 police stations, and the total number of UNTAG bases (including military posts) reached almost 200. Over 43,000 Namibians were repatriated prior to the elections from 40 different countries by the UNHCR, and 56 laws categorized as discriminatory were abolished. UNTAG produced and broadcasted as part of its voter education campaign 32 television and 201 radio programmes, the latter in 13 different local languages. More than 600,000 T-shirts, buttons, stickers, information brochures, and posters were distributed.

Most importantly, among an estimated total population of less than 1.5 million people, 701,483 voters were registered and 670,830 of them (97.4 per cent) made use of their voting right. People queued patiently for days at polling stations, monitored closely by observers, to exercise their right to cast a vote in a process with remarkably few reported irregularities. The collecting of ballot boxes and the counting of votes took place with the participation of all parties. The announced election results, providing an absolute (though not a two-thirds) majority to the liberation movement, were openly and enthusiastically celebrated by the majority of the population and accepted by the defeated opponents. A culture of fear had finally come to an end. The result of this exercise, leading to independence on 21 March 1990, was acknowledged by one of the local weekly newspapers in German with the headline "Danke, UNTAG".[19]

Even a critical approach to the UNTAG enterprise has to register with some degree of satisfaction an ultimately happy end and correct many of the originally more pessimistic doubts as to the possibilities of a success. This conclusion is mainly drawn under the given circumstances of judging UNTAG as a peacemaking or actually peacekeeping mission in the first place. It supervised the adherence to agreed democratic principles to ensure an acceptable result of the decision-making process on the political future of Namibia by the majority of the Namibian people. But it was not a mission with the mandate to establish democracy as a lasting political system. Seen in this context, UNTAG received praise mainly with regard to its efficient role as a peacekeeping force, thereby creating an enabling environment for free and fair general elections. To that extent the Namibian case and experience contributed in a positive way to the redefinition of the potential role of the United Nations as a global agency and institution enforcing rules applicable to humanity as a whole.[20]

The following sections explore the scope and limitation of Namibian democracy during the initial stage and the subsequent experiences of the first decade. The chapter then considers to what extent the United Nations might have missed an opportunity to enhance democratization in Namibia beyond the accomplished mission of a lasting and more or less peaceful transition towards independence under a democratically elected government.

Democracy at independence

With the proclamation of independence on 21 March 1990, Namibian society resembled all formal aspects of a democratic political system. This in itself can be regarded as a positive surprise. The introductory and concluding passages of the preamble of "The Constitution of the Republic of Namibia" provide explicit reference to a democratic society as the most effective system to maintain and protect the fundamental rights of the people:

Whereas recognition of the inherent dignity and of the equal and inalienable rights of all members of the human family is indispensable for freedom, justice and peace;

Whereas the said rights include the right of the individual to life, liberty and the pursuit of happiness, regardless of race, colour, ethnic origin, sex, religion, creed or social or economic status;

Whereas the said rights are most effectively maintained and protected in a democratic society, where the government is responsible to freely elected representatives of the people, operating under a sovereign constitution and a free and independent judiciary;

Whereas these rights have for so long been denied to the people of Namibia by colonialism, racism and apartheid; [...]

Now therefore, we the people of Namibia accept and adopt this Constitution as the fundamental law of our Sovereign and Independent Republic.

The constitutional democracy was formally institutionalized as a last step towards the formal sovereignty of the Republic of Namibia. Both its contents and the drafting procedures reflected a negotiated compromise. Since the constitutional document had to be adopted by a two-thirds majority, none of the parties involved in the negotiations had the power to impose a unilateral decision-making process upon the other interest groups represented in the Constituent Assembly. SWAPO, with 41 seats (57 per cent of the votes), had missed the two-thirds majority. The DTA (Democratic Turnhalle Alliance) with its 21 seats (28 per cent of the votes) failed to emerge as a powerful opposition. In this constellation, both parties preferred a negotiated settlement to continued conflict. The emerging process has been qualified as "an impressive example of successful bargaining by opposing political elites in a transitional democratic context".[21] This view was confirmed when, on the occasion of an international conference in mid-1992, many of the relevant individual actors participating in the Namibian transitional process towards independence recalled the final stages of decolonization. Looking back, the DTA opposition leader Dirk Mudge summarized:

On our first meeting I proposed we take the SWAPO draft as the working paper and try to improve on it. To them, it must have come as a surprise: to my colleagues it must have come as a shock. The reason for my suggestion was that I could not believe that after such a long struggle SWAPO and the DTA could come up with such similar proposals. At the most there were two points of material dispute: over the question of an executive president and whether or not there should be a second chamber. Other than that it was clear that we had moved closer together.[22]

Theo-Ben Gurirab, from 1990 to 2002 Namibia's first Minister of Foreign Affairs (and since then the country's Prime Minister), agreed: "our Constitution is the product of serious internal political negotiations. We debated every aspect of it until we reached consensus; only then did we instruct, in specific terms, the draftsmen to put that consensus into the appropriate legal language ... we never had to vote on a single issue."[23] The Namibian constitution, in the words of Theo-Ben Gurirab, "is therefore a collective brainchild of all those who served on that committee".[24] These statements could serve as evidence to confirm the hypothesis that the negotiated settlement in Namibia resembled aspects of an "élite pact" as defined by O'Donnell and Schmitter.[25] Dobell adds further evidence to support this by quoting from an interview with another leading local politician involved in the negotiations, who told her in August 1991 that "everybody wanted to be seen as a democrat during these negotiations".[26]

The memory of the two political "old-timers" quoted above might, however, be a bit too reconciliatory when recalling these events. They fail to acknowledge the full implications of the fact that the constitutional negotiations were the final chapter of a decolonization process "closely supervised by international forces, and facilitated by a 'transitional pact'", which "alongside at least an instrumental commitment to democracy on the part of opposing forces, has surely also made a difference".[27] As Erasmus points out in retrospective, the international settlement plan as designed in Security Council Resolution 435 (1978) "gained an important additional element when it was decided to determine the basic content of Namibia's Constitution in advance. Constitution-making became part of the international peace-making operation."[28] He further points out that the adoption of these principles implied "that Namibians actually did not enjoy a completely free hand in writing their own constitution".[29]

It was the same Theo-Ben Gurirab who, on behalf of SWAPO:

formally proposed the incorporation of the 1982 constitutional principles, a proposal that was adopted to resounding applause. These 1982 principles laid down ground rules for a multiparty democracy with regular elections by secret ballot, an independent judiciary, and a declaration of fundamental human rights, including recognition of property rights. The reassertion of these principles laid to rest the spectre of a one-party state that had worried some of SWAPO's opponents.[30]

In other words, the negotiated settlement started under UN supervision continued to acknowledge the externally defined rules of the game and the parties involved were eager to document their constructive approach.

In general, agreement came about quickly, and there was little sign of old animosities. All parties seemed more anxious to get on with the business of running their own country without the South Africans than giving lengthy consideration to the principles that would govern political life in the long run ... The constitution was rushed through by all parties, eager to seize the reins of power.[31]

Most observers agree that the internal will to close the chapter of colonial rule was supported by external factors contributing decisively to the negotiated results. "The Namibian Constitution is a lengthy and detailed document," summarized Harring. "It was the product of a complex political compromise between a right wing, racist South African government and a leftist, nationalist SWAPO government in exile, brokered by the United Nations. As such it sets out a number of political relationships in a very detailed way."[32] Indeed, the Namibian constitution deliberately aims to reconcile previously antagonistic forces by means of one common framework. Next to the uncompromising establishment of clearly defined human rights, the constitution explicitly refers to the philosophy of national reconciliation. To that extent, far-reaching human rights provisions within Chapter 3 encompass a variety of civil and political rights, including the recognition and protection of property rights under Article 16, which also rules that any expropriation required just compensation. These civil and political rights are entrenched, which means that "it is not possible to amend that instrument so as to weaken any of them", and "for the most part, they are non-derogable, i.e. they cannot be set aside even on the declaration of a public emergency".[33]

The constitution was the final part of a negotiated compromise between the colonial power, its previous Western allies, and the forces of national liberation within a framework designed by and under the supervision of the United Nations. This constellation has "profoundly influenced the form of the new Namibian democracy".[34] The constitutional rooting of formal political liberties and human rights secured a "yardstick for good governance".[35] To that extent it offers a meaningful impact as a tool contributing towards a process of democratization. The *Grundnorm*, however, requires societal acceptance. Testing the essence against some features of social reality, a law professor at the University of Namibia observed a "discrepancy between the acclamation of the Constitution as the symbol of liberation and independence, and the translation of the Constitution into daily life".[36] The Under-Secretary for Legal Affairs at the Ministry of Foreign Affairs had another warning to offer. "To instil democratic and human rights values," he pointed out, "is not enough, however; we also need to insist that institutions themselves become more democratic." It is an irony, he continued, "that although we have a widely admired Constitution, the organizations which are supposed to provide the officials who will protect this constitution, namely our political parties, are the most undemocratic institutions in the country".[37]

The following section reviews some of the further developments in post-colonial Namibia. It explores the degree of consolidation or erosion of democratic virtues, norms, values, and practices between 1990 and 2000 with the aim of drawing some conclusions on prevailing tendencies. The question that then has to be answered is if, by which means, and to what extent the United Nations might have been able to contribute more actively towards a sustainable democratic perspective.

(Post-)colonial political culture

Each decolonization process can claim a degree of uniqueness, based on historically unique features of the particular society and its social forces. One should therefore abstain from premature generalizations. There are certain common features, however, shared between the liberation movements in Southern Africa which in the process of decolonization obtained political power. The emphasis on free elections and an agreed constitutional framework for a controlled transition in Zimbabwe, Namibia, and South Africa suggests similarities in terms of shaping the post-colonial environment. Their cases represent examples of liberation movements turning into parties to occupy political power. These parties have managed to consolidate their dominant position and expanded control over the state apparatus. In all cases their legitimacy is based on being the – more or less democratically elected – representative of the majority of the people. At the same time, however, the democratic notion is also a contested territory. Post-colonial policies in these countries display at times a lack of commitment to democratic principles and/or practices by those in political power and control.

John Saul proposes as a result of this sobering reality to question these changes as "liberation without democracy".[38] The track records of the liberation movements – both with regard to their internal practices during the wars of liberation and their lack of democratic virtues and respect towards the protection of human rights once in power – are far from positive examples. Victims are often turned as liberators into perpetrators. While these movements were fighting against systems of institutionalized violation of basic human rights, they were at the same time not always sensitive to human rights issues within their own ranks. Fighting against unjust systems of oppression, rooted in totalitarian colonial rule of a minority, did not protect them from falling prey to undemocratic practices applied by themselves against dissenting internal and external forces.[39] Lauren Dobell argues that there has been a lack of democratic convictions within the ranks of the organized social forces seizing political power.[40] The organization of a serious liberation struggle had much in common with the authoritarianism and hierarchical organization reflecting the totalitarian structures inherent to the colonial system opposed. To this extent, features of the colonial character are reproduced in the fight for their abolition and the emerging concepts of power applied in the post-colonial reconstruction phase.

During the first decade of Namibian independence a political system emerged which displayed tendencies towards a factual one-party state under increasingly autocratic rule. Based on its reputation as the liberating force and in the absence of serious political alternatives, SWAPO managed firmly to entrench political dominance by means of obtaining a continuously higher proportion of votes in a basically legitimate way. An increasingly repressive atmosphere during the election campaign in late 1999 might in contrast be perceived as a "lack of consolidation of Namibian democracy".[41] The far-reaching mandate encouraged the misperception that the government is supposed to serve the party and that the state is the property of the government. In line with this tendency, the SWAPO election manifesto of 1999 denounced any political opposition in a way that made a mockery out of the same democratic notion upon which the party bases its legitimacy. It declared that "saving democracy, or more appropriately saving the opposition, is the latest version of Europe's burden to civilise the natives".[42]

Notwithstanding such flaws, Namibia's first decade of independence witnessed a constant gain and consolidation of political power and control by the former liberation movement. The election figures over the first 10 years, however, illustrate a striking feature (see Table 10.1[43]). The numbers disclose only a comparatively small increase in votes received by SWAPO from the electorate during this period. In fact, while SWAPO increased its representation in the National Assembly by 17 per cent in 1994 compared to 1989, the absolute number of votes had declined. In the 1999 national elections, SWAPO received just 6.1 per cent more votes than in 1989. But due to 22.1 per cent fewer votes being cast during the election, the party increased its representation by almost 2.3 per cent to 76.15 per cent.

Table 10.1 Election results for the bigger parties, 1989–1999

Election	Votes	SWAPO	DTA	UDF*	CoD**
1989 Constituent	687,787	384,567 (56.90%)	191,532 (28.34%)	37,874 (5.60%)	– –
1992 Regional	381,041	256,778 (68.76%)	103,359 (27.68%)	9,285 (2.49%)	– –
1992 Local	128,973	73,736 (58.02%)	42,278 (33.26%)	7,473 (5.88%)	– –
1994 National	497,499	361,800 (73.89%)	101,748 (20.78%)	13,309 (2.72%)	– –
1998 Local	63,545	37,954 (60.35%)	15,039 (23.91%)	4,191 (6.66%)	– –
1999 National	536,036	408,174 (76.15%)	50,824 (9.48%)	15,685 (2.93%)	53,289 (9.94%)

*United Democratic Front
**Congress of Democrats (founded in 1999)

SWAPO managed to obtain exclusive control over the parliamentary decision-making process with the results of the national elections in December 1994. The two-thirds majority allowed the party to initiate the first amendment of the country's constitution in 1998. Despite strong objections from most other political parties, SWAPO's politically elected representatives in both houses (the National Assembly and the National Council) adopted the constitutional modification allowing its president a third term in office as head of state. From a formal point of view, such policy interventions are legitimate and based on the mandate received through general elections by secret vote of all citizens registered. But it could suggest that Namibia is not yet a sustainable democracy. According to Abbink, this would in contrast require "the consolidation of institutional, social and legal frameworks which make the process of open political communication independent of the persons who happen to be in power".[44] Instead, loyalty to Namibia is increasingly equated with loyalty to SWAPO's policy. Namibia's political culture reveals more than a decade after independence some disturbing features of deterioration.[45] A survey conducted at the turn of the century among six African countries by the Southern African Democracy Barometer ranks Namibia last in terms of public awareness of democracy.[46] A summary of the report concludes, with reference to Namibia and Nigeria, "the consolidation of democracy is a distant prospect in both these countries".[47] A survey by the Helen Suzman Foundation among six Southern African states during the late 1990s produced another sobering result: Namibia was the only country in which a defeat of their own party would not be accepted by a large majority. The survey results furthermore diagnosed "a complete collapse of confidence in the future", while finally "not much more than one third of respondents felt confident of democracy's future".[48] The most recent survey among Namibians aged 18 to 32 concludes: "Namibia does not have sufficient young Democrats to make the consolidation of democracy a foregone conclusion".[49]

Development and democracy: The role of the UN system

External support for the post-colonial transformation of Namibian society is widely perceived as a matter of development assistance confined to socio-economic issues. But a meaningful and profound social change requires considering the political culture as part and parcel of a transition process towards more egalitarian structures too. In the introduction to his collection of lectures, *Development as Freedom*, Amartya Sen concludes that "Freedoms are not only the primary ends of development, they are also among its principal means".[50] He points out that freedoms of different kinds are linked with one another. They include political freedoms, social opportunities, and access to economic resources. If one shares such an integrated approach, it might well be argued that external support to socio-economic changes implies a certain degree of political intervention too.[51] Hence there might be opportunities in supporting Namibian post-colonial developmental strategies in a way which at the same time enhances a democratic culture.

This section presents an overview on the international development cooperation with the Namibian authorities. It aims to explore if and to what extent external support might be able to contribute towards an environment conducive to further democratization. The United Nations had assumed and executed special responsibility for Namibian independence. It is hence an interesting question if and to what extent the United Nations might have been able to exercise a more active role in the further consolidation of democracy in Namibia.[52]

Efforts of the local UNDP office to compile a comprehensive overview on the dimensions and priorities of external support to Namibia had achieved meaningful results by the end of the 1990s. As 1997 figures show, Namibia is the highest recipient in terms of external assistance of total net ODA per capita in the region.[53] While Namibia is ranked as a lower-middle-income country in terms of its average per capita income (close to US$2,000 per year), it had been temporarily classified on an "as if" basis as a least developed country (LDC) by the UN General Assembly in December 1990. This status had been reconfirmed by ECOSOC in 1996: "Widespread poverty and the backlog of development needs present a challenge, which the international community has been keen to meet by providing external assistance on a concessional basis."[54] Both Namibia's head of state (on the occasion of the World Food Summit in November 1996) and Namibia's Foreign Minister (during his speech to the thirty-first session of the UN General Assembly in September 1996) have appealed to the members of the international community to grant Namibia an LDC status. This appeal has been reiterated at a donor conference organized in support for external assistance to the implementation of the second National Development Plan in February 2003.[55]

As Odén argued in one of the first assessments of the impact of aid to Namibia, donor funds are not a dominant source of government finance.[56] Aid has nevertheless played an essential role throughout the years. External assistance has therefore gained macro-economic importance that might exceed its relative size. Over the years, disbursements by foreign donors have averaged 5.0 per cent of GDP per annum, peaking at 6.0 per cent in 1998. The *Development Co-operation Report* for 1998, in presenting data of this nature, concludes that since 1991 "external assistance has been equivalent, on the average, to some 15.1% of current public expenditures"[57] (see Table 10.2).[58]

Figures concerning disbursements until 1999 do not confirm features of an "aid fatigue" yet. Quite the opposite:

External assistance disbursements during 1999 were US$ 207 million, the largest since independence, an increase of 10.7% over the revised 1998 level of US$ 187 million. As such, 1999 was the peak year for external assistance.[59]

The most important component of overall external support is bilateral agreements, with Germany being the biggest single donor. Another ma-

Table 10.2 Macro-economic importance of external assistance to Namibia, 1990–1998

	1990	1991	1992	1993	1994	1995	1996	1997	1998
Assistance (US$M)	64.1	116.4	139.8	130.8	115.9	157.1	175.6	162.1	184.9
Assistance as % of government expenditure	11.1	16.3	15.7	14.0	12.3	15.2	16.8	15.3	19.2
Assistance per capita (US$)	46	83	100	93	83	95	106	98	109
Assistance as % of GDP	3.4	5.5	5.6	4.9	3.9	4.9	5.5	5.0	6.0

Table 10.3 Sources of external assistance to Namibia, 1995–1998

	1995		1996		1997		1998	
	Amount US$000	%	Amount US$000	%	Amount US$000	%	Amount US$000	%
UN	13,789	8.8	10,854	6.2	8,469	5.2	9,398	5.1
EU	17,764	11.3	29,593	16.8	23,845	14.7	61,290	33.2
Bilateral	120,643	76.8	126,353	71.9	125,183	77.2	107,675	58.2
NGOs	4,905	3.1	8,848	5.0	4,597	2.8	6,511	3.5
Total	157,101		175,648		162,094		184,874	

jor donor (ranking second in terms of 1998 and 1999 disbursements) is the USA, followed by the group of Nordic countries (notably Sweden, to a lesser extent Norway and Finland). The second most important source of external assistance has been the EU, contributing in 1998 one-third of the total financial volume to Namibia (a marked increase, compared to a marked decrease in bilateral assistance). NGO activities have remained rather low, but this is the area with the highest uncertainty in terms of measured input. Of interest here is that drastic changes over the years can be recorded in the decline of UN assistance in both absolute and relative terms, which is a marked contrast to the sharp increase in EU assistance (see Table 10.3).[60]

The 1999 figures show an increase again in total disbursements of the UN agencies (including the UNDP) by some 19.7 per cent to US$11.417 million (5.5 per cent of total external assistance) compared to the previous year.[61] However, there are visible trends that important members of the donor community have already decided upon a reduction of their degree of involvement in Namibia. Relevant bilateral partners have downscaled their involvement (Denmark at a rather early stage, Norway and the Netherlands more recently). Finland has announced a phasing-out of current programme support by 2007, among other reasons due to Namibia's involvement in regional military conflicts. Others (such as the UK through the British High Commissioner) have indicated similar plans. This is significant since Sweden, Norway, the UK, and Finland were after Germany and with the USA the most important donors throughout the 1990s. Some of them replace the "traditional" country cooperation by support to projects devoting their efforts to issues such as the improvement of good governance, strengthening of civil society, and protection of human rights. The "honeymoon" that Namibia enjoyed, resulting from the preferential status of internationally negotiated and successfully implemented independence, seems to have come to an end – partly but not only due to the deteriorating performance in terms of a commitment to the democratic principles and the notion of "good governance".

Given that this might represent a new challenge to external support in strengthening good governance initiatives, it is somehow disappointing to see the actual distribution of funds under the Country Cooperation Framework (CCF) between 1997 and 2000.[62] The total funds disbursed for this period by the UNDP amounted to US$7.36 million, out of which a mere US$254,000 or 3.5 per cent were allocated to a budget line "support to good governance".[63] It might be noteworthy, in this context, that during a workshop on the UN Development Assistance Framework (UNDAF) for 2001 to 2005 the stakeholders participating in the working group on governance, human rights, and gender pointed out "that the UN has a broader role than just being a technical expert provider. The role of the UN is also to remind the Government of the global values it represents."[64] The tentative conclusions presented by Santiso are therefore also of considerable relevance for the Namibian case and the potential role of UN development agencies in the post-colonial reconstruction process:

to promote democracy and good governance, donors will need to address the underlying interests and power relations in which institutions are embedded. This will entail thinking about development cooperation as a political endeavour and establishing development partnerships grounded in pacts for governance reform. Democracy assistance can have a real influence in the shape and direction of democratization.[65]

A survey exploring donor assistance for the consolidation of democracy in Namibia identified a lack of capacity by the people to exercise their democratic rights in spite of democratic and functioning legal institutions. It asks for more concerted efforts by donors: "There is a clear need to increase the demand for democracy through improving education, increasing capacity building and ensuring that the civil society and media institutions can function properly."[66] If the UN system is willing to perceive its obligation towards the people of Namibia not only as being confined to a historic mission as midwife to formal independence, but defines its mandate also as contributing towards the consolidation of a sustainable democratic environment, it needs to reconsider its current role.

Conclusion

The Namibian case of decolonization was guided by the goal of achieving a more or less democratically legitimate transition towards independence, but not the firm entrenchment of democracy. After all, rather logically, the democratically elected representatives of the Namibian population should have the discretion and power to decide themselves upon the character of the political system. On the other hand, as a study based on several fact-finding missions to Namibia during March to November 1989 concluded, the United Nations did succeed in redirecting a profound (also military) conflict into electoral competition and provided a democratically oriented solution: "The Settlement Plan was not just a device for instituting independence; it also helped Namibians develop a democratic system of government, where meaningful elections are held periodically and where human rights are generally respected."[67]

What has been maintained with reference to the subsequent changes in neighbouring South Africa applies as much to the Namibian case:

South African society, with its massive inequalities, racial and ethnic sensitivities and authoritarian legacies, is hardly an ideal environment for textbook liberal democracy. However although South Africa may not have the democracy it deserves, it may well have the democracy that it can sustain.[68]

Given the legacy of a century of foreign occupation, the process towards independence in Namibia produced remarkably positive results. But it also has to be kept in mind the word of warning extended by Hyden: "Applying the principles of good governance to post-conflict situations is taking them to a new frontier, where the unknowns prevail."[69] He therefore urges caution and prudence as salient attributes of any approach by the international community to promoting reconciliation and democratization in post-conflict situations. This touches at the same time upon the aspect of democratization as "a transitional phenomenon involving a gradual, mainly elite-driven transformation of the formal rules that govern a political system". Such a process is thus "not an end-game; rather, it is a means to an end, which is democracy".[70]

With explicit reference to the positive example set by the UN intervention in the Namibian case, Johansen identifies the emergence of a global political process which humanizes local political processes by linking them to global supervision and enforcement.[71] International norms and processes, he concludes, could hence be utilized by people in many countries. Transnational coalitions for the purpose of securing peace are having better chances to be successful, he predicts, after the Namibian experiences.[72] To that extent the decolonization of Namibia, which at least partly has been a result of UN intervention and implemented in its final stages under the UNTAG supervision, might not have been mainly a decisive factor in establishing democracy, but was certainly a relevant contribution towards creating a better environment for the further efforts towards democracy and the protection of human rights. To end, in the words of the UNTAG special representative who was in charge of the mission accomplished:

Namibia taught us the need to develop flexible, integrated task-oriented approaches to our new responsibilities in the area of peacemaking. There are, however, no easy analogies and we should beware of mechanistically repeating any operational plan. If the UNTAG experience is to provide a starting point for what could be a new dimension of international involvement in peaceful change and peacemaking in the last decade of the century, the foundation for a successful operation remains, as ever, the full cooperation of the parties concerned.[73]

Notes

1. Melber, Henning. 2003. "From controlled change to changed control: The case of Namibia", *Journal of Contemporary African Studies*, Vol. 21, No. 2.
2. Melber, Henning. 2003. "'Namibia, land of the brave': Selective memories on war and violence within nation building", in Jon Abbink, Mirjam de Bruijn, and Klaas van Walraven (eds) *Rethinking Resistance: Revolt and Violence in African History*, African Dynamics, Vol. 2. Leiden: Brill.
3. The chapter benefits in parts from previously published analyses which offer additional arguments and insights on certain issues less directly related to the topical focus of this chapter: Melber, Henning. 2000. "Development and aid", in Henning Melber (ed.) *Namibia – A Decade of Independence 1990–2000*. Windhoek: Namibian Economic Policy Research Unit; Melber, Henning. 2000. "The culture of politics", in Henning Melber (ed.) *Namibia – A Decade of Independence 1990–2000*. Windhoek: Namibian Economic Policy Research Unit, 2000; Melber, Henning. 2001. "Liberation and democracy in Southern Africa: The case of Namibia", in Henning Melber and Christopher Saunders *Transition in Southern Africa – Comparative Aspects. Two Lectures*. Uppsala: Nordic Africa Institute; Melber, Henning. 2002. "From liberation movements to governments: On political culture in Southern Africa", *African Sociological Review*, Vol. 6, No. 1.
4. Melber, Henning. 2000. "Economic and social transformation in the process of colonisation: Society and state before and during German rule", in Christiaan Keulder (ed.) *State, Society and Democracy. A Reader in Namibian Politics*. Windhoek: Gamsberg Macmillan.
5. With Resolution 2145 the UN General Assembly terminated on 27 October 1966 South Africa's mandate over South-West Africa and subsequently qualified its continued presence as illegal occupation.
6. This was subsequent to Resolution 2145(XXI), decided upon by the General Assembly on 19 May 1967, to create an entity representing the interests of the Namibian people within the UN agencies.
7. UN General Assembly Resolution 3111 of 12 December 1973 recognized SWAPO as "the authentic representative of the Namibian people". This was amended in UN General Assembly Resolution 31/146 of 20 December 1976 to "sole and authentic", endorsing an exclusive status and political monopoly of SWAPO in the negotiations on behalf of the Namibian population.
8. A wide range of literature has been produced on the Namibian case, much of it characterized by a preference to one of the parties involved in the conflict and reflecting the

bias of the Cold War period. Informative though not necessarily non-partisan overviews on the different aspects of the complex issue and the variety of political interests at work are offered by Dore, Isaak. 1985. *The International Mandate System and Namibia*. Boulder, CO and London: Westview Press; Dreyer, Ronald. 1994. *Namibia and Southern Africa. Regional Dynamics of Decolonization 1945–1990*. London and New York: Kegan Paul; Du Pisani, Andrew. 1986. *SWA/Namibia: The Politics of Continuity and Change*. Johannesburg: Jonathan Ball; Kaela, Laurent C. W. 1996. *The Question of Namibia*. Houndmills and London: Macmillan Press and New York: St Martin's Press; Nyangoni, Wellington W. 1985. *Africa in the United Nations System*. London and Mississauga: Associated University Presses; Rocha, Geisa Maria. 1984. *In Search of Namibian Independence. The Limitations of the United Nations*. Boulder, CO and London: Westview Press; Singham, A. W. and Shirley Hune. 1986. *Namibian Independence: A Global Responsibility*. Westport: Lawrence Hill; UN Institute for Namibia. 1987. *Namibia: A Direct United Nations Responsibility*. Lusaka: UN Institute for Namibia.

9. Dobell, Lauren. 1998. *Swapo's Struggle for Namibia, 1960–1991: War by Other Means*. Basel: P. Schlettwein Publishing.

10. In particular the chapters by Adam Przeworski ("Some problems in the study of the transition to democracy") and Alfred Stepan ("Paths towards redemocratization: Theoretical and comparative considerations") in Guillermo O'Donnell, Philippe C. Schmitter, and Laurence Whitehead (eds). 1986. *Transitions From Authoritarian Rule: Corporate Perspectives*. Baltimore: Johns Hopkins University Press.

11. Dobell, note 9 above.

12. *Ibid*.

13. One might argue that the constitutional principles, which were drafted in the early 1980s by the Western Contact Group and adopted by (if not to say imposed upon) the conflict parties (SWAPO and South Africa) as a common denominator and prerequisite for the implementation of Resolution 435 (1978), were characterized by a democratic notion. Others might counter-argue that this democratic notion was mainly crafted to maintain a *status quo* under a controlled change in terms of securing the existing property relations and former privileges by those who benefited from the minority rule.

14. "Interview with the President of the Republic of Finland, Martti Ahtisaari, 29.1.1966", in Soiri, Iina and Pekka Peltola. 1999. *Finland and National Liberation in Southern Africa*. Uppsala: Nordic Africa Institute.

15. A detailed but unashamedly biased pro-South African description of the events is offered by Stiff, Peter. 1989. *Nine Days of War. Namibia – Before, During and After*. Alberton: Lemur.

16. See, for example, the remarks in President Sam Nujoma's autobiography where he accuses Martti Ahtisaari, the highest UN official in charge of Namibian decolonization, of being "more concerned with his career at the United Nations than with his responsibilities towards the oppressed people of Namibia". Nujoma, Sam. 2001. *Where Others Wavered. The Autobiography of Sam Nujoma*. London: PANAF.

17. See the debates in Weiland, Heribert and Matthew Braham (eds). 1994. *The Namibia Peace Process: Implications and Lessons for the Future*. Freiburg: Arnold Bergstraesser Institut. See also passages of an interview with Martti Ahtisaari, who stated, *inter alia*, in defence of the passivity: "The sad thing is that when you are in a position like I was to implement an agreement, you had to be as tough with your friends as your foes because at that time you could hardly say that the South Africans were my friends. But you had to give them credit that they behaved correctly." Soiri and Peltola, note 14 above.

18. Soiri and Peltola, *ibid*.

19. *Namibia Nachrichten*, 25–26 March 1990.

20. Johansen, Robert. C. 1990. "UN peacekeeping: The changing utility of military force", *Third World Quarterly*, Vol. 11, No. 2.
21. Forest, Joshua Bernard. 1998. *Namibia's Post-Apartheid Regional Institutions: The Founding Year*. Rochester: Rochester University Press.
22. Quoted in Weiland and Braham, note 17 above.
23. *Ibid*. The pragmatic give-and-take approach has also been confirmed in the biography of Namibia's first head of state, who reiterates that "we agreed without argument that Namibia would be a multi-party democracy with an independent judiciary and a strong bill of rights". Nujoma, note 16 above.
24. Quoted in Weiland and Braham, *ibid*.
25. O'Donnell, Guillermo and Philippe C. Schmitter (eds). 1986. *Transitions From Authoritarian Rule: Tentative Conclusions About Uncertain Democracies*. Baltimore: Johns Hopkins University Press.
26. Dobell, note 9 above.
27. Bauer, Gretchen. 2001. "Namibia in the first decade of independence: How democratic?", *Journal of Southern African Studies*, Vol. 27, No. 1.
28. Erasmus, Gerhard. 2000. "The constitution: Its impact on Namibian statehood and politics", in Christiaan Keulder (ed.) *State, Society and Democracy. A Reader in Namibian Politics*. Windhoek: Gamsberg Macmillan. In this context it is relevant to acknowledge the impact of the UN Security Council's adoption of Document S/15287 of 12 July 1982 ("Principles concerning the Constituent Assembly and the Constitution for an independent Namibia"), introducing next to procedural rules for the planned election under UN supervision several "Constitutional Principles".
29. Erasmus, *ibid*.
30. Cliffe, Lionel, Ray Bush, Jenny Lindsay, and Brian Mokopakgosi. 1994. *The Transition to Independence in Namibia*. Boulder, CO and London: Lynne Rienner.
31. *Ibid*.
32. Harring, Sidney. 1995. "The constitution of Namibia and the land question. The inconsistency of Schedule 5 and Article 100 as applied to communal lands with the 'rights and freedoms' guaranteed communal land holders", paper presented to a workshop on "Traditional Authorities in the Nineties – Democratic Aspects of Traditional Government in Southern Africa", Centre for Applied Social Sciences/Faculty of Law at the University of Namibia, 15–16 November.
33. Szasz, Paul. 1994. "Creating the Namibian constitution", in Weiland and Braham, note 17 above.
34. Saunders, Christopher. 2001. "From apartheid to democracy in Namibia and South Africa: Some comparisons", in Henning Melber and Christopher Saunders *Transition in Southern Africa – Comparative Aspects. Two Lectures*. Uppsala: Nordic Africa Institute.
35. Erasmus, note 28 above.
36. Hinz, Manfred O. 2001. "To achieve freedom and equality: Namibia's new legal order", in Ingolf Diener and Olivier Graefe (eds) *Contemporary Namibia. The First Landmarks of a Post-Apartheid Society*. Windhoek: Gamsberg Macmillan.
37. Pickering, Arthur. 1995. "Instilling democracy and human rights values in Namibian society", in *Human Rights Education and Advocacy in Namibia in the 1990s. A Tapestry of Perspectives*. Windhoek: Gamsberg Macmillan.
38. Saul, John. 1999. "Liberation without democracy? Rethinking the experiences of the Southern African liberation movements", in Jonathan Hyslop (ed.) *African Democracy in the Era of Globalisation*. Johannesburg: Witwatersrand University Press.
39. As Lamb has recently put it with regard to SWAPO's violation of human rights in exile: "The international community turned a blind eye to human rights abuses, viewing the goal of Namibian independence as of greater importance. In particular, SWAPO had to

be seen as morally superior to the South African security forces. This contributed to an environment in which human rights violators continued to act with impunity." Lamb, Guy. 2001. "Putting belligerents in context: The cases of Namibia and Angola", in Simon Chesterman (ed.) *Civilians in War*. Boulder, CO and London: Lynne Rienner.

40. Dobell, note 9 above.

41. Glover, Susan K. 2000. "Namibia's recent elections: Something new or same old story?", *South African Journal of International Affairs*, Vol. 7, No. 2.

42. SWAPO Party Department of Information and Publicity. 1999. "Election manifesto".

43. Source: Keulder, Christiaan. 1998. *Voting Behaviour in Namibia – Local Authority Elections 1998*. Windhoek: Friedrich Ebert Stiftung; official figures from the Directorate of Elections for 1999.

44. Abbink, Jon. 2000. "Introduction: Rethinking democratization and election observation", in Jon Abbink and Gerti Hesseling (eds) *Election Obsevation and Democratization in Africa*. London: Macmillan.

45. According to a recent survey among citizens in Lesotho, Mozambique, Namibia, and Zimbabwe, only 57 per cent among interviewed Namibians (less than in the other countries) disagreed with the opinion that freedom of movement should as a basic human right transcend national boundaries. Eighty per cent (more than in the other countries) shared the opinion that it is important for a country to draw borders which make it different from other states. See Frayne, Bruce and Wade Pendleton. 2000. "Namibians on South Africa: Attitudes towards cross-border migration and immigration policy", in D. A. McDonald (ed.) *On Borders. Perspectives on International Migration in Southern Africa*. New York: St Martin's Press.

46. Mattes, Robert, Yul Derek Davids, Cherrel Africa, and Michael Bratton. 2000. *Public Opinion and the Consolidation of Democracy in Southern Africa: An Initial Review of Key Findings of the Southern African Democracy Barometer*, The Southern African Democracy Barometer Working Papers. Cape Town: Institute for Democracy in South Africa.

47. Bratton, Michael and Robert Mattes. 2001. "How people view democracy. Africans' surprising universalism", *Journal of Democracy*, Vol. 12, No. 1.

48. Johnson, R. W. 1998. "Six countries in search of democracy", *Focus*, No. 9.

49. Keulder, Christiaan and Dirk Spilker. 2002. "In search of democrats in Namibia: Attitudes among the youth", in Henning Melber (comp.) *Measuring Democracy and Human Rights in Southern Africa*, Discussion Paper No. 18. Uppsala: Nordic Africa Institute.

50. Sen, Amartya. 1999. *Development as Freedom*. Oxford: Oxford University Press.

51. This is not considered to be an argument in favour of conditionality. It only suggests that support for socio-economic development cannot be considered in isolation from the political environment and its impact on other sectors of society.

52. As a recent example illustrates, the prospects are currently not very encouraging: the *Human Development Report 2000* for Namibia had a focus on "gender and violence" which stated that "a decade after the end of the liberation struggle, military rhetoric and symbols play still play a large part in the political life of the country. The images and vocabulary of violence continue to receive significant attention. The names of the national soccer teams, the Brave Warriors and the Young Warriors, perpetuate images of violence in popular culture." UNDP with UN Country Team. 2000. *Namibia Human Development Report 2000*. Windhoek: UNDP Namibia.

53. UNDP, Development Co-operation Namibia. 1999. *1998 Report*. Windhoek: UNDP Namibia.

54. *Ibid.*

55. *The Namibian*, 24 February 2003.

56. Odén, Bertil. 1994. "Namibia: Macro-economics, resource distribution and the role of

aid", in Bertil Odén, Henning Melber, Tor Sellström, and Chris Tapscott (eds) *Namibia and External Resources. The Case of Swedish Development Assistance*. Uppsala: Nordic Africa Institute.

57. UNDP, Development Co-operation Namibia, note 53 above.
58. Original source: national accounts 1983–1998 and Development Co-operation Analysis System. Source: UNDP, Development Co-operation Namibia, note 53 above.
59. UNDP, Development Co-operation Namibia. 2001. *2000 Report on External Flow for the Calendar Year 1999*. Windhoek: UNDP Namibia.
60. Source: UNDP, Development Co-operation Namibia, note 53 above.
61. UNDP, Development Co-operation Namibia, note 59 above.
62. The CCF is the result of a consultative process that involved the Namibian government, the UN agencies, the donor community, and the UNDP country office.
63. UNDAF. 2001. *United Nations Development Assistance Framework 2001–2005. Co-ordination and Co-operation of the United Nations System in Namibia*. Windhoek: UNDAF.
64. *Ibid.*
65. Santise, Carlos. 2001. "International co-operation for democracy and good governance: Moving towards a second generation?", *European Journal of Development Research*, Vol. 13, No. 1.
66. Laakso, Liisa, Iina Soiri, Zenebework Tadesse, and Konjit Fekade. 1998. *In Search of Democratic Opposition – Constraints and Possibilities for Donors' Support in Namibia and Ethiopia*. Helsinki: Swedish School of Social Science, University of Helsinki.
67. National Democratic Institute for International Affairs. 1990. *Nation Building: The UN and Namibia*. Washington, DC: National Democratic Institute for International Affairs.
68. Schrire, Robert. 2001. "The realitites of opposition in South Africa: Legitimacy, strategies and consequences", in Roger Southall (ed.) *Opposition and Democracy in South Africa*. London and Portland: Frank Cass.
69. Hyden, Göran. 2000. "Post-war reconciliation and democratisation: Concepts, goals and lessons learnt", Working Paper 2000:8. Bergen: Chr. Michelsen Institute.
70. Gros, Jean-Germain. 1998. "Introduction: Understanding democracy", in Jean-Germain Gros (ed.) *Democratization in Late Twentieth-Century Africa. Coping with Uncertainty*. Westport and London: Greenwood.
71. Johansen, note 20 above.
72. One needs to keep in mind, however, a word of caution by Hearn, who points out that "the conflict in Namibia had largely been resolved prior to the deployment of UNTAG; the role of the UN was to facilitate the settlement plan. This is clearly different from intrastate conflicts where the UN has entered a country or a region where a conflict has not been resolved, with the aim of pacifying or resolving that conflict." See Hearn, Roger. 1999. *UN Peacekeeping in Action: The Namibian Experience*. Commack, NY: Nova Science Publishers.
73. Ahtisaari, Martti. 1991. "Foreword", in Dawid van Wyk, Marinus Wiechers, and Romaine Hill (eds) *Namibia. Constitutional and International Law Issues*. Pretoria: VerLoren van Themaat Centre for Public Studies/University of South Africa.

11

The UN's modest impact on Cambodia's democracy

Sorpong Peou

The best that can be said for the UN role in democratizing Cambodian politics, particularly as a result of the direct intervention by the UN Transitional Authority in Cambodia (UNTAC) in 1992–1993, is that it has been positive but modest. Some authors have argued that the UN's intervention actually had a negative impact.[1] Others contend that the country's structurally deep-seated problems were such that they thwarted any attempt to impose liberal values from outside; therefore, coercive attempts to transform Cambodian politics could only possibly have superficial, neutral, or temporary effects.[2] This chapter leans toward a third perspective: namely, the United Nations has made a modest but real contribution to the process of democratization.[3]

Properly assessing the UN's influence is a difficult methodological challenge because there are external actors other than the United Nations which form what may be called an "international aid regime". Between 1992 and 1997 there were 29 bilateral donors to Cambodia and several other multilateral ones, and the United Nations was only one of them, albeit a large and potentially influential one. As recently as June 2002, foreign donors from 22 countries and seven international organizations made annual pledges. The fact that the United Nations achieved only modest success can be explained by a growing imbalance of political power between the Cambodian regime, which has been increasingly dominated by one party, and the United Nations, a body appearing to be quite powerful but, in comparison to the authoritarian internal force, only having a relatively weak influence. This is not meant to suggest that other domestic factors – cultural and socio-economic – are unimportant. Obviously Cambodia was hardly a country that could be transformed into a democracy overnight, given its centuries-old undemocratic leadership culture and poor socio-economic conditions. The anti-democratic cultural factors have obviously hindered attempts by democracy promoters to accomplish their mission, but culture is dynamic and subject to change.[4] Poor countries, even without democratic traditions, can be more democratic than wealthy ones.[5] The point is that, within an extremely weak state, the process of democratic transition is fragile, often thwarted by unbalanced factional politics that perpetuates economic stagnation and social upheaval. The imbalance of power among the political élite often makes it difficult for them to reach any meaningful democratic compromise, especially at the early stages of democratic development.

Thus, the imbalance of social/factional power is the central concept of this case study, which treats the implantation of a democratic culture as the dependent variable and Cambodia's domestic power structure as its crucial independent variable. UN and other international assistance is treated as the intervening variable, because it helps condition the relationship between the dependent and independent variables.

This chapter is divided into four parts. The first provides some historical background to the conflict during the 1980s, and asserts that Cambodia would have remained undemocratic had the United Nations (and of course individual member states of the UN system) not intervened. The tenets of liberal democracy are used to assess Cambodia's current progress. The next part further evaluates the UN legacy and discusses the UN's modest record in the process of democratization. Part three shows some correlation between the UN's involvement and Cambodia's political trends over the decade since UN intervention. Specific examples of the UN's limited ability to change Cambodian politics are discussed. The fourth part explains the UN's several weaknesses in terms of its moral commitments, technical assistance, political will, and legal mandate.

UN intervention: Normative issues

In view of the country's tragic past, tainted as it is by repressive violence, civil wars, mass murder, and foreign interference, combined with its strategic geographic location in the heart of South-East Asia, Cambodia became the subject of intervention by the United Nations. After gaining independence in 1953, Cambodia enjoyed a short period of political stability. This came to an end in 1970, when Lon Nol and other members of the government of Prince Norodom Sihanouk staged a successful bloodless coup. The Prince's paternalistic regime gave way to what came to be known as the Khmer Republic, which quickly plunged into a bloody civil war and turned to authoritarian ways. The revolutionary movement known as the Khmer Rouge or "Red Khmer", led by a group of Marxist-Maoist intellectuals (most notably Pol Pot), challenged the regime and eventually won power in 1975.[6] The conflict was brutal and claimed an estimated minimum of 1.5 million lives. The new regime was repressive and totalitarian and turned the country into "killing fields" in a matter of days. Between 1 and 1.5 million additional people lost their lives under its reign of terror. Many scholars believe the Khmer Rouge committed genocide.[7] Indeed, the new term "auto-genocide" was first employed to describe the Cambodian tragedy.[8]

The revolutionary totalitarian Pol Pot regime was brought to an end in 1979 by an invasion by close to 200,000 Vietnamese troops. History's irony replayed itself in a tragic way. During the 1970–1975 period, the civil war was waged between the Khmer Republic (with military assistance from the USA and its allies) and the Khmer Rouge (with military assistance from socialist allies, particularly North Viet Nam). But during the period 1979–1989, socialist Viet Nam assisted the anti-Pol Pot socialist regime, an ally of the Soviet bloc, known as the People's Republic of Kampuchea (PRK), which came into existence in 1979 and changed to the State of Cambodia (SOC) in 1989.

China, leading Western states, and other anti-communist states in South-East Asia rushed to assist the Cambodian resistance movement, which included the Khmer Rouge remnants under the firm grip of Pol Pot and his loyalists. Under immense pressure from these states, especially China, the Khmer Rouge agreed to form an alliance with two other major resistance armies: the anti-communist, anti-Vietnamese Khmer People's National Liberation Front (KPNLF) and the royalist National United Front for an Independent, Neutral, Peaceful, and Cooperative Cambodia (FUNCINPEC). The resulting émigré Coalition Government of Democratic Kampuchea (CGDK) was formed in 1981 to fight the PRK/SOC regime. Throughout the 1980s neither side could prevail over the other through military means. Even after the final withdrawal of Vietnamese troops from Cambodia in 1989, the war continued unabated.

The *realpolitik* of the situation pointed to the need to combine all forces opposed to the PRK/SOC regime, and indeed the inclusion of the Khmer Rouge in the peace process was believed by some to be a recipe for lasting peace.[9] In reality, the promotion of democracy was jeopardized by the UN acceptance of the genocidal Khmer Rouge faction in the electoral process, though it can be argued that the Paris Agreements were possible only because they included the Khmer Rouge. Also, the civil war continued after the 1993 election because of the government's decision not to accept its inclusion. Cambodia was an extremely fragile state that could not afford a protracted war. The country has since 1998 experienced peace and stability after a series of amnesties were given to some Khmer Rouge leaders, whose army disintegrated with remnants integrated into the national armed forces.

Any argument that UNTAC acted more or less as a "colonial power" seeking to impose its will and a set of alien values on another sovereign state could not be more misleading. The UN mission did not aim to transform Cambodia into a colony of any kind, the way the French had turned Cambodia into one of its protectorates in the nineteenth century. The Paris Agreements defended the sovereignty, independence, territorial integrity, neutrality, and national unity of Cambodia. Cambodia and 18 other states agreed on a comprehensive political settlement, which was based on "full observance of the principles of non-interference and non-intervention in the internal and external affairs of States". The agreements reaffirmed "the inalienable rights of States freely to determine their own political, economic, cultural and social systems in accordance with the will of their peoples, without outside interference, subversion, coercion or threat in any form whatsoever". In this context, the UN mission also sought to restore Cambodia's rightful place as a sovereign member of the international community, and pulled out of the country shortly after its tasks came to an end.

The UN mission also helped prepare the way for future assistance in the process of national reconstruction. Part IV of the Paris Agreements was devoted to a declaration on the rehabilitation and reconstruction of Cambodia as a sovereign state. Paragraph 2 even prohibited any attempt to impose a development strategy on the country from any outside source or to deter potential donors from contributing to its reconstruction. It added that "the main responsibility for deciding Cambodia's reconstruction needs and plans should rest with the Cambodian people and the government after free and fair elections". Furthermore, the declaration made it clear that the process of rehabilitation and reconstruction as well as economic aid to Cambodia should not leave out any area of the country or any level of society, especially the more disadvantaged.[10]

The "neutral" or "temporary effect" argument has more merit than the "harmful effect" one, but remains empirically weak. The contention that nothing in Cambodia has really changed over the last 10 years is false. If we treat Laos and Viet Nam as a control group and subject them to analysis, the differences today are striking: Cambodia and its former allies belong to different types of political system because the communist parties of Laos and Viet Nam retain a complete monopoly of political power.

When examined closely, Cambodia is no longer a socialist state under the control of one vanguard communist party. Looking at 1982–1991 as the baseline for analytical purposes, the regime clearly did not fit any definition of liberal democracy. The key components – including electoral contestation, representation and protection of diverse interests, aggregation of diverse individuals as well as groups, the state as impartial referee, a system of checks and balances to prevent the tyranny of the majority, constitutional safeguards of individual rights, and equality before the law – were patently absent. Liberal democracy contains several attributes that serve as useful indicators for measuring the process of democratic transition. Government leaders do not inherit their positions; they must compete for public office through an electoral process in which others are also allowed to take part. Such electoral competition means there are at least two political parties contending for power and entails three features: repeatability, *ex post* irreversibility, and *ex ante* uncertainty. Elections must be repeated or held on a regular basis; and the winner must not use the power of incumbency to make it impossible for challengers to compete in future elections and/or win. Electoral outcomes are temporary. Losers do not forfeit the right to compete again. *Ex post* irreversibility means that whoever wins elections is allowed to form the next government. *Ex ante* uncertainty means the incumbent party could lose in the next free and fair elections.[11] Others go beyond these basic indicators of liberal democracy, adding another: political rights and civil liberties. George Sorensen lists three dimensions of procedural democracy: "competition, participation, and civil and political liberties".[12]

The PRK regime came to power in 1979 through bullets, not the ballot box. The majority of the people who survived the "killing fields" were generally unhappy about living under another regime they considered "communist" and led by some of those who had been part of the brutal Pol Pot regime, despite their claim to have freed Cambodia from genocide. The People's Revolutionary Party of Kampuchea (PRPK) had fewer than 30,000 members, representing only about 0.36 per cent of the population. An election was held in 1981, but only one party was allowed to run for public office. The party leadership was made up of former Communist Party of Kampuchea cadre, who had rebelled against the Pol Pot group but then acted under Vietnamese direction. For the next 10 years, not a single national election was held.

Although it was far less repressive than the Pol Pot regime and it did its best to present the polished image of a legitimate state to the international community, the new socialist regime granted few political rights or civil liberties to its citizens. Citizens were forbidden to form any political parties to challenge the ruling Communist Party. Although restrictions on religious belief and freedom of movement were gradually loosened, the regime did not allow free and independent media. No independent judiciary was put in place, either. People accused of supporting the "enemies" were imprisoned and tortured. Although the state did not seek to control every aspect of social and personal life, as the Pol Pot regime had, property rights were restricted. The SOC regime, however, did officially adopt a market economic policy in 1989.

This was the Cambodian political landscape the United Nations had to deal with. The permanent members of the UN Security Council, especially the USA and France, managed to get the warring factions to accept agreements that included provisions in support of democracy and human rights. Parts II and III of the Paris Agreements focused on elections and human rights. Article 12 stated that "[t]he Cambodian people shall have the right to determine their own political future through free and fair election of a constituent assembly, which will draft and approve a new ... Constitution in accordance with Article 23". According to Article 23, Cambodia would adopt a constitution built on basic principles promoting human rights, fundamental freedoms, and Cambodia's status of neutrality as a sovereign state.

On human rights, Article 15 of the agreement clearly stated: "All persons in Cambodia and all Cambodian refugees and displaced persons shall enjoy the rights and freedoms embodied in the Universal Declaration of Human Rights and other international human rights instruments." Article 16 allowed UNTAC to take responsibility to foster an environment that would ensure respect for human rights. Article 17 permitted the UN Commission on Human Rights to continue monitoring the human rights situation in Cambodia after the end of the transition period.

Annex 5 of the Paris Agreements further laid down specific fundamental principles for a new constitution. Paragraph 2, for instance, stated that "Cambodia's tragic recent history requires special measures to assure protection of human rights. Therefore, the constitution will contain a declaration of fundamental rights, including the rights to life, personal liberty, security, freedom of movement, freedom of religion, assembly and association including political parties and trade unions." Other fundamental rights included due process and equality before the law, protection from arbitrary deprivation of property or deprivation of private property without just compensation, and freedom from racial, ethnic, religious, or sexual discrimination.

The UN's modest record: 1992–2002

In order to understand better the UN's success in its attempted democratic and human rights transformation of Cambodia, it will be important to determine whether this has had any lasting effects on Cambodian attitudes. This section therefore examines the UN's record over the 1992–2002 period and its impact on Cambodia's political progress, and reveals it to be modestly successful. Political progress is "measured" in the qualitative context of what is termed "democratic acculturation".[13] At the risk of oversimplification, democratic acculturation is treated as the dependent variable and defined as attitudinal progression towards respect for the liberal rules of the democratic game.

One positive indicator in the early process of democratic acculturation is associated with the continuing effects of the constitution (largely drafted by UN advisers and adopted after the 1993 election), which was fairly liberal, although far from perfect by Western standards. The king no longer enjoys absolute power; he reigns, but does not rule. Khmer citizens enjoy constitutional guarantees of rights. Representatives of the people are to be elected to the National Assembly, and soon to the new Senate. The executive is to be held accountable in parliament for its actions. The judiciary is intended to have independent power. The Constitutional Council has the duty to safeguard respect for the constitution, and to interpret it as well as legislation.

A second positive indicator is that Cambodia continues to have a multi-party electoral system and has thus far held national elections on a regular basis. In the 1993 election there were about 19 political parties; in the 1998 election the number rose to 39; in the 2002 commune elections, eight political parties[14] with more than 76,000 candidates competed for local power. This multi-party electoral system proves that Cambodian citizens now have a basic level of rights to organize political parties and other competitive groups of their own choice. The July 2003 national election was held on schedule. All this shows regularity in holding elections.

A third positive indicator might be seen in the fact that political parties seem more readily to accept election outcomes. After the 1993 election the Cambodian People's Party (CPP) contested the outcome; some of its leaders even threatened to divide up the country militarily. In July 1997 the CPP overturned the compromise flowing from the 1993 elections when it drove First Prime Minister Ranariddh out of power and Second Prime Minister Hun Sen took sole charge of government affairs.[15] After the 1998 election FUNCINPEC and the Sam Rainsy Party (SRP) staged large demonstrations to protest the irregularities that led to their defeat, but the royalists finally agreed to form a coalition with the CPP. The SRP chose to remain the main opposition party in parliament. There was no open military conflict among them. The 2002 commune elections saw even fewer outcome-related controversies. It is not suggested that the opposition parties have no reasons for complaint, as the 2002 election was marred by irregularities. During the voter registration period alone, election observers such as COMFREL, COFFEL, and NICFEC examined only 3,711 of the 12,378 registration stations and found 7,477 cases of technical irregularities.[16] Breaches of the campaign law, poor conditions for campaigning, intimidation of voters, vote buying, threats and violence against candidates, and deaths were subsequently reported.[17] But opposition leaders filed far fewer election-related complaints than in 1998 and staged no massive protests against the CPP, as they had in 1998. The real test for this indicator, however, would be CPP acceptance of an electoral defeat, an unlikely prospect at this stage.

If the decline of political violence over the 1992–2002 period is treated as an indicator of democratic acculturation, numerous sources of evidence clearly suggest that the overall level of political violence against opposition parties has decreased noticeably. Before the 1998 election 22 politically motivated killings took place, but this number represented a marked decrease in violence from the 1993 election, which claimed at least 200 lives. According to the representative for the UN High Commissioner for Human Rights (UNHCHR), who issued a report on the commune elections, "there has been a decrease in acts of violence and intimidation compared to previous national polls".[18]

The overall number of deaths appears to have decreased from 1998 to 2002, a period leading to the commune election. In 1999 there was a zero death rate, but the following year witnessed the killing of four political activists as the commune election was being considered. The number increased to 12 in 2001. The period from January to 3 February 2002 alone saw five deaths. The number of deaths in the three-month period leading to polling day was 13 for the 1998 election, compared to 11 for the 2002 election. Several killings before the 1998 election also involved torture and mutilation, whereas only one such death occurred in the 2002 election.[19] Moreover, the 2002 election saw less severe political intimidation when compared with the 1993 and 1998 national elections. During the commune election, "political parties were [also] able to resolve disputes arising from polling day and vote counting in a manner that avoided further conflict" and "there have been fewer retribution problems than in 1998".[20]

But the regular holding of national and communal elections, increasingly peaceful transfers of power, and less political violence alone do not qualify Cambodian democracy as liberal and embedded. In fact, the Cambodian style of democracy appears to be becoming more illiberal. One negative indicator that shows stagnation in the democratic process is that election outcomes have become more certain. The CPP has fought its way back to power – from its defeat in the 1993 election to a near-monopoly of political and military/police power – and appears certain to win in further foreseeable elections. Trends in the last 10 years confirm this prediction. An impressive show of public interest in regime change was evident on polling day in 1993, when the majority of the voters gave a resounding approval to FUNCINPEC rather than the CPP, despite the latter's political violence and intimidation. In this election FUNCINPEC won, having collected 45.5 per cent of the total vote, which translated into 58 seats, compared with 51 seats garnered by the CPP. Had the political environment been subject to less control by the SOC and to more control by UNTAC, the other parties would have collected even more seats.

Although it was the loser, the CPP successfully forced FUNCINPEC to share power within a coalition government that kept political control from the royalists, and in July 1997 Minister Hun Sen seized power as Cambodia's sole Prime Minister. Few, if any, had expected the CPP to lose in the 1998 election. The CPP gained 64 out of the 122 seats in the National Assembly; the FUNCINPEC seats were reduced to 43, whereas the SRP picked up 14 per cent of the vote (15 seats). The 2002 commune council elections legitimized the CPP's almost complete control over the communes. The CPP was left in charge of more than 98 per cent of the country's 1,621 communes. FUNCINPEC and the SRP may have broken the CPP's absolute monopoly of commune control, but they only won a handful of communes, virtually all in urban areas.

The pattern suggests that political stability is likely when the CPP believes it has the upper hand in elections, but that the party may resort to violence and intimidation the moment its leaders believe that their party faces defeat. There is nothing to indicate the CPP is prepared to let opposition parties win future elections. The ruling party may simply have adopted a new political strategy – one that appears to rely less on brute force and more on structural constraints to keep opposition parties at bay.

This is another key negative indicator; the growing certainty of electoral outcomes in favour of the CPP results not from its performance in office, but rather from its ability to use its powers of incumbency to control various institutions, thus neutralizing opposition parties, especially during elections. Since the coup in 1997, the CPP has gained more control over the news delivery system. News coverage in the 1998 election tended to focus on the activities of the government and the CPP.[21] During the 30-day campaign period, each party received only five minutes of free television time, hardly enough for opposition parties to get their messages across to voters. UN reports on the 1998 election further concluded that access to press, radio, and television by political parties and candidates was far from fair. The CPP strongly dominated state and quasi-state electronic media stations. The activities of opposition political parties and their candidates went unreported.[22]

A UN report confirms that media access before the 2002 election "was less fair than in 1998 ... Problems relating to the ownership structure of media companies and imbalance in news coverage remained. News coverage both by state-owned and private television and radio focused overwhelmingly on the activities of the government and the [CPP]. Only marginal coverage was given to FUNCINPEC and the Sam Rainsy Party."[23] Other sources made similar assessments. According to Carlos Costa Neves, chief observer of the EU Election Observation Mission for the Cambodian commune election, "State TV and radio failed to meet their obligation to provide voters with adequate information on the election or fair and balanced coverage of the campaign. State TV devoted over 75% of coverage to government and a further 12% to CPP." His statement adds that "In contrast, FUNCINPEC received 2% of coverage and Sam Rainsy Party less than 1%. The President of the National Assembly, Prince Norodom Ranariddh, who is leader of the CPP's main rival party, FUNCINPEC, received some 8% of coverage." Moreover, "Coverage by private TV showed a similar bias. Private stations also declined to accept party advertising, apparently fearing any involvement in politics."[24]

The extent to which the CPP-dominated system has a negative effect on the process of democratic acculturation is difficult to assess, but evidence shows that the CPP has sought to control the electoral environment. The balance of power among the 11 members elected to the National Election Committee (NEC) on 26 January 1998 favoured the CPP. Although the committee had a representative from each of the political parties represented in the National Assembly, the CPP still had the upper hand, albeit mitigated to some extent by the presence of foreign – EU and Canadian – advisers. Thousands of local election observers were also known to have political links to the CPP.[25] It is not difficult to understand why the CPP-dominated NEC sought to impose greater restrictions on freedom of expression during the 2002 election campaign period.

After the commune elections in 2002, the CPP took further steps to consolidate its political control over the NEC. Opposition parties sought to make the committee more politically representative. FUNCINPEC, for instance, drafted a proposal aimed to create a six-member NEC board represented by two members of each of the three major parties, to prevent vote buying and ensure more equitable access by all parties to the media. But the CPP rejected the proposal and succeeded in amending the electoral law to empower the Ministry of Interior to nominate NEC candidates. The new five-member NEC is now made up three CPP-affiliated members and two royalists, thus maintaining the balance of decision-making power within the committee in favour of the CPP. The main opposition party, the SRP, still has no representative in the NEC. In October 2002 three opposition parties threatened to stage demonstrations if the coalition government controlled by the CPP and FUNCINPEC refused to reorganize the NEC.[26]

The limited impact of UN "democracy" assistance

UNTAC laid a good foundation for democracy and human rights in Cambodia. Its electoral component was the most successful part of the mission. Its human rights component engaged in human rights education and the investigation of human rights abuses.[27] In October 1992, UNTAC launched an appeal for the Human Rights Education Programme. The impact was immediately noticeable. The recent growth of indigenous human rights organizations engaged in public education and investigation in Cambodia should not be overlooked. They are by-products of the UN intervention.

The post-UNTAC liberal constitution was also a major legacy of the Paris Agreements and the UN role in Cambodia. To this day, the Cambodian government remains rhetorically committed to the protection of democratic and human rights enshrined in the constitution. In September 2000, for instance, Prime Minister Hun Sen was among the heads of state and government gathered at the UN headquarters, where they reaffirmed their commitment to democracy and human rights in the UN Millennium Declaration.

Since 1993 the United Nations has also served as a useful mechanism for exposing political violence or violations of human rights in the country. The Cambodian Office of the UN High Commissioner for Human Rights (COHCHR) reports to the Commission on Human Rights and publishes numerous reports. UN offices have served as useful repositories of information and documentation related to political development. Other agencies and institutes working to promote democracy and human rights have relied on their reports. One of the advantages of the UN offices is that their officials are often given more access to information than other agencies in the country. The special representative of the UN Secretary-General in particular has the important responsibilities of maintaining a political dialogue with the Cambodian government, monitoring the political and security developments of the country, and reporting to the Secretary-General through the Under Secretary-General of the Department of Political Affairs.

The United Nations has been influential to the extent that it has at least put the Cambodian government on the defensive in regard to human rights violations. For instance, the government responded quickly to a memorandum by the UN special representative for human rights containing details of summary executions, missing persons, and torture during and after the 1997 coup. Then Foreign Minister Ung Huot accepted that:

the Royal Government promptly initiate investigations into the information provided [because] there is a need for a serious criminal investigation into each of the cases referred to in the appended document. Those responsible for summary executions or other serious crimes ... in this context must be brought to justice.[28]

The various UN bodies also played a useful role in helping to facilitate the process leading to the election. Before the 1998 election, they assisted in the electoral process. Alongside the ASEAN "Troika", Australia, Canada, Japan, the USA, and the EU (members of the "Friends of Cambodia", which put pressure on the government to hold elections with all political parties present), the United Nations offered support, equipment, and technical assistance for the creation of an electoral administration. Since late 1998 and before the 2002 commune elections, UN agencies such as the UNDP were also involved in model decentralization projects to help promote good governance.

One must, however, understand the limited power the United Nations can wield in at least four broad areas. First, in respect of political violence, UNTAC was unable to disarm the Cambodian signatories, a circumstance that perpetuated the war until 1998. This is not to blame UNTAC, although the mission was unable to take effective action in part due to the slow deployment of its troops, but to point to the limits of what it could do at the time. The United Nations could not prevent attacks on opposition party members, nor indeed prevent the coup in 1997. Nor could it restore the pre-coup political *status quo*, though the UN special representative was able to facilitate the return of exiled politicians who had fled after the coup. But to do so, the UN special representative needed the active support of the "Friends of Cambodia"[29] to put pressure on the CPP leadership to allow opposition parties to compete in a free and fair election. Thus, the United Nations played a useful role when backed by key members, especially the major donors and permanent members in the Security Council.

Second, the United Nations has had a very limited impact on the promotion of equitable media access during elections. During the run-up to the 1998 election, for instance, the special representative of the UN Secretary-General for human rights in Cambodia, Thomas Hammarberg, reported on the unfair access to press, radio, and television by political parties and candidates. The CPP showed no signs of taking any serious action in response. Subsequent UN attempts to ensure equitable media access were equally unsuccessful. Before the 2002 elections, UN special representative for human rights Peter Leuprecht recommended a number of steps for the Cambodian government to ensure the prevention of political rights violations, including repeated calls for equitable access to the media. He received assurances from the NEC that the parties and candidates would receive equal access to the media during the 15-day campaign period but "this did not happen".[30] As noted, media access during the 2002 elections was even less equitable than in 1998. According to a UN report, "instead of promoting media access, the NEC played an active role in hindering the broadcast of party messages, roundtable discussions and candidate debates through delays in decision-making, ill-considered directives, and administrative obfuscation".[31]

Third, the Cambodian authorities not only failed to respond to UN pressure for equitable media access, but also failed to have the NEC comply with UN demands for law enforcement in relation to electoral laws, including in the case of the 2002 communal elections.[32] At first, the NEC appeared to respond favourably to the demands. On 4 November 2001 the NEC instructed all commune election committees "to hold a hearing to punish offenders of the electoral law ... and to ensure the effectiveness of the hearing process". However, the NEC itself failed to enforce the penal provisions in the Law of Commune Council Elections. It did not use its mandated powers and took no serious action when numerous violations were brought to its attention. According to a UN report, "in no cases were the sanctions stipulated by law enforced. Hearings into complaints resulted, in a few cases, in warnings being issued to the officials."[33]

Under pressure from the United Nations and donor countries, the government established a Central Security Office for the Defence of the Commune Elections in August 2001, a body to investigate any incident related to the election. The UN special representative for human rights also put pressure on Cambodian authorities to curb violence and intimidation. In November 2001 he managed to get Hun Sen to call for non-violence in the election period, but CPP officials only paid lip-service to this pledge. Although he mentioned it about 15 times before polling day, Human Rights Watch was "not aware of any steps taken by the government to turn the Prime Minister's words into official policy to ensure the security of both candidates and voters".[34] By early 2002, the Central Security Office had remained ineffective and had failed to conduct any investigations.[35]

CPP officials also tended to deny any violation of political rights and civil liberties. In a statement put out on 6 February 2002, for instance, the Ministry of Interior contended that the commune elections were free, fair, and just, as well as non-violent, and that "since before the beginning of the electoral campaign until the present, there has been no politically motivated crime". Instead, the statement condemned a number of the local and international media for "reporting misleading information of crimes…"[36]

Fourth, Cambodian authorities also tended to ignore repeated UN calls for political justice. On 6 November 1998, Thomas Hammarberg, before the Third Committee of the UN General Assembly, made known his concern over the continuing culture of impunity in Cambodia and complained about the political intimidation and violence before and after the 1998 election. He gave details concerning the 182 deaths since the March 1997 grenade attack on the demonstrators led by the SRP and the coup against Prince Ranariddh in July 1997. Subsequently, on 18 November 1998, the Third Committee of the UN General Assembly adopted a resolution that "[called] upon the Government of Cambodia to investigate urgently and prosecute, in accordance with due process of the law and international standards relating to human rights, all those who have perpetrated human rights violations".[37] The resolution expresses "grave concern at the situation of impunity in Cambodia and stresses that … bringing to justice those responsible for human rights violations … remains a matter of critical and urgent priority".[38] In spite of the strong assurance by the then Foreign Minister, Ung Huot, that his government would promptly investigate the human rights cases associated with the coup in July 1997, no one involved in the summary executions or torture of royalist members has been brought to justice.

The UN demands for justice were never heeded; few perpetrators of subsequent political crimes, if any, have been prosecuted.[39] The most galling example of the UN's limitations in promoting justice had been its inability to pressure the government in Phnom Penh to allow the judicial process to bring former Khmer Rouge leaders to justice.[40] But in June 2003 Cambodia and the United Nations signed an agreement concerning the prosecution under Cambodian law of crimes committed during the period of Democratic Kampuchea. The 32-article agreement between the United Nations and the government of Cambodia provides for the establishment of "extraordinary chambers" within the existing court structure of Cambodia. The chambers will have jurisdiction to try senior leaders of Democratic Kampuchea and "those most responsible for the crimes and serious violations of Cambodian and international law during the period from 17 April 1975 to 6 January 1979". They will comprise one trial court and one Supreme Court, and there will be a mix of international and Cambodian judges. Decisions in the two chambers will be taken by a majority of four and five judges respectively.[41]

In short, then, the UN successes in promoting democracy should not be exaggerated. The world organization was in a position to take some firm actions to pressure Cambodia, such as leaving the Cambodian seat in the UN General Assembly unoccupied after the 1997 coup, but the United Nations could do little to restore the pre-coup political power-sharing arrangement agreed to by the winner of the 1993 election. Nor could the United Nations do much to increase respect for the rules of liberal democracy, most notably in the areas of equitable media access, electoral law enforcement, and justice for the victims of political violence, especially opposition party members.

Explaining the UN's modest record

The UN's modest record can be best understood if its "democracy" assistance is treated as an intervening variable that had some effect on the domestic power relations between the Cambodian signatories of the Paris Agreements. As shall be discussed later, it was not the UN's main objective to create a more symmetrical power structure in the country. In the event, it contributed to Cambodia's increasingly asymmetrical structure of power relations.

It is worth emphasizing that Cambodia's cultural and socio-economic factors made it difficult for the United Nations to play a more effective role in the country. At the time of UNTAC's arrival, as noted, Cambodia had no genuine democratic culture. Between 1946 and 1981, 10 elections for legislative assemblies were held: three before Cambodia gained independence in 1953, four from independence to 1970, one under the Khmer Rouge regime, and one under the PRK/SOC regime. Although the first three elections were considered reasonably free and fair, the subsequent ones were not.[42]

The majority of Cambodians are also said to show little interest in democracy, a conclusion drawn from a 1995 study by the National Democratic Institute (NDI).[43] According to a survey conducted in 2000 by the Center for Advanced Study, "most Cambodians still favor feudal or paternalistic local government, over either democratic or authoritarian forms".[44] The majority (56 per cent) of the respondents held a paternalistic view of the government as a father and the people as a child. Only 27 per cent of them believed that government and people are equals, thus reflecting a low level of civic culture in Cambodia.

While culture matters, it should not be viewed as deterministic. Even if only 27 per cent of Cambodians understood the meaning of democracy, this would represent progress and reveal that culture is not immutable. Moreover, it should not be forgotten that the last two national elections saw extremely large voter turnouts, with 98 per cent of the entire voter population participating in 1998. Although the rate of voter turnout declined to 83 per cent in the commune election, it should not be taken to mean most Cambodians prefer an authoritarian form of government. Such decline, even if it continued in future elections, should be seen more as a by-product of disillusionment among voters.

Socio-economic perspectives shed more light on why Cambodians may have grown disillusioned with the country's new democratic politics and why the United Nations could not do much more than it has.[45] The socio-economic conditions in the early 1990s were still appalling. After a decade of war and destruction in the 1970s, the national economy was brought to its knees. The Khmer Rouge policy reduced Cambodia to a Stone Age economy. In 1983 the Ministry of Agriculture claimed that the country's per capita income was only about $50. In 1986 the Economist Intelligence Unit (EIU) cited a mid-1988 PRK figure of $70.[46] Out of the approximately 500 medical doctors before the Khmer Rouge period, only about 40 remained in 1979. By the late 1980s, Cambodia had one doctor for every 30,000 people. The PRK/SOC regime also rebuilt the educational system from scratch.[47] The country's Human Development Index (HDI) value in 1992 was 0.337. The UNDP placed Cambodia at 153 out of 174 countries, with a life expectancy rate at birth of only 51.6 years, a life expectancy index of 0.44, an adult literacy rate of 37.8, and an education index of 0.35. The real GDP per capita was only $1,250, and the GDP index was only 0.22.[48] All of these socio-economic problems presented a formidable challenge for the United Nations to help democratize Cambodia. After almost a decade of rebuilding since the UN intervention, the country's socio-economic conditions have improved noticeably: the UNDP promoted Cambodia from among those with low human development to among those with medium human development (now standing at 130 among 173 countries). In 2000, its life expectancy at birth was 56.4 years; its life expectancy index was 0.52; its adult literacy rate was 67.8; its education index was 0.66; its GDP per capita was $1,446; its GDP index was 0.45; and its Human Development Index value was 0.577.[49]

These improved socio-economic factors alone, however, do not seem to be a sufficient condition for democratic acculturation. Relatively steady GDP growth between 1993 and 1996 (4.1 per cent in 1993, 4.0 per cent in 1994, 7.6 per cent in 1995, and 7 per cent in 1996) did not prevent political violence, especially the coup in July 1997, which brought GDP growth down to 3.7 per cent in 1997 and 1.8 per cent in 1998.[50] While the economy began to rebound in 1999 and 2000 (5 per cent and 5.5 per cent growth respectively), the country's democracy continued to stagnate.

There is no clear correlation between technical and economic aid and direct political influence or steady democratic acculturation, either. The UN agencies and institutions, for instance, together constitute a major donor presence in Cambodia, but cannot impose much influence on the government. From 1992 to 1997, for instance, they disbursed more than $400 million (larger than the EU disbursement of $183 million or the Asian Development Bank's of $130 million over the same period), but clearly their efforts prevented neither the 1997 coup nor other violent incidents. As mentioned earlier, the decline in the overall level of political violence over the last 10 years has been more strongly correlated with the CPP's growing confidence in its ability to consolidate its political power base. Japan, Cambodia's largest donor, did play a useful role in helping to bring the Cambodian factions back into the electoral process in 1998.

One important factor that kept Cambodia from democratic acculturation is that as the CPP has grown stronger, the United Nations has lost much of its influence over the Cambodian regime. From the earliest UNTAC days, the CPP leadership quickly learned that the United Nations was not mandated to restrict the party's power to any real extent. The United Nations spent US$2.2 billion on UNTAC work, but was not able to tackle the underlying political restraints hampering Cambodia's transition to democracy. UNTAC succeeded in holding the 1993 election, but could not effectively influence the political consequences following the election results. The international community's ambiguous record on the Khmer Rouge position gave the CPP ammunition to present itself as the most credible party to prevent the return of Khmer Rouge "genocide". To this day, however, the CPP leadership has ridiculed UNTAC's failure to bring peace to Cambodia, and has instead given itself the credit for being the only party that could effectively bring an end to the war.

A harsh reality that has emerged in Cambodian politics today is that none of the opposition parties is in a serious position to defeat the CPP in an election. The most credible challenger – FUNCINPEC – has suffered from numerous internal political frictions. In early 2003 it was reported that about 20 of the royalist generals would leave FUNCINPEC for the SRP.[51]

The UN's political role has inevitably grown weaker with the passing of time, especially since 1998 after the CPP's electoral victory. The COHCHR role in promoting respect for human rights can hardly be said to be influential. It was unique in that it was the first office outside the UNHCHR headquarters in Geneva, but it operates on a budget of only US$2 million (1998). The UN representative for human rights visits Cambodia a few times a year. As a result, the CPP-dominated government has become more confident in resisting the United Nations. While agreeing in November 1999 that the UN Human Rights Centre in Cambodia could remain, Hun Sen contended that the United Nations should instead focus its efforts on providing technical assistance in such areas as the drafting of laws and judicial reform, not in monitoring human rights abuses. He even asked the UN Secretary-General to close down the office of the special representative in Cambodia, claiming that its presence was not based on any agreement. This coincided with the intention of the United Nations to close the office in any case for fiscal reasons. The Prime Minister further said he now wanted to see a return to normalcy in Cambodia-UN relations, arguing that the Cambodian representative at the UN headquarters in New York should serve as the official channel between them.

The office of the special representative of the UN Secretary-General in Cambodia exercises little political power. In 1994, because of the ongoing war, the Cambodian government elevated him to semi-diplomatic status and invited him to all diplomatic functions; however, he "was not equipped to deal with effective preventive diplomacy and peacemaking"[52] and "carried neither the stick nor the carrot".[53]

Another factor is the changing nature of the UN's efforts. The centre of gravity of UN involvement in Cambodia quickly shifted from the UNTAC mission to different UN agencies: the UN Development Programme (UNDP), the World Bank (WB), and the International Monetary Fund (IMF). They, along with the other UN bodies active in Cambodia, have devoted almost all of their efforts to helping to reconstruct the Cambodian economy rather than to consolidating any democratic gains.

The United Nations is now in the position of attempting to achieve broad democratization objectives with limited resources, although the UN coordinator (the UNDP resident representative) played a useful role in ensuring that the material and technical assistance was focused and avoided redundancies. When given the task of coordinating the Joint International Observers Group (consisting of some 500 observers from 40 countries) during the 1998 election, for instance, the UN role was strategic but necessarily tailored to the limited resources of the Electoral Assistance Division of the UN Department of Political Affairs.

Limited resources and narrowed objectives became the norm in the UN's work in Cambodia. The UNDP office was given the responsibility of coordinating the activities of UN agencies (especially in technical areas, such as mine clearing and military reintegration and demobilization) and has also provided election assistance, but it has not always considered it as part of its mandate to defend democracy. It was even seen as being soft on the Cambodian authorities. During the 2002 election, its electoral team issued a paper before the election taking the legalistic position that the NEC had neither the duty nor the legal right to ensure the "coverage of the electoral campaign in state-run newspaper and TV".[54] This position raised critical questions about the UN agency's political understanding and drew editorial criticism.[55] The World Bank has served as one of the two co-chairs for the annual aid-pledging conference on Cambodia, but the major UN financial institutions, the World Bank and the IMF, involved in Cambodia do not have a mandate to promote liberal democracy but tend to be satisfied, along with other UN bodies, with promoting the processes of electoral democracy, which have seen Cambodia in effect turn into a one-party "democracy". Although the UNDP office had the responsibility to promote good governance in Cambodia (of which democracy is an aspect), democracy promotion has never been high on its agenda in Cambodia in view of the reality of having to deal with a dominant incumbent political party.

Cambodia has had political allies inside and outside South-East Asia to help it defend the principle of non-interference in its domestic affairs. The CPP has been successful in enhancing its international legitimacy by relying on the support of many UN members that are not democratic. And, in early 1999, Cambodia was admitted as the newest member of ASEAN, a regional organization that operates on the principle of non-interference in domestic affairs. ASEAN did intervene in Cambodia after the coup in 1997 by sending three of its foreign ministers (the ASEAN troika) to help resolve the conflict and by postponing Cambodia's admission into the group, the objective of which was to re-establish conditions for a pluralistically contested election. But Hun Sen maintained that his decision to join ASEAN had to do with, among other things, the ASEAN norm of consensus and its principle of non-interference. On 20 October 1999, when Cambodian, Lao, and Vietnamese leaders held their first "unofficial" Indochina summit, a meeting that sparked concern about the role of subgroups within ASEAN, they discussed their joint opposition to outside intervention in East Timor.

It may be worth recalling that the UN intervention in Cambodia from 1992 to 1993 was possible primarily because of cooperative great-power politics. Soviet decline, changes in Chinese interests, and the so-called American triumph in the Cold War made this possible. But the USA cannot fully impose its will on other powers, especially China and Russia, or indeed even on Cambodia, and this may help explain why the Paris Agreements did not go as far as to ensure concrete steps for effective democratic acculturation. In recent years, cooperation among the permanent members of the UN Security Council has become even less evident. After the violent coup in 1997, for instance, the Council's president issued a statement condemning the violence, but this statement did not blame any party and even refused to call the situation a coup. The Council members acted neither decisively nor in unity. The CPP-dominated government has since failed to gain the confidence of the USA, which considered the 1997 incident a coup and spearheaded action within the UN Credentials Committee to deny the Cambodian seat in the UN General Assembly that year. But the Cambodian government has since become more successful in cultivating close bilateral relations with China. As noted, China was not even among the "Friends of Cambodia" who met to discuss Cambodia after the coup. Russia was, but abstained from any form of intervention.

Chinese influence on Cambodian politics has been subtle, but should not be underestimated. China has emerged as a great regional power that has been successful in expanding its economic and political influence on mainland East Asia. A leading China expert characterizes the region in bipolar terms: the USA dominates the region's maritime areas, whereas China dominates its mainland.[56] China remains politically tied to its insistence on single-party governance even though it has accepted the concept of a market-based economic system. China has consistently supported the principle of non-interference in the domestic affairs of UN members, leading it to defend the authoritarian system of Myanmar and the socialist system of Viet Nam.

Conclusion

The United Nations has without a doubt done the right thing in trying to spread liberal democratic values in Cambodia, and has done a decent job in helping to keep its government at least rhetorically committed to the promotion of political rights and civil liberties. Overall, however, the last 10-year period has brought the United Nations only modest success when "measured" in terms of its limited ability to transform the attitude of the Cambodian political élite and in particular the ruling party towards liberal democracy.

Several major lessons can be drawn from this study. First, the United Nations remains far better equipped than regional organizations, such as ASEAN, when it comes to democracy promotion in extremely weak states which do not have a democratic culture nor the favourable socio-economic conditions necessary for democratic acculturation. Without achieving a much higher level of economic development, Cambodian democracy cannot be expected to mature. With a per-capita income of only about $300, it may even die.[57] Second, one-time UN intervention may be an important step in the process of democratic transition if an election can be held, but this alone offers no guarantee for democratic acculturation. Third, the infusion of democracy and human rights, the existence of constitutional safeguards, and the regular holding of elections may not result in deepening democratic attitudes in states where adversaries remain locked in deadly "winner-take-all" struggles. Fourth, technical and economic assistance is a necessary but not a sufficient condition for promoting democracy given local power relations. Fifth and most important, external pressure from organizations like the United Nations on national regimes dominated by one political group have clear limitations. It is unlikely to bear much fruit unless the United Nations can translate its assistance into political influence and until UN members, especially the permanent members of the Security Council, agree to promote democracy and take firm collective action in that direction.

Acknowledgements

The author would like to thank Gordon Longmiur (former Canadian ambassador to Cambodia), Benny Widyono (former special representative of the UN Secretary-General to Cambodia), and the two co-editors of this volume for their valuable comments on earlier drafts of this paper. That said, the author is alone responsible for any misjudgement or factual errors that still exist.

Notes

1. A representative of this perspective is the work by Yale historian Ben Kiernan. See Kiernan, Ben. 1993. "The inclusion of the Khmer Rouge in the Cambodian peace process: Causes and consequences", in Ben Kiernan (ed.) *Genocide and Democracy in Cambodia: The Khmer Rouge, the United Nations, and the International Community*. New Haven: Yale University Southeast Asia Studies.
2. For a representative of this perspective, see Lizée, Pierre P. 2001. "Adding '98 to 93' and still coming up with zero: The international community, peace-building, and democratic maturation in Cambodia", in Amitav Acharya, Michael Frolic, and Richard Stubbs (eds) *Democracy, Human Rights and Civil Society in South-East Asia*. Toronto: University of Toronto-York University Joint Centre for Asia Pacific Studies.
3. See Peou, Sorpong. 2000. *Intervention and Change in Cambodia: Toward Democracy?* New York, Singapore, and Thailand: St Martin's Press, Institute of Southeast Asian Studies, and Silkworm.
4. Several Asian societies without any democratic tradition have become more democratic, especially since the early 1990s. See Morley, James W. (ed.). 1999. *Driven By Growth: Political Change in the Asia-Pacific Region*. Armonk, NY: M. E. Sharpe; Diamond, Larry and Mark F. Plattner (eds). 1998. *Democracy in East Asia*. Baltimore and London: Johns Hopkins University Press.
5. In South-East Asia, Singapore is the wealthiest country but is less democratic than both Thailand and the Philippines. For more on this see Laothamatas, Anek (ed.). 1997. *Democratization in Southeast and East Asia*. Singapore: Institute of Southeast Asian Studies. According to Adam Przeworski and his associates, "transitions to democracy are random with regard to the level of development: not a single transition to democracy can be predicted by the level of development alone". Przeworski, Adam, Michael E. Alvarez, Jose Antonio Cheibub, and Fernando Limongi. 1996. "What makes democ-

racies endure?", *Journal of Democracy*, Vol. 7, No. 1. But high levels of economic development make democracy endure.

6. For more background, see Kiernan, Ben. 1985. *How Pol Pot Came to Power: A History of Communism in Kampuchea, 1930–1975*. London: Verso.

7. Kiernan, Ben. 1996. *The Pol Pot Regime*. New Haven: Yale University Press.

8. Ponchaud, François. 1978. *Cambodia: Year Zero*, translated by Nancy Amphoux. New York: Holts Rinehart and Winston.

9. See, for instance, Mahbubani, Kishore. 2001. *Can Asians Think?* Toronto: Key Porter Books.

10. Cambodia has been heavily dependent on foreign aid, which has helped to bring about social stability. Since the 1993 election it has never resisted any attempt by the donor community to help in the process of economic reconstruction. In addition to the US$2.2 billion spent on the UN mission, the donor community has pledged more than US$500 million every year to assist Cambodia's economic and institution-building.

11. Przeworski *et al.*, note 5 above.

12. Sorensen, G. 1993. *Democracy and Democratic Maturation: Processes and Prospects in a Changing World*. Boulder, CO: Westview Press.

13. The term "democratic transition" or "consolidation" is avoided because the author emphasizes the importance of attitude change rather than regime change and because it is desired to treat attitude change as an incremental process. Democratic transition and consolidation are often treated as two separate processes. "Democratic acculturation" implies progress toward accepted attitudes that give full respect to the liberal rules of the democratic game and signal a very considerable degree of democratic stability.

14. The CPP, FUNCINPEC, Sam Rainsy Party, Khmer Democratic Party, Chamgoeun Niyum Khmer Party, Vongkort Khmemarak Party, Khmer Angkor Party, and Khmer Women's Party.

15. For more details on the coup, see Peou, Sorpong. 1999. "Hun Sen's preemptive coup: Causes and consequences", in *Southeast Asian Affairs 1998*. Singapore: Institute of Southeast Asian Studies.

16. COMFREL, COFFEL, and NICFEC. 2001. "Joint Statement on the Voter Registration for the Commune Council Elections", Phnom Penh, 7 September.

17. Asian Network for Free Elections. 2002. "Final Statement on Cambodian Commune Council Elections", Bangkok, 15 February; COMFREL, COFFEL, and NICFEC. 2002. "Joint Statement on Findings of Pre-Polling, Polling and Ballot Counting Periods", Phnom Penh, 12 February; EU Election Observation Mission. 2002. "Preliminary Statement", Phnom Penh, 5 February; COFFEL. 2002. "Campaign Assessment Report", Phnom Penh, 3 February.

18. Special Representative of the UN Secretary-General for Human Rights in Cambodia. Undated. *Commune Council Elections 2002*. Phnom Penh: United Nations.

19. *Ibid*.

20. *Ibid*.

21. Center for Advanced Studies and the Asia Foundation. 2001. *Democracy in Cambodia: A Survey of the Cambodian Electorate*. Phnom Penh: Asia Foundation.

22. Special Representative of the UN Secretary-General for Human Rights in Cambodia. 1998. *Media and the Elections: Updated Statistics*. Phnom Penh: United Nations, 23 July.

23. SRSG, note 18 above.

24. Neves, Carlos Costa. 2002. "Preliminary Statement by EU Election Observation Mission on Cambodia Commune Elections 2002." Phnom Penh: EU Office in Phnom Penh, 5 February.

25. COMFREL. 1998. "Pre-Election Assessment Statement." Phnom Penh: COMFREL, 24 July.

26. Their criticism was that the new NEC favoured the two ruling parties.
27. For more background, see Duffy, Terence. 1994. "Toward a culture of human rights in Cambodia", *Human Rights Quarterly*, Vol. 16, No. 1; Duffy, Terence. 1994. "Cambodia since the election: Peace, democracy and human rights", *Contemporary Southeast Asia*, Vol. 15, No. 4; Marks, Stephen. 1994. "Forgetting 'the policies and practices of the past': Impunity in Cambodia", *The Fletcher Forum*, Vol. 18, No. 2.
28. Ung Huot's letter to Thomas Hammaberg, HR REC 13/97, 22 August 1997.
29. China was not part of this group; Russia was, but abstained from intervention of any kind.
30. SRSG, note 18 above.
31. *Ibid.*
32. Report of the Special Representative of the Secretary-General for Human Rights in Cambodia, Peter Leuprecht, in accordance with Resolution 2001/82, UN Doc.E/CN.4/2002/118, December 2001.
33. SRSG, note 18 above.
34. Human Rights Watch. 2002. *Cambodia's Commune Council Elections: A Human Rights Watch Backgrounder*. New York: Human Rights Watch, available at www.hrw.org/backgrounder/asia/cambodia_elections.htm.
35. *Ibid.*
36. Statement of Spokesman of Ministry of Interior, Phnom Penh, 6 February 2002.
37. UN General Assembly, Third Committee, A/C.3/53/L.39, 18 November 1998, para. 10.
38. *Ibid.*, para. 11.
39. In recent years only a few of those who killed opposition party members have been convicted and sentenced to many years in prison. However, the judges tended to make their decisions with a view that the killings were not politically motivated. On 12 October 2001, for instance, the Kampong Som Provincial Court sentenced the prime killer of an SRP commune council candidate to 15 years in prison, but declared that the victim "was a sorcerer ... practised black magic". See *Phnom Penh Post*, 26 October–8 November 2001. In early May 2002, the Provincial Court in Kampong Cham acquitted two police officers identified as killers of two commune council candidates, justifying that the killings were not politically motivated. The court, however, sentenced two other killers to 18 years in jail, but did so in absentia.
40. For more background analysis, see Marks, Stephen P. 1999. "Elusive justice for the victims of the Khmer Rouge", *Journal of International Affairs*, Vol. 52, No. 2.
41. Office of the United Nations Resident Coordinator in Cambodia, press release, 6 June 2003, Phnom Penh.
42. Heder, Steve. 2002. "Cambodian elections in historical perspective", in John L. Vijghen (ed.) *People and the 1998 National Elections in Cambodia: The Voices, Roles and Impact on Democracy*. Phnom Penh: Experts for Community Research.
43. National Democratic Institute. 1996. *Public Attitudes toward Democracy in Cambodia: A Focus Group Study*. Washington, DC: NDI.
44. Center for Advanced Study and the Asia Foundation. 2001. *Democracy in Cambodia: A Survey of the Cambodian Electorate*. Phnom Penh: Center for Advanced Studies and the Asia Foundation.
45. Researchers have discovered that most Cambodians care more about their socio-economic well-being than about democracy. See Hughes, Caroline. 2002. "Political parties in the campaign", in John L. Vijghen (ed.) *People and the 1998 National Elections in Cambodia: The Voices, Roles and Impact on Democracy*. Phnom Penh: Experts for Community Research. According to the Center for Advanced Study, "In all the regions, the principal local problem is the same as that cited at the national level, poverty, which is mentioned by 66 per cent as one of the two most important local problems.

However, the second most mentioned local priority differs from the national number two. It is a concern with water supply (either quantity or quality) and was mentioned by 19 per cent, particularly by rural dwellers and by people in the Southeast and Southwest regions. It is followed by concern for lack of infrastructure (15 per cent), health care (8 per cent), and corruption (7 per cent)." Center for Advanced Study, *ibid.*

46. Muscat, Robert J. with Jonathan Stromseth. 1989. *Cambodia: Post-settlement Reconstruction and Development*. New York: East Asian Institute, Columbia University.

47. *Ibid.* The Khmer Rouge policy resulted in the death of almost three-quarters of the 20,000 teachers. Although the government claimed to have trained or retrained about 50,000 teachers, the quality of education was extremely low. Teachers earned as little as $3 per month.

48. UNDP. 1995. *Human Development Report 1995*. New York and Oxford: Oxford University Press.

49. UNDP. 2002. *Human Development Report 2002*. New York and Oxford: Oxford University Press.

50. Royal Government of Cambodia. 2000. *Interim Poverty Reduction Strategy Paper*. Phnom Penh: Royal Government of Cambodia.

51. *Phnom Penh Post*, 28 February–13 March 2003.

52. Widyono, Benny. 1998. "The SRSG in the Context of Post-Conflict Peace Building in Cambodia", unpublished draft made available to author, dated 1 December.

53. *Ibid.*

54. UNDP Electoral Team Paper, 1 February 2002.

55. Kumar, Rajesh. 2002. "UN agency condemned for lobbying tactics", *Phnom Penh Post*, 15–28 February.

56. Ross, Robert. 1999. "The geography of the peace", *International Security*, Vol. 23, No. 4.

57. According to Adam Przeworski and his associates, a democracy can be expected to last an average of about 8.5 years in a country with per-capita income under $1,000. Only democracies with per-capita income above $6,000 can be expected to live forever. See Przeworski *et al.*, note 5 above.

12

Kosovo: A permanent international protectorate?

Ylber Hysa

Apartheid and war in Europe

Eleven weeks after the North Atlantic Treaty Organization (NATO) air strikes on Yugoslavia, NATO troops along with the UN international administration entered Kosovo. Kosovo effectively came under a new administration. This move was followed by a military technical agreement in Kumanova which created a five-kilometre Ground Safety Zone, raising the question of whether Kosovo also had new frontiers.

This short summary of the epilogue of an air military operation that lasted two-and-a-half months gives the impression of a speedy resolution to a regional problem on the edge of Europe. For Kosovars, however, this was simply the most decisive step in what had been a much longer struggle dating back centuries. This struggle came to a head in recent history when the Socialist Federal Republic of Yugoslavia lost its *raison d'être* at the end of the Cold War.[1] Belgrade declared a state of emergency and, in 1989, established martial law which affected the lives of Kosovars over the next 10 years.

The regime in Belgrade seized control of every institution in Kosovo, from the parliament to the police. In response to the demonstrations of trade unions in Kosovo, the Serbian regime took drastic measures and expelled more than 150,000 workers, a majority of the Kosovo workforce, from their jobs. Virtually no Albanians remained employed in state administration, including the police force, and the majority of Albanian workers were dismissed in the economic sector. Soon after, the schools and universities were closed. Health services were almost paralysed, and within the education system students were not allowed to continue their studies. The Albanian community, making up 90 per cent of the Kosovar population, had no choice but to establish a parallel education and governance system that continued for the next decade.

The parallel system established by the Albanian population was organized in many segments of public life: education, healthcare, sport, media, trade unions, and political parties. This parallel system was part of a broader strategy of non-violent resistance that took place over 10 years. Elections were held for the parliament and the presidency. Ibrahim Rugova, leader of the Democratic League of Kosovo (LDK), was elected as president. Of course these elections were not recognized by the Serbian regime, but they had a deep symbolic meaning for the Albanian population.

As a result, a system of ethnic segregation – an apartheid – was installed and existed in this small part of Europe for the next 10 years. Shocking though it may seem, there was a positive side to this bitter experience. A strong, peaceful movement developed during that period, when Kosovars built a viable civil society capable of opposing Belgrade's expansionist and repressive policies through these parallel institutions. This parallel system came to be appreciated as a principal asset in Kosovar society during the post-conflict period.

Although the Dayton Conference in November 1995 aimed to discuss, among other issues, the situation in Kosovo, all attention was focused on the immediate problem of Bosnia and the issue of Kosovo was neglected. The Serbs in Bosnia were establishing a state entity bolstered by waging a terrifying war against other ethnic groups. These aggressive Serbian policies in the region emanated from the ruling clique of Yugoslav President Milosevic in Belgrade. In those circumstances, the Kosovar public began to question whether a resolution could be reached by peaceful means alone.

Belgrade's unyielding refusal to resolve problems through dialogue resulted in the emergence of a group of Albanian guerillas named the Kosovar Liberation Army (KLA). By 1997 the KLA had begun targeting Serb police forces. Belgrade's security forces took action against the KLA over the ensuing two years with such a violent campaign that humanitarian catastrophe was the inevitable result. The Belgrade regime's reaction was tantamount to genocide and resulted in the "ethnic cleansing" – to continue an expression that will hopefully disappear from the world's political lexicon – of half of the 2 million population in Kosovo.[2]

It was against this background that the NATO air strikes took place.

All peaceful means had been exhausted and, after Milosevic refused to sign the Rambouillet Accord in February 1999, little alternative was left.

NATO acts, the United Nations reacts

The NATO air strikes have triggered serious debates. NATO intervention and the use of military force was not a UN decision. The United Nations generally has difficulty with the concept and staging of large military enforcement measures. However, UN action was blocked due to disagreements in the UN Security Council, especially disagreements relating to the possibility of Moscow and Beijing vetoes. This resulted in NATO taking the lead without UN endorsement. This intervention laid bare the inadequate state of international law in responding to acts of genocide. Those arguing for humanitarian intervention asked the simple question: should we allow genocide to happen simply because some members of the UN Security Council will not give the green light to humanitarian intervention due to their conflicting interests based on domestic agendas and concerns over the possible "negative precedents"?[3]

NATO's military intervention against Serbia underscored the tensions between two principles enshrined in the UN Charter: state sovereignty and the defence of human rights. Since the early 1990s, a consensus has developed that massive human rights violations can sometimes justify encroachment on state sovereignty. This emerging consensus is buttressed by UN Security Council (UNSC) resolutions and practices of UN member states. However, it has not yet crystallized into clear rules establishing the right to "humanitarian intervention", nor has it been accepted by significant powers such as Russia and China.[4] Yet, through NATO's humanitarian intervention, genocide was averted and the Kosovo case demonstrates that action can be justified in certain circumstances.

Belgrade officials had little option but to accept a peaceful agreement after 11 weeks of the air campaign. According to NATO, the air war caused serious damage to Yugoslav forces. Although there are contradictory figures about the damage, based on independent sources about 6,500 people, including 1,500 civilians, were killed during the bombing of Yugoslavia.[5] Forty-five bridges were put out of commission and 57 per cent of all petroleum reserves in Yugoslavia were destroyed. The cost of the NATO operation has been estimated at US$4 billion.[6] Total economic damage for Serbia as a result of NATO's air war is estimated at approximately US$30 billion, including projected loss of GDP. This amount includes damage to infrastructure, economic infrastructure, non-economic civilian objects, natural wealth, human capital loss, and other losses in GDP.[7] However, the Kosovo campaign achieved its objective without a single combat fatality on the NATO side.[8] The air strikes and UN Security Council Resolution 1244 resulted in more than 850,000 Kosovar Albanian refugees returning to Kosovo in what can be regarded as history's most rapid return of refugees.

UNSC Resolution 1244 was reached on 10 June 1999 after key decisions about political solutions to the Kosovo crisis had already taken place at the G8 meeting of 6 May 1999. Resolution 1244 established a peace agreement and served to legitimize the presence of an interim international administration in Kosovo the – UN Interim Administration Mission in Kosovo (UNMIK) and its peacekeeping force, the NATO-led Kosovo Force (KFOR). Interestingly, many of the key provisions of Resolution 1244 are in the two annexes based on G8 and NATO documents.

Democratization: Picking up the pieces

For more than 10 years Kosovo suffered from the most extreme human rights violations in Europe. Through the parallel system that was established after Belgrade's introduction of martial law in Kosovo, a period of national segregation was installed, effectively creating apartheid in one part of Europe.

The Serbian repression had left more than 10,000 civilians dead, a lot of them women and children. Thousands of woman were raped, more than 120,000 houses were destroyed, the economy collapsed, and almost one-third of the territory was sown with land-mines. This legacy has its reflection in the post-war period. Ethnically motivated revenge killings have taken place after the war, especially against the Serbs. Figures from the International Committee of the Red Cross (ICRC) show that during and after the war there were 5,313 missing persons. While many cases have been resolved there are 3,525 persons remaining missing: 2,746 are Albanian, 516 are Serbian, 137 are Romanian, and there are 126 others.[9]

Under these circumstances, democratization becomes a very difficult task for Kosovo. War largely destroyed the spirit of organized civil society and people relied on the international administration to pick up the pieces. However, the rebuilding and reconstruction efforts brought renewed entrepreneurial spirit and initiative amongst Kosovars. Small economic efforts kick-started immediately, and about 80 per cent of housing reconstruction efforts were carried out by Kosovars themselves. During the first few months following the war, international police could not establish full control and so citizens showed a great deal of self-restraint and adherence to law and order.

Democratization in the post-war chaos was pursued by the international administration and was shortly to become the responsibility of

UNMIK.[10] Democratization in Kosovo was predominantly linked with Pillar III, the Democratization and Institution-building Pillar, of UNMIK and was under the control of the Organization for Security and Cooperation in Europe (OSCE) mission. UNMIK applied the principle of joint administration to deal with programmes and projects of democratization. One international expert and one local expert were appointed to deal with the wide scope of democratization initiatives, ranging from issues of public participation to aspects of gender equality.

Through the election process, the OSCE promoted greater inclusion of women. Under electoral regulations the number of women candidates in the local elections increased. Greater gender balance is now reflected in several public sectors. For example in the traditional male-dominated domain of the Kosovo Police Service there are 764 women (19 per cent).[11] According to the head of the OSCE mission in Kosovo the issue of women and gender in Kosovo is complex:

During the war and the post-war period, women are faced with gender specific forms of violence. In the case of Kosovo this means increased domestic violence against women and children; trauma and stress as consequences of rape (and the other forms of violence); enormous psychological, social and economic pressure on women in those families where men have disappeared, were killed or imprisoned, resulting in women becoming the main breadwinners and the head of the household; trafficking of women and forced prostitution. Unemployment, lack of education and health care severely affect women due to their disadvantaged position in society.[12]

In this sense, women who are political activists in Kosovo think that the "vision for Kosovo women in the new millennium" should imply building an institutional framework for empowering women in general, and more specifically within politics.

The strategy would comprise the following elements: Creating a political platform for women's empowerment and equal opportunity for both genders; Designing a legal framework for women issues; Building up instruments for the implementation of the political framework; Setting up state mechanisms and other governmental and non-governmental agencies to deal with women's issues.[13]

Reform of the education system is an essential component to democratization within Kosovo, because under the Serbian apartheid-style rule Albanians were denied full access to education services. Reform is already under way and should benefit the 70 per cent of Kosovar society who are under 35 years of age.[14] In the meantime young people are faced with low levels of employment and an education system lacking reform.

The parallel system developed within the media during the repressive regime of Belgrade had a positive impact on education. The majority of the media were able to report effectively and inform the public but serious problems remain, especially in relation to the suppression of "hate speech" in the media. While democratization of the media is already having a positive impact in Kosovo, UNMIK has passed laws prohibiting the media from openly criticizing the administration. Those reporters previously repressed under the old regime are still being punished for their work,[15] and it is evident that the democratization process has a long way to go in this sector.

In the complex process of democratization, international (and local) NGOs emerged as an important agent for change. Immediately following the war, more than 400 international NGOs became involved in Kosovo, many supported by international donors. While international NGOs played a vital role in democratization, the lack of coordination between these NGOs led to duplication of efforts and hindered their ability to maximize impact. However, when these international NGOs withdraw from Kosovo this too will become a serious problem, as the much-needed international donations will drastically reduce.

Kosovar NGOs are effective partners in democratization projects as they are able to address the diverse needs of the population. They have played an important role in post-war democratization, particularly during elections. While they require more formal training, Kosovar NGOs experienced working during the non-violent struggle and within the parallel system, and they need to draw on this experience in the post-war period. The role of Kosovar NGOs is particularly important given the post-war apathy and disappointment of civil society towards the Kosovar political parties. They have been able to generate serious debates about tolerance towards ethnic differences and have successfully influenced local power structures through public participation within newly established democratic institutions. The political culture of civil society contributed to their active engagement in public debates on issues of common interest during these elections. Kosovar NGOs also played an important role in election monitoring.[16]

The most problematic aspect of democratization in Kosovo is the position of minority groups, especially the Serbs, within Kosovar society. A stronger commitment and concrete initiatives are needed if there is to be greater tolerance towards this minority. One avenue for promoting tolerance may be the participation of Serbs in Kosovar elections. The issue of the Serbian minority is complex and impinges upon aspects of the state system and institutions, for example the police and the judiciary, and upon the issue of war crimes. Dealing effectively with minority groups will remain one of the most important aspects in determining the success of democratization within Kosovar society.

Resolution 1244: The numerous interpretations of the Kosovar Bible

Although Resolution 1244 dictates substantial autonomy and meaningful self-administration for Kosovo, it has in many ways brought about a contradictory situation for post-war Kosovo. Depending on the nature of the problem, Resolution 1244 can be interpreted in a number of ways. While this resolution claimed to embrace the acceptance of the Federal Republic of Yugoslavia (FRY) sovereignty over Kosovo, Regulation 1/ 1999 of July 25 1999 – the first legislative act of UNMIK – determined that all legislative and executive power in Kosovo was to be exerted by UNMIK under the chairmanship of the special representative of the UN Secretary-General. Sovereignty was, in practice, frozen the moment that the UN interim administration took over governance of Kosovo. This issue continues to pose a quandary for the Security Council, and has become further complicated after the democratic changes in Belgrade with Milosevic's overthrow. Resolution 1244 respects the sovereignty and territorial integrity of the Federal Republic of Yugoslavia, including Kosovo. However, this presents a contrast with the reality on the ground, where certain territories are under the full control of KFOR and the international administration. After the trauma of war, the vast majority of the population see any reference to "Yugoslavia" as a serious obstacle to a peaceful transition.

In analysing Resolution 1244 it is interesting to see the distribution of responsibilities as well as the interrelation between different multilateral and international diplomatic and military mechanisms. In Resolution 1244 the responsibilities given to KFOR for international security include "maintaining and where necessary enforcing a cease-fire", demilitarization of the KLA, the establishment of a secure environment and public safety, supporting and coordinating the work of the international civil presence, conducting border monitoring, and "ensuring the protection and freedom of movement of itself, international civil presence, and other international organizations".[17] Civil administration is reserved for UNMIK. Resolution 1244 requires UNMIK to provide transitional administration, oversee the development of provincial democratic self-governing institutions, and, at some point, transfer administrative responsibilities to these institutions under a political settlement.

The division of responsibilities envisaged in Resolution 1244 basically outlines a division between NATO and the United Nations. External security aspects are tasked under NATO and civilian administrative aspects are purely the responsibility of UNMIK. The explicit mentioning of the role of NATO is outlined in Annex 2, point 4.[18] This division of responsibility flows from the Military-Technical Agreement in Kumanovo and

Resolution 1244. At the time Resolution 1244 was adopted, NATO was already implementing certain enforcement measures based on the provisions from the annexes in the Rambouillet talks.[19]

While Resolution 1244 clearly states that UNMIK's mandate is to build democratic institutions and hold elections, interpretations of the resolution in different situations have at times been rigid and at other times contemptuous of local views. In this sense, even though the mandate of UNMIK is focused exclusively within Kosovo territory, the need to encourage democratic processes in Serbia to defeat Milosevic's authoritarian regime has influenced UNMIK's political considerations when Serbian and Yugoslav elections have occurred. Serbs in Kosovo participated in both the Serbian and Yugoslav elections which were permitted in Kosovo.[20] However, Kosovar Serbs decided not to participate in Kosovar local elections, claiming that the elections lacked security and thus prevented them from participating. This provoked a strong reaction from Kosovar Albanians. They did not accept the Serbian argument because the Serbs had taken part in the Serbian election under similar conditions.

UNMIK has continued to operate in spite of such political difficulties. Other difficulties included the varying quality of UN personnel, the slow implementation of decisions from both local officials and the UN and NATO headquarters, and, at times, the conflicting national agendas of personnel during field missions. The UN mission in Kosovo was both complex and unique. It was attempting to build new institutions in a region that is virtually an international protectorate at the same time as undertaking the physical reconstruction of existing institutions and delivering good governance.

UNMIK's decision to accept a more cohesive policy regarding the role of local political forces was an original concept. UNMIK employed the local and international political forces, creating two instances of co-governed structures: the Joint Administrative Council (JAC) and the Kosovo Transitional Council (KTC). The first resembled an advisory administrative body, while the latter was similar to a pre-parliamentary institution. Both structures provide examples of consultative institutions, since actual power remains in the hands of the SRSG. However, the co-governed structures were an innovative move aimed at reducing tensions and avoiding possible misunderstandings between international and local political forces. These structures also contributed to consultations on a broader basis as a means of facilitating decision-making and implementation of policies. Another positive outcome was the facilitation of an understanding between competing local political forces, all of which found a place at the table.

A broad basis for cohabitation between the international administration and local forces came about quite quickly, although at times it did not appear as the ideal formula to overcome some of the more problematic situations. Upon entering Kosovo so quickly after the military campaign, the United Nations, much to its surprise, found the situation relatively peaceful. However, given that Kosovo had suffered quite a lot of destruction the mission faced significant practical problems. With 120,000 houses destroyed and 850,000 returning locals to be accommodated, half a million people within Kosovo were without a home. Ultimately, the provisional international administration in Kosovo accomplished its goals through an improvised agenda rather than a strategy that had been elaborated thoroughly beforehand.

The position of Serbs in Kosovo

It is also important to mention the inclusion of Serbian representatives in the new provisional joint structures between UNMIK and the Kosovar population. This was an important step that helped to overcome tensions in the post-conflict period. The inclusion of Serbs also served as a confidence-building measure between the Albanians and Serbs. Ten years of segregation and violence meant that they had not worked together within governance institutions. The Belgrade government under Milosevic did not encourage any form of cooperative mechanism. It called on the Serb community to boycott the local Kosovar elections and it criticized the Serbian National Council (SNV)[21] community. UNMIK decisions reinforced the separateness of the Kosovo Serbs by allowing the Yugoslav dinar to remain in circulation in their areas and by allowing Kosovar Serbs to patrol parts of the border with Serbia.

The post-Milosevic era has produced a new political climate in which the Serbian government is trying to work with the Kosovar political process. Serb representatives have been encouraged by the Serbian government to take part in UNMIK structures and cooperate with the SRSG. The provisional framework for the constitution of Kosovo offers an advanced model of positive discrimination for minorities, especially Serbs. Privileges are secured for minorities such as the Serbs within the electoral system. A system of reserving seats has been combined with the proportional system and a closed list, offering the Serbs significantly more seats in parliament than would be offered on the demographic make-up of Kosovo. Ten seats are reserved for Serbs, in addition to those coming from direct voting. Together with other minorities, this can produce a situation where, from a total of 120 seats in parliament, about 30 seats are reserved for minority representatives, most of whom are Serbs.

Despite the good intentions behind the international administration and Kosovar Albanian parties, the Serb minority face a difficult situation in post-war Kosovo. A number of Kosovo Serbs and their political representatives face serious problems of security and a lack of free movement. Many are showing resistance towards legitimizing the new Kosovar democratic institutions. Others argue that Serbian participation in the elections and institution-building process will be a confidence-building measure and a strong political card. They believe that if Serbs were to boycott the elections, the Albanian majority would take this to be a lack of political will to live together and to build a common future for Kosovo. The issue of Serb participation is important in the post-war institution-building process. Participation by Kosovar Serbs in this process would enable them to become stakeholders in the future of Kosovo's democratic society.

Another aspect of the elections, the institution-building process, and the participation of Serbs within this process concerns the problem of the final status of Kosovo. Based on Resolution 1244, UNMIK should initiate, organize, and assist in the process of institution-building, organizing elections and monitoring the process of the substantive autonomy as a provisional form of governance before the final status is agreed. Some Serbian political representatives of Kosovo are afraid that their participation in this political process may result in the full independence of Kosovo. However, those supporting Serbian involvement argue that the only way to address this issue is to be part of the process. This is because no final status can be achieved if these institutions are not functioning. The formation and functioning of a "state-like entity" able to provide order, security, and services for its citizens is the pre-condition for any final-status solution and has thus become a target in itself.

It is therefore important to include all Kosovar minorities, especially the Serbs, in the process of institution-building. In this way it is possible to build a society with sustainable democratic values that respect the diversities of different communities. In order to achieve this, both the majority and the minorities have to understand their role and responsibilities.

Establishing a secure environment

The Kosovo operation is a complex mission with civil and military aspects. If one of these aspects fails, regardless of the other's success, the mission will be considered a failure. In the case of Kosovo, characterized by a post-war, post-communist, and post-apartheid society, the objective of providing law and order has been severely tested. There were virtually no policemen out in the streets for the first five months after the war. Local people regarded the lack of policing to be as big a problem as the lack of electricity and water supplies. The lesson learnt from Kosovo's example is the need for an international mission to integrate the work of the military, civilian, and police services. Because NATO does not have a police counterpart, the police function has proven to be the most difficult.

The slow progress in building a local police force and making the international police operational led to many criminal cases remaining unsolved. The low "clearance rate" of criminal cases at the beginning of a mission can cause the population to lose confidence in the international effort as a whole. In this respect, lacking knowledge of the local language and mentality is an additional obstacle for an international mission. Isolation and lack of communication with the local culture are characteristic of an international staffing situation. UNMIK international administration employees do not mix and rarely communicate with the local people. Most contact with locals is undertaken by those whose duty it is to have such contacts. This impedes the efficient and normal operation of an international police force. The Kosovo experience suggests that the role of the police is just as important as that of the military in a post-conflict situation. Soldiers are not trained to carry out policing tasks and they made this fact clear during the Kosovo mission, proving that military staff do not feel comfortable with duties beyond their established mandates.

The international policing capacity within Kosovo is based on the individual capacity of those countries that represent the international force. National police are not organized in the same way as military staff and may not be in a position to undertake a task within an international mission. They may not have the necessary training or understanding of the situation at hand. Furthermore, national policing methods, particularly the use of firearms and other coercive tactics, may not be appropriate when transported to a foreign environment. A police force comprising policemen with different experiences and practices that are not standardized is not always helpful for missions such as the international police mission in Kosovo. The Kosovo police mission comprises policemen from more than 50 countries – America, Europe, countries in transition, the Far East, and post-colonial countries in Africa. These policemen differ not only in their perception of the role played by the police in a democratic society but in their understanding of when and how weapons are to be used.

The problem of appropriate policing is a magnification of the more general problem of personnel engaged in international administration of "Chapter VII" entities. The training of professional staff members within the UN administration requires further thought. One must ask what the best qualifications are for the selection of such personnel. In Kosovo, locals were under the impression that a major criterion was previous participation in UN missions and familiarity with the UN system rather than familiarity with the problem area. This assumes that problem areas are somehow generic, which is an assumption that may lead to future problems. In Kosovo, the hazard pay for working under dangerous conditions was well known. However, with the situation improving this pay was removed, thus inciting many critical reactions among UNMIK staff despite the fact that no foreigner participating in the mission in Kosovo ever came under direct attack.

Transformation and demilitarization of the Kosovar guerillas

The transformation of the Kosovar guerilla force, the KLA, deserves special mention because no doubt similar problems will arise in many UN missions. The KLA was identified at an early stage as a key agent in the resolution of Kosovo's problems. Of course, including the KLA in the political process was not easy, for reasons such as the international community's reluctance to accept insurgents as discussants. However, the Kosovo Albanians had exhausted all political and diplomatic possibilities of resolving the crisis throughout the decade of peaceful resistance. It should be recalled that in this period of non-violent protest, the international community allowed its attention to focus on other aspects of the Yugoslav tragedy. As a result Kosovo Albanians did not consider that their peaceful policies were sufficiently rewarded. The lessons of the recent bloody wars that followed Yugoslavia's disintegration have reinforced the importance of including combatants in the peace-building process. There was also widespread acceptance of the idea that the KLA were reacting to problems caused by Milosevic and his genocidal policies.

After some hesitation, the KLA was finally accepted as a crisis-resolving player and was thus invited to the international conference held in Rambouillet in France. In many ways this was a decisive turn for Kosovo and has determined the resolution of the crisis as we have witnessed it over the past couple of years. The issue of demilitarization – as international diplomacy wanted it portrayed – was initiated immediately after KFOR's arrival in Kosovo. The annex of the Rambouillet Agreement foresees the transformation and demilitarization of the guerilla forces, the KLA, and their active role in creating a new police force, the Kosovo Protection Corps (KPC), in Kosovo. The official establishment of the KPC occurred on 21 September 1999 after the respective UNMIK Regulation 1999/8 was promulgated by the first SRSG, Bernard Kouchner. Another document, including technical-military aspects, was signed afterwards by the commander of KFOR, General Jackson, and General Çeku on behalf of the KPC. According to this agreement, the KPC shall have 5,000 members: 3,000 active members and 2,000 reservists. Based on the agreement, the KPC is a "civilian emergency service", tasked to:

- provide disaster response services including medical assistance
- perform search and rescue
- provide a capacity for humanitarian assistance in isolated areas
- assist with de-mining
- contribute to rebuilding infrastructure and communities
- provide training and communication services.

The agreement stresses that the KPC will not be tasked to provide protection and it "shall not have any role in law enforcement or that of law and order". Under the auspices of the SRSG and the commander of KFOR, the KPC will have central staff in Pristina directing activities through regional task groups, with bases planned in towns within Kosovo.

The transformation of the KLA guerilla force into the KPC marks one of the fastest transformation processes of a former armed liberation movement. Within four months the 5,000-member KPC emerged after demobilization of the KLA, which had claimed a membership of 30,000 during the war. This initiative was based on a combined military, political, and diplomatic mechanism backed by NATO, the European Union, the USA, and Kosovar political parties, including those that emerged from the KLA. The process, managed by the International Organization for Migration (IOM), facilitated a number of projects designed to train former guerrilla members in areas such as electrical work, construction, and, for more senior soldiers, general management skills. The IOM developed income-generating activities for those former soldiers not enlisted in the KPC.

The KPC has continued its planned activities, in spite of accusations that some of its members, who are previous members of the guerilla force, are involved in organized crime. The KPC has maintained its original transformation plan, although its ultimate fate depends on the final status of Kosovo.

Former KLA members not involved in the KPC were able to become part of the KPS (Kosovo Police Service). It was initially planned that the KPS was to have 5,000 members, but this number has increased to 7,000, of whom half may be former KLA fighters. The old police models in Kosovo had to be jettisoned because they were either based on communist values or had been employed in maintaining apartheid practices.

The economy: Local entrepreneurs face political restrictions

Inaction within Kosovo on the issue of privatization flows from a rigid interpretation of the Resolution 1244 guidelines and the acceptance of Belgrade's sovereignty in Kosovo. Rigid interpretation of Resolution 1244 has meant that Kosovo is the only place in the former communist bloc where privatization has not been integrated into the system. There is, however, a substitute for privatization, called "commercialization", which provides short-term credit for enterprises with old governing structures. These old governing structures belong to the communist period before the Serb annexation at the beginning of the 1990s.

The approach to Kosovo legislation is an example of an irrational way of dealing with a problem based on a legalist interpretation of Resolution 1244. Resolution 1244 accepted the Yugoslav applicable laws up to 12 June 1999, the date of adoption of Resolution 1244. This implied UNMIK's acceptance of Milosevic's decision to revoke the autonomy of Kosovo, to enforce that revocation coercively, and to legalize the Serb *anschluss* with 47 discriminatory laws against Albanians in Kosovo. These discriminatory laws included a prohibition on commerce in real estate between Albanians and Serbs. While understanding the need for legal continuity, it struck local people as odd that the United Nations would perpetuate an apartheid situation in this way.

Rigid interpretation and implementation of Resolution 1244 are also evident with the issue of currency. The first SRSG in Kosovo, Bernard Kouchner, introduced the German mark as the best available currency. For years the German mark had been used within Kosovo, and no one considered the devalued Yugoslav dinar as a serious alternative. New York, however, reacted negatively and called this far-sighted decision an infringement of Yugoslav sovereignty. This was argued despite the fact that the Yugloslav republic of Montenegro had also started using the German mark as currency, thus proving Kouchner's decision to be both practical and valid. Authorities within the Bank and Payment Authority (BPA)[22] presented a programme for linking Kosovo to the euro, and this was introduced in January 2002. Therefore, the decision to use the German mark, leading naturally to the later use of the euro, appears to have been one of the most effective strategies of the interim administration. Through the euro, Kosovo was able to further its long-term strategic aim of becoming part of the European integration process.

Unemployment in Kosovo continues to be high at 74 per cent. For the severely damaged local economy, new employment opportunities with UN agencies and other international organizations have provided a much-needed boost. The knock-on effect of this has been noticed by small businesses such as restaurants and catering. These positive consequences were not, however, uniform across Kosovo. New unintended barriers divided people into those privileged to be associated with the United Nations and those who were not. Even Kosovars with prestigious positions, such as judges, doctors, teachers, and policemen, derived their salaries from the Kosovo consolidated budget. They were paid four times less than Kosovar UNMIK drivers paid by the United Nations.

The Kosovo consolidated budget sits just under DM5 billion, comprised mostly of European donor assets. This budget amounts to less than the cost of a NATO one-day air strike against Yugoslavia. Attempts to revive the Kosovo economy have been hindered by a lack of institutional support. Privatization and a transparent economic policy would help pave the way for a prosperous market economy. However, the fiscal policy of the political economy controlled by UNMIK does not stimulate local produce and relies heavily on imports. There is no legal framework or effective functioning of banks to help ensure the development of effective fiscal policy. Furthermore Kosovo, as a place that actually exported electricity for decades, is now experiencing frequent electricity restrictions. The independent media has accused public companies under the control of UNMIK of corruption and weak management. Despite this harsh criticism there has never been any serious investigation or legal measures undertaken.[23]

On a positive note, certain economic indicators prove Kosovars are increasingly able to provide a large percentage (72 per cent in 2002) of budget assets currently allocated by international donors. But despite the progress being made, Kosovo can be considered to be at a stage of *terra contradictorum*. The country is yet to enter into actual transition.

Elections: The "best in the region" but an uncertain outcome

After much debate it was decided that Kosovo should hold local elections in 2000. In the beginning there were several hesitations motivated by different concerns. One concern was whether holding elections was the best way to build governance institutions. This was followed by the fear that elections may result in political violence. Arguments in favour of holding elections were motivated by the need to prepare groundwork within Kosovo for carrying out and sharing responsibilities with the locals. Elections were also seen as the first phase of an "exit strategy" for the international community. The need for elections also flowed from one of the main mandates of Resolution 1244, which stated the importance of holding elections in order to build democratic institutions in Kosovo.

The local elections, held on 28 October 2000, were qualified as the best in the region.[24] No serious incident was reported and, in spite of the clumsiness of the OSCE in organizing the elections, citizens waited in queues for several hours with amazing self-discipline. Ibrahim Rugova's Lidhja Demokratike e Kosovës (Democratic League of Kosovo – LDK) won a majority, followed by Partia Demokratike e Kosovës (Democratic Party of Kosovo – PDK) and Aleanca për Ardhmërinë e Kosovës (Alliance for the Future of Kosovo – AAK). The latter two parties were born out of the KLA. These elections allowed for the creation of municipal assemblies in 30 municipalities of Kosovo.[25] Despite free elections, the laws of the local administration dictate that the international municipal administrator has the exclusive right to administer and veto all decisions. That the SRSG could have the final word in decision-making did not sit comfortably with the need to develop democracy in Kosovo.

After the local elections, there was a plan for national elections in Kosovo. This also generated debate despite the initial success of local elections. National elections were viewed as important because they would affect the unresolved issue of the final status of Kosovo. This was especially pressing after recent destabilizing events in Kosovo's neighbourhood, particularly in the Presheva Valley that bordered with Serbia, and the armed conflict in Macedonia where Albanian guerillas fought with Macedonian armed forces.

In preparation for the national elections, the SRSG at the time, Hans Haekkerup, adopted a new strategy that opposed that of his predecessor. Haekkerup insisted that there be no national elections until a legal framework was established. In this way he was seen to "blackmail" not only local political groups but the international community. As a result, after a two-month effort by a working group comprising local and international representatives, a document was drafted which has generated much debate. The text gives absolute priority (power) to the SRSG, with the right to veto any decisions made by the future Kosovar Assembly. Aside from this, other problematic issues included the name of the drafted document. The Kosovars insisted that the document be named a "Constitution" or "Provisional Constitution". Haekkerup and several international bodies, after insisting that the document be named "Legal Framework" or "Basic Law", finally named the document "The Constitutional Framework for Provisional Self-Government in Kosovo".

Another vital point of contention was whether to hold a referendum in Kosovo. A referendum was insisted upon by the Kosovars. They supported the Rambouillet Accord where it stated that, at the end of the international administration mandate, the final status of Kosovo would be decided by the Kosovo people. This request by Kosovars, however, was not considered by the SRSG or by UN officials in New York.

February 2002 saw the arrival of the third SRSG, Michael Steiner, a German diplomat with Balkans' experience. The political philosophy of Steiner's "Standards before Status", in which he outlines the importance of improving standards within Kosovo on issues such as crime, the economy, and multi-ethnicity before establishing the status of Kosovo, was welcomed in New York and in Western capitals. However, the concept of building democratic institutions before addressing the final status of Kosovo posed a considerable dilemma.

Steiner began his appointment as SRSG at a time when Kosovar political parties had not yet created a suitable coalition government. The inability of the political parties to transform the successful elections into a process of building governance institutions was due to a number of reasons.

The first reason was the complicated electoral system that was combined with a unique electoral zone. This system was structured with set-aside seats for minorities; it established standards for gender balance and did not require a threshold with which to enter parliament. The second reason was that the Kosovar political parties lacked parliamentary experience. The final factor hindering the development of governance institutions was the involvement of the international community imposing its own differing preferences.

After a hard debate between political parties and mediations by diplomats in Kosovo, the parties agreed to a large-scale rainbow coalition between Ibrahim Rugova's LDK (Rugova was later elected as President of Kosovo), leader of the PDK Hashim Thaqi, the ex-leader of the political wing of the KLA, and finally a minor party, the AAK, led by the charismatic ex-guerilla commander of Dukagjini Zone. The position of prime minister should have been allocated to the PDK, which won approximately 27 per cent of the vote. However, agreement as to who could be prime minister seemed to be imposed, and limited, by the international community. In this way, the chosen candidate was not the leader of the PDK, Hashim Thaqi, but Bajram Rexhepi, an agreed-upon moderate figure. Hashim Thaqi was a doctor in the KLA during the war and had earlier been the mayor of a municipality in Mitrovica, a problematic divided city in northern Kosovo. Nexhat Daci, from the biggest political party, the LDK, was elected President of the National Assembly. This combination of problems did not allow the Kosovar government to build its credibility as the first democratic government of Kosovo. The Kosovo government was restrained not only by a lack of experience but by limited legal competencies. These skills were not transferred from the bureaucratic offices in New York to Kosovars at the local level.

In creating a large coalition government that controlled 81 of 120 seats in the Kosovo parliament, the SRSG was creating a weak local partner for UNMIK. Discrepancies between the sometimes non-transparent agenda of the SRSG and the weak "Kosovar partner", lacking experience and with limited competencies, produced disharmony in the strategy of development and institution-building. Increasing local ownership is important for the institution-building process. In the beginning it was easier for the international administrator to make decisions without consulting broadly.[26] However, the dilemma remains: allocating a large proportion of decision-making power to UN officials will not necessarily result in the building of local institutions required to establish a final status for Kosovo.

Conclusion

The UN interim mission in Kosovo is unique and one of the most ambitious UN engagements. Not only is it a peacemaking mission and a peacekeeping mission, but at the same time it is a mission engaged in the administration and building of democratic institutions. It has required the creation of a completely new administration that started with a transitional phase and ended with the emergence of free local and general elections. This mission has required the creation of a legal framework and police service in the country.

From this mission there are many lessons to be learned. The problems of implementation of an international UN mission flow from both domestic factors and UN involvement. There are practical problems in the field that can, to a certain extent, be foreseen but cannot be planned for precisely. There are also problems that relate to the administrative, operational, and implementation structures of UN involvement.

A distinct characteristic of the mission in Kosovo is the relationship between the mission's military and civil sides. The dynamics of their engagement, coordination, and implementation differ. The military components often face difficulties in coordinating activities when their armies rely on national contingents and, in part, military alliances such as NATO. The UN mission in the field comprises personnel with different experiences and different requirements. Interlinking the civil and military sides has complicated the process of nation-building within Kosovo. To succeed, the relationship between the United Nations and NATO needs careful ground rules and coordination.

The Kosovo experience demonstrates that police operations are also an important element. The police appear to play the major role, especially in places where reconstruction must recommence and institutions must be built in inter-ethnic post-conflict areas. Police are effective in providing the interface element between those forces engaged in maintaining the external security and safety of a mission and those forces engaged in territorial administration of the mission.

From this prospect one gets the impression that the mission in Kosovo is of vital importance to the United Nations itself. It is important that missions conducted in Europe succeed because circumstances are even more difficult in the developing world. There is a need to ensure successful coordination between different international agencies and multilateral structures. UNMIK has four pillars within its internal organization structure, and some of them are headed and managed by the OSCE and the EU. It is imperative that the various agencies prove that they can work together.[27]

Even though the United Nations is seized with the importance of its mission in Kosovo, its bureaucratized structure and its multiplicity of external actors place it in a poor position to discharge the ambitious objectives set for it by the international community. Ultimately, it must be the people of Kosovo who determine the fate of their land and who must provide the decisive input for the successful democratization of Kosovo.

Notes

1. There are different views about this problem. Some authors suggest that "Kosovo is in its essence a leftover of nineteenth-century Balkan irredentism and twentieth-century ethnic cleansing". Veremis, Thanos. 1998. *The Kosovo Puzzle, Kosovo: Avoiding Another Balkan War*. Athens: Eliamep-University of Athens.
2. "It has been estimated that over 90 per cent of the Kosovar Albanian population – over 1.45 million people – were displaced by the conflict by 9 June 1999." OSCE. 1999. *Kosovo/Kosova, As Seen, As Told. An Analysis of the Human Rights Findings of the OSCE Kosovo Verification Mission, October 1998 to June 1999*. Warsaw: OSCE Office for Democratic Institutions and Human Rights.
3. See Independent International Commission on Kosovo. 2000. *Kosovo Report*. Oxford: Oxford University Press.
4. Guicherd, C. 1999. "International law and the war in Kosovo", *Survival*, Vol. 41, No. 2. The author notes that: "NATO nations have been at a loss to justify their Kosovo campaign in terms of international law. Rather than claiming that the Kosovo intervention is an exception, not to be repeated, Alliance members should lead a drive to adjust international law by developing clear rules for humanitarian intervention."
5. At the end of the war Yugoslav authorities announced the number of dead members of the Yugoslav security forces to be around 600. Referring to data from Yugoslav military officials, they reported around 1,800 dead soldiers during the war. Ten days prior to the end of the war, NATO officials reported 5,000 dead Yugoslav soldiers. Group 17. 1999. *Final Account, Economic Consequences of NATO Bombing: Estimate of the Damage and Finance Required for the Economic Reconstruction of Yugoslavia*, edited by Mladjan Dinkic. Belgrade: Group 17.
6. Source: www.cnn.com/SPECIALS/1998/10/kosovo/. The most concrete figures are to be found in the accounts of Belgrade-based Group 17, *ibid*.
7. *Ibid*.
8. "From a military standpoint, this is an unprecedented achievement. From an ethical standpoint, it transforms the expectations that govern the morality of war." Ignatieff, Michael. 2000. *Virtual War, Kosovo and Beyond*. New York: Metropolitan Books.
9. Zëri. 2001. "Loja me të vërtetën për të zhukurit në Kosovë", *Zëri*, 29 August.
10. Conclusions from the OSCE's report on the human rights findings suggest the following: "The international community, through UNMIK, has the opportunity to positively influence the development of civil society in Kosovo/Kosova. Support for UNMIK's efforts to establish the rule of law is central, and critical, to this." OSCE, note 2 above.
11. Singh, Neeraj K. 2002. "Një polici për popullin, Femrat Kosovare më të dhunuara tani se një dekadë më parë", *Koha Ditore*, February.

12. Everts, Daan. 2000. "The importance of women's participation in politics in a post-war society", in *Women in Politics*. Pristina: OSCE/UNMIK.
13. Tahiri, Edita. 2000. "Vision for Kosovo women in new millennium. A strategy for empowerment of women", in *Women in Politics*. Pristina: OSCE/UNMIK.
14. For analysis of the demographic trends in Kosovo, see Islami, Hivzi. 1990. *Kosovo dhe Shqiptarët, çështje demografike*. Pristina: Pena.
15. The daily paper *Dita* was punished under UNMIK regulations because it published the name of a Serbian UNMIK staff member accused of being a war criminal. Soon after, this man was found dead.
16. Elections were monitored by two domestic Kosovar NGO networks: the Kosovo Action for Civil Initiatives (KACI) Fryma e Re campaign and the Council for the Defence of Human Rights. These NGOs mobilized 1,200 observers for the October 2000 local elections.
17. UNSC Res. 1244 (1999), para. 9.
18. "The international security presence with substantial North Atlantic Treaty Organization participation must be deployed under command and control and authorized to establish a safe environment for all people in Kosovo and to facilitate the safe return to their homes of all displaced persons and refugees", UNSC Res. 1244, Annex 2, point 4.
19. UNSC Res. 1244 incorporates the Rambouillet Agreement. See UNSC Res. 1244, para. 11, point (e).
20. Based on reports from the media, Serbs from Kosovo have voted largely for the pro-Milosevic party, the SPS. For many years Kosovo Serbs have been considered to be strong supporters of Milosevic's regime.
21. Srpsko Nacionalno Vece (SNV).
22. The BPA is a form of the Central Bank of Kosovo under the auspices of UNMIK employing previous Kosovar staff from the Central Bank.
23. Schwartz, Stephen. 2003. "UN go home", *Koha Ditore*, 14 April.
24. *International Herald Tribune*, 30 October 2000; KACI. 2000. *Local Election Observation of the Kosovo Municipal Elections*. Pristina: KACI.
25. Resolution 2000/45 of UNMIK has provided the legal basis for local government.
26. As Kosovo Prime Minister Bajram Rexhepi said: "Sometimes UNMIK acts as if they are the bosses and we are just cosmetic." See Sell, Louis. 2003. *Kosovo: Time to Negotiate Final Status*. Boston: Public International Law and Policy Group.
27. UNMIK has 20 departments and works through four "pillars". The first pillar, Police and Justice, is under the supervision of the UNHCR. The second pillar, Civil Administration, is administered by the UN Department of Peacekeeping Operations (UNDPKO). The third pillar, Democratization and Institution-building, is led by the OSCE. The fourth pillar, Reconstruction and Economic Development, is under the direction of the EU. See www.unmikonline.org/intro.htm.

13

Delivering feudal democracy in East Timor

Tanja Hohe

Just six months after East Timor gained its independence, the capital Dili was shattered by student demonstrations that developed into riots and left at least two people dead. The Prime Minister's residence and an Australian-owned supermarket were burnt down and the parliament building was threatened.[1] The international community was surprised by the violence, since its state-building efforts in East Timor had been declared largely a "success". The UN Transitional Administration in East Timor (UNTAET) had been given a mandate to rebuild and administer a country that was reduced to ashes by the Indonesian military and local militias after a successful vote by the East Timorese for independence in 1999. Within two-and-a-half years the United Nations established some basic institutions of governance and administration. On 20 May 2002 the country's administration was handed over from its international officials to the East Timorese. After such a supposedly successful transition, what were the reasons for another outbreak of violence? Three possible causes were explicitly identified: extremist forces taking advantage of the uncertain local conditions, the tenuous economic situation, and a dysfunctional judiciary.[2]

However valid these triggers may be, the underlying problems are more fundamental, and they indicate that state-building and democratization, with all their implications and consequences, are particularly difficult to achieve. State-building in East Timor, the most comprehensive effort ever conducted by the United Nations, was ultimately insufficient and inappropriate in its approach. It ignored local realities and functioned without specialized "local knowledge". The international community focused solely on the establishment of Western institutions at the national level. Three factors contributed to the shortcomings in the process of democratization.

First, the Timorese social structures and cosmologies have emerged over the centuries to serve specific needs of local communities. Their mechanisms are not comparable to those of citizens of a state which relies on formal institutions to assure law and order and to arrange political life. This distinction is typical of "traditional" societies. Specific features have developed to address the requirements of small populations, to guarantee their security, and to assure their survival. Kinship relations are an integral part of the local social structure and provide the basis on which society and the cosmos are ordered. Many colonial and occupying powers have often placed state institutions (and geographical boundaries) "on top" of local structures, without actually attempting to transform these features. "Indirect rule" in the British colonies is a good example, as it relied on these local structures to keep order at the local level. Now, in post-colonial times, local social structures are often marginalized as state institutions develop that are incompatible with their logic. Many conflicts, and indeed the causes of fractured and failed states, can be diagnosed in this way. Timorese ritual life has little contact with state institutions, and traditional political concepts contradict the elected parliamentary state model.

Second, a significant part of the Timorese élite mobilized and manipulated these local paradigms. Some politicians acted out of genuine connection to that cultural heritage. Others used it to garner the population's support. As a result, the majority of political leaders behaved in accordance with local paradigms, which in turn have been transformed into the political culture at the national level. But even at this élite level the idea of the democratic state, though widely expressed, is barely understood.

Third, the ignorance of such local dynamics by the UN personnel, and therefore the absence of any accommodation of them, constituted its own constraint. An uninformed international community was not aware of how different local politics were from the forms taken by modern democratic states, and how they could undermine any state-building programme.

The net result is that the institutions of Western democracy have not taken root in East Timor. The result of the mix of local social hierarchy, national political factions competing for exclusive authority, and the UN's centralization and absolutism has been the establishment of a type of feudal political culture. These factors can be detected in nearly all post-conflict scenarios. While internal constraints of the UN organization have been widely addressed,[3] the intricacies of local realities on the ground are an additional dimension yet to be adequately appreciated. If the United Nations is to remain in the state-building business, it had better begin to address them.

Grass-roots hierarchy

Local "traditional" concepts are still very prevalent amongst East Timorese communities. They serve to ensure a good harvest, environmental protection, reproduction of the family, conflict resolution, power distribution, and other aspects of communal life – some of the very things that in modern state societies are the responsibility of state institutions.

When creating a state, it is the new legal and political concepts that clash most with local values. Traditional political concepts, sometimes labelled "local democratic" ways, often differ fundamentally from the concepts underpinning Westminster-style institutions. Some of the principal local values even run counter to basic Western democratic principles. Other features that seem to resemble democratic processes have to be understood in the frame of their holistic socio-cultural system, where they have a very different role and meaning.

In the modern state there is generally a separation between secular state bodies and religion, with limited interaction between the two. However, in the traditional Timorese arrangement of power, the main divide is between political authority and ritual authority. In the socio-cosmic systems, ritual and political authorities are in an essential relationship with each other. They form a dual pair of opposites that determine the organization of the community and explain the cosmos. Several families share the identity of a community (kingdom[4]) in which they are ordered in a hierarchical manner. The "highest" family is the one believed to have arrived first on the land. Hence it is the "opener" of the land for planting, and the one that holds ritual authority. This ritual authority is closely connected to the value of fertility, to the earth, and to the ancestors. It plays a crucial role for the survival of the community. The second family in the hierarchical order is mostly the "newcomer" and was appointed the "political authority" by ritual leaders.

Whereas in a Western democracy the powers of the judiciary, legislature, and executive are separated, political authority in Timorese society is the acknowledged single power that takes decisions in an unchallenged manner. Its rationale is not based on a party ideology, but flows from the ancestral will expressed through ritual authorities. Opposition can only exist between different political rulers, for example between neighbouring kingdoms. Therefore, kingdoms used to have well-defined relationships. They either considered each other as quasi-related by classifying each other as marriage partners or blood brothers, or they were enemies. Marriage partners are characterized by two families in which women are passed in an asymmetric direction from one family to the other. The "wife-giver" family is in a superior position. The same then is true for two kingdoms involved in such a marriage relationship; the "wife-giver" kingdom is in the superior position and reinforces a peaceful arrangement.[5] In the case of animosity, the interaction between kingdoms is defined by violence. There is not necessarily a permanent war situation, but it is not a relationship analogous to peaceful political opposition. The entire indigenous social structure is based on the idea of hierarchy, between families as well as between kingdoms.

The local political authority traditionally deals with issues like the defence of borders and conflict resolution. Usually one specific person from the family entitled to "political authority" conducts the relevant tasks. He is appointed by a league of elders, who are knowledgeable in the history of families and their intermarriages. Important political decisions are taken by a council of those holding "political authority". They sit on a woven mat and discuss an issue until consensus is reached. No opposition remains when they leave. While titles are inherited, change in political power is supposed only to happen within the "right" families, and it is up to the ritual leaders to choose the right individual.

Since the official abolition of the kingdoms, the former kings often have become village chiefs or subdistrict leaders. While the Portuguese in many cases did not have any impact on internal power structures, the Indonesian administration prescribed democratic elections of village chiefs. Yet in many cases the traditional political leaders were reaffirmed through elections. In cases of external Indonesian appointments, communities constructed ways to justify the change of leaders in keeping with the feared ancestral powers.[6] In the past, where relations between groups were classified as violent, paramilitary forces and resistance groups exploited the divisions. Consequently, today, it is not uncommon for one village to adhere to one political party only, because the hostile neighbouring village votes for another.

Occupying powers throughout history have underestimated the resilience of local concepts of political legitimacy and the influence that a local political ruler can have on his community.[7] Especially in a post-conflict scenario, societies attempt to reproduce their traditional order for the sake of creating stability. During UNTAET, identifying the legitimate local leaders was one of the most critical issues.

Immediately after the rampage in 1999, whereas the National Council of Timorese Resistance (CNRT), the umbrella organization for all resistance parties, appointed representatives from all levels, the hamlet to the national level, UNTAET's administrative structure extended only down to the district level. A team of UN officials set up the district administration and then slowly employed Timorese counterparts, to whom they eventually handed their executive responsibilities. From district capitals, international district field officers (DFOs) were responsible for the subdistricts, where they worked with the "unofficial" CNRT subdistrict representatives. They constituted the interface for UNTAET at the local level, while in Dili the UN leadership decided not to recognize the CNRT officially.

Today, local-level governance is still plagued by confusion, deriving from the unclear local governance structure that was left behind by the United Nations. The present plans of the government are similar to the former Indonesian structures: the village chief should be popularly elected, and the rest of the administration appointed. Opposition politicians fear that the government's ruling party, Fretilin, will dominate such elections. The idea of a neutral, non-politicized, technical administration as introduced by UNTAET is a foreign concept that finds little support. Currently, the former CNRT representatives and many of the UNTAET recruits are in opposition to the ruling party. One district administrator remarks: "The national government has only a roof but no roots."[8]

Early local-level elections could have avoided some of this confusion and some of the present political exploitations of it. Elected local leaders would have been formally recognized and have gained a more solid position. A stronger means of representation could have been created through a better-managed democratic exercise. As this was not achieved at the national level, at least it could have changed the face of UNTAET at the grass-roots.

Similar ideas were behind the World Bank's Community Empowerment and Local Governance Project. At an early stage the project was to support village council and subdistrict council elections to let the population decide on how to spend developmental funds. The project was planned to fill the void below the UNTAET structures and to create local accountability. At a later stage, the councils were to be integrated into the official governance structure at the local level. UNTAET initially rejected the project, and only later accepted it after intervention from the UN and World Bank leadership.

While local-level elections can be successfully personalized, a nationwide multi-party system contradicts the fundamentally hierarchical and unitary indigenous political idea, in which peaceful political opposition is logically impossible.[9] The term "multi-party" brought back the fear of the civil war in 1975, when competition between the newly emerging political parties led to violent conflict. That is why many village chiefs today claim that in their village "of course everybody is from the same party", making political opposition appear as something unnatural.

Introducing the term "democracy" to the population brought further confusion. Villagers used the term "democratia", which was introduced into Tetum as a Portuguese loanword, to argue for their total, individualistic, freedom even from the community. They denied their obedience to the village chief whenever it was uncomfortable. Local restrictions on the exploitation of public goods – such as coconut trees or game in the forest – were in some cases violated. "Democracy" also meant the demand of total equality in the distribution of aid goods. If an NGO did not bring enough goods for everybody, some communities refused the aid altogether. The word also seems to have had its impact on traffic rules: a vehicle winding around the island's serpentine roads annoyed the driver of the car behind, who said "they cannot go so slow, now that we have democracy".[10] The education coordinator in one of the eastern districts complained that the village population did not accept his distribution of teachers to the different schools. Villagers were demanding their right to vote for the replacement of a primary school teacher.[11] For the local population, "democracy" meant "paradise", it meant peace and anarchy at the same time, and it meant they could do whatever suited them. In their eyes it is a good invention, but not if it means a multi-party system is introduced!

There is still no clear understanding about the right to choose the representative with the best political programme in a government. The majority of the population continue to adhere to local concepts of hierarchical political institutions, centralized power, and vertical decision-making processes. Making the logic of the modern state part of local thinking is still a distant prospect.

National factions

Following the violence in 1999, East Timor's population was effectively represented by the CNRT. Former commander of the National Liberation Armed Forces of East Timor (FALINTIL), Xanana Gusmão, was President of the CNRT. Yet inside the CNRT the different factions that had developed during the independence struggle through different personalities and ideologies were still ever-present. The resistance was not characterized by internal harmony and agreement.

Nevertheless the CNRT displayed a strong unified front towards the outside world and appeared more monolithic than it was. Playing on the strong cultural value of unity, the CNRT denied the existence of any internal opposition for the sake of the appearance of stability. The internal agreement was that none of the CNRT member parties would attempt to exert influence below the district level or try to gain hold of the grass-roots, well aware that real strength flows from the political conceptions of the population at that level.[12]

Internal tensions, however, eventually boiled over. In August 2000 the CNRT held its first big congress in Dili. The outcome of the congress re-emphasized its enshrined principles of unity (by the "Pact of National Unity") while at the same time calling for democracy.[13] A multi-party system was identified as one of the main challenges. The rhetoric of unity and the prospect of multiple competing parties were in tension. The CNRT continued to try to manage this tension between the promise of democratic governance for the country and at the same time the need to maintain unity among its political factions. Xanana Gusmão called for political parties to make decisions on a "consensual" basis to "safeguard national interests".[14]

The biggest resistance party, the Revolutionary Front of Independent East Timor (Fretilin), whose capacities were underestimated by the CNRT leadership, refused to join the Permanent Council of the CNRT or to adhere by the various internal agreements. It subtly organized at the village level and effectively took control of the grass-roots. From October 2000 onwards, Fretilin started local-level elections for party representatives. It established a countrywide structure with representatives from the village up to the national level, parallel to the already existing CNRT structure. In some cases the CNRT appointee coincided with the new Fretilin representative; in other cases a dual power situation arose, causing confusion for the grass-roots. The CNRT continued to maintain the display of unity.

A former CNRT member points out: "We had the first big national CNRT Congress in August 2000, we should have never had a second one."[15] The second congress in June 2001 was a gathering leading to its own dissolution, only two months prior to the Constituent Assembly elections. The suspended unity umbrella was immediately replaced by the "official" signing of the Pact of National Unity, under the watch of the transitional administrator.[16] Fourteen out of 16 parties agreed to it. The concept of unity promised peaceful elections as it reaffirmed the socio-political values of the grass-roots. The socialization of the Pact of National Unity in the villages was much more successful than any voter education or political campaign conducted at the same time. Yet it ran counter to the development of the idea of a multi-party system.

When the CNRT through its dissolution finally gave the green light for political parties to act under their own auspices, Fretilin was already well established throughout the country. For the other parties, either entirely new or re-established older parties, two months was not sufficient time to develop a political profile and introduce themselves to the people. The subsequent Constituent Assembly elections turned into a battle over historical issues and traditional symbols. People felt obliged to vote for the main resistance party, with their flag and the original name of the nation (Democratic Republic of East Timor: RDTL), for which "family members had given their lives".[17] No party made attempts in the election campaign to explain democratic objectives. In the Constituent Assembly that was formed, the most heated debates were over matters like the revival of the RDTL flag. As a result of the effectiveness of a coalition between Fretilin and the traditionalist Social Democratic Association of East Timor (ASDT), newly created political parties were voted out of existence. This gave Fretilin an unrivalled opportunity to insert its ideology in the constitution. The constitution created a powerful prime minister with centralized official powers.[18] The population's democratic will had essentially resulted in a limited democratic space in which there was little room for opposing ideologies.

Fretilin turned what was announced to be a "government of national unity" into a government of "inclusion". Competent members of other parties were allowed to join the government, but had to act in accordance to the Fretilin party line. Some of the opposition parties had forlornly hoped that UNTAET could insist on the promised "government of national unity". In their eyes such a government would have limited the perils inherent in a multi-party process, and instead placed more emphasis on the development of the country first. UNTAET meanwhile hurried to leave behind a pseudo-democratic system following "free and fair" elections, in keeping with the UN's age-old exit strategy.

Fretilin as the governing party has continued to emphasize its historical heritage. Part of this was the dangerous renaming of the Defence Force (FDTL) after the old guerrilla force "FALINTIL-FDTL" (Armed Forces of National Liberation of East Timor, FALINTIL).[19] The present attempt at top-down politicization of the administration as opposed to the conduct of local-level elections indicates a tendency towards an authoritarian-style rule.[20] Recognizing the shortcomings of the current administrative apparatus, President Xanana Gusmão delivered a speech 100 days after independence and for the celebrations of "independence day" on 28 November 2002. He criticized the dominance of Fretilin in the government and the focus on historical issues as a cover for self-interest.[21] He also asked for the dismissal of the Interior Minister, thus unleashing further tensions in the country.[22]

The President, quietly siding with the main opposition parties, compensates for his lack of support in the executive and legislative branches through his outstanding popularity. The constitution grants him the power "to exercise competencies inherent in the function of Supreme Commander of the Defence Force".[23] The Defence Force is also where his unofficial loyalties lie. At the same time he tries to avoid the polarization of his popularity. In the presidential elections, which preceded the country's independence in May 2001, he strongly rejected the support of specific parties. This was played out in a battle between the two presidential candidates, Xanana Gusmão and Francisco Xavier do Amaral,[24] over the use of party flags on the ballot paper. Gusmão threatened to withdraw his candidacy if the party logos supporting him as a candidate were to appear. In line with the former CNRT policy of unity, he continued to deny the necessity of open political competition.

The divide between the government and the President plus the Defence Force is overshadowed by the development of factions within Fretilin[25] and various alliances with ex-FALINTIL groups.[26] The factions within Fretilin are unable to split apart, as each splinter ultimately draws its power from Fretilin's historic and traditional symbols. A Portuguese-educated diaspora is at odds with a younger generation of Indonesian-educated intellectuals. Tension also exists between the Australian diaspora and the diaspora from ex-Portuguese colonies. A conglomerate of internal ex-guerrillas has been attempting to forge old alliances. All claim to be working in the interests of democracy.

The Minister for Internal Affairs, Rogério Lobato, has attempted to undermine the police force with ex-guerrillas. The new recruits for the Timorese police force were all supposed to be ex-FALINTIL fighters.[27] The new recruitment strategy for police officers shows the intent to reward resistance fighters' achievements with jobs. The system of rewards is locally much better understood than the modern concept of meritocracy. The "awarding" system now becomes a tool of each of the Fretilin factions in power. This also includes the distribution of higher governmental positions. The factional conflict was played out in clashes between members of the police force and soldiers of the Defence Force in November 2002.[28]

Considering that the factions are not based on differences in political ideologies, but rather on a struggle for personal power and cultural denominators, a precarious partition and fragmentation are taking place. Expressions of differences have not been channelled into non-violent democratic forms, but are articulated through historical means and a mixture of political and military alliances. Executive power, the rule of law, and the use of military force find no conceptual division in the current administrative environment.[29]

This reflects, to a wide extent, indigenous political concepts. Local value systems keep the issues of war and violence in the same category as that of political authority. Whereas the main distinction lies between the political and ritual authorities, no such distinction is made between war and politics. Political authorities become even greater politicians by fighting a successful war. Therefore it concerned nobody when the head of the Defence Force took sides in the presidential elections and announced his support for presidential candidate Xanana Gusmão.[30]

Through Fretilin's 2001 electoral win, which was an expression of the population's will, the grip of historical events determined the constitution for the future of the country. The early democratic political process in East Timor was tied to local political culture, emphasizing the importance of historical remnants, instilling fear, and assuring the impossibility of outspoken political opposition, all of which are part of the cultural concept of unity.

In the new country, national means of decision-making and power exertion are similar to processes existing at the local community level in that both are based on concepts of hierarchy and seniority. Hence, part of the national élite are genuinely operating accordingly to local paradigms, which also promises more success as their actions are better understood by the local communities. On the other hand, the well-educated diaspora are attempting to operate outside this paradigm to gain power.

International feudalism

The United Nations was mandated in October 1999 to act as a transitional administration in East Timor. It was tasked to rebuild, administer, and prepare the country for independence. It received all legislative and executive authority over the territory of East Timor.[31] The transitional administrator was to act as civil governor with political authority over the country. The establishment of political institutions on the basis of democratic structures and "capacity-building for self-government"[32] does not only imply developing the technical skills of local civil servants. It also means creating a political environment in which different opinions can be expressed through a democratic multi-party system.

UNTAET attempted to build an indigenous public administration, oversaw the creation of political parties, and convened elections for a constituent assembly that was to draft a constitution based on democratic ideas. The only UNTAET initiatives that reached the grass-roots level were a civic education programme and the constitutional hearings. UNTAET's first plan for a civic education campaign was a typical UN-run project without local leadership. The introduction of democracy was to be run like an election. After Timorese civil society groups had expressed their dissatisfaction, the initiative was handed over to the UN Political Affairs Office to establish a national committee for civic education.[33] A different strategy was developed that focused on a partnership with Timorese civil society. Timorese community-based organizations from districts were involved and the exercise was supposed to create

Timorese ownership of the process. Yet, instead of persisting with the established partnership, the civic education campaign became a short-term process. An opportunity to build on the established relationships and increase Timorese institutional ownership and capacity was lost. The resultant UNDP civic education campaign concentrated on the experience of the international staff and did not pay sufficient attention to local ownership.[34]

Following a UNTAET proposal to encourage local involvement in the drafting of the constitution,[35] 13 constitutional commissions were established. They consisted of Timorese people and received logistical support from UNTAET. The idea was to give the opportunity to the Timorese to express "what they themselves want and believe is right for East Timor".[36] Villagers were gathered and invited to discuss issues like government structure, administration, political systems, the economy, language, citizenship, the currency, the national flag, and so forth. The results were delivered to the Constituent Assembly during their inauguration in September 2001.[37]

Though the constitutional hearings were not meant to be civic education, they encouraged people to listen and discuss issues of a modern state. Yet, instead of discussing the national government, the hearings made people talk seriously about relevant concerns in their daily life: questions like who was to collect the honey in the forest.[38] Whether a semi-parliamentary system is appropriate for the nation did not really seem to be of concern for them. People heard terminology that had no meaning for them. They were to decide about issues without any relation to these terms. The outcome of the hearings might have been that the majority of the population favour a presidential system, but what is the real value of such a statement if the majority do not know what a presidential system is?

Both initiatives, civic education and constitutional hearings, covered the entire country and introduced new concepts. The grass-roots in Timor have no experience with democracy and bad experiences with previous institutions. During the transitional administration only Timorese (CNRT-Fretilin) were active at the grass-roots, none of whom had experiences of democracy – thus raising the question of from where the understanding of democracy and a modern state structure was to come. UNTAET should have attempted to set standards at the local level and shaped future local governance, as opposed to its absence altogether from that level. There was a lack of a common language between the international and local community regarding the democratic state-building exercise.

UNTAET's performance with national actors was more in the spotlight than was its relationship with the grass-roots. The first obvious issue

UNTAET had to deal with was the presence of the CNRT all throughout the country. Whereas the Security Council mandated UNTAET as the sole formal authority, the CNRT had complete local recognition. UNTAET's options for dealing with the CNRT ranged from dissolution to recognition, or at least involvement. In the East Timor case, the classic setting of conflicting local parties that the United Nations often has to deal with, and in which the United Nations traditionally acts as neutral arbiter, did not exist. The United Nations did not want to recognize the CNRT as a government, because the "popular consultation" was not a vote for the CNRT but was only a vote for independence from Indonesian rule.[39] The CNRT was considered to be a fact, but official engagement was avoided. This constituted a difficult environment on the subnational level. The CNRT was present at the grass-roots and enjoyed local legitimacy. The sparsely staffed district administration had to rely completely on their help.

At the national level it was more difficult to deny collaboration with the CNRT. The National Consultative Council (NCC), which was established in December 1999 under the transitional administrator, was the first political institution to involve Timorese actors. As the CNRT insisted on the exclusion of any other pro-independence parties or civil society figures, only representatives from the pro-autonomy groups and the CNRT were appointed to this advisory body.

By April 2000 pressure on UNTAET to engage more with Timorese had mounted. The first East Timorese transitional government was formed, with five Timorese and four international ministers. Important portfolios, such as police and emergency services, political affairs, justice, and finance were still in the hands of UN officials. The NCC was turned into the National Council (NC), which consisted of additional district representatives, appointed through the international administrators in the districts. At the district level district advisory councils (DACs) were established to advise the DA in his decision-making.

The CNRT and its standing political committee made recommendations for the timetable for political transition.[40] Disappointed by their small share of power, anticipation for a complete handover of authority was increasing. In December 2000 the CNRT recommended elections for the Constituent Assembly. In February 2001 the CNRT brought forward a detailed plan for the subsequent handover of power, which was mostly followed by UNTAET.[41] Because of UNTAET's lack of understanding of the political culture of local actors, the strategy to build democratic political institutions was too generic. Ultimately, many of these institutions were only established in response to Timorese pressure.

The question of the "representativeness" of the Timorese who were employed or consulted by the United Nations was relevant throughout the UNTAET period. In the beginning, the transitional administrator used Xanana Gusmão as a single interlocutor. Fretilin's regaining of strength was underestimated in the early period, and when "Timorization" started, Timorese counterparts were appointed who later proved to have no popular backing.[42] Meanwhile Fretilin was winning over the grass-roots and surprising the international community with its overwhelming win in the Constituent Assembly elections. UNTAET, for the first time, now chose to work with the Fretilin leadership as principal interlocutors. In a difficult process the transitional administrator partly let the winning party determine the membership of the second transitional government.

On the subnational level the problem was more one of the legitimacy rather than the "representativeness" of Timorese leaders. The choices made by international administrators, as in the case of the DACs, often revealed a lack of knowledge about the local social and political situation. Though international officials might have chosen intellectually very capable people, they often lacked local legitimacy.[43] This then turned into a lack of legitimacy for UNTAET itself on the ground.

In most cases the positions of Timorese district and subdistrict administrators formerly had been filled with due regard to the indigenous power structure. When the new administrative staff under UNTAET were chosen, their appointments were made on the basis of their educational background and not their heritage and age. The result was a lack of local legitimacy as the population felt the wrong individuals occupied power positions. A district or subdistrict head traditionally stems from a family with political authority. The "modern" concept of the purely technical appointment in the administration was new to people. The discrepancy between the "modern" and non-political way of selecting administration staff and local ideas about legitimate personnel in these positions was never resolved.

The international staff members in the transitional administration itself suffered from a similar problem, in that none of them had been elected. The Timorese never had the opportunity to cast their vote about who governed them at the national and district levels during the transitional period. There was an insufficient attempt to ensure local participation in the overall process. This significant detail, which is the main pillar of any democracy, was downplayed. The administration, consequently, had little accountability to the population.

Another strong Timorese cultural concept is that of the dominance of the "centre" in the hierarchical power structure. Transferred to a governmental level, this logically had the effect of favouring a type of centralized and authoritarian rule. UNTAET, though, claimed to promote decentralization. Yet the actual power that was delegated to the district administrations was minimal, and Dili inevitably developed as the power centre. While decentralization and devolution are presently one of the biggest foci in international development strategy, they were never an issue for UNTAET. The government that came to power after UNTAET inherited the centralized system. So, while the constitution is committed to decentralization,[44] the words are sounding rather hollow.[45] In fact, the trend is in the opposite direction.

Timorese leaders – at the receiving end of the UN's democratization – were well aware of the lack of democratic culture and structures within UNTAET itself. In a general UN fashion, decisions were taken top-down from the special representative of the Secretary-General. Yet in the case of UNTAET the SRSG at the same time acted as the transitional administrator. Therefore, authoritarian-style decision-making was not only conducted internally within the mission, but also in the administration of the country. The transitional administrator had technically the last say in any matter. While in most democratic countries there is a divide between legislative, judicial, and executive powers, under UNTAET all powers were combined in a single individual. His extreme powers, which have been referred to as "benevolent despotism",[46] might prove to be – if that person makes the right decisions – the fastest way to rule in a post-conflict state but they did not provide a good example by which to prepare the local population for a democratic country. Rather, they facilitated the acceptance of top-down rule – in this case internationally legitimized. Whereas one dictator might be benevolent and competent, his successor might not; democracy is a casualty.

UNTAET's anti-democratic features may be defended by comparison with the operational difficulties inherent in a more democratic model. Yet, in terms of promoting democracy, the UNTAET structure was self-defeating. Democratic institutions in East Timor were to be built in a short amount of time in an environment that had never experienced a truly democratic system before, nor were the upcoming Timorese political élite coming from a particularly democratic background. Now, even in this short-term international intervention, there was no precedent set by the United Nations in which the local population could have been exposed to a democratic process. Any kind of message conveyed through civic education was lost in abstraction.

Conclusion

The lack of democratic structures or state institutions does not mean that a vacuum of power exists. Every society, even after a conflict, has an understanding of who should be in power and why, and who should make decisions and how. In the case of East Timor, this perspective differs drastically from that of Western democracy and therefore forms the strongest constraint for democratization. As long as democratic institutions of a state are built upon a fundamentally different view of the world than that understood by the people, state-building operations are doomed to build a fragile nation.

The grass-roots therefore need special attention, as this is where the majority of the population live and their understanding is an important ingredient for success. Their participation in the state-building process and their basic understanding of state institutions are crucial. The engagement with communities for these purposes is much more common in the democratization and development fields. The United Nations has not yet developed effective methods to involve local populations, and has not even focused adequately on this problem in its state-building exercises.

The term "participation" needs to be rethought, as genuine participation can only take place through the incorporation of local paradigms. To include the local population in the political process, sufficient understanding has to be gained about local political concepts and power structures. Only then does a reference point exist from which democratization can begin.

Understanding local perceptions and creating local participation go far beyond the pure idea of "civic education" and are essential ingredients for a successful international role. In East Timor, the "modern state system" was simply placed on top of an existing indigenous structure, however poor the fit.

Similarly, on the national level, the mere technical establishment of democratic political institutions is not sufficient. Factions need to be untied from their socio-cultural and historical background that prevents them from functioning properly within democratic institutions. A profound understanding of political factions and the mechanisms that make them function is a necessary first step. Political space has to be created in which local actors can be shown how to express differences democratically. In addition, the United Nations itself, in the case of a transitional administration, has to become an example to different factions of how to be a political player, and has to manage the political arena.[47] Only then can differences in ideology be expressed non-violently and democratically.

A decision has to be made between building a Westminster-style state and developing an alternative, more locally adapted model – or maybe something in between. Both approaches require a more flexible approach to state-building.

To introduce the Westminster model successfully, social engineering, a term that is mostly replaced by more polite words, inevitably has to be conducted. Local societies with all their traditional mechanisms have to be transformed into state societies. A genuine change of their political ideas will result in transformation of the entire social structure. On the national level this means forcing national players to adapt to a Western paradigm, and to use democratic channels of expression. Yet such an approach requires a much greater time and financial commitment. In East Timor, the United Nations was reduced to only the rhetoric of democratization. The mere conduct of "free and fair" elections as an introduction to democracy is not sufficient. Elections cannot become the measurement of the mission's success. Superficial as they are, they are likely to leave behind an unstable environment. Too often they are undermined by religious, historical, or cultural motivations, and they do not necessarily express a population's political will. East Timor has certainly achieved entry into the family of nations, but its governance system may have only international but not local legitimacy.

In a more locally sensitive approach, local institutions with non-state mechanisms would be left intact for longer. They would be integrated into the state institutions and could be reduced in phases. Societies should have space to transform gradually into a state society. In this case, intense knowledge about local structures is no less essential.

The result of the state-building approach in East Timor was dissatisfying: the international community has a lot to learn before being able to deliver a well-functioning state with its grass-roots as responsible and participating constituents. As long as the difference in the paradigms of the grass-roots population and the national élite on the one hand, and on the other hand the Westphalian state, is not taken into account in state-building and democratization, international interventions in the twenty-first century will continue to create pleasing shells with disappointing substance.

Acknowledgements

The author is indebted to Alessandro Righetti, Sarah Niner, and Jarat Chopra for comments on an earlier draft of the chapter.

Notes

1. Joliffe, Jill. 2002. "Police opens fire as riots and arson grip Timor", *The Age*, 5 December; Dickens, Jim. 2002. "Five killed in Dili riots", *Herald Sun*, Australia, 5 December.
2. See for example "East Timor. Legal system in crisis", Radio Australia, 19 December 2002, transcript at www.goasiapacific.com/specials/etimor/map.htm; "Outside elements linked to Dili riots", *The Age*, 6 December 2002.

3. See for example "Report of the Panel on United Nations Peace Operations", accessed at www.un.org/peace/reports/peace_operations/.
4. When the Portuguese first arrived, they found that the island of Timor was divided into numerous autonomous kingdoms.
5. In a case in which the two kingdoms are classified as brothers, one would usually be considered as older brother.
6. See Hohe, Tanja. 2002. "Clash of paradigms. International administration and local political concepts in East Timor", *Contemporary Southeast Asia*, Vol. 24, No. 3.
7. *Ibid.*
8. Interview with a district administrator, East Timor, November 2002.
9. Therefore the present idea of the government to run party elections on the village level could turn out to be dangerous.
10. Driver in Ermera, during Constituent Assembly election campaigns, August 2001.
11. Interview with district education coordinator, November 2002.
12. Interview with ex-CNRT leader, Dili, September 2002.
13. See "Outcomes of the CNRT National Congress, 21–30 August 2000", English version. Dili: CNRT National Congress.
14. Public Announcement of the First National CNRT Congress Conclusions, Address by the CNRT/CN President Xanana Gusmão, 9 October 2000, CNRT Headquarters, Dili.
15. Interview with former CNRT representative in Maliana, September 2002.
16. 8 July 2001.
17. See also Hohe, Tanja. 2002. "Totem polls. Indigenous concepts and 'free and fair' elections in East Timor", *International Peacekeeping*, Vol. 9, No. 4.
18. Although lip-service to decentralization is payed. See Constitution of the Democratic Republic of East Timor, Part I, Sec. 5. Dili: Constituent Assembly of East Timor.
19. See Pinto, Julio Tomas. 2002. "Antara Falintil dan FDTL", *Gevatil News*, April/June.
20. Fretilin is solely planning village chief elections, while the rest of the administrative structure will consist of political appointments. The most radical Fretilin elements want to transfer the Fretilin party structure into the official administration, arguing that they were all democratically elected. Interview with Fretilin representative, Dili, September 2002.
21. Speech by President of the Republic Kay Rala Xanana Gusmão at the official ceremonies commemorating 28 November, Dili, 28 November 2002.
22. Address to the nation by President Kay Rala Xanana Gusmão on 100 days of independence, Dili, 30 August 2002.
23. Constitution, note 18 above, Chapter II, Section 85b.
24. The President of the unilaterally announced Democratic Republic of East Timor in 1975.
25. Pinto, Julio Tomas. 2002. "Internal reform of Fretilin", *Timor Post*, Weekend Analysis, 16 November.
26. See also Pinto, Julio Tomas. 2002. "Militer yang gelisah", *Lian Maubere*, 21–28 June.
27. See "500 Eks Frente Klandestin-Falintil direkrut jadi PNTL", *Suara Timor Lorosae*, 23 September 2002.
28. See for example "Anggota Falintil-FDTL bentrok dengan polisi", *Suara Timor Lorosae*, 9 November 2002.
29. See also Pinto, Julio Tomas. 2002. "Militer dalam Politik (Disiplin dan Perilaku Politik Perwira)", *Timor Post*, 25 June.
30. See for example "FDTL dukung Xanana presiden TL", *Suara Timor Lorosae*, 4 December 2001; "Kol. Lere Anan Timor. UNTAET dan KPI ikuti kemauan rakyat dan Xanana", *Suara Timor Lorosae*, 13 March 2002.
31. UNSC Res. 1272 (1999), 25 October 1999.

32. *Ibid.*
33. Stewart, Colin. 2001. "Civic education carried out by Timorese people", *Suara Timor Lorosae*, 5 April.
34. Interview with Kieran Dwyer, Secretariat of the Truth and Reconciliation Commission in East Timor, Dili, November 2002.
35. See Galbraith, Pete. 2001. "East Timor's political transition. Testimony to the National Council", 20 January, www.gov.east-timor.org/old/civedu/20010120_poltran.php.htm.
36. UNTAET. 2001. *Report on the National Constitutional Consultation in East Timor.* Dili: UNTAET, June–July, foreword.
37. *Ibid.*
38. In a public hearing in Oecussi, June 2001.
39. Although the CNRT flag represented the rejection of the autonomy proposal on the ballot paper.
40. Kay Rala Xanana Gusmão, Committee on Political Affairs, 23 December 2000; "Report on the Political Transitional Calendar" by the National Council Standing Committee on Political Affairs, Dili, 22 February 2001.
41. National Council Standing Committee, *ibid.*
42. As for example Joao Carrascãlao, whose party got 2.36 per cent on the national list in the Constituent Assembly elections, but who was appointed as minister in the first transitional government.
43. Some of the district NC representatives were young students: according to the principle of seniority they had no local acknowledgement in such a position.
44. Constitution, note 18 above, Part I, Section 5.
45. See UNDP. 2002. *Ukun Rasik A'an. The Way Ahead. East Timor Human Development Report 2002.* New York: UNDP.
46. See Beauvais, Joel. 2001. "Benevolent despotism. A critique of UN state-building in East Timor", *New York University Journal of International Law and Politics*, Vol. 33, No. 4.
47. Chopra, Jarat. 2002. "Building state failure in East Timor", *Development and Change*, Vol. 33, No. 5.

14

The United Nations and democratization in Afghanistan

Amin Saikal

The United Nations has had a long involvement in Afghanistan, directed at bringing peace and stability to the country. Its engagement has been in several phases, beginning shortly after the Soviet invasion of Afghanistan in late December 1979. Although in the early phases its achievements were very modest, the 11 September 2001 terrorist attacks on New York and Washington by Osama bin Laden's al-Qaeda activists, harboured by the Taliban's medievalist Islamic regime in Afghanistan, changed the picture dramatically. The US-led military intervention in Afghanistan and its successful dismantling of the Taliban and dislodging of al-Qaeda in the country opened a rare opportunity for the United Nations to play a central role in helping the Afghans to settle their internal differences and build a lasting, popularly legitimated political order. The United Nations has ever since sought vigorously to promote democratization as the best process by which to achieve this objective. However, its journey on this path is fraught with difficulty. The Afghan people, who are made up of various traditional Muslim micro-societies, divided along ethno-tribal, linguistic, sectarian, and personality lines, have never had a tradition or culture of democracy. The only period during which they were subjected to a limited "experiment with democracy" was from the early 1960s to the early 1970s – an experiment which resulted in total failure. Building democracy can be very complex and a hazardous goal at the best of times, let alone in the ruined conditions of Afghanistan after 23 years of devastating conflict. Even so, the United Nations has been given a chance to achieve a lasting impact on the Afghan political, social, and economic landscape. Its success and failure in this area will be critical not only to the future of Afghanistan, but also to the credibility and functions of the international body itself.

This chapter has four main objectives. The first is to explore briefly the history of the Afghan conflict and the UN's role in search of a peaceful end to it. The second is to evaluate more specifically the UN's role in the post-Taliban settlement of the Afghan conflict, and to investigate what the United Nations wishes to accomplish in terms of helping the Afghans to create the necessary conditions for the growth of a stable and workable political order. The third is to discuss the steps which have been taken and in which the United Nations has been involved in support of democratization in Afghanistan. The fourth is to assess the challenges facing the United Nations in terms of achieving its objectives in Afghanistan over the next few years. The overall purpose is not to analyse every aspect of the UN's role, but only to focus on those UN efforts that deal with the construction of stable political order in Afghanistan.

Early phases

The UN's involvement in Afghanistan dates back to 1980, when shortly after the Soviet invasion of the country the United Nations was called upon to play a peace-promoting and conflict-resolution role in the country. Its role over the next 21 years until the US-led intervention evolved in four distinct phases. The initial phase lasted until the Soviet withdrawal from Afghanistan by February 1989. The second phase encompassed the period from the Soviet troop pullout to the collapse of the Soviet-installed government of Najibullah in Kabul and the assumption of power by the Islamic resistance forces, the Mujahideen, in late April 1992. The third phase, lasting over the next nine years, was marked by the failure of the Mujahideen Islamic government to consolidate, and the rise to power of the Pakistan-backed Taliban and transformation of Afghanistan into a source of international terrorism. The fourth phase, which forms the main concern of this chapter, began with the US-led military campaign in Afghanistan, which finally enabled the United Nations to commence a key role in the process of state reconstruction and democratization in Afghanistan.

During the first three phases, the UN's political role could not progress beyond mediation and attempts at peacemaking. In the first phase, the United Nations was mostly focused on how to broker a peace deal which could ensure the withdrawal of the Soviet forces from Afghanistan, end the Afghan conflict as a Soviet-American Cold War proxy conflict, and restore the independence and non-aligned status of the country. The UN role was by and large managed by various representatives of the UN Secretary-General, namely Javier Perez de Cuellar, Diego Cordovez, Benon Sevan, and Mahmoud Mestiri, the first two of whom shuttled between the capitals of major protagonists – Kabul, Islamabad, Tehran, Moscow, and Washington – as well as some of the second-rank players, such as Saudi Arabia and Britain.

During the first phase, the UN's peacemaking role was constantly frustrated by the incompatible positions of the parties involved, with the policy attitude of the Soviet-installed Afghan government fixed very much by Soviet priorities. The postures of its Afghan Islamic opponents, the Mujahideen, were determined largely by what their key supporters – that is Pakistan, Saudi Arabia, Iran, and the USA – wanted to achieve from the conflict, not only in opposition to the Soviets but also in support of their own conflicting regional and international interests. The UN representatives achieved little until the Soviet Union under Mikhail Gorbachev decided in late 1985 to find an "honourable" way out of Afghanistan. It took the UN Secretary-General's personal representative, Diego Cordovez, another three years to broker the Geneva Accords on Afghanistan, signed in 1988 between the Afghan and Pakistani governments and guaranteed by the USSR and the USA.[1] Under the Accords the Soviets undertook to withdraw their troops by May 1989, and in return Pakistan pledged not to interfere in Afghanistan's internal affairs. Meanwhile, the Soviet Union and the USA reserved a right to continue to supply arms to their clients – a development which ensured Afghanization of the war. The Accords did not provide for a cease-fire, let alone peace and a political settlement,[2] but they allowed the Soviets to claim an "honourable" exit and the Americans to inflict a humiliating defeat upon the Soviets, possibly comparable to what the Soviets had given to the USA in Viet Nam.[3] The continuation of the conflict also meant the prolongation of the UN role in search of a lasting settlement.

The second phase was distinguished by a substantial reduction in US involvement in Afghanistan, the failure of various Mujahideen groups to present a viable alternative, and Najibullah's exploitation of inter-Mujahideen division to promote a policy of token "national reconciliation" under his leadership. It was also marked by manoeuvres by the Mujahideen's regional supporters, especially Pakistan, to advance their rival interests in alliance with different resistance groups in Afghanistan. It coincided with the tenure of Benon Sevan as the UN Secretary-General's personal representative. Sevan's task was to help secure an orderly settlement of the Afghan conflict, based on an "intra-Afghan dialogue", in order to shape "a credible and impartial transition mechanism" that "would enjoy the confidence of the Afghan people and provide them with the necessary measures to participate in free and fair elections, taking into account Afghan traditions, for the establishment of a broad based government", and "cessation of hostilities during the transition period".[4]

However, Sevan achieved remarkably little. This was partly because he never gained a firm grasp of the complexity of the Afghan conflict and worked misguidedly on the assumption that the Mujahideen could be reconciled with Najibullah's regime in a coalition government. The fact that the Soviet Union sank deeper into domestic crisis, eroding the bargaining capacity of Najibullah's leadership, also undermined his mission. He could neither bring the parties together for an internal settlement nor put in place an effective transition mechanism to ensure a smooth transfer of power from Najibullah's government to the Mujahideen. In the end, as Najibullah's government faced collapse, there was a scramble for power. Najibullah sought to flee the country, but failed and obtained refuge at a UN office in Kabul until his murder at the hands of the Taliban more than four years later. The forces of the distinguished Mujahideen commander Ahmad Shah Massoud took over much of Kabul by 25 April 1992, opening the way for the establishment of the first Mujahideen Islamic government, in which he remained the strong military man. Since Sevan had not established any prior meaningful contacts with Massoud, he could neither influence Massoud's operations nor for that matter play any role in impacting on the composition, structure, and direction of the Mujahideen government. Ultimately, he made a rather unceremonious exit from the Afghan scene.

Yet Massoud's initial victory rapidly turned sour as other Mujahideen groups, especially that of Pakistan-backed Gulbuddin Hekmatyar, decided to fight for power and control of Kabul, resulting in a bloody inter-Mujahideen power struggle. Given the fact that the Soviet Union no longer existed and the USA decided not to be involved in the post-communist management of the Afghan conflict, Afghanistan also became more vulnerable than ever before to interference by regional powers (particularly Pakistan), which now sought to back their various Afghan clients in pursuit of regional ambitions. Pakistan, or more specifically its military intelligence (ISI), which had been in charge of Pakistan's Afghanistan and Kashmir policies since the early 1980s, at first stood by Hekmatyar to achieve its objective of securing a receptive government in Kabul.

Within five months of Massoud's takeover of Kabul, Hekmatyar's forces, which were subsequently joined by the Iranian-backed Shi'ite Mujahideen group of Hezbi Wahdat (Party of Unity) and troops of the Uzbek warlord, Rashid Dostum, began rocketing Kabul intermittently at the cost of thousands of lives and the destruction of half of the capital.

The aim was to block off the efforts of the new government, headed by Burhanuddin Rabbani, to secure its position. The United Nations found itself once again compelled to launch a mediatory and peacemaking role. The UN General Assembly adopted a resolution in December 1993, requesting the Secretary-General "to dispatch to Afghanistan ... a United Nations special mission to canvass a broad spectrum of the leaders of Afghanistan, soliciting their views on how the United Nations can best assist Afghanistan in facilitating national *rapprochement* and reconstruction, and to submit its findings, conclusions and recommendations to the Secretary-General for appropriate action".[5]

In February 1994 the Secretary-General appointed a veteran Tunisian diplomat, Mahmoud Mestiri, to head the Special Mission to Afghanistan. Although Mestiri began his mission in earnest, consulting a wide range of relevant officials in New York, Afghanistan, and Pakistan, he faced an uphill battle from the start, for a number of reasons. He had not only to deal with the problem of helping the Afghans to work out a lasting power-sharing arrangement for a broad-based government as a prelude to creating a stable political order, but also to persuade various regional actors, most importantly Pakistan and Iran, that they should support his mission at the cost of their rival regional agendas. Pakistan by now had emerged as the key player, capable of wrecking any UN-brokered Afghan internal settlement that did not suit its purposes. Mestiri quickly opted to go down the same path as Sevan: that is to secure a transitional mechanism as a pre-condition for creating a broad-based, popularly legitimated government. He did so by relying too much on advice that he received from Pakistani authorities and the US embassy in Islamabad, which was sympathetic to Pakistan, as well as some New York-based UN sources which were remote from the Afghan scene. He rapidly found it expedient to lean on the Rabbani government, of which Massoud was the key military figure, to accommodate Pakistan's demand for a determining role for Hekmatyar in the government, without any guarantees that this would deliver stability.[6]

As relations deteriorated between Kabul and Islamabad, with most of Afghanistan beyond the rule of the Rabbani government, the United Nations had to engage in a greater humanitarian and political role. However, it appeared paralysed in managing such a role. When in 1994 Kabul came under heavy rocket attacks and more and more of Kabul's citizens became dependent on food hand-outs from the United Nations and other humanitarian agencies, the United Nations withdrew its international staff, and Mestiri concluded that the Rabbani government could no longer be a nucleus around which a broad-based government could evolve. In effect, Mestiri sided with Islamabad on the issue and openly criticized the Kabul government at an aid donor conference in Stockholm. From that point he could expect little or no cooperation from the Rabbani government, which Islamabad had condemned as "illegitimate". Meanwhile, the ISI woke up to the fact that Hekmatyar could never become an effective and credible client, given his unpopularity among the Afghans and his poor strategic sense. It thus set about orchestrating the Taliban as a fresh force, routing not only Hekmatyar's forces but also forcing Massoud to retreat from Kabul to the north in September 1996.

As Mestiri failed to highlight Pakistan's increasingly flagrant interference in Afghanistan, especially with the rise of the Taliban, he lost the trust of the Rabbani government and many factions associated with it. Following the Taliban take-over of Kabul in September 1996, Mestiri was replaced by a German Foreign Ministry official, Norbert Holl, whose tenure proved to be undistinguished. Holl was too cautious in his approach to the Afghanistan problem and refrained from identifying Pakistan publicly as a main culprit (although in private he could not contain himself about Pakistan's destructive role in Afghanistan).

A more successful UN role came with the appointment of Lakhdar Brahimi as the Secretary-General's special envoy for Afghanistan in July 1997. A veteran Algerian diplomat and former Foreign Minister of his country, with a strong background in the United Nations, which he had served in various capacities for several years prior to his Afghan mission, Brahimi quickly distinguished himself as perceptive and proactive in dealing with the Taliban and their Pakistani backers, as well as the opposition, led by Commander Massoud. His credentials as a good and honest Muslim also helped him in this respect, although his public criticism of Pakistan as the main obstacle to finding a resolution of the Afghan conflict led Islamabad to be wary. When the Taliban's sweep into northern Afghanistan in late 1998 and killing of nine Iranian consular officials and two associates in Mazar-e Sharif resulted in an Iranian border mobilization against the Taliban, Brahimi's success in defusing the crisis won him much admiration as a mediator and peacemaker in the region. However, ultimately he could do little to persuade Pakistan and the Taliban to choose the path of a peaceful settlement as long as they were on the offensive and firmly believed they could secure a final military victory over an increasingly isolated and weak Massoud-led opposition. In October 1999 Brahimi suspended his mission until such time as the conditions were right for him to play a meaningful role. Those favourable conditions arose in the wake of the terrorist attacks in the USA of 11 September 2001, the Taliban's refusal to denounce their alliance with al-Qaeda and hand over its leader Osama bin Laden to the USA, and Pakistan's sudden about-face under American pressure to join the US-led war on terror against its Taliban clients.

On 3 October 2001 the UN Secretary-General appointed Brahimi as his special representative for Afghanistan to begin the task of transformation of Afghanistan from a theocratic state and a nest for international terrorism under the Taliban to a democratic state under a broad-based and internationally backed and acceptable government. Brahimi was "entrusted with overall authority for the humanitarian, human rights and political endeavours of the United Nations in Afghanistan". He was also to "initiate preparations for the transition to the post-conflict peace-building phase, through the development of plans for the reconstruction and rehabilitation of that country", and "oversee the activities of, and ... be supported by, the two existing pillars of the United Nations system regarding Afghanistan: the United Nations Special Mission to Afghanistan (UNSMA) and the Office for the Coordination of Humanitarian Assistance".[7] These two bodies were subsequently absorbed into a single body – the UN Assistance Mission in Afghanistan (UNAMA), which was established under Brahimi by UNSC Resolution 1401 (28 March 2002) as the principal face of the UN system in Afghanistan.

The United Nations and democratization

It was from this point that the United Nations was granted an unprecedented and critical opportunity to assist the Afghans to build a government and construct a lasting political order which would be democratically legitimate, responsible, and accountable. In other words, the United Nations was entrusted with a pivotal role to establish a kind of democratic order which Afghanistan had never had, but which it would need to have if the Afghan people were to have a viable future within a properly governed, stable, and securely reconstructed modern state. Rightly, no UN Security Council resolution specified the kind of democracy Afghanistan should have, but Resolution 1378, adopted on 14 November 2001, authorized the United Nations to play a "central role" in helping the Afghan people to establish a transitional administration for the formation of a new government. The UN role was very much personified by Lakhdar Brahimi.

In an extraordinary act of political and ethno-linguistic balancing, Brahimi was able to convene talks between representatives of four Afghan groups. One was the United Front (or the so-called Northern Alliance), which was largely composed of non-Pashtuns and had fought the Taliban and aided the USA and its allies in the ground war against the Taliban. Another was the "Rome group", which was made up of a mixture of Pashtuns and non-Pashtuns from the Afghan diaspora, and which had revolved around the former Afghan King Zahir Shah, who had lived in exile in Italy since his overthrow in July 1973. It is worth stressing that most of this group's members had played little or no role in the Afghan resistance to Soviet occupation in the 1980s or its aftermath. The third and fourth groups, although both very small, were selected from bases in Pakistan in order to enable various strands of Pashtuns to have a stronger representation as part of an ethnic balancing act. Pashtuns, who are divided into various tribal and sub-tribal entities, have historically constituted the largest ethnic cluster, although not the majority of the population in Afghanistan, and provided the ruling élite during most of Afghanistan's existence since its creation as a political unit in the mid-eighteenth century. And indeed the bulk of the Taliban belonged to this cluster.

Brahimi's role in selecting these groups and in persuading them to join forces together, as well as in enlisting the support of the German government to host their meeting in Bonn, and in chairing the meeting for nearly two weeks from late November, cannot be overstressed. Similarly, his mediation skills in helping the delegates to chart their way through some very difficult issues and compromises and in ensuring that their outside supporters were restrained from excessively influencing the outcome could not be overpraised. The final outcome was the Bonn Agreement Pending the Re-establishment of Permanent Government Institutions, which was signed by the parties on 5 December 2001. It endorsed the institution of an Interim Authority, presided over by a chairman, to be inaugurated by 22 December as the repository of Afghan sovereignty. It also prescribed the establishment of a Special Independent Commission for the Convening of an Emergency Loya Jirga (the traditional Afghan grand assembly), to be convened within six months of the enactment of the Interim Authority. The function of the Emergency Loya Jirgah was to create a transitional authority:

to lead Afghanistan until such time as a fully representative government [could] be elected through free and fair elections to be held no later than two years from the date of the convening of the Emergency Loya Jirga. A Constitutional Loya Jirga ... [was] to be convened within 18 months of the establishment of the Transitional Authority, in order to adopt a new constitution for Afghanistan. A Constitutional Commission [was] to be established by the Transitional Authority (with the help of UN) within two months, to assist the Constitutional Loya Jirga.[8]

Furthermore, the agreement contained provision for the establishment of a Supreme Court of Afghanistan as well as such other courts as the Interim Authority decided. It carried an agreed list of names to fill the positions of the chairman and cabinet posts of the Interim Authority, with Hamid Karzai confirmed as the compromise choice for the chairmanship.

In essence, the agreement provided for the urgent formation of a central power-sharing authority and a set of procedural steps and mechanisms as well as a timetable for the institution of a culturally relevant political order that could ensure the transformation of Afghanistan into a peaceful, secure, and stable democratic state within the shortest period of time possible. It contained three essential elements. One required the immediate establishment of the Interim Authority as the nucleus of a central government. It defined the interim arrangements "as a first step toward the establishment of a broad-based, gender-sensitive, multi-ethnic and fully representative government", and added that they were "not intended to remain in place beyond the specified period of time". Another set the broad parameters within which a series of processes and mechanisms – some of them with roots in Afghan traditions, such as a Loya Jirga, and others universal in character, such as a constitution and elections – were to be enacted to legitimize and institutionalize that Interim Authority in several stages, and turn it into a permanent variable. The agreement did not specify what form the Interim Authority should eventually take and whether the governmental system should be presidential or parliamentary, or for that matter of any other kind. It left the details to be worked out amongst the stakeholders in a sequential order, and thus let the Afghans feel that ultimately they were in charge of charting their destiny. The third element specifically empowered "the United Nations, as the internationally recognised impartial institution" to play "a particularly important role ... in the period prior to the establishment of permanent institutions in Afghanistan". In effect, it endorsed the position of Lakhdar Brahimi to act as the overall UN supervisor of Afghanistan during the country's transition from being a dysfunctional, disrupted state to being a viable state with a stable democratic political order.

However, the United Nations was not the only key international player in either the transition of power or the process of democratic transformation. It had to contend with two other influential outside actors in helping to shape the peace talks and their outcome, as well as the post-Taliban politics of Afghanistan: the USA and NATO. Given its position as the main military operator and security provider against the Taliban and their al-Qaeda allies, the USA from the start was instrumental not only in ensuring the success of the anti-Taliban forces, but also in facilitating the UN's role. Representing the USA at the peace talks were the Afghan-American Zalmay Khalilzad, who in early 2002 was appointed as President George W. Bush's special envoy for Afghanistan, and a State Department official, James Dobbin. However, given his position as a Republican loyalist, an adviser to President Bush on West Asia, and a long-standing protégé of Vice President Dick Cheney, with an intimate involvement in the conduct of the Republican Party's Afghanistan policy under President Ronald Reagan and his successor George Bush, Khalilzad proved to be the main driver of America's interests at the talks. He could use the leverage of the USA's pre-eminent power in Afghanistan to cajole and reward the delegates and play a determining role in pursuit of American interests. Meanwhile, NATO, in conjunction with the European Union, was also positioned to discharge an important role. The organization's influence stemmed from its contribution to the US-led military campaign (and subsequent substantial participation in the International Security Assistance Force (ISAF), which in accord with a UN Security Council decision became fully operational in February 2002 to maintain order in Kabul in support of the Interim Authority), and from its provision of considerable aid to assist Afghanistan's reconstruction.

Although no serious conflict of interests existed between the United Nations, the USA, and NATO, Brahimi and the UN agencies working under him or in association with him nonetheless had to be conscious of the fact that without America's military presence and political influence as well as economic muscle the United Nations would not have the necessary space and security to operate effectively in Afghanistan. This meant that Brahimi had to steer through delicate passages not only among the Afghan parties but also in relation to what the USA and its European allies wanted in terms of their interests. The USA was understandably focused on an outcome which would put Afghanistan on a path of secular rather than religious reconstruction and development, and would transform the country into a US Muslim ally that could vindicate the USA's war on terror and provide it with a bastion from which it could exude wider influence against defiant radical political Islam in the region. NATO, while sharing the USA's concerns, appeared keener to help empower the Afghans to determine their future, without outside powers being too intrusive in achieving that goal. This was a position that tallied more with that of the United Nations than that of the USA. As such, the Bonn Agreement and its implementation in various stages had to be from the start based on reconciling the different approaches and objectives of not only the Afghan participants, but also a number of international players which were now set either deliberately or by force of circumstances to influence the direction of Afghan politics.

The implementation of the Bonn Agreement

To implement the Bonn Agreement, in early December the United Nations established the Integrated Mission Task Force for Afghanistan to oversee and execute the UN agencies roles in helping Afghanistan, and, at the request of Brahimi, the UN Development Programme (UNDP) established the Afghanistan Interim Authority Fund. Brahimi and his staff as well as the team of the UN Special Mission to Afghanistan, which had hitherto been located in Islamabad, moved into Kabul one day before the formal inauguration of the Interim Authority. Presided over by Brahimi, the institution of the Interim Authority could not have gone more smoothly. While the United Front forces maintained security in Kabul and the American forces acted to keep any possible major attack by the Taliban and their al-Qaeda allies at bay, Chairman Karzai and other members of the Interim Authority took oath of office in a ceremony which was attended by all those Afghan and foreign delegates who really mattered.

If any disagreements arose in the days leading up to the inauguration among the Afghan power brokers, they were skilfully and resolutely resolved or capped by the United Nations and the USA. For example, shortly before the inauguration ceremony President Rabbani, whose government's powers were transferred to the Interim Authority, expressed some dissatisfaction with the process and voiced a reluctance to support it, and the powerful governor of the western provinces, Ismail Khan, adopted a similar approach, although for different reasons. In response, the United Nations and the USA showed no hesitation in cajoling them both directly and indirectly to secure their compliance.

The Karzai Interim Authority provided the United Nations with the core operative political mechanisms that it needed to engage in state-building in Afghanistan. The United Nations moved rapidly to assist the Karzai administration to establish the Special Independent Commission for the Convening of the Emergency Loya Jirga as the main traditional instrument of indirect popular political legitimation to transform the Interim Authority into the Transitional Authority. It played a determining role in facilitating the establishment of ISAF, and in moving to set up public service, judicial, defence, and human rights commissions.

From the start Brahimi's approach appeared to emphasize the intertwined character of governance, development, and security as bases for state-building. He matched his efforts in the political arena by similar endeavours in the realm of social, economic, and security reconstruction, and humanitarian requirements. The United Nations organized a major aid donors' conference hosted by the Japanese government in Tokyo for Afghanistan's reconstruction, resulting in the promise of $4.5 billion in aid over the next five years. Of this figure $1.8 billion was earmarked for 2002 – something that the donors largely met, but most of which was spent on UN offices and urgent humanitarian needs. Contrary to expectations, about 2 million Afghan refugees returned home in 2002, obliging the Karzai government and the United Nations to spend a lot more on humanitarian emergencies than on reconstruction. The difficult task of reconstruction, with an emphasis on infrastructure-building, began, but only at a very modest level. The main project in this respect was the reconstruction of the Kabul-Kandahar-Herat highway, although even this project soon fell far behind schedule. In the area of security, various bodies were set up and agreements with outside powers were signed to expedite the processes of establishing an Afghan police force and national guard and army, and to disarm the local militias.

The Emergency Loya Jirga, convened in Kabul from 11 to 19 June 2002, consisted of over 1,600 delegates. A majority of the delegates were elected from various parts of Afghanistan, based largely on ethnic attachments; a proportion of delegates were appointed by various power brokers and local power-holders; and a number of them came from abroad, representing Afghans living around the world. Of the delegates, 1,295 voted for Karzai as the head of state, 171 for a woman candidate, Massouda Jalal, 89 for a third candidate, Mahfouz Nadaei, and 83 abstained.[9] Despite some irregularities, including intimidation and arm-twisting, in the election and selection of the delegates, despite procedural difficulties, despite behind-the-scenes dealings, and despite some blatant external cajoling, especially by Zalmay Khalilzad, who allegedly pressured the former King, Mohammed Zahir Shah, not to compete with Karzai, the Loya Jirga proved to be historical in many ways. Unlike many of its predecessors in Afghan history, this was the first moderately democratic Loya Jirga to confer indirect popular legitimacy on an Afghan head of state. It served as a major venue for the Afghans to air their differences openly through robust discussions and processes after 23 years of conflict. It set the foundation for democratic practices which the Afghan leaders could follow to govern and chart the future of Afghanistan. It also enabled Afghan women, who had been a main target of the Taliban's repression, to have an important voice in the post-Taliban politics of their country.[10]

Although the Jirga failed because of serious disagreements to leave behind an elected representative council from its ranks to function as the legislative arm of the Transitional Authority, Karzai invited some delegates to stay behind for this purpose. However, the council did not materialize, depriving the government of a legislative arm, which together with the creation of an independent judiciary was necessary to complete a somewhat democratic structure of governance. From the mere fact that it conferred a kind of public legitimacy on Karzai and some of his key ministers, and provided a forum for national participation in shaping post-Taliban politics, the Loya Jirga served as a useful mechanism to the Transitional Authority and to a new political order, with some links to the past Afghan traditions of legitimation. It positioned Karzai and the

United Nations to institute the next steps on the road to political legitimacy and democracy.

The challenges

It is too early to be confident about the growth of democracy in Afghanistan. The Karzai leadership team is far from claiming a national base of
support. Karzai has personally had no solid national standing, and in fact
before his assumption of the interim headship few had heard of him inside or outside Afghanistan. He was only known to the extent that he had
participated in the Mujahideen resistance against the Soviet occupation
of Afghanistan in the 1980s and had served briefly as deputy Foreign
Minister in the first Mujahideen government of President Burhanuddin
Rabbani (1992–1996). During the Taliban period he spent most of his
time in Pakistan and the USA, where his family had run businesses for
many years. He raised his credentials as a Kandahari Pashtun leader
when in November 2001 he decided, with full US political and combat
support, to fight the Taliban.

Although he has emerged as a conciliatory, moderate, and forward-
looking leader, this does not mean that he has been able to claim widespread acceptance among the tribally heterogeneous Pashtuns. There are
also many elements among the non-Pashtun segments of the population –
especially those living in the western provinces led by Ismail Khan, central areas dominated by various Shi'ite Hazara groups, and north-western
provinces populated by Uzbeks – who have not widely embraced either
Karzai or his administration. Some of the members of his transitional
cabinet are there simply because they represent a particular ethnic or
power group, but have few qualifications and little experience in relation
to the portfolios they hold.

In short, whereas the Interim Authority functioned largely through the
goodwill of the signatories of the Bonn Agreement, the Transitional
Authority has come to function mainly at the behest of key power players
in Kabul and various other parts of Afghanistan, with continued dependence on the United Nations, the USA, and ISAF. These three actors
may well prove to be the backbone of any central government in Kabul
for the foreseeable future. These players continue to set the limits within
which Karzai can operate, despite his pledge at the Loya Jirga that he
will use the Jirga's mandate to the maximum to follow and protect the
religion of Islam, rebuild Afghanistan, bring peace, security, and prosperity to the country, and safeguard its independence.[11] It is now seriously doubtful whether the Transitional Authority and therefore the
United Nations will be in a position to achieve the next major goal to

which they are subjected under the Bonn Agreement: to hold a free and fair general election by mid-2004. It will depend on the achievement of security and stability in the country, the setting up of a proper electoral system and political parties, the establishment of effective legal and administrative structures, the readiness of the essential institutions to facilitate institutionalized power-sharing and public participation, and the preparedness of the key players to pledge that they will accept the outcome of the election whatever it may be. While the processes are still unfolding, progress in all these areas has so far been painfully slow and fraught with corrupt administrative practices. Ethnic and factional politics, and family connections, have hampered the government's ability to staff various commissions and ministries with qualified people and to create an environment whereby it could attract increased talents from the Afghan diaspora. Nepotism and bribery appear once again to have become normal practice in Afghan politics.

During the transition phase, the danger is that the question of national unity may at any time take a back seat in favour of parochial interests and local hegemonies. A number of autonomous actors, ranging from Ismail Khan to Gul Agha, the governor of Kandahar, to the Uzbek warlord Abdul Rashid Dostum, and a host of others who have their own personalized armies and income, are in a position to frustrate or undermine the efforts of any central authority to create a national system of governance. This situation tends to be reinforced by the US practice of arming various strongmen and according them differential treatment for the purpose of using them to hunt down the Taliban and al-Qaeda remnants. The USA has considered this as necessary until such time as there is a strong central government.[12] However, this practice, together with the persistent US resistance to the expansion of the role of ISAF to cover the areas outside the capital, could prove to be a major catalyst for instability in the long run.

One factor that could reduce the chances of Afghanistan again going down the path of political fragmentation will be the rise of an inter-ethnic force which could cut through social divisions and strengthen national unity in conjunction with national reconstruction and growth of democratic values and practices. At present, such political forces appear to be in very short supply. Both the former United Front and the Rome group are now quite fractured. Many components of the former United Front have grown disgruntled with the Tajik, or more specifically the hard-core Panjsheri, followers of the late Commander Massoud, who have controlled the key ministries of defence and foreign affairs, as well as intelligence services in the Transitional Authority.[13] Meanwhile, all has not been well within the Tajik component either: some tension seems to have developed between the Defence Minister and Vice President Mohammed

Fahim, who succeeded Commander Massoud, and some other major players in their camp. Fahim is viewed as somewhat self-centred and distant from Commander Massoud's vision for Afghanistan. Further, a rift has surfaced between the Badakhshi faction, led by the former President Burhanuddin Rabbani, and the Panjsheri faction. These developments will make the task of establishing a national democratic framework and viable political parties beyond sectional interests very difficult, if not impossible.

On the other hand, the situation does not look very promising in Zahir Shah's camp. Zahir Shah's return to Kabul in April 2002 after 29 years of exile in Rome, to act as a symbol of national unity, has been somewhat sidelined, for three main reasons. First, he is very old and vulnerable to manipulation by younger members of his family, many of whom have never had the experience of living in Afghanistan. Second, during the King's absence conditions in Afghanistan have changed so much that some two generations of Afghans cannot easily identify with him. Third, there have been signs of rifts between those followers of Zahir Shah who have wanted the ex-King to play a greater role in the Transitional Authority and those who have opted for a compromise in favour of Karzai. This has been in addition to a simmering rivalry that has somewhat bedevilled the relations between the ex-King's youngest son, Mir Wais, and his grandson, Mustafa, who is now Afghan ambassador to Italy. This has been reminiscent of the debilitating rivalry between the ex-King and his ambitious cousin and brother-in-law, Mohammed Daoud, which dogged Afghan politics in one way or another for some 30 years until Daoud succeeded in overthrowing the monarchy in 1973 and declaring Afghanistan a republic. The rivalry was instrumental in opening the way for radicalization and disintegration of Afghan politics, and therefore the bloody conflict and ideological extremism that gripped the country from 1978 to 2001. This all may have contributed to the final decision by Zahir Shah not to contest the position of head of state in the Loya Jirga and to rest content with the title Karzai bestowed upon him as "Baba" or Father of the Nation.

Afghanistan continues to provide a classic case of a weak state with a strong society. Historically, Afghanistan's micro-societies have operated both individually and in alliance with one another, and the dynamics of their relations amongst themselves and with a central authority have been critical in defining the powers of the central authority and the nature of the Afghan state. The 24 years of warfare that followed the seizure of state power by a cluster of pro-Soviet communists in Kabul in April 1978 affected the boundaries of the micro-societies and the pattern of power and authority relations within and between them. However, it did not ultimately alter their internal dynamics to the extent that could reduce their relevance and influence in shaping the post-Taliban politics of Afghanistan. The traditional khans, sardars, mullahs, and pirs have certainly diminished in number. But they have in many instances been replaced by new kinds of local power-holders, who have commonly become known as "warlords", with local communities or micro-societies revolving around their dispensary and patronage power. Some of these local power-holders are linked to external forces, especially in the context of Afghanistan's extensive cross-border ethnic ties with the country's neighbours, and the new role of the USA as a dominant power in Afghanistan.

This development is set to play a central role in the post-conflict political, economic, and security reconstruction of Afghanistan. It confronts the Transitional Authority of Hamid Karzai and the United Nations with serious challenges, and may ultimately dictate the shape and direction that Afghanistan's political order and overall reconstruction may take. The predominant view in the Karzai administration is that in its present situation Afghanistan needs a centralized, unitary, presidential system of governance. Some members of the administration claim that this is to some extent embedded in the Bonn Agreement, and it is something which is apparently favoured by the UN mission in Kabul and which the new constitution is set to prescribe. However, if one looks at the Bonn Agreement carefully, it essentially leaves this issue to be worked out and determined by the power-holders and the Afghan people. As the situation stands, the political and social realities on the ground seem to demand something other than a unitary system of governance.

A regionalized federal structure

An alternative is a regionalized federalist system, based on the creation of a central authority whose powers are determined in an interactive relationship with seven political-administrative regional units to replace the existing 32 provinces, which have made the task of governance burdensome. Each region could be composed of several micro-societies that hold common references of ethnic identity and thus can be defined more naturally than in the artificial way that has characterized the current provincial set-up. It can have a regional administration with a considerable degree of autonomy in its regional affairs. The seven regions could be in the order of two in the north, one at the centre, one in the west, and three in the south and east, where the non-Pashtun and Pashtun segments of Afghanistan's are respectively concentrated.

The central government in Kabul can be composite and parliamentary, based on separation of powers, with authority emanating from a properly instituted federal parliament through regular fair and free elections. The parliament would be responsible for electing from amongst its deputies a seven-member executive council, with one member representing one region, and a chair of the council as President for the duration of the life of the federal parliament. The President and the council would have the right to form the cabinet from members coming from inside and outside the parliament, but the parliament would be empowered to confirm the cabinet and other senior appointments, including those in the judicial branch, and approve appropriation bills. While the federal government would have full jurisdiction over national defence, security, finances, development, and foreign affairs, the council and its chair alone would be in charge of a federal professional army, police force, and border guards.

Such a system would open up the opportunity to all stakeholders to have a share in the power and governance structures and would diminish the chances for open conflict, which has marred Afghanistan for most of its existence in modern history. Of course, the generation and stability of this system, like any other system that might emerge in Afghanistan, would depend very much on the creation of appropriate national conditions: the enhancement of interrelated social and economic reconstruction and the prevalence of security. This would in turn depend on the commitment of the international community, especially its most powerful member, the USA, to remain constructively engaged in Afghanistan for a period of at least another decade.

This system cannot be constructed over as short a period of time as envisaged in the Bonn Agreement. The time-frame allowed under the agreement is very short. It is necessary for the current Constitutional Commission to take into consideration such a proposal in drafting the new constitution. The task of the Constitutional Loya Jirga, planned for 2004, should be expanded not only to ratify the new constitution but also to extend the tenure of Karzai's Transitional Authority for a further two years.

The constitution should be implemented in several stages, with a general parliamentary election to be held as the first substantive step no earlier than mid-2006. This time-span will be needed for two purposes. One is to organize the necessary logistics and mechanisms, including formation of political parties, for holding such an election. Another is to create the much-needed economic and security conditions that could enable the Transitional Authority to educate the voters away from a culture of conflict towards a culture of democratic practices within a stable national environment. Once this phase is completed then work can begin on constructing the regional set-ups, which could take as long as four years or the duration of the first parliamentary government. Meanwhile, the processes of security and economic reconstruction will have to be prioritized and managed in such a way as to strengthen interdependent relations between the central government and the regions, and amongst the latter. The details for such an extended transitional phase should be worked out by the Constitutional Commission as a supplement to the draft of the new constitution for the Loya Jirga's ratification.

Whatever the outcome of the debate about whether Afghanistan should have a centralized or mixed system of governance, it is a matter which requires national debate and wise counsel from the United Nations. Although the Afghan situation is still unfolding, the form of the government that will emerge will be critical to creating not only a stable political order but also stability in Afghanistan. So far, the UN's role in guiding Afghanistan on a path of democratic stabilization has been encouraging, but not conclusive. It has produced something similar to what the organization has succeeded in achieving in Cambodia and East Timor – which has been somewhere between stability and volatility. Its ultimate success in helping the Afghans to develop a stable, democratic political order and culture will depend very much on how long and how extensively the international community, and the USA in particular, will be prepared to remain engaged in Afghanistan, with a determination to deter any further interference in the country by its neighbours. The problems of Afghanistan cannot be solved simply by legitimizing and protecting a government in Kabul and keeping at bay the remnants of the Taliban and al-Qaeda whenever necessary. They must be addressed in a systematic and comprehensive fashion, with the international community investing a lot more in the country's security and reconstruction than has hitherto been the case. If the United Nations fails in Afghanistan it will not be for lack of trying, but rather a result of the unwillingness or inability of its members, especially the USA and its allies, to do what it takes to create human security in every sense of the word on a massive scale over the next decade.

Notes

1. For an inside account, see Cordovez, Diego and Selig S. Harrison. 1995. *Out of Afghanistan: The Inside Story of the Soviet Withdrawal*. New York: Oxford University Press.
2. See Maley, William. 1989. "The Geneva Accords of April 1998", in Amin Saikal and William Maley (eds) *The Soviet Withdrawal from Afghanistan*. Cambridge: Cambridge University Press.
3. For a comparative study of the Afghan and Viet Nam conflicts, see Borer, Douglas A. 1999. *Superpowers Defeated: Vietnam and Afghanistan Compared*. London: Frank Cass.
4. For details of the Secretary-General's settlement plan and the Mujahideen's reaction to it, see *Afghan Information Centre Monthly Bulletin*, Nos 123–124, June–July 1991.

5. United Nations. 1994. *Progress Report of the Special Mission to Afghanistan*. UN Doc. A/49/208, 1 July.
6. For a detailed discussion, see Saikal, Amin. 1996. "The UN and Afghanistan: A case of failed peacemaking intervention?", *International Peacekeeping*, Vol. 3, No. 1.
7. UN Press Release BIO/3397, 5 November 2001.
8. For the full text of the agreement, see "Agreement on Provisional Arrangements in Afghanistan Pending the Re-establishment of Permanent Government Institutions", UN Security Council, S/2001/1154, 5 December 2001.
9. "Karzai elected Afghan leader", BBC News, 13 June 2002.
10. See Maley, William. 2002. *The Afghanistan Wars*. London: Palgrave Macmillan, Ch. 11; Johnson, Chris and Jolyon Leslie. 2002. "Afghans have their memories: A reflection on the recent experience of assistance in Afghanistan", *Third World Quarterly*, Vol. 23, No. 5.
11. "Loya Jirga's mixed message", BBC News, 19 June 2002.
12. See the comments by US envoy Zalmay Khalilzad, *Afghanistan Online Press*, www.afghan-web.com/aop, 15 June 2002.
13. For details see Saikal, Amin. 2002. "Afghanistan after the Loya Jirga", *Survival*, Vol. 44, No. 3.

Acronyms

AAK	Alliance for the Future of Kosovo
ACE	Administration and Cost of Elections project
ADAB	Association of Development Agencies in Bangladesh
ANC	African National Congress
ASDT	Social Democratic Association of East Timor
ASEAN	Association of South-East Asian Nations
BPA	Bank and Payment Authority (Kosovo)
CAPEL	Center for Electoral Promotion and Assistance
CCF	Country Cooperation Framework
CGDK	Coalition Government of Democratic Kampuchea
CHR	UN Commission on Human Rights
CNRT	National Council of Timorese Resistance
CoD	Congress of Democrats (Namibia)
COFFEL	Coalition for Free and Fair Elections
COHCHR	Cambodian Office of the UN High Commissioner for Human Rights
COMFREL	Committee for Free and Fair Elections in Cambodia
COMKFOR	Commander of KFOR
CPP	Cambodian People's Party
DA	district administrator
DAC	district advisory council
DESA	UN Department of Economic and Social Affairs
DFO	district field officer
DTA	Democratic Turnhalle Alliance (Namibia)
EAD	UN Electoral Assistance Division

ECOMOG	ECOWAS Military Observer Group
ECOSOC	UN Economic and Social Council
ECOWAS	Economic Community of West African States
EIU	Economist Intelligence Unit
EMB	electoral management body
ETA	Basque Fatherland and Freedom
ETTA	East Timorese Transitional Administration
EU	European Union
FALINTIL	Armed Forces of National Liberation of East Timor
FDTL	Defence Force (East Timor)
FRETILIN	Revolutionary Front of Independent East Timor
FRY	Federal Republic of Yugoslavia
FUNCINPEC	National United Front for an Independent, Neutral, Peaceful, and Cooperative Cambodia
GA	UN General Assembly
GDP	gross domestic product
GPA	governance and public administration
HDI	Human Development Index
HDZ	Croatian Democratic Movement
IAC	Interim Administrative Council (Kosovo)
ICCPR	International Covenant on Civil and Political Rights
ICESCR	International Covenant on Economic, Social, and Cultural Rights
ICFTU	International Confederation of Free Trade Unions
ICRC	International Committee of the Red Cross
IDEA	International Institute for Democracy and Electoral Assistance
IFES	International Foundation for Election Systems
IFI	international financial institution
IMF	International Monetary Fund
IO	international organization
IOM	International Organization for Migration
ISAF	International Security Assistance Force (Afghanistan)
ISI	Inter-Services Intelligence (Pakistan)
JAC	Joint Administrative Council (Kosovo)
JIAS	Joint Interim Administrative Structure (Kosovo)
JIC	joint implementation committee
KACI	Kosovo Action for Civil Initiatives
KFOR	Kosovo Force
KLA	Kosovar Liberation Army
KPC	Kosovo Protection Corps
KPNLF	Khmer People's National Liberation Front
KPS	Kosovo Police Service
KPU	General Elections Commission (Indonesia)
KTC	Kosovo Transitional Council
LDC	least developed country
LDK	Democratic League of Kosovo
MICIVIH	International Civilian Mission in Haiti

MINURCA	UN Mission in the Central African Republic
MINURSO	UN Mission for the Referendum in Western Sahara
MONUA	UN Mission of Observers in Angola
MONUC	UN Organization Mission in the Democratic Republic of Congo
MPLA	Popular Movement for the Liberation of Angola
NAM	needs-assessment mission
NATO	North Atlantic Treaty Organization
NC	National Council (East Timor)
NCC	National Consultative Council (East Timor)
NDI	National Democratic Institute for International Affairs (USA)
NEC	National Election Committee (Cambodia)
NED	National Endowment for Democracy
NGO	non-governmental organization
NICFEC	Neutral and Impartial Committee for Free and Fair Elections in Cambodia
NP	National Party (South Africa)
OAS	Organization of American States
OAU	Organization of African Unity
ODA	official development assistance
OHCHR	Office of the UN High Commissioner for Human Rights
OIF	Organization of la Francophonie
ONUMOZ	UN Operation in Mozambique
ONUSAL	UN Observer Mission in El Salvador
OSCE	Organization for Security and Cooperation in Europe
PDK	Democratic Party of Kosovo
PLAN	People's Liberation Army of Namibia
PR	proportional representation
PRK	People's Republic of Kampuchea
PRPK	People's Revolutionary Party of Kampuchea
RC	UNDP resident coordinator
RDTL	Democratic Republic of East Timor
RS	Republika Srpska
RUF	Rebel United Front (Sierra Leone)
SC	UN Security Council
SDA	Democratic Action Party (Bosnia-Herzegovina)
SDS	Centrist Party (Slovakia)
SDS	Serbian Democratic Party
SG	UN Secretary-General
SIP	Inter-American Press Society
SNV	Serbian National Council
SOC	State of Cambodia
SRP	Sam Rainsy Party (Cambodia)
SRSG	special representative of the UN Secretary-General
SWAPO	South-West African Peoples Organization
TFET	Trust Fund for East Timor
TNC	transnational corporation

UDF	United Democratic Front (Namibia)
UDT	Timorese Democratic Union
UNAMA	UN Assistance Mission in Afghanistan
UNAMET	UN Mission in East Timor
UNAMSIL	UN Mission in Sierra Leone
UNCDF	UN Capital Development Fund
UNCHS	UN Centre for Human Settlements
UNDAF	UN Development Assistance Framework
UNDP	UN Development Programme
UNDPKO	UN Department of Peacekeeping Operations
UNHCHR	UN High Commissioner for Human Rights
UNIDIR	UN Institute for Disarmament Research
UNIFEM	UN Development Fund for Women
UNITA	National Union for the Total Independence of Angola
UNITAF	Unified Task Force (Somalia)
UNMIH	UN Mission in Haiti
UNMIK	UN Interim Administration Mission in Kosovo
UNMOGIP	UN Military Observer Group in India and Pakistan
UNOMIL	UN Observer Mission in Liberia
UNOMSIL	UN Observer Mission in Sierra Leone
UNOPS	UN Office for Project Services
UNOSOM	UN Operation in Somalia
UNPREDEP	UN Preventive Deployment
UNSC	UN Security Council
UNSMA	UN Special Mission to Afghanistan
UNTAC	UN Transitional Authority in Cambodia
UNTAES	UN Transitional Administration for Eastern Slavonia
UNTAET	UN Transitional Administration in East Timor
UNTAG	UN Transitional Assistance Group (Namibia)
UNV	UN Volunteers programme
WB	World Bank

Contributors

Simon Chesterman
  Executive Director, Institute for International Law and Justice, New York University School of Law

Tom J. Farer
  Dean, Graduate School of International Studies, University of Denver

Tanja Hohe
  Social Anthropologist – Middle East and North African Region, The World Bank

Ylber Hysa
  Director, Kosova Action for Civic Initiatives (KACI)

Robin Ludwig
  Senior Political Affairs Officer, UN Department of Political Affairs

Henning Melber
  Research Director, Nordic Africa Institute, Sweden

Edward Newman
  Academic Officer, Peace and Governance Programme, United Nations University

Sorpong Peou
  Associate Professor of Political Science, Sophia University, Tokyo

Richard Ponzio
  Democratic Governance Team Leader
  UN Development Programme Kosovo

Benjamin Reilly
  Senior Lecturer, Asia Pacific School of Economics and Government, Australian National University

Roland Rich
  Director, Centre for Democratic Institutions, Research School of Social Sciences, Australian National University

Amin Saikal
  Director, Centre for Arab and Islamic Studies, Australian National University

Laurence Whitehead
  Official Fellow, Nuffield College, Oxford University

343

Index

Catalogue Request

Name: _____

Address: _____

_____

Tel: _____

Fax: _____

E-mail: _____

To receive a catalogue of UNU Press publications kindly photocopy this form and send or fax it back to us with your details. You can also e-mail us this information. Please put "Mailing List" in the subject line.

 **United Nations University Press**

53-70, Jingumae 5-chome
Shibuya-ku, Tokyo 150-8925, Japan
Tel: +81-3-3499-2811 Fax: +81-3-3406-7345
E-mail: sales@hq.unu.edu http://www.unu.edu